D0099182

THE SECRET STATE

THE
SECRET
STATE

A HISTORY OF INTELLIGENCE
AND ESPIONAGE

COLONEL JOHN HUGHES-WILSON

PEGASUS BOOKS
NEW YORK LONDON

THE SECRET STATE

Pegasus Books Ltd
148 West 37th Street, 13th Floor
New York, NY 10018

Copyright © 2016 by John Hughes-Wilson

First Pegasus Books hardcover edition January 2017

ISBN: 978-1-68177-302-5

10 9 8 7 6 5 4 3 2 1

Printed in the United States of America
Distributed by W. W. Norton & Company, Inc.

This book is dedicated to the memory of:

Victor Andersen †
British Intelligence Services

Val Heller †
US Defense Intelligence Agency

Major Andrew Nightingale †
Intelligence Corps and Special Air Service Regiment

Colonel John K. Moon †
US Military Intelligence

Corporal Oliver Thomas †
Intelligence Corps

The Latin phrase *sub rosa* means 'under the rose' and is used in English to denote secrecy or confidentiality.

The rose as a symbol of secrecy has a history dating back to ancient Egypt. The Romans sometimes hung a rose above the table being used for diplomatic negotiations. In medieval times pictures of five-petalled roses were often carved on confessionals, indicating that what was said within would remain secret. In the council chambers of Henry VIII's palaces a stylised Tudor rose covered the ceiling of the private chamber where confidential decisions of state were made.

The rose is now used by many nations as the badge of intelligence and security.

Contents

'Now the reason the enlightened prince and the wise general
conquer the enemy whenever they move and their achievements
surpass those of ordinary men, is foreknowledge.'

Sun Tzu, *The Art of War*

Introduction

ABOUT THIS BOOK

This is a book that has its roots in *Military Intelligence Blunders*, first written in 1999. It sold well and a second, updated edition came out in 2004 after the 9/11 attack on the World Trade Center and the invasion of Iraq. That too became a best-seller and I was both surprised and heartened to see that the book has since been translated into six languages, including Turkish and Japanese, and has become recommended reading by intelligence agencies, as well as a text book for a number of university courses on intelligence.

Since 2004 much has changed however and in this new book, which is much wider in scope than its predecessors, I have tried to capture some of these changes and assess their impact to give the reader a much broader view of the whole subject of intelligence. Hence its title: *On Intelligence*. However, unlike Clausewitz's monumental 1832, *On War*, this work on intelligence is intended to avoid the pitfalls of the now dated German *meisterwerk*.

For a start it is meant to be *readable*. With a book that is an important issue. It would be interesting to discover just how many people (let alone academic military historians) have actually read all eight volumes and all the complexities of von Clausewitz in the original German. I suspect, rather like the Communist–Socialist bible, *Das Kapital*, very few folk have actually read and absorbed the master's deep thoughts, let alone understood the linguistic subtleties and nuances contained therein.

On Intelligence is therefore not intended as a ruminative academic stroll through historic events to reach some broad reflective conclusions, before getting completely lost in the thickets of philosophy and Hegelian dialectic. Rather it is intended as an up-to-date analysis of intelligence in the recent past, and how its impact has affected great events. Wherever possible, case studies and hard examples are analysed in some detail, looking for answers rather than the unfinished metaphysical reflections that so characterise *On War*. There are some tough lessons to be learned from intelligence failures especially today, and from intelligence successes, too.

But *On War* and *On Intelligence* do both share a common aim. In von Clausewitz's own words from long, long ago: 'To write a book that will not be forgotten after two or three years.'

Most of us have read press accounts and books about the events that unfold on these pages. But very few of us have seen the events from the *inside*. The inside implies knowledge: and knowledge means *power*.

By 'inside', I do not mean the views of politicians or the other self-satisfied classes like senior civil servants or even those very grand journalists who often write *memoirs* on the lines of, 'Well, as the president said to me . . .'

The real 'insiders' knowledge' is always the intelligence that was available *at the time*. It was that secret intelligence that shaped events and made the people who took the decisions into heroes or villains. This book tries to lift the veil on what really happened behind the scenes in the intelligence world during some of the most well-known military events that have shaped our lives. It tries to show why decisions were made, for good or ill, by a number of famous and not so famous characters, based on the intelligence and the secrets they had to work with at the time. This book tends to highlight intelligence mistakes and blunders (carefully concealed from the taxpayer who paid for them) for the simple reason that they are more interesting than the far more numerous successes of intelligence.

The book also identifies numerous deceptions, lies and cover-ups. Not all of these were committed to deceive the enemy. Turning over stones invariably lets a harsh light onto some creatures of the shadows.

There are many intelligence officers and government officials, in all regimes, who prefer to keep their role and decisions secret, and thrive on secrecy in order to protect their careers and way of life. It guarantees their income, their status and their pensions. Secrecy is everything to them and far too often it is not for any motives of 'national security.' In this desire to cover things up, they are too frequently encouraged – and joined – by their political masters.

In this they are only outclassed by their bosses, those very senior civil servants and 'securocrats' of every country's administration, who equally thrive and prosper in the sure and certain knowledge that access to secret intelligence has given them the ultimate benefit of the mistress or harem: power without responsibility. But, like their political masters, good intelligence officers should always have the courage of their convictions, and be ready to show moral courage by taking responsibility for their advice. Intelligence is, after all, about predicting the most likely future, not just regaling concerned decision makers with hot new facts. That is called news. CNN, the BBC, Fox, Sky News and now the immediacy of social media do the rolling 24/7 news agenda far better than any intelligence agency, as every professional modern intelligence officer knows. However, when careers are at stake that is a hard precept to follow.

If I had to offer a motto for any intelligence officer I would unhesitatingly quote the 1950s American Friends (Quaker) phrase, 'Speak Truth unto Power.' That phrase has since been long associated with the British Civil Service. To be able to give honest and objective advice to ministers has always been seen as something that all impartial civil servants and intelligence officers should be able to do. Sadly, in their complicity over the scandal of Tony Blair and Alastair Campbell's use of a notoriously misleading (if not downright mendacious) 'sexed-up' intelligence dossier to convince Parliament and the British people to enter the 2003 Iraq War, Whitehall's not so faceless intelligence bureaucrats let their calling – and their countrymen – down badly.

The various case studies in the book are intended to provide an accessible and readable narrative of the events they describe, accompanied by some professional intelligence insights into how those events came about and unfolded. They tread a delicate path between the laboriously footnoted and exhaustive detail of the academic PhD tome, and the trivial, flippant (and often inaccurate) 'popular history' of cheap journalism. Where possible, quotations are clearly indicated. For those who would like to delve into the stories in more detail, a short reading list is provided so that they can be better informed about events and individuals. History is, after all, 'a never ending argument'.

In putting together this book I have been aided across the years by the Director and staff of the Royal United Services Institute in Whitehall. Various members of the Study Group on Intelligence at the RUSI have made invaluable suggestions over the years on a variety of topics. In particular Professor Christopher Andrew and the late (and much missed) Professor M. R. D. Foot have been influential, as have their colleagues, Professors Richard Aldrich and Gary Sheffield. The Intelligence Corps Archives, now at Chicksands, have dotted many I's and crossed many T's on key reminiscences. For details of Vietnam I owe a considerable debt to my many American friends and colleagues over the years, especially the late Colonel John Moon and Colonel John Robbins of the United States Army for their perceptive comments on my drafts of American events, and also for their previously unpublished memories of Tet. The late Val Heller of the Defense Intelligence Agency contributed a number of reveal-ing dry – and wry – comments about the internecine inter-agency turf battles common to the alphabet soup that constitutes the US intelligence agencies.

Many others in the intelligence world of several nationalities have helped me, both on and off the record. I am particularly grateful to Andreas Campomar, late of Constable & Robinson (now Little, Brown) for recognising the need for a new, more all-embracing book on intelligence, and also to Andy Hayward, a *doyen* of the London publishing scene, for suggesting the idea in the first place. For a sharp professional scrutiny of the manuscript and the avoidance of any 'fouls' I can only express deep gratitude to my editor, Josh Ireland, who painstakingly checked the text and made numerous helpful suggestions to improve the finished product. No author likes (in the words of Robert Louis Stevenson) to 'murder his darlings'. Josh has been a skilful executioner of cherished – but redundant – text.

Any errors and omissions however are mine own, as are the opinions expressed. They represent the broad overview of over forty years working with, and thinking about, intelligence in general and military intelligence in particular. Having said that, this is most certainly *not* a theoretical text about international affairs. *On Intelligence* instead gives the reader a broad overview of a vast subject, ranging from biblical spies to modern satellites and cyberwar. Every one of the topics covered rates a complete book of its own; and in many cases, has already filled whole library shelves. The book's chapters aim to provide the reader with accessible, well-informed insights into a variety of issues, with many secrets and technicalities. Because, above all, *On Intelligence* is a book that is meant to be read and enjoyed by the general reader and the intelligence professional alike.

I genuinely hope both gain something from my labours.

John Hughes-Wilson, Cyprus

PART 1

SETTING THE SCENE

CHAPTER ONE

A Little History

'If you do not know others and do not know yourself, you will be in danger in every single battle.'

Sun Tzu, *The Art of War*

From the dawn of time, intelligence has mattered. The knowledge of where your enemy is, what forces he possesses, and what he plans to do, should help even the most dim-witted and stubborn politician or general.

Every great commander in history has relied on good intelligence as a 'force multiplier', or as a guide as to when and where he should strike. Those unfortunates without good intelligence have, in their turn, usually gone down to defeat, death and disgrace.

Some call intelligence the 'Second Oldest Profession' – experts say, however, that it is the first, because knowledge of where the enemy is and the need for self-preservation and survival rates above all other urges. Ask any bird hunting for worms in a cat-infested garden . . .

What is intelligence? There are many different meanings of the word, but we all admire it and we all recognise the real thing when we see it.

The Bible has some of the first evidence of military intelligence: in particular, its reference to Moses' famous spying expedition into present-day Israel. On the run from Egypt in the inhospitable

burning wastes of the Sinai desert, the wandering tribes needed somewhere to settle with abundant water, fertile soil and green trees. The
Hebrews knew exactly where to turn for assistance in their hour of
need: as the Old Testament says,

> And the Lord spoke unto Moses, saying, 'Send thou men that they
> may search the land of Canaan'. . . And Moses sent them to spy out
> the land of Canaan and said unto them . . . 'And see the land, what
> it is; and the people that dwell therein, whether they be strong or
> weak, few or many. And what the land is that they dwell in, whether
> in tents or in strongholds . . .'

In modern parlance, Moses had issued his 'critical intelligence
requirements'.

The Bible is full of such tales of military prowess, battles, deception
and, above all, intelligence gathering. This is hardly surprising, as many
modern scholars believe that the Hebrew's chosen god, 'Jehovah', was
the Israelites' original god of war from their pantheon. Later, Moses'
successor, Joshua, sends two spies to report on the walled city of Jericho
and its defences. According to the Bible story, the two spies are hidden
by a friendly prostitute called Rahab; the first, but by no means the last,
evidence of close collaboration between the two 'oldest professions'.
Betrayed by an informer, the Hebrew agents flee the city with Rahab's
help, for which service her house and life are spared when the well-
briefed Jewish army later storms and sacks Jericho. It is a classic
example of intelligence in action.

Another Old Testament example is the story of Delilah, the earliest
recorded example of a 'honey trap', or what the KGB called a 'swallow'.
The Philistines decide that she is the ideal tool with which to entrap
the Israelites' strongman, Samson, and Delilah lures the Jewish champion into her boudoir. Samson blurts out the secret of his strength (his
hair) before, like so many men before and since, falling into the deep
sleep of the 'just after'. Shorn of his strength by a gentle barber and
blinded by not so gentle Philistines, Samson languishes in captivity
before finally pulling down the columns – and the roof – of his prison
on his tormentors once his hair has grown back. It is a cautionary tale

of the power of women and the weakness of men confronted with a suitably seductive and available source of temptation.

There is other, more concrete, evidence of ancient intelligence in action. On the wall of the great temple at Karnak in Egypt is the graphic story of Tutmoses III's triumphant campaign against the Syrian uprising of 1488 BC. The warrior Pharaoh's speedy reaction to the rebellion was made possible by his secret agents in Megiddo. These undercover spies noted Khadesh's growing army in the north and promptly rode south to warn the Egyptian outpost fort at Tjuru (near present-day Port Said) of the gathering storm, months before the rebels were ready to move against their new young Pharaoh.

According to the Greek chronicler Herodotus, when Histiaeus the Milesian was sent to the court of King Darius, the Persians took him for a possible spy, briefed to report on any weakness in the Persian Empire. He was placed under house arrest and all his communications back home blocked. However, Histiaeus thought that he had identified the weak spot in the Persians' grip on their sprawling Empire; but how to tell his fellow Greeks and evade the Persians' total shutdown on messengers or letters?

Histiacus' solution was simple. He cut the hair off a servant's head, tattooed the crucial message onto the shorn scalp, and let the hair grow back. The servant was then despatched home. Darius's men let him pass, little knowing that his head bore the crucial words, 'Histiaeus bids thee to incite the Ionians to rise up and revolt against Darius.' The ruse worked. The simple servant returned home bearing the vital intelligence on, not in, his head.

Legend has it that the travel-stained servant was brought in to Histiaeus's son-in-law Aristagoras carrying the bizarre request, 'Thy father-in-law Histiaeus bids thee to shave my head . . .' The Greeks took note and Aristagoras duly incited Darius's Ionian vassals to rise against their unpopular overlord. If nothing else, the story stresses the need for very clear and very brief secret communications. There is, after all, only so much space on the human scalp.

The first known writer on intelligence in the ancient world appears to have been Sun Tzu, a serious soldier and government bureaucrat who lived and fought around the Yellow River province of Wu around 500 BC – well before Rome's pre-eminence. Like many professional soldiers before and since, Sun Tzu realised that there was far more to war than just battles. Sometime towards the end of his career he wrote a classic textbook called, *The Art of War* (*Ping Fa*), which placed a heavy emphasis on intelligence.

Realising that any half-decent and well-led enemy will rarely have the good grace or courtesy to conform to his own wishes, (and indeed, may even have some tiresome ideas of their own) Sun Tzu thought deeply about intelligence, and made it a priority for soldiers and statesmen alike.

Sun Tzu classifies his 'collection agents' into five main groups:

1. Local inhabitants.

2. Government officials in the enemy camp who would betray their government in order to stay in their jobs.

3. Enemy spies who could be 'turned' and doubled to play back disinformation.

4. Expendable agents who can be sacrificed to feed false information to the enemy.

5. Spies who can be relied on to penetrate the enemy, survive and report accurately from inside the enemy camp.

Sun Tzu realised that the relatively small resources spent on garnering intelligence in peacetime were in fact *investments*: insurance policies against having to spend far, far more if – or when – war broke out. To Sun Tzu, good intelligence in peacetime was as much a part of national defence as an army on the march in war: and a damned sight cheaper too . . .

His philosophy can best be seen by his clear understanding of intelligence, or 'foreknowledge':

Now the reason that the enlightened prince and wise general conquer their enemy is foreknowledge.

What is called foreknowledge cannot be divined from spirits, gods, comparison with past events nor from calculations. It must be obtained from men who know the enemy's true situation ...

Sun Tzu's judgements on intelligence were by no means isolated examples of the wisdom of the Orient. A century later in India, Kautilya, the *nom de plume* of the Indian statesman and philosopher Chanakya, chief adviser and Prime Minister to Emperor Chandragupta, first ruler of the Mauryan Empire, was explaining how collecting intelligence was the best way to secure the state and to disrupt an enemy. Kautilya, often called the 'Indian Machiavelli', had uncompromising views on how to be a successful commander and also on the vital importance of good intelligence. In the fourth century BC he set them down in his *Arthashastra*, or testament.

We have plentiful other evidence of the importance of intelligence in antiquity. Mithridates, the youthful King of Pontus, is alleged to have spent no fewer than seven years of his adolescent exile wandering Asia Minor collecting intelligence in the bazaars and markets dressed as a camel boy or a merchant, before finally taking up his crown at the age of twenty-one. Then, at the head of a small but tactically competent army in 88 BC, he launched a devastating assault on Asia Minor. His commanders seemed to know every pass, every road in advance. More dangerously, they knew the identities of the disaffected, the traitors and the would-be turncoats who would rally to their side everywhere they went. City after city yielded to him. Within a few short years, Mithridates ruled much of Asia Minor; a resounding victory based on good intelligence.

Rome relied on spies from its earliest days. According to Livy, as early as 300 BC the Consul Quintus Fabius Maximus had sent his brother undercover, disguised as an Etruscan farm worker to infiltrate the ranks of their Umbrian rivals and spy behind the enemy lines.

By the time Hannibal and his elephants had burst into Italy following their surprise march from Spain a century later, Rome found itself on the receiving end of someone else's very sophisticated intelligence effort. Hannibal used agents widely to keep himself informed about Carthage's arch-enemy, even infiltrating his spies deep into Rome itself. Well might Cato have thundered angrily from his seat in the Senate at the close of every speech, 'Carthage must be destroyed!' On the evidence, at least some of his distinguished Roman audience were probably paid agents of Carthage.

By the time Scipio Africanus took over the Roman effort against Hannibal in 210 BC he had learned that he must control his own intelligence effort. He even ordered some of his centurions to disguise themselves as 'slaves' to accompany a peace delegation into the enemy camp. As mere slaves they could wander around unchecked, while secretly reconnoitring the enemy positions, strengths and numbers.

Unfortunately, one of Hannibal's Numidians recognised one of the undercover soldiers, Lucius Statorius, as a centurion in the legions. Scipio denied the claim, promptly ordered the accused 'slave' to be publicly flogged as a demonstration of his servile status. The unfortunate Statorius endured his painful ordeal, doubtless consoling himself by reflecting on the republican virtues of fortitude and stoicism demanded in the service of Rome. His cover held. The dubious Numidians were convinced. No self-respecting Roman centurion would ever tolerate or endure such a public humiliation. Sometimes the price for securing intelligence can be a painful one.

By the time of Julius Caesar in the first century BC we can clearly see the first recognisably modern system of intelligence in action, although Roman intelligence organisations of the day were privately run, usually by the rich: senators, merchants and politicians. For example, Crassus, Caesar's senior partner and money lender, set up an intelligence network covering the whole of the Republic, designed to warn him of every development, whether a threat to Rome or, more importantly for the richest man in the city, any shift in the market forces that governed the Republic's far-flung trade.

Caesar developed this into the first real 'national' intelligence system. As a successful soldier he realised the importance of timely, accurate information on his enemies and the need for fast, secure communications to keep his own plans secret. His *Gallic Wars* contains numerous references to intelligence collection, the most notable being the reconnaissance of Britain by his agent Gaius Volusenus in 55 BC, just before Caesar's landing in Kent. However the organisation remained essentially Caesar's, not Rome's. Intelligence, even national intelligence, was still an individual venture, run by a successful general.

With Caesar's own murder in 44 BC, the network passed on to Octavius, later Caesar Augustus. As the final beneficiary of the bloody civil war, Augustus was taking no chances. He rapidly drew all the existing military and diplomatic intelligence into his own hands and established an empire-wide network of communications, the *cursus publicus*, which was to become the core of Rome's imperial secret service. With its thousands of waystations along the network of main roads it allowed people, taxes – and intelligence – to move swiftly. As Suetonius explained:

> To enable what was going on in each of the provinces to be reported and known more speedily and promptly, he [Augustus] at first stationed young men at short intervals along the military roads, and afterwards post-chaises. The latter has seemed the more convenient arrangement, since the same men who bring the dispatches from any place can, if occasion demands, be questioned as well.

Using this network, Rome could now build on Crassus's and Caesar's private foundations to establish an imperial police and intelligence service designed to give early warning of any threats to the imperial throne and of corruption and unrest in the Empire. Trajan and his successors further refined this Roman secret service. They created a network of spies and informers that covered the civilised world to support their need for intelligence on imperial security and commerce, and to back up the legions guarding the long frontiers. These undercover secret agents were controlled by official intelligence officers: the *speculatores*, drawn from the intelligence officers of the legions and from the military procurement system, the *frumentarii*, whose ostensible role was to obtain grain for the army at the best prices.

The *frumentarii* were aided by their more sinister counterparts the *peregrini*, who were based in a special barracks on the Caelian Hill. As their name implies the *peregrini* acted as a roving secret military police and enforcement unit for the emperor's orders anywhere in the Empire. The *peregrini* quickly acquired the happy reputation common to all such organisations: they were heartily detested by their fellow citizens.

The role of the *peregrini* as a kind of early Gestapo in the great cities started in the first century AD, with the Christians as one of their special quarries. Any political movement that advocated the equality of both slaves and freemen and the existence of a heavenly kingdom clearly posed a serious challenge to the Roman social order, and as such was considered deeply subversive of domestic security. The *frumentarii* were tasked to hunt down these dangerous revolutionaries.

Like most secret police and security services however, the *frumentarii* seem to have lacked imagination. One early Christian, Dionysius, evaded them by the devious expedient of hiding *in his own house*. This particularly cunning ploy confused the frustrated secret policemen as they scoured Rome for four days, fruitlessly searching for the tricky and dangerous dissident. Dionysius was eventually smuggled to safety by the Christian underground, thus proving the truth that a repressive regime will, as often as not, inspire an equally determined and resourceful resistance movement with its own intelligence networks and spies.

Despite this secret service reporting to the imperial palace, Rome's intelligence service does not seem to have been especially efficient. Many Roman emperors fell to the assassins' deadly stroke rather than peacefully in their beds. In the words of the distinguished historian of Rome's grubbier past, Professor Rose Mary Sheldon, 'Ironically, for all their reputation as empire builders, the Romans were never as good at watching their enemies as they were at watching each other.'

With the collapse of the Western Empire in AD 476, the surviving Eastern Empire remained to carry on the genius that was Rome. Byzantium's administrative institutions, dynastic complications and fortunes for the next thousand years depended to a large extent on the competence or otherwise of Constantinople's spy network; and the evidence is that Byzantium's secret intelligence service was very busy indeed.

Byzantium's long struggles were caused, in large part, by the constant threat from Islam and the heirs of the Prophet. Rampaging Islam absorbed a great deal of Constantinople's effort and was covered, over many centuries, by a comprehensive network of informants, agents and spies in the Mohammedan camp. The best sources were the major trading routes and flow of commerce that flourished across the Near East and followed the great caravan routes that linked Byzantium to Baghdad.

Baghdad, in its turn, showed equal zeal in keeping an eye on its own internal pre-occupations. The Abbasid Caliph, Harun-al-Rashid, who ruled between 786–809 AD and has been immortalised in the *One Thousand and One Nights*, was said to have been prone to disguising himself and wandering the streets and souks of Baghdad to collect his own intelligence on what the people really thought about their ruler. 'Uneasy lies the head that wears the crown.' But using secret police to keep a close eye on the views of the faithful has remained a feature of Islamic states over the centuries, and still remains a priority for authoritarian Islamic leaders today, as the citizens of Cairo, Damascus, Baghdad, Teheran and even Istanbul know only too well.

Byzantium's other great intelligence preoccupation highlights intelligence's handmaiden: security. Constantinople's principal counter-espionage problem was to prevent the secret formula of their ultimate terror weapon, 'Greek Fire', from falling into the hands of their Islamic foes.

Greek Fire appears to have been a viscous liquid mixture of naphtha, liquid bitumen, turpentine resin from pine trees, sulphur and quicklime. It could be dropped onto men or ships in clay pots, flung from catapults and, suitably diluted, even be projected from siphons or tubes like a flame-thrower. It burned with a tenacious, all-consuming flame and only sand, urine or vinegar could extinguish it swiftly; water merely helped the fire to spread. A small pot of Greek Fire hurled like a hand grenade into a cluster of Moorish warriors would ignite their flowing cotton surcoats and stick tenaciously to armour and skin, turning men into flailing human torches, burning in their own fat. It was an effective and terrifying 'secret weapon' – no wonder the Muslim armies wanted its recipe.

The Islamic agents of the Caliphate were as anxious to discover the secrets of Byzantium's terror weapon as the defenders of Christendom's Eastern Empire were to keep its secrets. For several hundred years, its formula was a Moorish intelligence priority. Astonishingly, and despite the systematic torture of thousands of captives over the years, and the lure of treachery and gold, the Byzantines appear to have kept their jealously guarded secret safe until about 1100.

The other major intelligence collectors of the Middle East at the time were the fanatical followers of Hassan-i Sabbah, known as the 'Assassins'. They took their name from hashish, not because they were regular users of the drug (*hashashin* means hashish eaters), but because, in the opinion of the moderate Muslim world of the time, anyone who behaved quite as wildly as the Assassins must have been drugged up to the eyeballs

> At his mountain stronghold at Alamut [in the Persian mountains north-west of Teheran] ... the old man kept a number of young men from twelve to twenty, each with a taste to be a warrior, and told them stories of Paradise, as had the Prophet before him ... When the old man wanted a lord killed, he would say to a youth, 'Go thou and slay so-and-so and if you return my angels will carry you straight to Paradise. Even if ye die, my angels will convey you thence, to the realm beyond Earthly joys ...
>
> Marco Polo

Such a sect relied almost entirely on good intelligence and inside knowledge to focus its murderous activities. By the twelfth century, the 'Old Man of the Mountains' allegedly had a spy, informer or paid agent 'in every lord's tent'.

Confronted by this far-flung network, attempts to stamp the Assassins out proved fruitless. Their excellent intelligence service forewarned them of impending attacks and allowed them to stop any threat well in advance. When, for example, Sindjar, Sultan of the Seljuks, decided to move against the order in the tenth century, Hassan-i Sabbah ordered his agents to ask the Sultan to desist – or else. Sultan Sinjar ignored the approach and the Assassins resorted to direct action. One morning, the closely-guarded Sultan awoke to find an Assassin's dagger thrust into the floorboards alongside his bed. As the shocked potentate was coming to terms with the implications of this rude awakening, a slave entered carrying a message. It read,

Were I not well inclined toward Sultan Sindjar, the hand that planted my knife in the floor would have plunged it into the sultan's bosom. Let him know that I, from my mountain far off, guide the hands of those who surround him. Peace be with you . . .

But a new threat was looming, one that relied on intelligence to grease the slipway of its victorious march through Asia. Fresh from his victories in the east, by the late 1230s the Great Khan's army was on the march west, looking for new conquests in Europe.

By 1241, when the Mongol Horde was poised to launch its assault on Eastern Europe from the Donets Basin, Yelü Chucai was the principal intelligence coordinator for the Mongol Empire. For over a decade, his agents had penetrated virtually every European court and major city and discovered not only the Europeans' capabilities and intentions but also their fears. To the Khan's intelligence service, Europe was an open book. Chucai, along with Subutai, the great Mongol general, appears to have been running a remarkably integrated – and modern – intelligence operation, building up a detailed picture of their next conquest and running advance spoiling operations against potential adversaries in Europe.

The papal legate Fra Carpini was sent as an envoy to the Mongols. From his chronicle we can piece together the basics of Mongols' intelligence system. First, sometimes years ahead, came the 'merchant spies', always travelling in pairs and reporting back, diligently hunting for every scrap of basic information on the potential victim: topography, climate, roads, bridges, cities, the political and demographic make-up of the region and the loyalty of its tribes.

Inevitably, military forces, weapons and fighting ability figured large in the Mongols' plans. It is reasonable to conjecture that such low-key but pervasive penetration of the enemy was reported back to the Mongols' commanders (and, ultimately, to the Great Khan himself) by means of the commercial codes used by merchants travelling along the caravan routes of Asia.

Genghis Khan's code of law, the *Yassa*, was a complex synthesis of tribal laws and customs. Of the twenty-two articles that we know of, two in particular reinforce the Khan's pre-occupation with intelligence:

...send out spies and bring in captured informers who must be questioned and made to give information that we can check off against the spies' reports ...

and, as a second order prescribes,

Spies and false witnesses are to be condemned to death ...

For the Mongols, intelligence was a priority – by law.

Genghis Khan and Sun Tzu's thoughts and observations have stood the test of time. They remain proof that intelligence has always been crucial: not just for survival, but for battlefield success and political power.

The Catholic Church's intelligence service rested on four principal pillars: the power of the confessional; a monopoly on literacy and learning; good communications; and the Inquisition. The terrors of hell and the powers of the priests enforced obedience and, more importantly, through the all-important confessional, they encouraged timely information on man's temporal intentions that could be used for the benefit of Holy Mother Church.

The sacrament of confession and penance rested on the simple theory that sin – except for mortal sin – could be forgiven after it had been confided to an ordained priest. This also happened to be a useful tool, both for collecting information and for social control. The confessional heard everything and forgave much. This marvellous intelligence apparatus pervaded the Church from top to bottom. To hold back was to risk damnation and so, either through faith or sheer superstition, for hundreds of years, millions of people, from peasants to princes, poured out their innermost secrets to Catholic priests across Europe. The confessional was quite simply a fabulous information gathering system.

Priests were supposed to keep the secrets of the confessional, but the system had an inbuilt flaw: the priests themselves had to confess. Thus guilty knowledge would be passed up the Church's hierarchy until it reached Rome itself. It was not supposed to happen, but it would be naive to pretend that it did not. Moreover, it flies in the face of all our experience of human nature and the way hierarchical organisations operate, to pretend that confessors did not curry favour by warning their bosses of impending trouble or heretical ideas.

For example, in about 1550, the Archbishop of Milan gave clear orders to his clergy that they were to reveal the names of any heretics or suspected enemies of the Church obtained through confession in order to collect intelligence on Rome's Protestant foes. It would fly in the face of reason to suppose that it was the *only* example over hundreds of years. The main beneficiary was the Inquisition.

By the early thirteenth century, the need to stamp out opposition to the authority of Rome and uncover 'heresy' led to the formation of the Inquisition by Pope Gregory IX in 1231. The teachings of Christ himself were even quoted as the basis of the Inquisition's most feared practice, burning at the stake: 'If anyone abide not in me he shall be cast forth as a branch and wither: and they shall gather him up, cast him into the fire, and he burneth.'

The first task of the Inquisition was to collect intelligence on the faithless. For this, the Church was well equipped with its new armies of friars: chief among them being the Dominicans, whose satirical nickname *Domini Canes* (Hounds of the Lord) sums up their task. By the year 1250, the secret service of the Church was no longer playing a passive collection role. Its 'hounds' were actively engaged sniffing out valuable intelligence.

The most notorious and most successful achievements of the Inquisition were in Spain, where the Inquisition's intelligence process was surprisingly modern. Spies, agents and informers built up a comprehensive 'database' on likely suspects long before the Inquisition proper made their entrance. The Inquisition's advance guard of friars would then arrive and preach a list of heresies. They would then offer an 'Edict of Grace' – effectively an inducement to denounce others. If the faithful came forward and confessed all, then their sins would be pardoned – for a price. This was used to defray the Inquisition's costs.

Hardly surprisingly, a blizzard of self-seeking denunciations and confessions usually assailed the Inquisition when they rolled into town. The Inquisition's police state was a chilling portent of the excesses of twentieth-century secret police, and often more efficient.

Further to the east, scheming Venice survived – and thrived – on a mercantile society deeply rooted in international trade. International trade meant money; and making money demands good information and intelligence. From 1250 onwards, Venice set up probably the finest intelligence system in the world, for its day. Although it was primarily commercial, Venice's prosperity and national security were indivisible from her market intelligence. The markets in their turn needed every scrap of political and military intelligence in order to operate for the greatest benefit of the oligarchy and citizens of Venice.

Although Venetian secrecy has hidden many details across the years, we have a unique mirror image of Venetian intelligence methods and an insight into just how they worked from the detailed records of one small city-state. Dubrovnik, or Ragusa, was an independent city state only 250 miles to the south, on the other side of the Adriatic. It prospered in the shadow of Venice during *La Serenissima*'s century of greatness and modelled many of its institutions on its large and dangerous neighbour, albeit on a much smaller scale.

Ragusa's security policy relied on a unique doctrine based on intelligence alone. From 1301, the Ragusan governing council formally decreed that,

> for the fortification and security of the City . . . to choose good and competent men to explore where they consider best, both inside and outside the Republic, all information and inform the Prince as necessary for the good and prosperity of the state.

One of the prime early targets was Venice itself. By 1348, we see the Ragusan Senate ordering the Council to assign '5 men of knowledge and wisdom to enquire and check on intelligence from Italy and Serbia'. Ragusa's main agents were, like Venice's, 'consuls' or ambassadors sent far afield with specific orders to report everything they saw or heard. Between 1250 and 1590, the number of deployed intelligence service agents abroad on the City payroll rose from three to over forty, all reporting back to Ragusa's senate. Intelligence was the Ragusans' key to survival.

Like Venice, Ragusa had to keep a close eye on the Ottomans, and often behaved as a vassal state. We know that her ambassadors to Istanbul/Constantinople rotated every two years and had written orders instructing them: '. . . if something happens you consider important, we order you to inform us and not to spare horse couriers, for we shall pay them. Be cautious in sending them . . .'

Ragusa's intelligence collection priorities went much wider than mere conventional spying and diplomatic reporting however. Like Venice, as early as the sixteenth century, the Ragusan Senate realised the value of the primitive news-sheets then beginning to circulate. Within the next hundred years Ragusa was formally buying, and using as an 'open source' of intelligence, the *Gazetto di Toscan*, the *Gazette de Leyde* from the Netherlands and inevitably, Venice's own very first news-sheet, the *Notizie del Mondo*. Like some latter-day Special Branch, Ragusa subscribed to and supported her adversaries' newspapers.

With the coming of the printing press, economic intelligence became more open and systematic. Venetian agents were collecting market intelligence at the great European trade fairs from the mid-1400s onwards.

By 1540 a recognisable commercial intelligence system based on the flow of trade and the markets of Europe was firmly established, certainly in Antwerp, where Venice's agent there, van Bombergen, had a clear brief not only to buy and sell items for his Venetian masters (he was on commission) but was also tasked to report formally on key items of market – and all other – intelligence. Such an intelligence network was far too important to be left to mere merchants in such troubled times. As the political upheaval of the Reformation exploded through Europe, the spy masters and intelligence collectors of the various courts and governments began to realise that, in this emerging network of money, market and commercial intelligence, there was an intelligence system that would work for their national survival too.

The English courtier and bureaucrat Francis Walsingham was a dedicated Protestant in the service of Queen Elizabeth. In his early twenties, during the reign of the Catholic Queen Mary, he had been forced to flee abroad, where he had learned the arts of intrigue as practised by the Venetians – the skilful use of diplomacy and secret intelligence to manipulate politics, trade and international influence.

Sir Francis Walsingham had actually witnessed the massacre of the French Huguenots in Paris on St Bartholomew's Day, 1572. He genuinely feared that if the Catholics ever took power again in England his own neck would be on the line.

Once the new Queen's reign made it safe to return to London, Walsingham's quiet, discreet efficiency made him a natural choice as the principal agent runner for Robert Cecil (later Lord Burghley) Elizabeth's principal Secretary of State.

A vicious undercover war was raging between the English secret service and the Jesuits, a fanatical new order of Catholic 'Soldiers of Christ', swearing direct allegiance to the Pope and the spearhead of Rome's Counter-Reformation. If the Pope could get Queen Elizabeth killed, then a Catholic regime could be re-installed in England. England desperately needed intelligence on the Vatican's plots. Walsingham put together a shadowy and highly effective network of agents.

In 1583 Sir Edward Stafford was appointed English Ambassador to Paris. He lacked any background in diplomacy and was soon in trouble, short of money and floundering at the sophisticated French Court. The secret compromisers of the day moved in to snare the unwary envoy. By 1585, de Mendoza, the Spanish Ambassador in Paris triumphantly informed Madrid in a secret letter that he could bribe the British Ambassador into showing him 'Secret Dispatches from London', adding, 'this ambassador is much pressed for money'. A delighted Madrid promptly authorised a bribe of 2,000 golden crowns.

But Walsingham already knew all about the Ambassador's treachery. He had been intercepting and reading the communications between Paris and Madrid and had a trusted informant on the inside, reporting on England's hapless Ambassador. Moreover, he had also identified Stafford as being in contact with Catholic agents of Mary, Queen of Scots and was convinced that the Ambassador was a courier and go-between for Catholic plotters in England and France.

Walsingham could have used his knowledge to send the treacherous Stafford to the block – or worse, 'hanging, drawing and quartering', the usual sentence for treason in Tudor England. But Walsingham was a professional intelligence officer and agent runner. He decided instead to play the treacherous Stafford back to his unseen Spanish masters.

Walsingham used the unsuspecting diplomat to unwittingly pass on disinformation and false intelligence back into Spain.

By 1586 Stafford's value as an 'unconscious' double agent was further reinforced when he became aware of the Spanish plans for an impending invasion of England a good two years before the Armada sailed. Walsingham was informed immediately.

Walsingham's intelligence network was well placed to frustrate Spanish intentions. Using his agents in northern Italy he got the Spanish government's invoices and bills for loans 'contested' when they were presented for payment to the banks at Genoa (who were lending the capital to bankroll the Spanish project to invade England). Delay followed delay and, by autumn 1587, Walsingham could confirm that the Armada was held up for at least another year as his secret hand choked off the vital supply of Italian gold that Spain needed to fund their 'Great Enterprise Against England'.

When finally the Armada did sail in the summer of 1588, two years late, surprise was lost from the moment the great expedition hauled anchor. Walsingham had deployed fishing boats off the Spanish ports and a network of harbour watchers to report the exact size, composition, course and speed of the approaching threat the minute it appeared. Harassed by the English fleet up-Channel, storm and shipwreck completed what the Navy Royal and Walsingham had already begun. Of the 130 ships and 15,000 men who set out, only thirty-five ships and 6,000 exhausted survivors finally limped home to Spain in September after their 3,000-mile voyage. It was Walsingham's greatest military intelligence triumph.

Walsingham was a master of false-flag operations. Once the Catholic Mary Stuart fled Scotland in 1568 for exile in England, she posed a permanent threat to Elizabeth and the Protestant regime. Although Elizabeth kept her rival under house arrest, the Queen of Scots inevitably became the focus of the Catholic cause, and attracted plots and plotters. After twenty years of intrigues, Walsingham decided to trap her once and for all. His tool was a double agent tasked to run a dangerous sting operation.

A convicted crook called Gifford approached Anthony Babington, the leader of yet another plot to free the Scottish Queen, claiming to be a trusted courier of Catholic messages. Babington was fooled and began a correspondence with Mary. Walsingham read it all and baited a trap suggesting a plot to 'rescue' Mary and kill Elizabeth. Unwisely the Queen of Scots wrote back, agreeing to the attempt; in doing so she signed her own death warrant. Babington and his accomplices were arrested and executed; Mary Queen of Scots went to the block herself in Fotheringay Castle on 8 February 1587 – victim of another of Walsingham's well-planned intelligence operations.

Christopher Marlowe was a *protégé* of Sir Roger Manwood, who had close links with Walsingham. It was almost inevitable that one of Manwood's clever scholars from the King's School in Canterbury would drift into the world of intelligence. Once Marlowe had gone up to Cambridge in 1580 he supposedly became a Catholic convert and was sent to a seminary at Rheims. However, his real mission appears to have been to smell out plots against Elizabeth and to identify Catholic agents under training on the continent. His job of identifying enemy agents done, Marlowe fled back to England and became a famous playwright.

Marlowe's mysterious death in 1593 points to some hidden hand at work. On 18 May 1593, he had been arrested and hauled before a special court of privy councillors charged with the correction of slanders, heresies, libels and riots. They released him on bail, but on 30 May, he spent the day in the house of a Mrs Bull at Deptford with three known government spies, all paid agents of the Walsingham intelligence web: Ingram Frizer, Nicholas Skeers and Robert Poley. A struggle took place and Marlowe was stabbed in the head. Frizer was tried and acquitted after pleading self-defence. The affair looks suspiciously like a cleverly executed 'wet job' – the killing of a dangerous and garrulous double agent who knows far too much and must be silenced at all costs. Spying has always been dangerous work.

Armand Jean du Plessis, better known as Cardinal Richelieu of France, was heavily involved in intelligence and intrigue. His greatest triumph was using a Capuchin monk called de Tremblay (the original '*éminence grise*') as an agent of influence to manipulate the Austrian Habsburgs during their long war with the Protestants in Germany. Richelieu's agent network spread lies, false intelligence and used active measures to influence events all over Europe to keep France's enemies fighting each other and weaken them.

His *'cabinet noir'* of letter openers and code breakers alerted him to Buckingham's abortive expedition to la Rochelle to help the rebellious Huguenots in 1627 long before it sailed to certain failure. The Duke of Buckingham's limp send-off, 'The courage of our soldiers and marines must make up for the want of intelligence' would have had intelligence professionals like Walsingham turning in his grave.

Daniel Defoe, of *Robinson Crusoe* fame, was an undercover agent for the government long before he became a famous author. In 1704 he was wandering the Highlands of Scotland posing as 'Alexander Goldsmith', with a brief to report on Scottish political attitudes to London.

The Duke of Marlborough ran a formidable intelligence apparatus during the war against France in the early 1700s. He famously asserted that 'No battle was ever won without good intelligence.' London had a network of spies and agents in Versailles and St Germain sending a steady flow of good intelligence on French dispositions, capabilities and intentions. In addition, Marlborough, in his independent post as Supreme Allied Commander in the Netherlands, ran his own parallel network of high-level agents. These were supplemented by roaming merchants and visitors reporting on the capabilities and deployments of the French as they travelled around the camps and garrisons in north-east France. Marlborough never failed to give this flow of intelligence the highest priority, even if it meant buying it. As *'Stadtholder'* of the Dutch armies he could use both their and Hannover's funds for this vital task: a financial initiative for which his fellow countrymen would later threaten to impeach him and which ended in his dismissal.

Across the Channel, the Chevalier d'Eon's mother had, for reasons best known to herself, dressed and raised her son as a girl since the age of four. The boy grew up able to pass himself off as a woman. He joined the French King's secret service and, in 1765, Louis XV despatched him to St Petersburg as Lia, the niece of a Chevalier Douglas, who was travelling 'for his health'. Douglas's attractive 'niece' was in fact charged with securing a clandestine audience with the Czarina and handing over a secret letter from France designed to block a proposed treaty with Britain.

This 'small and slight girl, with her pink and white complexion and pleasing gentle expression' attracted masculine attention everywhere she went. On arrival at St Petersburg, she was a sensation at Court and was presented to the Empress as 'this delightful flower of French maidenhood'. D'Eon, even became a Maid of Honour to the aged Empress. A glum British Ambassador wrote back to London shortly afterwards, 'I regret to inform you that it is impossible to induce her Majesty to sign the Treaty which we so earnestly desire . . .' D'Eon returned to Paris a hero.

In eighteenth-century Prussia, her warrior King was a great believer in intelligence. He drew up a list of 'Military Instructions to his Generals', which effectively codified national political and military intelligence requirements. Of his twenty-eight 'Articles', no fewer than five are directly tailored to intelligence and one, Article Twenty-Four, discusses 'Security', specifically warning of bad operational security as a direct consequence of treachery.

Article Five of Frederick's instructions lays out his intelligence collection priorities 'For the Knowledge of a Country', listing all the 'Basic Intelligence' needed by an attacker, such as topography, rivers, bridges and the civil population. Article Twelve talks of 'Spies, Deserters and Double agents' and urges generous payment to spies, 'even to the degree of extravagance'. Frederick concludes this article by saying, 'the man who risks his neck to do your service deserves to be well rewarded', which seems sound advice.

Frederick the Great well understood the difference between intelligence 'capabilities' and 'intentions': his Article Thirteen looks at the way that 'an enemy's intentions are to be discovered'. He concluded this article with the dry observation, worthy of a true student of Voltaire, that 'an intelligent enemy is likely to attempt that enterprise most likely to give you the greatest annoyance . . .' Article Fourteen looks at the advantages of fighting on friendly territory, 'where every man acts as your spy' and vice versa.

The fledgling United States of America was founded by a flourishing and highly sophisticated intelligence service run by one of the greatest intriguers and spymasters of his age: George Washington. Revered as a morally upright and almost god-like figure, Washington was in fact a cunning and unscrupulous intelligence officer and a spy-master of the first rank. Walsingham, Richelieu and Thurloe, Oliver Cromwell's devious spymaster, would have instantly recognised him as a worthy adversary, and a fellow spymaster capable of any immoral trickery in pursuit of his aims.

Washington always relied on good intelligence and ran chains of stay-behind agents deep behind British lines. With his intelligence chief, Benjamin Tallmadge, he operated a network of spies in self-contained intelligence cells using dead letter boxes to communicate. Above all, he was a master of disinformation. Again and again he fed false information to the British camp. He deliberately allowed over-inflated troop lists to fall into the hands of known British spies to mislead the enemy about the strength of the rebel forces and personally prepared fake correspondence in his own handwriting to add to the deception. It worked: the British didn't realise just how weak their opponents really were.

Washington also used disinformation as an offensive weapon. His planting of false 'intelligence' to protect the French landings at Newport in 1780 is a classic example of using disinformation to force the enemy into doing the wrong thing. Washington arranged for a fake copy of a 'top secret' plan to fall into British hands showing that his army was going to move to attack the main British base. The British commander abandoned a planned attack on the vulnerable French landing site and instead prepared to defend his headquarters against a non-existent onslaught. It was a classic example of 'warfare by other means' and it was as effective as any victory on the battlefield – and a lot cheaper in terms of lives and treasure. As president, George Washington put his money where his mouth was: he devoted 12 per cent of his first budget to the collection of intelligence.

His equally revered compatriot, Benjamin Franklin, American patriot, hero of the Revolution and champion of liberty, was in fact a British agent and spy throughout. The evidence is compelling. While American envoy to Paris he turns out to have had a code number, 'No. 72', as a paid-up agent of William Eden, the head of the British secret service in London. Franklin dealt openly with the British secret service's head of station in Paris and allowed suspected spies to read his secret correspondence. The truth is, that the cunning old man was playing both ends all along to make sure he was going to be on the winning side – whoever won.

As the new century dawned, France's new master, Napoleon Bonaparte, took an early interest in intelligence. To be a successful general, he realised only too well how much he needed local knowledge, as his ruthless orders about 'volunteering' local guides to 'assist' him in finding his way on campaign make clear:

> One orders the major to seize some peasant to be put at one's disposal, arrest his wife as a hostage and dress up a soldier as the man's farmhand ... Such a system always succeeds ...

The key to Napoleon's military system in the field was a well-organised headquarters that operated according to strict staff procedures. Savary, the principal military intelligence officer under Chief of Staff Berthier ran a surprisingly comprehensive intelligence operation. From cavalry reconnaissance on the battlefield to strategic 'HUMINT' with spies in the enemy camp, French military success was usually backed by timely and accurate intelligence.

Savary's greatest coup was to recruit one of history's master spies, a young Alsatian called Charles Schulmeister. In 1804 Schulmeister was provided with ample funds, servants and a coach, and 'kicked out of France', allegedly for having been overheard supporting the Austrian cause. Posing as a disgruntled nobleman, he fled to Vienna where he offered to tell the Austrian Commander-in-Chief, General Mack, 'everything he knew about the French army' as a revenge for his treatment at their hands. It was all lies, but ensured that, in the campaign of 1805, the Austrian armies were hopelessly fooled by the false intelligence planted by Napoleon's undercover agent.

At home, Napoleon relied on his chief of secret police, Joseph Fouché, to keep him informed, particularly about domestic plots against his despotic rule. The three attributes Fouché demonstrated to his peers were ruthlessness, bureaucratic efficiency and, like J. Edgar Hoover, a readiness to blackmail any potential enemies. Fouché's system of national intelligence was revolutionary and all-encompassing.

To the existing state intelligence structure of a secret chamber of decoders for intercepting diplomatic letters, spies abroad and informers at home, he added the whole revolutionary apparatus of internal spies, informers and denunciation.

The old idea of *intendants* was expanded, with a 'prefect' responsible to Paris in every one of the ninety-odd new Napoleonic *départements*. Within every *arrondissement*, or sub-district, 'sub-prefects' reinforced the flow of intelligence, and single spies and informers informed on *them*. For the first time ever, a country had a complete bureaucracy of internal intelligence agents reporting efficiently back on its population's every move.

From 1804 on, every day, except Sunday, Fouché sent an intelligence summary to the Emperor. In it he summarised events on a wide range of subjects:

Crime statistics

Intercepted letters

Enemy agents detained

Agents' reports

Interrogation reports

Rebellions against National Guard,
police or gendarmerie

Stock market and economic trends

Currency speculation

Public opinion

Army morale and desertions

Political trends, domestic and foreign

Agitators' reports

Prison population

Reports on suspects under surveillance

Royalist plots

Arrest lists

Napoleon's nemesis, the Duke of Wellington, also owed much of his success in Portugal and Spain to a surprisingly modern and highly successful intelligence organisation. He was an old India hand, experienced in fighting the large and well-armed armies of the Moghul rulers. Like Napoleon, Wellesley, or the Duke of Wellington as he became after 1814, knew only too well the importance of intelligence: 'All the business of war, and indeed all the business of life, is to endeavour to find out what you don't know by what you do: that's what I call "guessing what was on the other side of the hill".'

In 1809 he formed a specialist intelligence unit, the Corps of Guides. Its tasks were to scout forward, collect intelligence, interrogate prisoners, and liaise with the locals 'to gain information respecting the force and movements of the enemy'. Of all the Guides and 'Exploring Officers', Colquhoun Grant is perhaps the best known. His exploits would make most Hollywood adventure stories look tame. He rode deep into French-occupied Spain and, speaking fluent Spanish, was accepted by the local villagers around the hearth. More importantly, he was accepted by the leaders of the numerous guerrilla bands in the hills and caves.

Grant and his brother officers hoovered up reports of French movements, divisional and battalion locations, rations and ammunition dumps. It was priceless operational intelligence, made even more valuable by the occasional haul of a French courier's saddlebags, frequently blood-stained, containing coded orders, or letters between the French high command and Paris. These lists of meaningless numbers were handed over by the guerrillas to the Guides in exchange for British gold or weapons, and the precious ciphers passed back to Wellington's code-breaking expert at his headquarters.

Wellington's principal intelligence officer was George Scovell, whose talents lay not in dangerous escapades behind enemy lines but in code breaking. His fluent French and an enquiring, mathematically logical mind made Scovell an inspired code breaker. After 1811, he had even 'cracked' the French 'Great Paris Cipher' and could turn captured despatches into lucid, clear translations. Such a treasure trove of communications intelligence gave Wellington a priceless advantage over his French opponents. The Guides gave Wellington the enemy dispositions and capabilities: Scovell could now read the enemy's *intentions* as well.

After the collapse of France in 1815, revolution was in the air all over Europe. Police forces were everywhere expanded and networks of intelligence agents and informers recruited nationwide, to identify hotbeds of potential disaffection such as 'intellectuals', 'liberals' and nationalist movements. In Austria, Metternich doubled his domestic spy force in the 1820s, pushing thousands of government agents into every area of Austro-German rule where trouble might brew. Metternich was proud to sit like a spider in the middle of his wide intelligence web. He boasted of it.

In this he was far surpassed by the Russian Czar. By 1830, Nicholas I had turned Russia into a police state reminiscent of the bad old days of Ivan the Terrible and Peter the Great. A special 'Third Section' was set up, which acted as the Czar's personal secret political police. With orders to crack down hard on likely dissenters such as university professors, students, writers, musicians, even primary school teachers, Russians learned to fear the bone-headed dead hand of the Russian secret police, who would send a critic of the government to Siberia, 'just to be sure'.

Potential revolutionaries were hunted down by the secret police; few Russians dared to speak out openly. Academics and intellectuals were forbidden to travel abroad, and the villages of Siberia began to fill with well-educated exiles from St Petersburg and Moscow cursing their luck – and the Czar. Underground groups spoke openly of revolution. As Richard Deacon observed, '. . . he [Czar Nicholas I] created such resentment against himself and the office of the Czar that the ultimate fate of Czardom was sealed before 1850'.

When Britain entered the Crimean War in 1854, the first anguished question that went up in Whitehall was: where the hell exactly was the Crimea? Britain's War Office was forced to go and buy maps from a local stationer's before turning to a bootlegged supply provided by a retired officer called Jervis, who had found some maps of the Crimea in a Brussels antique shop.

The British Commander-in-Chief, Lord Raglan, was heard to remark on his departure for war, that, 'Sevastopol is as great a mystery to me as to Jason and his Argonauts.' Intelligence was so bad for the Crimean expedition that Raglan's Quartermaster-General, Sir James Freeth, actually re-issued exact copies of General Murray's intelligence orders from Spain, forty years before, which included such howlers as, '[Exploring Officer] and Assistant Quartermasters-General ... are to pay for such goods and services as are rendered in Spanish *Reals* ...'

In America when the Civil War finally erupted in 1861, both sides understood the importance of intelligence. The proximity of the combatants, a very open press and the porous 'border' between North and South ensured that intrigue and spies would play a notable role in the conflict. Both sides therefore had rudimentary intelligence and espionage networks in place from the beginning.

Lincoln's first choice as chief of the Union intelligence service was a detective, Allan Pinkerton. Pinkerton had fled Scotland with a price on his head to found 'Pinkerton's Detective Agency', which supplied security and intelligence services to a consortium of railroad companies. Pinkerton knew little about intelligence, but enough about basic police work, so concentrated on spying and catching spies.

He was greatly helped by the capture of an openly Confederate socialite, Mrs Rose Greenhow, who ran a Washington spy ring. Pinkerton and his team then 'staked out' the Greenhow household to identify any of her contacts. Alas, the watchers in the bushes and searching her house caught no-one. Rose Greenhow's eight-year-old daughter admitted years later that she had climbed a tree by the front gate, shouting to passers-by 'Mother's been arrested!' Unsurprisingly, there were no more visitors to the Greenhow residence for the rest of the day.

Pinkerton had great success with a remarkable undercover operator, Timothy Webster, a New York policeman. Webster set himself up in Baltimore once the war broke out, spending money freely in the local bars and shops and openly bad-mouthing the Union cause. Once he had been welcomed among the Confederate sympathisers and accepted by the Confederate underground, Webster began to run dangerous spying missions for the Confederacy, bringing valuable 'intelligence' from the Union.

In fact, Pinkerton's man was a classic double agent. The 'intelligence' from the North that Webster was passing over was 'chicken feed' (minimal information passed by a double agent to deceive the opposition into believing that they are receiving valuable, accurate intelligence). In reality he was spying for the Union and reporting *against* the Confederacy. His exploits soon allowed him access even to the Confederate War Minister's office. On one occasion from his base in Richmond, Webster sent Pinkerton a thirty-seven-page report of all the Confederates' military dispositions and plans.

Things went wrong when Webster became seriously ill. His Union spymasters sent two Britons to Richmond to find out why no reports had been received from their undercover agent. Unfortunately, both Scully and Lewis were well known to Confederate sympathisers as 'Federal Security Men' and were arrested by the Confederate Police. Under questioning, the two Pinkerton men broke and implicated Webster, who went to the gallows as a Yankee spy.

But the Confederacy had its share of espionage triumphs, too. One of the most remarkable was an officer using the cover name of 'Captain Coleman'. Hiding in a contraband expedition in Tennessee he and Sam Davis, his courier, were arrested. Coleman's secret despatches were discovered on Davis, who refused to identify who had given them to him. He was reminded that he would swing as a spy if he didn't tell the truth, but Davis refused to talk and the infuriated Union soldiers hanged him.

A relieved Coleman escaped to spy another day, thanks to his colleague's bravery. When, much later, the commander of the Corps of Scouts, General Dodge, learned of the remarkable story of how his chief adversary had slipped through his fingers, he contributed to a memorial being erected in Nashville to Sam Davis, the Confederate hero.

The South's most famous agent was a woman, called, appropriately enough, Belle Boyd. This intrepid Southern belle ran what was effectively a one-woman spy service for the Virginia Confederacy, on one occasion actually dashing onto the battlefield at Front Royal on 23 May 1862 under a hail of fire to warn General 'Stonewall' Jackson that three undetected Union columns were about to fall on his outnumbered force.

Eventually, like most amateurs, she over-reached herself and was arrested. Pinkerton himself interrogated her. However, this redoubtable young woman managed to pull the wool over the eyes of Lincoln's 'ace detective' and bluffed her way out of jail, only to be caught some months later by Lafayette Baker. This time she was held. After her release in 1864 she met a US naval officer, Sam Hardinge, who decided to marry her. The Union authorities were unimpressed and threw Belle's new Yankee husband into prison for his romantic impulse, where sadly he died. The beautiful Belle, ace rebel spy, ended her days giving dramatic lectures about her life to audiences around the country.

By 1863, the Union Army of the Potomac's new Chief of Staff, Daniel Butterfield admitted that, 'we're almost as ignorant of the enemy as if they'd bin in China . . .' Under the Union Army's Provost Marshal, a new intelligence and security organisation was formed called the 'Bureau of Military Information' under a former New York lawyer, Colonel George Sharpe.

His organisation was almost an echo of Wellington's in the Peninsula, half a century before. The Bureau of Military Information contained a 'scouting' wing of nearly 200 roving spies and scouts, a captured-document office, telegraph interceptors, code breakers, prisoner of war interrogators and even, for the first time in a major war, an aerial reconnaissance cell.

But intelligence cannot win battles by itself. One of the all-time classic examples of this universal truth comes from the American Civil War. Just before the bloody clash at Antietam in September 1862, two Union soldiers discovered an envelope containing cigars. The cigars were wrapped in a secret copy of Robert E. Lee's 'Special Order No. 191': the Confederate general's detailed orders for the invasion of Maryland. Despite this clear insight into his enemy's plans, General McClellan, the Union commander, failed to use this intelligence coup and, in a disastrous, bumbling battle, was defeated by the weaker Confederate force – even though he had a complete copy of their battle plan in his hand.

It was lack of intelligence that finally sucked Lee into the decisive battle of the war. Ordered to locate any enemy forces on Lee's flank, his cavalry commander Stuart instead took the Confederate cavalry off on a pointless *chevauchée,* deep into Union territory, leaving Lee completely blind at a critical moment. Lacking vital information on the presence of the enemy, the Confederate commander pushed a whole corps across the mountains into the small town of Gettysburg to find out what was going on, just as Meade's leading Union units blundered into the town from the other side. In a rolling encounter battle, Lee's soldiers battered themselves to death against a desperate Union defence, until after three days of savage fighting he was forced to retreat.

The Union was helped enormously by its ability to take advantage of the most effective espionage network of the whole civil war, running deep inside Richmond itself. Its leader was an eccentric little spinster called Elizabeth Van Lew. Colonel Sharpe himself paid tribute to this unlikely super-spy's success: 'the greater portion [of our intelligence] from Richmond in its collection . . . and its transmission, we owed to the intelligence and devotion of Miss Van Lew.'

Elizabeth Van Lew was known as 'Crazy Bett'. She was an open abolitionist and had long since freed her own black slaves. She visited the sick and wounded, including the Federal prisoners of war armed with permits signed by General Winder, the man who ran the Confederate prisons, himself. 'Crazy Bett' was able to collect a vast amount of raw information on everything the Union POWs had seen behind Confederate lines and supplement it with her own observations. Her greatest coup was to get one of her black helpers, Mary Bowser, into the Confederacy's White House as a waitress at President Davis' own table, where every indiscretion or revelation was promptly relayed back to 'Miss Bett'.

She sent her intelligence to the North by a complicated series of black couriers 'runnin' errands for Miss Bett'. The ciphered messages were hidden in dummy eggs and servants' frocks and were never intercepted. It enabled Miss Van Lew to keep up a steady flow of high-grade intelligence for most of the war. By 1864, Elizabeth Van Lew's house had become the nerve centre of the biggest spy ring in the South, with sub-agents in the Confederate army and navy headquarters, food and ammunition suppliers, the Confederate White House and links with a railway network to record and report all train movements.

Elizabeth Van Lew survived the Civil War. However, her help for the North meant that she spent the rest of her days as a social pariah in Virginia. An ungrateful US Congress refused to vote her any money for her efforts and she passed her last years alone and in poverty: a sad end for a genuine master spy who ran an extraordinarily successful undercover operation.

Wilhelm Stieber was a Saxon. He was a two-faced, lying, treacherous, double-dealing, amoral, duplicitous, conniving bastard: in fact he had all the qualities of a very effective intelligence officer. He trained as a Prussian lawyer but became an informant for the Berlin police, eventually joining them as an inspector. During the 1848 revolution he helped 'save' the King from a mob (which may well have been paid off by Stieber himself in his role as agent provocateur) and was promoted to Chief of Police. His methods closely followed Fouché's and he has considerable claim to be the man who invented modern 'intelligence'.

Stieber's greatest coups were in support of the Prussian Army and the expansionist plans of Otto von Bismarck. Between them they invented and organised one of the secret powerhouses of the nineteenth century, as Stieber became Bismarck's 'sleuth-hound' for the next twenty years. The 'Prince of Spies' and the 'Chief to 40,000 spies' (some of the nicknames given to Stieber by admirers and enemies alike) carved out a brilliant career that set the agenda for modern espionage.

The heart of his empire was a massive network of underground informants ('The 40,000 spies') from which reports and dossiers flowed on the internal situation in Prussia. Secondly, he conducted extremely detailed reconnaissance and spying missions (which he, unusually for a spymaster, undertook himself) against Bismarck's diplomatic 'targets'. Last, but not least, he analysed and combined all this material into comprehensive intelligence reports for Bismarck and von Moltke, the Chief of Staff. It was a tour de force and Prussia's – and Bismarck's – success owes as much to Stieber's clear intelligence reports as to any great diplomatic 'genius' on the part of the Iron Chancellor.

During the summer of 1865, the chief of Prussia's secret police even dressed up as an itinerant pedlar and roamed Austria and Bohemia in a horse and cart. Stieber stopped at towns and villages, talking to the locals and happily selling his goods to any Austrian units on manoeuvres. To the villagers he sold religious trinkets and pictures of saints; to the soldiers, especially the rich young Austrian officers, he peddled an interesting line in pornographic pictures. By the time he returned to Berlin, he was able to draw up a highly detailed report on the Austrians for Bismarck and von Moltke's planned invasion routes into Austria. Prussia's crushing victory in 1866 owed much to Stieber's detailed and accurate intelligence.

For Bismarck's planned attack on France in 1870, Stieber established what was, up to then, probably the most comprehensive intelligence and espionage system ever seen. While he travelled as a 'Greek entrepreneur' looking to invest in French industry (backed by a large bag of gold), two of his acolytes quietly hired dozens of whores in the French garrison towns. The Prussians also recruited a thousand young women 'of good upbringing', to act as servants and chambermaids in French officers' messes, smart hotels and the residences of local prefects and mayors. As if such a spy network was not enough, Stieber got permission from Bismarck to recruit several thousand 'farm labourers' to help the French farmers with their harvest.

This vast network, estimated by Prussian sources to have been 35,000-strong at its peak, was controlled by a selected group of retired German officers who set up businesses in key military garrisons at Paris, Lille, Valenciennes, Strasbourg, Bordeaux, Lyons and Marseilles. They and their 'young captains', posing as clerks, gathered in the individual reports from a huge number of dead letter boxes and despatched them in cipher to regional controllers set up by Stieber at Brussels, Geneva and Lausanne. It was a prodigious undertaking, controlled directly by Stieber himself.

By the start of the Franco-Prussian war Stieber had brought back over three trunk loads of documents and compiled over 1,650 separate intelligence reports on every possible aspect of the invasion of France, from up-to-date maps to the locations of draught horses. Von Moltke's armies could not have asked for more when, in the summer of 1870, Bismarck struck. The Prussians knew exactly where to go, which farms had livestock and food and where every French official lived. Stieber's intelligence ensured the French defeat.

After the war, Stieber returned to Berlin as chief of Bismarck's secret police. There he set up a high-class bordello in Berlin called 'The Green House', staffed by a carefully selected group of his agents and patronised by foreign diplomats, German aristocracy and senior officers. Intelligence, security and whores came together in a natural synergy. His recruited prostitutes – both male and female – soon made him aware of their high-born clients' likes and dislikes, especially individual perversions. Armed with this insider's knowledge of sexual habits and illicit liaisons, Stieber was now able to blackmail much of Berlin society and a number of important foreign visitors too.

Although Stieber had over twenty decorations for his contribution to Bismarck's dream of a united, powerful Germany, he never gained the social acceptance he craved. When he died in 1892, a huge crowd of nobility came to the funeral and followed his coffin. At the time it was noticed that the mourners were unusually cheerful. One Berlin wag pointed out that, 'the reason that so many toffs came to the funeral was because they wanted to confirm that Stieber really was dead'.

Stieber's work lives on to this day. He was the first national intelligence chief to use agents to monitor and control the press, the banks, business and industry. Long before Franco, Stieber devised the idea of a putting a 'fifth column' in place before an invasion. He regularised mass postal censorship and used it to spy on both the army and the population, and to enhance his own power. His Central Information Bureau virtually invented modern 'psyops' – psychological warfare designed to raise the morale of his own side, and weaken that of his opponent, by publicising enemy blunders, bad news and casualties. Stieber's techniques poisoned the atmosphere throughout Europe, demonstrated the power of intelligence, created a spy fever that is with us to this day, and helped to set the international climate for the Great War of 1914–18. Stieber's achievement on behalf of Bismarck, Prussia and modern intelligence is awesome – and frightening.

As Ireland's growing demand for Home Rule encouraged a wave of terrorism in Ireland and London in the 1870s and 1880s, there was a loud call for more intelligence. London tried to stamp out Fenian dynamite bombings on its doorstep, while the Royal Irish Constabulary clamped down hard on terrorism across the water. The murder of the Chief

Secretary for Ireland, Lord Frederick Cavendish, in Dublin's Phoenix Park in 1882, was the last straw. London set up 'The Special Irish Branch' – Britain's political police, a unit within the Metropolitan Police – specifically to cope with Irish terrorism. It has been busy ever since ...

As the nineteenth century drew to its close, what was known as the 'Great Game', began to become an imperial pre-occupation. This was the name given to the undercover war between Britain and Russian on the wild North West Frontier of Pakistan. It was a *Boy's Own Paper* myth fostered by men like Baden-Powell, founder of the Scout Movement, who spent some time on the frontier having what he described as 'some jolly larks', before graduating to pottering around the Mediterranean, drawing pictures of fortifications whilst pretending to be sketching butterflies.

Reflecting his time and his caste, he wrote, 'the best spies are unpaid men doing it for the love of the thing', and, memorably, 'For anyone who is tired of life, the thrilling life of a spy should be the finest recuperation.' One wonders quite what William Buckley, the CIA Beirut station chief murdered by Hezbollah in 1985, would have made of Baden-Powell's imperial nonsense about 'the thrilling life of the spy' as he lay in his own excreta, chained to the water pipes of his filthy underground prison.

Across the Channel, harsher disciplines prevailed. Stieber's legacy of distrust and deceit pervaded diplomatic exchanges at every level and bred suspicion, especially in Paris. The most notorious case of all was the Dreyfus Affair, the worst political scandal in modern French history. It had all the hallmarks of Stieber's methods. This time the evil genius was not German but French, and there were many accomplices to help him.

Alfred Dreyfus was an artillery officer – and a Jew. In September 1894, he was called to the office of the Chief of the General Staff, asked to draft a letter and then arrested and imprisoned on the grounds that 'his handwriting was that of a known spy for the Germans'. Dreyfus was court-martialled and, on the evidence of a suborned handwriting expert, duly convicted of passing top-secret plans to the Germans. A stunned Dreyfus was led away, weakly protesting, and sent to a living death on Devil's Island.

However, a Colonel Picquart pointed out that that Dreyfus had never had access to the operational plan that he was alleged to have sold to the Germans. Picquart did however find a document linking Captain Ferdinand Esterhazy of the French Operational Plans Branch with Colonel von Schwartzkoppen, the German attaché who allegedly received the secret plans from Dreyfus. In August 1895 Picquart, believing he had uncovered the real spy, took his evidence to the Chief of Staff.

To his astonishment, Picquart was transferred to North Africa. It was clear by now that nothing must be allowed to undermine the reputation of the General Staff. The Army had found Dreyfus guilty and so he must be – never mind the embarrassing facts later uncovered by the nosy Colonel Picquart. The scandal erupted into the newspapers, with Émile Zola thundering *'J'ACCUSE!'* against the Army and the government. He was arrested too and had to flee France.

It took ten long years to clear Dreyfus's name. On his deathbed Esterhazy's agent handler's last words were reputed to have been, 'Tell them that Dreyfus was innocent!'

The Dreyfus Affair signalled the start of a Europe-wide spy mania, well before the First World War. William Le Queux in Britain invented a villain, called 'Gaston la Touche', as improbable a creation as any of Ian Fleming's later villains. By the time 1914 erupted, Erskine Childers and John Buchan – aided and abetted by the newspapers of the day – had ensured that Germany replaced France as Britain's enemy of choice. Intelligence and spy fever became public obsessions.

Governments everywhere began to translate these public fears into national organisations. By 1906–10, the idea that Britain was riddled with a huge army of undercover German spies posing as waiters, barbers and commercial travellers was accepted as gospel by many. That Germany was one day planning to invade the British Isles seemed only too believable so, in 1909, Britain's Committee for Imperial Defence recommended a new organisation to keep itself informed about espionage.

As a result, an obscure captain of the South Staffordshire Regiment was appointed to lead a domestic security service: the Secret Service Bureau, which later became known as MI5. Vernon Kell, bureaucratic-empire-builder extraordinaire, was to cling on to his post for another thirty-one years, until the summer of 1940, when Winston Churchill sacked him. Ironically it was Churchill as Home Secretary who supplied the initial legislation that enabled Kell to expand his 'office and one clerk' into a major bureaucratic organ of state security linked into every police station, dockyard and factory in the land, and able to intercept mail at will.

Armed with these powers, Kell was remarkably successful. In the last hours before war, he ordered police to lift twenty-one of the twenty-two known German agents operating throughout the country. This MI5 coup totally disabled the German intelligence network in Britain for the rest of the war. Britain's pre-war spy fever may have been exaggerated and farcical. It did, however, indirectly lead to the very result it advocated: the complete eradication of German spies in England.

Kell's counterpart at the War Office's 'Special Intelligence Bureau' was Mansfield Cumming, who had been invalided out of the Royal Navy in 1885. Since his retirement he had dabbled in some undercover intelligence trips abroad for the Naval Intelligence Department. In 1912 he was appointed as head of the 'Special Intelligence Section', the new overseas arm of Britain's Secret Service Bureau, later to be known as MI6 or the Secret Intelligence Service.

New technology played a significant role in World War One. Within its first month, the French were collecting signals intelligence on their enemy. A wireless listening station on the Eiffel Tower brought the news that von Kluck was heading south to the Marne.

The first British aerial reconnaissance of the war revealed massed German columns marching southwest from Brussels. Intelligence from aerial reconnaissance soon turned out to be a crucial factor in the conflict. On all sides, aircraft had assumed the role previously played by the cavalry – as the eyes of the commander, enabling him to keep his 'contact intelligence' up to date and to discover exactly where his enemy was and what he was up to. It was but a short step to using photography to lay hard facts before doubting generals. This kind of near real-time photographic intelligence revolutionised warfare.

The first priority of aerial photography was to improve mapping for the troops and for the artillery. Aerial photography's contribution grew as the war progressed. By 1918, the British had processed over half a million aerial photographs on the Western Front.

Churchill's aggressive plans after the Great War for an expedition to crush the Bolsheviks petered out when Britain withdrew from Russia. At home, a surly army awaiting demobilisation mutinied 'twenty times a week', waiting to join an even surlier workforce, crippled by class war, strikes and unrest. The mood in Britain, as with Russia and Germany, was revolutionary; soldiers were used to guard key points. The 'Red Menace' seemed very real in 1919. Securing intelligence on the threat to national security became a Whitehall priority.

The threat of subversion at home was the order of the day. Suspicion of the Bolsheviks' activities pervaded the whole country. The British Establishment of 1924, thoroughly alarmed at what they regarded as their own Socialist government in power – the first Labour government had just been formed – and what looked like an imminent rising of the working class, had every reason to fear the Bolsheviks and their 'Red friends' in Britain. Events exploded in 1924 with the publication of an intercepted letter from a senior Soviet official, Grigory Zinoviev, to the British Communist Party (CPGB). The letter openly called for intensified agitation in the United Kingdom.

Although there is some evidence that the letter was a forgery, probably authored by White Russians, an extensive investigation by Gill Bennett, the Chief Historian of Britain's Foreign Office in 1999 was unable to give a definitive ruling.

She said that the letter – supposedly sent to MI6 from one of its agents in the Latvian capital, Riga – was written as a result of a campaign orchestrated by White Russians who had good contacts in London who were strongly opposed to any Anglo-Soviet treaty.

Forgery or not, her report made clear that MI6 deceived the Foreign Office at the time by asserting that the Zinoviev letter was genuine. There can be little doubt that it reflected the prejudices held in Whitehall and had some impact of the general election that swept the Conservative government to power.

Despite Prime Minister Ramsey MacDonald's specific instructions that no action was to be taken, the Conservative opposition promptly passed the letter to the *Daily Mail* for publication. By next day the story was all over all the newspapers – just four days before the voters went to the Polls. Labour lost the election (though they were heading for defeat even before the letter was publicised) and Anglo–Soviet diplomatic ties were broken off.

By the 1920s every nation recognised the importance of secure codes. The Germans brought the supposedly unbreakable Enigma machine into service for all their classified signals in the late 1920s. In 1939 the Poles gave it to the British to complete the job. It would go on to play a significant part in the upcoming conflict – a vindication of the key role intelligence can play.

MI6 had a disastrous start to World War Two. In December 1939 their two senior agents in Holland were trapped by a clever German sting operation. Posing as 'Disaffected German Officers' Sicherheitsdienst (SD) operators lured the unsuspecting SIS men to the border and captured them. They talked and revealed SIS's whole European network.

But Britain had its successes too. In 1939, MI5 recruited a double agent called Owens and passed him off to the Germans as a fanatical Welsh revolutionary. Agent 'Snow' came back to Britain clutching instructions and a nice new Abwehr (the German military intelligence) code book to use when he sent his messages to Germany. Soon he was chattering away to the Germans on his 'secret' radio – courtesy of MI5. It was the first seeds of what would later grow into the British Double Cross radio game, which would turn the Abwehr inside out and eventually leave MI5 controlling virtually every German spy reporting from Great Britain.

However, the British were not the only ones who played 'radio games'. In occupied Holland the British Special Operations Executive (SOE) ran into serious trouble. 'Operation North Pole' saw every British agent trapped by the Germans on landing. They were then either sent to a concentration camp or pressed into service as a double agent, sending back false messages on their radios.

To the east, Stalin had numerous warnings of Hitler's intention to invade the USSR in 1941 – 103 in all. The Soviet dictator ignored them all and his staff were too scared to tell him anything with which he might disagree. Thanks to Stalin's obduracy, Operation Barbarossa took the USSR by surprise on 22 June 1941. Twenty-five million Russians died in the subsequent 'Great Patriotic War'.

As the war progressed, the need for intelligence grew and intelligence agencies proliferated. The British had no fewer than *nine* secret agencies during the conflict. Many of these intelligence agencies are still with us in one form or another to this day. For instance, the American Office of Strategic Services (OSS) would evolve into the Central Intelligence Agency (CIA) and America's code breakers eventually re-emerged as the National Security Agency (NSA).

The development of the atom bomb in 1944–5 was supposed to be the most closely guarded secret of all time. However, even if Hitler was in the dark, Stalin knew all about the 'Manhattan Project' from the start, thanks to a group of committed Communist spies, who kept the Soviet leader well informed.

The result was that the Cold War was an intelligence war from the start. Communist expansion and Western containment clashed first in Europe and then all over the world. As the arms race escalated into a nuclear stand-off by the late 1950s, both sides tried to find out as much as they could about the weapons programmes of the other camp. The Cold War was fought with spies, intelligence-gathering ships, planes and submarines, and with constant espionage. It also spawned a whole new genre of spy literature and films.

The Cold War encouraged technical intelligence gathering on an unprecedented scale even using submarines as secret intelligence collectors. In 1979, the USS *Halibut* placed a bug on the Soviets' cable in the Sea of Okhotsk and, by the mid-nineties, the NSA and the US Navy began to tap directly into deep undersea cables, a dangerous and illegal task. They used the USS *Parche*, a specially converted submarine to slice into a Russian fibre-optic cable in the Barents Sea – but details on this are sketchy, as information about interception methods are still among the most highly classified US government operations.

Between 1978 and 1992, even Australian submarines got involved in Cold War spying, carrying out top-secret missions against Russia and China in some very unusual locations. One operation was believed to have taken an Australian submarine as far as the waters off Libya.

The Cold War was not the only undercover battle of its time. In the unremitting struggle between Israel and its Arab neighbours, Mossad has carved an enviable reputation as an intelligence agency. But even the much-vaunted Mossad can be fooled. At Yom Kippur in 1973 the Israelis got the shock of their lives when the combined armies of Syria and Egypt fell on them by complete surprise. Although Israel eventually threw the invaders back, the Yom Kippur War of 1973 was Israel's worst intelligence failure.

Markus Wolf, the legendary East German spy chief, didn't accept failure. He penetrated every level of West German life – running agents from Günter Guillaume in President Willi Brandt's office to humble office cleaners. He even personally controlled the second in command of the West German military intelligence service, the MAD, for eight years. His Stasi specialised in using smooth male gigolos to pick up NATO secretaries and seduce them into giving up their secrets. He boasted that: 'I may have perfected the use of sex in spying.' After re-unification the West Germans sentenced Wolf to three years for 'detention, coercion and bodily harm'.

With the end of the Cold War priorities changed.

The Falklands War in 1982 however proved an old rule: nothing beats good intelligence. It started as an intelligence disaster – for both sides. Galtieri and his Junta refused to believe that the British would fight: the British Foreign Office suppressed warnings from its attaché in Buenos Aires. British intelligence was reduced to photocopying pages from *Jane's Fighting Ships* before sending the fleet off to the South Atlantic.

Hardly was the Falklands over when conflict erupted in Beirut in the mid-eighties to be followed by Saddam Hussein's 1990 grab for Kuwait's oil. The Iraqi eviction from Kuwait followed swiftly but by then the Middle East was aflame, from Algeria to Afghanistan. The attack on America in 2001 by hijacked civilian airliners shocked the world. President Bush's response in 2003 was to invade Iraq, for reasons that still remain unclear. Many are convinced – in spite of their protestations to the contrary – that the evidence shows he and Prime Minister Blair deliberately manipulated intelligence to mislead their electorates.

From 1950 onwards, technology changed intelligence. The USA began developing intelligence satellites in the mid-fifties and after the Soviets' launch of the first *Sputnik* in 1957 and the debacle of the shooting down of Gary Powers' U-2 over the USSR in 1960 invested heavily in 'spy satellites'. In America the National Reconnaissance Office is the responsible intelligence agency. Most satellites are designed to either photograph or provide radar imagery of ground targets, IMINT, with others dedicated to SIGINT, the collection of radio transmissions; others are collecting electronic signals, or ELINT.

Today, satellites can see a great deal. Modern digital technology from low orbit means that a golf ball, a newspaper headline or a car licence plate are all visible. However, what none of these can do is see through the roof.

For that you still need an old-fashioned spy on the ground. Some things in intelligence never change.

PART 2

CHAPTER TWO

On Intelligence

It is hard to lose a game of cards when you can see the other fellow's hand.

In war and in politics, this ability to 'see the other fellow's hand' has always been of crucial importance. It is with some surprise therefore that we discover that intelligence features little in many otherwise influential writings on great events and military campaigns. Many authoritative military historians somehow manage to skip over intelligence completely. The great Clausewitz himself, in his 1832 masterwork, *On War*, treats intelligence with something amounting to disdain. This may be the result of his experiences in the Prussian army: in their campaigns against Napoleon the Prussians frequently found themselves at a loss for military intelligence. Clausewitz's dismissive conclusions, certainly at the tactical and operational level, seem to be rooted in what we call 'the fog of war', which meant that, to the great military theorist, much of military intelligence was questionable at best and frequently late or wrong.

And, in all fairness, Clausewitz's assumption that surprise on a strategic level is well-nigh impossible is generally true, as the massing of forces both before the 1812 Moscow campaign and equally in the desert around Kuwait before the first Gulf War in 1991 demonstrate. It really is difficult to avoid telegraphing hostile intent when you are moving a million men on the border. Nonetheless, Clausewitz's lofty dismissal of the merit of intelligence as a force multiplier and war winner is clearly misguided and is (along with his ignoring of logistics and seapower) a major flaw in his supposedly magisterial analysis of war.

His rival Antoine-Henri Jomini, in his *Summary of the Art of War* (1838) made no such mistake and goes to some lengths to avoid falling into the same trap. Jomini had been schooled by Napoleon and had observed just how much importance the Emperor attached to timely and accurate intelligence. Jomini leaves us in no doubt about the value of intelligence, even writing, 'intelligence is one of the chief causes of the great difference between the theory and practice of war'.

Modern writers like Martin van Creveld and Edward Luttwak have confirmed in robust terms just how vital intelligence is in war. It is irritating therefore that many otherwise much admired writers on military history skim over its vital role. For example, David Chandler's masterly *The Campaigns of Napoleon* manages to record the French Emperor's martial feats in great detail with hardly a mention of intelligence. Likewise John Keegan's magisterial *The Face of Battle*, *Mask of Command* and *The Price of Admiralty* have no mention of intelligence in their indexes and very little in their text. This is strange. To name but two highly successful commanders – George Washington and Napoleon Bonaparte – their great victories are matters of national celebration to this day: but rarely is the extent to which their triumphs were based on good intelligence acknowledged.

Clearly there is something seriously wrong here. Why has intelligence been treated as the Cinderella of the martial record by serious politico-military writers?

Two reasons immediately spring to mind: first, secrecy. Intelligence coups are usually best left in the shadows. When you have an ace up your sleeve, or your idiot opponent is playing cards with a mirror behind him, stay quiet. That way you'll win. Second, intelligence has, for a long time, been regarded as a poor relation in the armoury of many nations' security measures. Pilots get glory for punching holes in clouds and sailors advance their careers by commanding warships at sea. Generals get promotion for fighting and winning battles. Precisely how they achieve that is often forgotten or overlooked. (Ask any embittered logistical staff officer.)

And politicians with secret intelligence to guide their seemingly brilliant decisions tend to stay very quiet as to just how well informed they were when they made them; preferring instead to luxuriate in the limelight. Not for nothing did Sir Alexander Cadogan, Permanent Under-Secretary for Foreign Affairs at the British Foreign Office from 1938 to 1945, describe intelligence as 'the missing dimension from most diplomatic history'.

This perception of intelligence as some secret Cinderella is reinforced by the old joke, 'Military intelligence is a contradiction in terms.' However, it is a commonly held view, because history is littered with disastrous intelligence mistakes. From the earliest recorded times down to the many wars, big and small, in our world today, politicians and soldiers of all kinds have been taken by surprise. How could these supposedly intelligent and supposedly well-briefed leaders have been so stupid?

Yet 'surprise' is one of the cardinal principles of war. Every military academy and staff college in the world teaches the need to achieve surprise – and to guard against it – to every single student of the military art. Despite this, political and military decision makers appear to have been caught out with almost predictable regularity. Is the failing one of endemic stupidity or of an opponent's cunning?

The answer is both. Just as every military commander hopes not to be taken by surprise, potential adversaries strive equally hard with every trick and resource to mislead, to deceive, and to catch their enemy unawares. Machiavelli understood this very well: 'Never attempt to win by force what can be won by deception.' And Sun Tzu still goes to the heart of the matter: 'Thus, what enables the wise sovereign and the good general to strike and conquer, and achieve things beyond the reach of ordinary men, is FOREKNOWLEDGE.'

To avoid being surprised, and to surprise their foes, commanders and politicians rely on intelligence and their intelligence staffs far more than they generally let on. Sometimes they are successful, sometimes not. On the success of intelligence hinges the decisions taken by politicians and military commanders alike; and very often the future of their country and its population too.

Whilst other professionals in a host of occupations make key decisions, none of them carry such an awful responsibility or can have such disastrous consequences. If a banker makes a fatal error, economies crash and people lose their savings and jobs. If a surgeon makes a dreadful mistake, a patient or two dies. But when a politician, general, admiral or air marshal blunders in war, soldiers and civilians alike die, sometimes in appalling numbers. To take just one example, Hitler and Paulus sent no fewer than quarter of a million men to their doom around Stalingrad. Of that number, only five thousand broken men finally came back from Russia in 1955. Would Hitler have ordered the Sixth Army to stand fast if he had had accurate intelligence about the Soviet generals' plans? And, perhaps more telling, would Hitler ever have unleashed his legions against the USSR in 1941 if he had known that the USSR would be able to draw on nearly 600 divisions in the coming twelve months? Twice as many as his intelligence advisers had forecast.

An even more chilling example is the Cuban Missile Crisis of 1962, when the USA and the USSR came to the brink of nuclear war. If secret backstairs diplomacy saved the world from nuclear Armageddon that autumn, then it was intelligence that identified the threat and helped the protagonists to negotiate their way out of the nightmare.

Good intelligence helped make good decisions. Bad intelligence invariably leads to disaster, both political and military. That is a simple truth, whether in our own lives or the affairs of nations.

However, although intelligence can help, it cannot make commanders' decisions for them. Even when confronted with crystal-clear reports, accurate, up to date, and supported by first-hand evidence, history has shown us over and over again that stubborn, ambitious or misguided politicians and military commanders will simply ignore the cast-iron proof before them. They are only human. We do not have to go very far to find a particularly striking example.

In September 1944, General 'Boy' Browning disregarded Major Brian Urquhart's black-and-white aerial intelligence photographs clearly showing the presence of German SS Panzer divisions refitting near Arnhem. Not only that, he raged that Urquhart had risked compromising the operation by flying reconnaissance Spitfires over the target and promptly dismissed his unfortunate intelligence officer on the grounds that, 'he was mentally disturbed by stress and overwork'.

A distressed Urquhart was escorted out of the headquarters by a grim-faced Director of Medical Services and sent off on convalescent leave. Days later, the Paras dropped to their doom, right into the lap of two SS Panzer divisions.

The consequences of Browning's orders led to the catastrophic loss of British 1st Airborne Corps on the ill-fated Operation Market Garden. It need never have happened, but for Browning's decision (which seems to have been based primarily on a desire 'not to be left out of the action' when the war's end was thought, wrongly, to be in sight). The soldiers of the British and Polish airborne brigades paid a terrible price for Browning's determination, conceit, arrogance, desire for glory – call it what you will – which motivated his wilful refusal to acknowledge the accurate information put before him by his intelligence staff. Commanders and politicians are, after all, only fallible human beings; and greedy and ambitious as other men – often more so.

Ironically, years later, when Urquhart was the senior adviser on security operations to the Secretary-General of the United Nations, he recounted the story of that fateful wartime autumn in sad, almost humorous, terms, ending with by saying: 'But I don't really blame General Browning; in his shoes, what else could he have done?'[1]

But, by and large, politico-military commanders are not stupid. Even the most intellectually challenged national leader has always understood that war is a matter of at least two sides and wants, understandably, to be on the winning team. Victory will bring him honours, riches, rewards and the applause of his countrymen. Why then, with such incentives, do approximately 50 per cent of them get it so consistently wrong? In the great majority of cases, defeat can often be traced back, among other things, to a lack of knowledge of the enemy. Whether from over-confidence, ignorance, gullibility, or just a failure to comprehend the facts, military defeats are almost invariably associated with *intelligence* defeats. In Malaya in 1941, British and Imperial commanders believed that the Japanese were puny little Asiatics, incapable of fighting in the jungle, let alone operating modern combat aircraft, and posed little or no threat at all. They were wrong.

---

1. Private communication with the author, Cyprus, 1975.

It is hard for us to grasp just how such appalling misjudgements were ever allowed to become part of a nation's military policy. We must therefore look closely at the actual mechanisms of intelligence itself, long regarded as a black and mysterious art practised by anonymous men and women, far from the limelight. Are their failings and failures the true reason behind so many military blunders? How can 'intelligence' ever get it so badly wrong?

Yet we should not be too surprised. Despite its undoubted importance, governments have rarely been lavish in the support they have accorded their intelligence operations. With its fellow battle-winning partner, logistics, intelligence is often treated like a backwater or a mysterious haunt of clever but difficult individuals.

Part of the problem is that intelligence does not exist in a political or bureaucratic vacuum. The real task of intelligence is to tell the truth to powerful decision makers, *whether they like it or not*. The relationship between the providers of intelligence and any nation's political decision makers is therefore of paramount importance. It invariably requires a great deal of moral courage on the part of any intelligence officer when it comes to briefing unpalatable news.

Although in liberal democracies we tend not to literally shoot the messenger, bearers of unwelcome news can quickly become unpopular and find themselves sidelined and overlooked. The temptation is there for intelligence agencies therefore to pander to the preconceptions and whims of their masters. In their turn, decision makers all too often try and trim and even ignore intelligence that does not coincide with their priorities.

Different nations have handled this in different ways, reflecting their political system, cultural values and their needs. Stalin's insistence that only intelligence with which he agreed could be accurate, completely undermined the biggest and best intelligence organisation of its time, as a climate of fear and conformity hollowed out and distorted the NKVD's intelligence assessments in early 1941. Lyndon B. Johnson's war cabinet took a different approach over the war in Vietnam in 1968. Confronted by clear evidence of the North Vietnamese intention to fight on and take a pounding, whatever terms were offered, in order to reunite their country, the American leadership just ignored the facts before their eyes.

This realisation that vital intelligence can be disregarded or challenged as being unpalatable or inaccurate has forced modern intelligence services to try and make their intelligence ever more accurate and robust. The aim is to force their 'customers', be they military or political, to acknowledge the truth staring them in the face. To achieve this, military intelligence nowadays has been turned into a system designed to reduce error and anomaly to a minimum.

The process of turning information into intelligence is known as the 'Intelligence Cycle'. It is important for us to understand these basic processes of the intelligence world. Only then can we understand what went wrong in the past, and why. Only then can we understand just what intelligence can, and cannot, do.

PART 3

HOW INTELLIGENCE WORKS

CHAPTER 3

The Intelligence Cycle

Intelligence might best be described as information that has been systematically and professionally processed and analysed. There are many definitions of intelligence, but every professional intelligence officer understands precisely what he or she is required to deliver. For the professional, intelligence is simply defined as:

> 'Processed, *accurate* information, presented *in sufficient time* to enable a decision maker to take whatever action is required.'

The key point is that intelligence is a rigorous, cyclical process. The intelligence cycle is usually presented graphically as a circular process.

THE INTELLIGENCE CYCLE

DIRECTION
The commander or political leader states his *intelligence requirement*, usually in the form of a question.

DISSEMINATION
Dissemination can take any form: a written brief, an urgent signal, a routine intelligence summary, or, more usually in urgent cases, a verbal brief to the political leader or commander.

COLLECTION
The intelligence staff convert the commander's intelligence requirement into a series of essential elements of information (EEIs) and task the intelligence agencies using a *collection plan*.

INTERPRETATION
Interpretation is where the collated information is analyzed and turned into intelligence. This is usually done by asking the key questions: Who is it? What is it doing? What does it mean?

COLLATION
The intelligence staff collates all the information from the various sources into a readily accessible database. It is essential that all the information collected can be *retrieved*.

Two key points colour all intelligence: accuracy and timeliness. *Inaccurate* information speaks for itself; no-one gets credit for wrong facts. Even junior reporters are fired for failing to check their sources and getting facts wrong. Equally, to shout 'Duck!' *after* the roof tile crashes to the ground is hardly *timely* intelligence. But the intelligence officer confronts another, more subtle, problem: that of capabilities versus intentions.

Understanding the difference between a potential enemy's *capabilities* and his *intentions* is crucial to understanding the difficulties facing the purveyor of intelligence. For example, if I have a gun gathering dust in a drawer, then I have the *capability* for violent action. But there is no evidence of *intention*. I pose only a *potential* threat, based solely on my possession of an object designed for killing.

If, on the other hand, I have a sharpened pencil, *but I am waving it in front of your face, absolutely determined on stab it into your eyes*, then I am an extremely dangerous individual. Despite an apparently limited aggressive capability, (every household or even primary school has a sharp pencil or two) my intention makes me a major threat. We need to recognise that capabilities and intentions are in fact very different things.

This problem of separating intentions and capabilities will recur throughout our examination of intelligence failures. The intelligence cycle makes an effort to separate the two; it has to be admitted, not always very successfully. But the distinction is clear.

The reason is simple. Capabilities are relatively easy to measure. Anyone can count ships, tanks or aeroplanes – but determining an adversary's true plans or intentions is fiendishly difficult to measure or quantify. And a man's intentions can change like the weather. Even the most sophisticated intelligence breaks down when confronted by the whims and vagaries of the changing human mind. Just what were Saddam Hussein's real intentions before Kuwait in 1991? Just what did President Putin and the Russian Army intend when they intervened in Eastern Ukraine?

In fact, the classic Cold War intelligence briefing invariably centred around the issue of Soviet capabilities (lots of tanks and missiles) versus Soviet intentions for their use. During the Cold War the 'Bean Counters' (that is, the capabilities men), ruled the intelligence roost with a vengeance. For the first time in history, technology enabled intelligence organisations to collect information on a massive scale. 'Intelligence' was reduced to acquiring huge quantities of information, often in very expensive and career-enhancing ways – and then drawing (often false) conclusions from the evidence.

CHAPTER 4

On Direction: 'What Exactly is Your Intelligence Requirement, Minister?'

In order to better understand the intelligence process, we must return to our military or political decision maker and his or her wishes. The very first stage of the intelligence cycle is the definition by the commander or decision maker of their intelligence requirements. What precisely do they want to know? What is the precise question he or she wants answering?

One of the first lessons hammered into trainee staff officers is the most important principle of all: 'the selection and maintenance of the aim'. That same lesson is absorbed just as swiftly by CEOs in business, editors of newspapers, publishers – in fact almost every successful enterprise has a clear mission. Curiously, democratic politicians, with their ever-flexible desire to trim their sails to every passing breeze, and tomorrow's headlines, are notoriously reluctant to commit themselves to a clear and single-minded purpose. But without a clear aim it is impossible to know what we are trying to achieve or obtain.

However, with a little prompting, most sensible decision makers will usually come to address this key question. For example, 'Will the Argentinians invade the Falkland Islands? If so, when, where, and in what strength?' is a classic and clear example of a 'commander's intelligence requirement', enabling the intelligence cycle to begin. If the British Joint Intelligence Committee had debated these particular questions in such clear terms in late 1981, the Falklands crisis might never have erupted in the way it did. So, the first priority of the intelligence officer and the intelligence process should always be to ask: 'What precisely do you want to know, Minister?'

'You tell me,' is the usual limp response . . .

We should not be surprised at this. Politicians are usually ignorant of what is required to make intelligence work. Although the decision maker is clearly responsible for spelling out his Essential Elements of Information (EEI), in practice, government ministers very rarely exercise this role. The Israeli Shlomo Gazit, one time head of the Israel Defense Forces' military intelligence, spelled it out very clearly at a high-level meeting of retired intelligence officers and academics in 1999:

> In most cases the decision maker simply doesn't understand the problems involved in producing the EEI. In most cases he doesn't even understand just what you want from him. Thus the head of the service in charge of the national intelligence assessment and in charge of coordinating the collection effort has to bring along his suggested plan . . . for the decision maker's signature.

Even the most reluctant politician can be induced to put their name to a policy or plan, once they realise that any failure to take responsibility might mean the loss of their departmental budget and power.

CHAPTER 5

On Collection

The Collection Plan

Having wrung a clear intelligence question out of the decision maker, the various requirements are then tasked to the collection sources and agencies as part of a collection plan. To construct a collection plan, it is essential that the intelligence users understand the strengths and weaknesses of all the various agencies, because sources and agencies lie at the heart of intelligence collection.

For example, HUMINT (human intelligence, the business of agent running, traditionally the province of the CIA, MI6 and the James Bonds of fiction) is good at reporting on an enemy's *intentions*, and satellite photography (the province of the USA's top secret National Reconnaissance Office, or NRO) can assess an enemy's *capabilities*, measured in tanks or rockets (provided it can see them). Both agencies would find it difficult, if not impossible, to do it the other way round, given their sources of information. Plainly, it makes little sense to task an intelligence agency with a job for which it is ill suited. No-one but an idiot would expect a maritime search radar to provide up-to-date intelligence on a land-based nuclear research programme.

The digital revolution has spawned a fierce debate nowadays both within and without the intelligence community based on the impact of 'social media' and open sources, and its value as a collection source. On the one hand there are those who argue that 'Open Sources' (OSINT) now supersede much of the time, effort and money hitherto spent on clandestine intelligence collection. 'The world has changed in the digital age,' they say. This is a fair point and one that most intelligence agencies now accept without question, generally focusing their efforts and resources on seeking by clandestine means that which cannot be obtained openly.

However the question then arises: how do you know what cannot be obtained openly? To know that, you have to have clandestine sources anyway. The debate goes on; but no sensible intelligence officer, military commander or politician is going to be so stupid as to rely solely on open sources for all intelligence, however cheap it appears to be.

A TYPICAL (VERY SIMPLIFIED) INTELLIGENCE COLLECTION PLAN

INTELLIGENCE REQUIREMENT – WILL FANTASIA INVADE?
IF SO: WHEN, WHERE, AND IN WHAT STRENGTH? (KEY INDICATORS)

SOURCES →	SIGINT	HUMINT	IMINT	TECHINT	OSINT	DIPLOMATIC & GOVERNMENT	ETCETERA... →
ESSENTIAL ELEMENTS OF INFORMATION (EEIs) FROM AGENCIES ▼	NASA, GCHQ	SIS/MI6 CIA	SATELLITE, DRONES	RADARS, SONARS	JOURNALISTS, TV, TOURISTS	MILITARY ATTACHES	
LOCATION OF SE, AIRBORNE & MARINE UNITS?	X	X	X	X		X	
WARSHIPS AT SEA?	X	X	X	X	X		
LOCATION OF SUBMARINES?	X		X	X			
AIRCRAFT AT READINESS?	X	X	X		X	X	
PILOTS RECALLED FROM LEAVE?		X				X	
EXTRA SECURITY AT MILITARY BASES?		X	X		X	X	
AMMUNITION OUTLOADING?		X	X				
TROOP MOVEMENTS?	X	X	X		X	X	
CYBERWAR ATTACKS?	X	X		X	X	X	
MOBILISATION & RESERVISTS CALLED UP?		X			X	X	
UNUSUAL RADIO TRANSMISSIONS?	X		X				

In this detailed example of an intelligence collection plan, the 'Requirement' has been broken down into even more specific 'Essential Elements of Information' (See Example). Thanks to the advent of 'social media' in the accelerating digital age, today's collection plans boast a vast new spectrum of sources – reliable or not.

Collation – Putting it all together

Once the information has been collected, it has to be collated. This can be laborious and unglamorous, but the greater part of the intelligence operative's world is taken up with collating a mass of information rather than collecting it. This is the province of clever and industrious clerks and their computers and databases, and is far removed from the exciting world of guns, missiles, special forces and the battle front, so beloved of the popular media and computer games. In the digital age, collation systems and records data are computerised; in Napoleon's day they relied on quill pens, card indexes and good memories. Sometimes they were just as efficient . . .

Interestingly, Hitler's prime expert on the Soviet Army, Colonel Gehlen, who had painstakingly collated the best card index and records on the Eastern Front, was promptly recruited by the US Army at the end of 1945. After all, a unique, well collated, accurate and up-to-date intelligence database can overcome almost any scruples.

Collation is important for another, almost laughable reason; in today's technical age it is, perhaps for the first time, possible to over-load an intelligence system with *too much* data.

For example, in the Vietnam War the Americans famously held drawers full of aerial photographs of Vietnam that nobody had ever looked at. This 'foot drawer of photographic intelligence' became a derisive symbol of the failure of US military intelligence to cope with the mass of information available, let alone present it to their masters. There simply was not time or the manpower to look at every single image collected.

It is increasingly difficult for collation systems to maintain that essential 'rapid retrieval response capability' – being accessible to users when they need to get at data. Think of the multiplicity of police surveillance cameras: for once, the image of finding needles in haystacks is apt.

The sheer volume of social media, the 24/7 rolling-news cycle and new cyber threats risks overwhelming even the most modern computer-based collation systems, as Edward Snowden's intelligence revelations demonstrated. For the collator, the cardinal sin is to have vital evidence and not know it, or to not be able to find it to interpret it, let alone pass it on to decision makers. Even with the most powerful computers in the world that task is becoming more and more difficult.

Interpretation – What does it all mean?

Once collated, information then has to be interpreted or processed. This analytic process is what turns information into intelligence. In its simplest terms this means that each bit of information is compared with all other existing information in order to answer four basic questions: 'Is it true?' 'Who is it?' 'What is it doing?' and, 'What does it mean?' On the objective answers to these deceptively simple questions the whole expensive intelligence effort can stand or fall.

Maddeningly for the technocrats, the human brain, with its flair, expertise, experience and intuition, cannot be bettered. Even the smartest computer cannot assess intentions. Interpretation remains firmly the province of the analyst who knows and understands the subject. In intelligence there is no substitute for linguists, country experts and experienced analysts. Ironically they are often the first to be sacrificed when defence cuts beckon and, irony of ironies, they are invariably the first to be missed when some unexpected crisis blows up and politicians demand, 'Action this day!' studiously ignoring the truth that you cannot grow an army of foreign linguists overnight.

Dissemination – Telling the boss

This final part of the intelligence cycle is perhaps the most fraught. No bureaucracy relishes the prospect of passing on unwelcome information to its political or military masters. Intelligence officers are as human as the rest of us, and the temptation for the nervous, ambitious or sycophantic intelligence reporter to tailor the story to suit his boss's wishes, or avoid his displeasure, can be very strong. Who, for example, would have relished saying to Mrs Thatcher, at the height of her powers, 'Prime Minister, I'm afraid you're not exactly 100 per cent correct on that . . .'

Interpretations can, and often are, twisted to suit political preconceptions, with no basis in fact. Perhaps the most egregious case has been the manipulation of the British Joint Intelligence Committee's infamous 'Dodgy Intelligence Dossier' of 2003 on Iraqi nuclear weapons. It wasn't intelligence: it was plain manipulative politics; and the FCO, SIS and the JIC's reputations for honesty and objectivity took a blow from which Whitehall has still not recovered.

But manipulation of intelligence for political purpose is not the worst crime of all. In 1917, Haig, the British Commander-in-Chief on the Western Front had key intelligence deliberately withheld from him by his senior intelligence officer, Brigadier Charteris, who told his subordinates, 'We shouldn't disturb the Chief with this sort of news . . .'

Against this sort of bureaucratic manipulation there is little defence. In a university, such behaviour could be airily dismissed as 'intellectually dishonest'. In the First World War it led to the slaughter of hundreds of thousands of men. Military decisions carry a grimmer responsibility than others.

Dissemination, then, should be accurate, timely and should clearly distinguish intelligence *fact* from interpretative *comment* or assessment. It should also be secure and free from prying eyes and ears. (If the enemy knows precisely what you are up to, he will probably change his plans, which is why 'security' should always be the reverse face of the intelligence coin.) Above all, final intelligence reports should be brutally honest and objective. These are easy sentiments; but who in reality would really like to confront an all-powerful politician or general with the knowledge that his plans are either nonsense, or that they soon will be, because the enemy refuses to cooperate, or worse; the politician or general has simply got it wrong?

Hitler, the supreme warlord who dictated both the strategic and the tactical dispositions of the Germans in the Second World War, could fall into towering rages if he was contradicted by his staff. On one occasion, before the final Russian attack at Stalingrad, a brave intelligence officer briefed him on the growing Soviet capability in the Don Bend sector. The Führer exploded with rage, shouting: 'I won't have that sort of talk in my headquarters . . . ridiculous pessimism!' He then physically attacked the unfortunate individual before his astonished generals, and had him sacked from his staff.

As every intelligence officer has known throughout history, telling the truth, particularly to a dictator, can sometimes be a *very* bad career move.

Indicators and warning

The pinnacle of the whole intelligence process is often a device called the 'indicators and warning display'. Indicators and warning is the most important way of keeping track of an enemy's capabilities and intentions. It effectively fuses all known intelligence from every source onto an easily read matrix, usually coded, like the traffic lights, green, amber and red for danger. Black usually means unknown.

Indicators and warning, done properly by objective third parties, and using rigorous techniques of critical source analysis, can successfully fuse intelligence from all sources to give realistic estimates of potential enemies' capabilities and intentions; and even where it cannot, a good indicators and warning display will highlight even for the most obtuse minister or commander precisely which critical elements of information they lack to complete the full picture.

A TYPICAL (VERY SIMPLIFIED) INDICATOR AND WARNING DISPLAY

INTELLIGENCE REQUIREMENT - WILL FANTASIA INVADE?
IF SO: *WHEN, WHERE, AND IN WHAT STRENGTH? (KEY INDICATORS)* (BLACK = *Unknown*)

SOURCES ➞	SIGINT	HUMINT	IMINT	TECHINT	OSINT	DIPLOMATIC & GOVERNMENT	ETC... ➞
ESSENTIAL ELEMENTS OF INFORMATION (EEIs) FROM AGENCIES	NASA, GCHQ?	SIS/MI6 CIA?	SATELLITE, DRONES?	RADARS, SONARS?	JOURNALISTS, TV, TOURISTS?	MILITARY ATTACHES, EMBASSIES?	
LOCATION OF SF, AIRBORNE & MARINE UNITS?	RED Moving to borders	Deployed from barracks				AMBER Unusual activity reported	
WARSHIPS AT SEA?	AMBER At sea		RED Not in port	AMBER Radars detected		RED Not in port	
LOCATION OF SUBMARINES?		RED Not in port		AMBER Unusual sonars detected			
AIRCRAFT AT READINESS?	GREEN Radio silence	GREEN In hangars	GREEN In hangars	GREEN No activity	No aircraft to be seen	GREEN In hangars	
PILOTS RECALLED?		GREEN Pilots on weekend leave			GREEN Aircrew absent	GREEN Pilots away weekend	
EXTRA SECURITY AT MILITARY BASES?		RED Army bases on lockdown			RED Army bases on lockdown	RED Army bases on lockdown	
AMMUNITION OUTLOADING?		Many trucks seen			AMBER Many vehicles	RED Many trucks seen at depots	
TROOP MOVEMENTS?	AMBER Unusual activity	RED Units leaving barracks	RED Many troop movements		RED Many troop movements	RED Units leaving barracks	
CYBERWAR ATTACKS?	RED Some jamming	RED Widespread DOS attacks		RED Widespread attacks	RED Widespread DOS attacks	RED Widespread DOS attacks	
MOBILISATION & RESERVISTS CALLED UP?		AMBER Only specialists				AMBER Specialists only	
UNUSUAL RADIO TRANSMISSIONS?	AMBER Unusual activity detected		AMBER HQ comms vehicles on move	AMBER Unusual activity and frequencies			

This is a classic chart from which the intelligence analyst can see that, while there is much *preparatory* activity going on (army, special forces [SF], ship movements, etc.) there is no hard evidence of an *imminent* attack. The outloading of ammunition indicates a distinct readiness for action; the stand down and radio silence at airfields may well be a deception, because airpower can mobilise and strike quickly. But the Fantasians aren't ready to go just yet, *although they appear to be mobilising for something.*

Time to give the Minister a telephone call . . .?

Technically developed governments, like the USA and high-tech agencies such as North American Air Defence Command (NORAD) rely, inevitably, on highly sophisticated computer driven indicators and warning displays. Traditional, politically-conscious organisations (such as the mandarins of Britain's Foreign & Commonwealth Office, and the Joint Intelligence Committee) have historically tended to look down on such an obvious technical tool as lacking the intellectual subtlety of the more elegant 'Diplomatic Assessment' – a *very* carefully phrased exposition of the pros and cons of any situation by Whitehall's supposedly 'Rolls-Royce' minds ...

However, the deceptively simple indicators and warning display is invariably more reliable than the vagaries of individual minds, however brilliant or experienced, because it applies a ruthless academic logic to the situation at hand. For example, in the Cyprus crisis of late 1974, the British Cabinet was worried that Turkey was going to have a third bite at the Cyprus cherry and Whitehall flew into a panic. However, if Whitehall had been displaying a simple indicators and warning board that gave answers to simple key questions such as, 'Are the Turkish Air Force's aircraft at flight dispersal or not?' 'Are the planes bombed-up?' 'Are the Turkish pilots at readiness or off for the weekend?' they would have learned that the Turkish Air Force were far from ready to fight and the situation need never have embarrassed the Foreign Secretary and forced an apology at Cabinet level, a fact which is still concealed with some chagrin.

Even then the game is not over. As the chapters that follow will make clear, even after it has been disseminated to decision makers, perfectly sound intelligence can be tainted; distorted by other factors (usually disbelief); ignored; or just arrive too late to be useful. To further complicate matters, 'intelligence' is living through the very same digital revolution that is blowing hurricane-like across the world, and needs to adapt accordingly. The good old traditional intelligence cycle is now under threat from advanced technology.

The civilian money markets have already identified this changing model of intelligence collection and dissemination for financial gain and have invested accordingly. Those with responsibility for market 'intelligence' now rely almost entirely on high-speed computers and high-frequency traders to deal in milliseconds with vast quantities of information for Wall Street and the City of London's benefit. This represents a challenge to traditional intelligence methods.

It will be interesting to see how the military copes with organising and managing the emerging integrated digital age, with its new all-in-one discipline of C4I STAR (Command, Control, Communications, Computers and Intelligence – plus Surveillance, Target Acquisition and Reconnaissance). This change already represents a formidable – and very expensive – challenge for governments and their intelligence agencies in the future.

Armed with a better understanding of the basic mechanics of the intelligence process, and able now to discern the true role of 'intelligence', we can look more closely at the truth behind some of the intelligence activities that have shaped armies, battles, great events and the destinies of nations.

PART 4

ON HUMINT AND SPIES

Human intelligence – HUMINT – has been with us from the start. Spies are at the heart of intelligence and have been from time immemorial. While signals intelligence has been around for over a century, imagery intelligence for just about a century, and electronic intelligence for only seventy years, human intelligence – spies and spying – represents the oldest form of intelligence – and the most numerous. From Sumeria to tomorrow's headlines, from all-out war to stealing commercial secrets, there will always be spies. Spying is all about trust and betrayal, hope and fear, love and hatred. Spying to collect information on 'the other' is eternal; and it has always been centred on people and personalities. Families spy; businesses spy; nations spy.

What the spy can do, above all, is to identify *intentions* in a way that mere technical or mechanical methods of intelligence frequently cannot. And knowing the other guy's intentions is vital. Intelligence has always been more than just bean counting: How many tanks? How many terrorists? A key requirement, once we have identified an adversary's capabilities will always be, 'What do they intend to do?' This basic intelligence requirement never goes away and so the spy with access, recruited by whatever means, will always have his or her part to play in providing the answer. Case officers around the world, even as we read this, are daily trying to persuade individuals with access to become traitors, and using methods as old as time to encourage or coerce them to do so.

Human intelligence is a very wide field. It is much more than just spies and James Bond fantasies. For a start, there are many forms of

HUMINT – from debriefing defectors and refugees to interrogating prisoners of war, and from running agents behind enemy lines to exquisitely discreet polite diplomatic exchanges at cocktail parties. As its name implies, HUMINT means dealing with that most treacherous, fallible and unreliable source of information of all: human beings.

So the spy has ever been with us in one form or another, good and bad. Looking back at the history of intelligence, a truth emerges: very often spies are not nice people. The American CIA and FBI went through a phase in the 1990s of issuing guidelines that barred the recruitment of sources guilty of human rights violations or who 'might embarrass the Agency'. The problem is that if, for example, you want to really know what is going on inside criminal terrorist organisations, or a bloodthirsty jihadi group, then you have to get your hands dirty.

As every detective knows, if you want to stop crime, you have to get into the gutter, go down to the sleazy bars, and consort with crooks. If you want to collect human intelligence on militant Islamists, then you have to, at the very least, talk to bloodthirsty and experienced decapitators. HUMINT – agent handling – sometimes requires an amoral heart of stone and is not for the squeamish, because revulsion and avoidance will not collect hard intelligence. HUMINT can be very messy, for all concerned.

The key element in recruiting a human source is the most basic question of all: does he or she have *access* to the intelligence we need? Though even this can be an assessment based on their potential access. Back in the thirties the Soviets actually recruited young graduates *without* any access at all with the aim of letting them gradually worm their way into the fabric of the British Establishment to gain the glittering prize of access to secrets in the long term. The successes of Philby, Burgess, MacLean, Blunt and Cairncross speak volumes for the triumph of this slow-burn policy.

Modern technological toys, such as a fake rock with a hidden computer that can be 'loaded' with secret intelligence by a passing agent using a mini-transmitter, attract the attention of the world's press when they surface amid the usual cloud of scandal and recriminations. But these are mere technical gizmos aimed at making the tradecraft of the secret agent easier. A 'brush pass' with a rock or a tree is still a brush pass in all but name. The real need for HUMINT still remains. The trusted undercover agent in place with access to the enemy's camp remains at the heart of most intelligence operations.

With this wider and much longer appreciation we can examine spies and HUMINT in greater detail. This deeper examination of the spy is justified, because spies and spying are by far the biggest, longest and most diverse of all intelligence sources, and have been since the dawn of time. HUMINT is a bigger subject than all the other subjects combined. The motives for spying are traditionally represented by the acronym 'MICE', with the four main triggers of treachery identified as: Money; Ideology; Compromise/Coercion; and Ego. However, experienced intelligence and security officers know that behind these big four lurks the most powerful motive of all: the festering grievance.

Let us now look at these various kinds of spies in some detail and why they did what they did.

CHAPTER 6

Money: The Walker Family's Unusual Business

On a cold December day, just before Christmas 1967, a man calling himself 'John Harper' walked into the Soviet Embassy in Washington with an unusual business proposition. Mr Harper calmly offered to spy for the Russians, offering a bundle of authentic US Navy top-secret documents in return for payment.

The mysterious 'Mr Harper' identified himself as Chief Warrant Officer John A. Walker, US Navy. He claimed to be the Keylist Custodian of all the classified communications materials for CINCLANT, the US Atlantic Fleet's naval base at Norfolk, Virginia. To prove his credentials he showed Soviet KGB General Boris Solomatin, his handler, who oversaw the Walker case from start to finish, his US Navy ID Card and gave him a copy of a month's classified communication keylists in advance.

Walker made it quite clear that he wanted to spy – but only for money. He knew exactly what he was doing and exactly what his product was worth. He expressed derision for Marxism and Communism – no ideology here. As far as the American was concerned, this was strictly business.

Walker was given several thousand dollars cash as a down payment. The amazed Russians then bundled this intelligence equivalent of Santa Claus out of the back of the Embassy in the trunk of a car and set up a regular monthly income of up to $1,000 a month. The US Navy's worst security nightmare was just beginning.

Walker had enlisted in the Navy in 1955 after having confessed to several other crimes. A kindly judge had offered him the choice of joining the Navy rather than serve jail time. Walker was based at Charleston, South Carolina, where he slowly slid into debt. He even drove a cab on his shore assignments and shuttled rental cars among cities, but it was not enough.

So, like any resourceful businessman, he looked around for a product to sell. As a specially vetted and security-cleared communications chief, he was one of the few people who had access to all the code settings for the US Navy's top secret encryption device, the KW-7.

The key point was that only the sender and receiver of the signals knew those daily code settings, which were kept in security sealed packets and stored by specially cleared custodian officers. Those sealed packages and their daily key settings were worth a king's ransom to hostile intelligence agencies.

That is precisely what John Walker was offering the Soviets. With a KW-7 crypto machine and the secret daily settings, Moscow would be able to instantly read all classified US Navy traffic as quickly and as easily as the daily newspaper – from nuclear firing messages to ships' deployment stations. It was truly the intelligence opportunity of a lifetime.

But first the Soviets had to acquire a working KW-7.

On 23 January, off the coast of Wonsan, the USS *Pueblo*, a top-secret spyship stuffed full of highly-classified radio recording equipment and documents was approached by a North Korean sub chaser and ordered to heave-to. Trapped and hopelessly outgunned, the tiny and vulnerable *Pueblo* surrendered.

The *Pueblo*, with her captured crew, was escorted to Wonsan. The SIGINT material was flown straight to Moscow. Within a month of John Walker volunteering his services, the Soviets had managed to hijack a United States Navy SIGINT ship along with its priceless cipher machines.

Moscow now had both parts of the puzzle. They had the coding machines from the *Pueblo* and they had an American spy in place, at Fleet HQ in Norfolk Virginia, with the vital code cards and promising access to more. It was an intelligence coup of staggering value. And, much, much worse, the US Navy and its cryptographers in the NSA hadn't the faintest idea that their nation's greatest naval secrets had been compromised. Thus was the Walker spy business born.

Within six months Walker's treachery had become a regular commercial exchange. The Russians assured Walker that they were prepared to pay handsomely for any cryptographic materials that he could supply. The KGB even slipped Walker a specially built rotor detector for the new KL-47 series of American machines, which could detect and 'read' encoded rotor settings automatically. Their scientists had developed it from the KW-7 machines captured on the *Pueblo* and from those lost in Vietnam.

For the next nine years, until he retired in 1976, Walker set up what amounted to an organised cryptographic spy business inside the US Navy. Philby, Burgess and MacLean's treacheries pale into insignificance against this deeper betrayal; and just for money too.

Walker had two serious problems. First, despite KGB warnings, he had involved his wife in his treachery. Barbara had become suspicious about the sudden easing of the family's money problems. When she then found a store bag stuffed full of classified documents, she confronted Walker. At first he tried to claim that his moonlighting was the source of his money but, eventually, he admitted that he was spying. Amazingly, he even took his difficult wife along on a dead drop to involve her. This was a mistake, as Barbara was drinking heavily and their marriage was in trouble.

His second problem was less urgent. Once he retired from the Navy, Walker's access to the supply of his 'product' would dry up; but if he could recruit a colleague and pay him a salary plus commission, then he would be better able to manage his 'business'. In 1975 he found what he was looking for and recruited an old Navy friend, Senior Chief Petty Officer Jerry Whitworth, another communications specialist, who was told that he was working as 'a friend of Israel'.

By the summer of 1975, when Walker put in for an early retirement, he was actively running Whitworth as a paid agent, tasked with supplying secrets while on board the USS *Niagara Falls*, in the very post that Walker had once held. When the ship went into dry dock, Whitworth was reassigned to the Naval Communications Center,

Alameda, California, where he spent his lunch hours in a van in the parking lot photographing classified documents. The Soviets paid handsomely and so did Walker, now a freelance private investigator. Everyone was happy.

Whitworth soon found out that he wasn't working for Israel but for the KGB. Undeterred, he carried on, but became greedy and troublesome. When he finally pulled out of the ring in 1983 (having delivered a treasure trove of documents on the key lists for the KW-7, KY-8, KG-14, KWR-37, and KL-47 cryptographic systems as well as the newest secure STU phone system) it looked once again as if Walker's business selling secrets was over.

However, like all good businessmen, Walker rose to the challenge by diversifying. He approached his son, Michael, a yeoman in the administration office of the carrier USS *Nimitz* and asked him to join the family business in return for cash. Michael duly obliged by photocopying more than 1,500 documents for the KGB on a wide range of subjects including nuclear weapons storage and release procedures, new weapon systems, command operating procedures, identification methods, and contingency target lists. Walker now believed that, by keeping it in the family, he was safer and more secure and that the more 'employees' he had, the greater the flow of product from his suppliers – and therefore the greater the flow of money from the grateful Soviets.

He next turned to his older brother Arthur, now a retired Navy lieutenant commander, who owed him some money. Arthur Walker was employed by a defence contractor working on classified repair records of US warships. Walker took them all on as partners. All were paid 'by results' through John Walker's unusual pyramid-selling operation, using Soviet supplied funds.

By 1984 the Navy's Investigation Service (NIS, now NCIS) was becoming suspicious. In retirement, Jerry Whitworth had begun an anonymous correspondence with the FBI in San Francisco, offering dark secrets of naval espionage. The FBI agents involved were unable to track down the mysterious informant calling himself 'RUS', but passed what information they had to the NCIS.

Walker's other problem was his ex-wife, who was by now a bad tempered drunk threatening to reveal all to the FBI. Sure enough, in

November 1985 Barbara Walker denounced her ex-husband to the FBI field office in Boston. The spy's ex-wife told an agent of her husband's confession, and how she had accompanied Walker to dead drops near Washington.

Unfortunately, Barbara Walker was half-drunk at the time (she was drinking vodka even during the official FBI interview) and the field agent decided that she was probably acting out of spite towards her ex-husband. He sent the report to Boston, where it was quietly filed away. However the problem did not go away. The Norfolk, Virginia office re-opened the case. One of the first interviews was with Walker's daughter, Laura Walker Snyder, who told the startled FBI investigators that her father had tried to recruit her as a spy when she was serving as an Army sergeant some years before. A full FBI counter-intelligence unit investigation was then launched, code-named operation Windflyer.

The net was now closing in on Walker. The FBI set up a sting with Laura Walker-Snyder. She telephoned her father and he encouraged her to re-join the service or even the CIA, with the FBI listening in. On board the USS *Nimitz*, NCIS investigators confronted a frightened Michael Walker. He broke down and confessed.

The investigators then moved in for the kill.

On the evening of 19 May 1985, after making certain no-one was watching him, John Anthony Walker Jr stopped his van alongside a deserted road just north of Washington DC and stepped out to drop a paper grocery bag near a utility pole and a tree with a 'No Hunting' sign nailed on it. The 'bag of trash' contained 129 copies of classified US Navy documents; and Walker's every movement was being monitored by a major FBI surveillance operation. Not far away, someone from the KGB was dumping a paper grocery bag with $200,000 in used $50 and $100 bills.

However, when Walker arrived at the KGB's drop point to collect his bag of money he couldn't find it. He retraced his steps and discovered that his bag of Navy secrets had also disappeared, along with the safety signal, a discarded soda can. FBI officers watched the puzzled spy as he frantically checked both sites several times – but both bags had gone. Shortly before midnight, he gave up and drove to a motel, checking in to room 763.

No-one knows what went through the traitor's mind at that point. He may not have been too worried, as the Soviets had screwed up on their dead drops a couple of times before. However, when the telephone rang at 0330 hours in his room he was awake and alert. An excited voice yelled, 'This is the front desk. Is the blue-and-white van out front yours?'

'Okay,' replied Walker. 'Be right down'.

However Walker had a problem. He was carrying the envelope containing the KGB's very detailed instructions on how to locate this particular dead letter box and his missing $200,000. So the worried spy took out his .38 revolver and walked into the corridor to check it was empty. There was no-one there, so he grabbed the incriminating envelope and started to hide the envelope behind the ice machine – just in case. As he did, two armed FBI officers came out of the neighbouring rooms, guns drawn, shouting, 'FBI! Drop the gun!'

A stunned Walker dropped his pistol.

While Walker was still reeling from the shock of capture, FBI Agent Hunter produced a typewritten letter that the traitor had sealed inside the Navy documents that he had stolen for the Russians. Walker was caught red-handed. The KGB had warned him several times against putting anything personal in his dead drops. Now he had incriminated himself. It was over.

Walker tried to bargain with the legal authorities, looking for some form of deal that would land his son with a lighter sentence. He pleaded guilty and offered to give a full confession and to testify as a prosecution witness against his old comrade Jerry Whitworth.

His old 'business partner' was eventually convicted by a Federal jury of espionage for his participation in a Soviet spy ring that the government called the most damaging espionage conspiracy in decades. Whitworth was sentenced to 365 years in prison and fined $410,000.

Walker's son, Michael, who had a relatively minor role in the ring, and who agreed to testify in exchange for a reduced sentence, was released from prison on parole in 2000. Barbara Walker was not charged. Walker himself was found guilty on all charges and sentenced to life.

The Walker story shines a light into some of the darker corners of the American dream. Ever since the unmasking of his businesslike commercial spy ring in 1985, it has been quite clear that Walker's motive was purely financial, never ideological. Walker was not some foreigner or 'outsider' committed to the triumph of international Communism.

Despite his claims after his arrest that, 'The farce of the Cold War and the absurd war machine it spawned, was an ever-growing pathetic joke to me,' the traitor's real reason was money.

Characterising John F. Kennedy's father – correctly – as a bootlegger and a crook, Walker told investigators that 'enough money buys respectability; you can even send your son to the White House'.

The Walker spy ring was undoubtedly one of the most harmful ever in United States history. The extent of the damage is difficult to assess; but the US government had to spend more than $1 billion changing all the codes and equipment compromised by Walker's activities, let alone suffering the loss of confidence amongst serving sailors.

The uncomfortable fact is that, from 1967 until 1985, by providing the KGB with every detail of the US Navy's plans and capabilities, John Walker had completely compromised America's ability to fight the Soviets at sea if war had ever broken out. His handler, Boris Solomatin, later called him, 'the most important spy ever recruited by Russia. John Walker gave away the keys to your most secret code machines', adding, 'he gave us the equivalent of a seat inside your Pentagon where we could read your most vital secrets'.

KGB officer Vitaly Yurchenko was even more blunt: 'Walker was the greatest case in KGB history. We deciphered millions of your messages. If there had been a war, we would have won it.'

CHAPTER 7

Ideology

Cambridge's Famous Five

The most familiar examples of ideological spies are the so-called 'Cambridge Five' – Burgess, MacLean, Philby, Blunt and Cairncross – who spied for Stalin's USSR in the 1940s. All of them, certainly at first, appear to have been seduced by the utopian possibilities of a Marxist-Communist state. Blunt – the oldest – visited the Soviet Union in 1933, and was possibly recruited in 1934.

What bonded many of them together was the impact of their sexual preferences on their treachery. A number were members of a closed society at Cambridge called 'The Apostles'. This frisson of sexual conspiracy and secrecy came together to breed a hothouse climate in which other conspiratorial secrets could be encouraged and to flourish. The Apostles became the secret recruiting centre for ideologically committed young men to worm their way into the fabric of British society, and the NKVD were incredibly patient with their new espionage assets.

The defining moment for the 'idealistic' spies of the Cambridge conspirators came in August 1939 when Ribbentrop and Molotov signed their Non-Aggression pact. From then on, any pretence that the Cambridge spies were working for some great moral cause went out of the window. A cynical stroke of realpolitik suddenly made Hitler's Nazis and Stalin's Communists sworn allies and bosom friends – at least on paper.

However, the intellectual gymnastics required to surmount this ideological obstacle posed no problem to the agile minds of Cambridge men from Trinity. By claiming that they were working for the Communist International's interests (and not the USSR) they could salve their consciences. The truth is that Burgess, Philby and MacLean hated their own society and fellow countrymen so much that they were prepared to sell their soul to the Devil – for that is what the Cambridge traitors did.

Besides, as many a spy has found, it was too late to turn back now. They were quite happy to continue spying for the Revolution: and there was always a threat of blackmail or exposure in the background if they did not carry on cooperating with the Soviet Union. Their past treachery trapped them, like flies on a web. The Famous Five had no choice but to keep on spying, for Moscow and for glorious Comrade Stalin – whatever intellectual gyrations and deceits they may have performed.

They were phenomenally successful. The wider Cambridge Ring eventually penetrated the innermost secrets of the British State and, from 1940, was providing Moscow with virtually every secret known to the British. Cairncross worked directly for Lord Hankey who was effectively Churchill's Controller of Secret Services; Leo Long sold out Bletchley Park's Enigma secrets; Donald Maclean was First Secretary of the British Embassy in the USA and betrayed all things Anglo-American; Anthony Blunt was spying on MI5: and Kim Philby was running the Iberian Desk inside MI6/SIS. So successful were they that, at times, Moscow Centre found it difficult to process, let alone believe, the sheer mass of material being forwarded by their spy ring.

Inevitably they came under suspicion. In 1948, long before Blunt's public exposure, Philip Hay, a newly demobilised army officer, attended an interview at Buckingham Palace for a post of private secretary. After passing Blunt in a corridor, Sir Alan Lascelles, the King's Private Secretary, quietly warned Hay: 'By the way, that's our Russian spy.'

By the end of the 1950s the KGB's 'Magnificent Five' were all gone, exposed in one way or another: but the damage the arrogant intellectual spies had done was immense. Their memorial is that their names are remembered as bywords for treachery.

Where Ideology and Ego Mix: Ana Montes

The case of Ana Belen Montes, a senior DIA (Defence Intelligence Agency) analyst who spied for Cuba from 1985 until 2001, highlights the curious mix of ideology and ego that often combine to drive a spy onward. Nicknamed 'the Queen of Cuba' by her colleagues, Montes gave away every secret she saw to her handlers at Cuba's DGI (Intelligence Directorate) for sixteen years. She appears to have hated America and idolised Cuba. The FBI believe that she was probably the DGI's most valuable mole inside the American defence establishment.

Raised by a dominating Puerto Rican father, Montes spoke Spanish as her native tongue. She was articulate, clever and hard working. In 1979 she earned a degree in foreign affairs from the University of Virginia.

According to a declassified report, Montes's decision to spy for Cuba was 'coolly deliberate'. With her outspoken anti-American rants, especially about US support for the Contras (the rebels fighting the leftist Sandinista government in Nicaragua) as well as her praise for Castro's Cuba, she had soon been talent-spotted by a Cuban agent while working at the Department of Justice in Washington. Montes was recruited as a spy during a clandestine trip to New York in December 1984. There she met undercover Cuban intelligence officers attached to the United Nations and she 'unhesitatingly agreed' to work for Castro and the Cubans.

In those days there was no mandatory polygraph check for low-level DIA officers. So, in September 1985 Montes, despite her confirmed left-wing political views and strong criticism of the Reagan administration's policy in Central America, was hired by the DIA for their Central American desk. The agency had hired an intelligence-trained Cuban spy.

In her subsequent meteoric career, Montes was promoted rapidly, as she was soon regarded as a brilliant analyst on Cuban affairs. She also showed herself to be unusually well informed on Cuban internal politics; and her insights and judgement on Cuban matters went a long way to influencing (and in many cases softening) US policy toward Castro's isolated island.

With hindsight it is hard to see how the Cuban DGI would have

allowed her to be anything else but 'brilliant and well informed.'
Castro's Mata Hari was well rewarded for her achievements. The
KGB-trained Cubans were undoubtedly skilled in manipulating and
controlling their prize asset. After her arrest, Montes insisted to interrogators that she had the 'moral right' to provide information to Cuba
and that she considered herself the equal of her 'Cuban comrades, not
some menial espionage tool'.

Montes said her Cuban handlers were 'thoughtful, sensitive to her
needs, very good to me'. They went to 'special lengths to assure her they
had complete confidence in her'. As they were not paying for her
extraordinary services, she believed that she was in control, not the
DGI, an arrogant and foolish assumption for one being manipulated
by skilled and ruthless KGB trained agent handlers.

She was run through regular weekend meetings in Washington,
according to the Pentagon's later damage assessment, and even managed another visit to Cuba, but any details of this second covert trip
has been redacted in the Pentagon report.

In 1991, Montes was nearly caught. During a routine security review
she was asked about foreign travel, and lied. Questioned about inaccu-
racies in her original application for employment, she confessed that
she had misrepresented an incident in her past. Feigning innocence,
Montes claimed that she 'did not understand the seriousness of being
truthful and honest at the time'.

Her security case was then reviewed at a higher level. Mindful of
her 'brilliant work' for the agency, a senior security officer ruled however that, 'while Montes seemed to have a tendency "to twist the
truth" to her own needs and her honesty was still a cause of concern,
adverse security action was unlikely'. Montes retained her high-level
clearances.

Soon she was briefing the Joint Chiefs of Staff, the National Security
Council and even the President of Nicaragua about Cuban military
capabilities. She even helped draft a controversial Pentagon report
stating that Cuba had only a 'limited capacity' to harm the United
States and could pose a danger to US citizens only 'under some circumstances'. And she was about to earn yet another promotion, this
time a prestigious fellowship with the National Intelligence Council.

But the net was closing in on the 'Queen of Cuba'. By 1996, an anonymous DIA employee reported concerns about her loyalty and security. She was questioned by a DIA special agent who raised doubts about Montes' puzzling demands to see classified papers about subjects that were not her concern.

Investigators raised more doubts about her statements but there was no proof and seemingly no motive. This was partly due to Montes' scrupulous care not to breach the DIA's clumsy – but rigid – internal security procedures. As far as investigators are aware, she never took classified documents home, never stayed on in the office and was punctilious over security.

What the DGI spy actually did was to read and memorise everything she saw and then type it up to send to the DGI on her laptop every night. The well-trained Montes listened to her shortwave radio for coded instructions from her control officers and then slipped packages to agents on brush passes in public places. Montes did take risks. She sometimes actually met her handlers in Washington's Chinese restaurants, where the spy would slide a fresh batch of encrypted diskettes hidden underneath dishes of Chinese delicacies. When challenged, she claimed that these contacts were invaluable sources in the Cuban community. She also used her vacations on sunny Caribbean islands to make clandestine drops of 'masses of secret material' to her Cuban handlers. The Cubans even taught Montes how to beat a US polygraph test 'by tensing the sphincter muscles'.

However, by April 1998, American security was getting reports from several sources that there was a high-level DGI mole operating in Washington. A long-running inter-agency search for a Cuban spy was launched. According to the Pentagon report it was thought at first that it must be a CIA employee.

If we can believe the Pentagon's final report on the case, Montes appears to have been discovered almost by accident. 'We got lucky,' as a counter-intelligence official observed, without further explanation. Investigators had two other crucial clues: the unknown spy had apparently travelled to the Guantanamo naval base – just as Montes had done on official DIA business – and the spy had bought a Toshiba laptop. Cuba's ace spy was now in the frame. Pressure intensified to bring Montes in for questioning. However the FBI preferred to wait in order 'to monitor Montes's activities with the prospect that she may have eventually led the FBI to others in the Cuban spy network'.

In May 2001, armed with a Federal Warrant, the FBI took a big risk and mounted a black-bag operation to search Montes' apartment while she was out of town with her new boyfriend. The danger was that, as a skilled agent, she could have booby-trapped drawers and cupboards to warn her of any intruders, however careful. Just a hair across a desk drawer, or a dropped cork behind a closed door would give the game away to the trained spy on their return.

Despite the risk, FBI specialists searched everything, going through the pages of hundreds of books and photographing dozens of personal papers. In a cardboard box in the bedroom they discovered a Sony shortwave radio and then a concealed Toshiba laptop. The FBI techies copied the hard drive, shut down the computer and were gone.

Little did they know it at the time, but they had hit gold dust. A few days later, the translated contents of the hard drive were revealed. Before arresting Montes, the FBI wanted the secret crypto codes that investigators believed that she carried at all times in her handbag. They came up with a plan to lure her out of her office with a sudden invitation to say a few words at short notice to a prestigious gathering on the next floor. A flattered Montes left her office – and her handbag – and went upstairs.

As soon as she was gone the FBI team quickly copied the contents. Inside her purse were pager warning codes and a phone number, US area code 917, which was quickly traced to Cuban intelligence.

On 21 September 2001 Montes was arrested. The FBI spent hours ripping her apartment to pieces. Hidden in the lining of a notebook they found the handwritten cipher Montes used to encrypt and decrypt messages, scribbled shortwave radio frequencies, and the address in Mexico, where she was meant to flee in an emergency. The radio and code crib sheets were written on water-soluble disappearing paper.

Under questioning she confessed, even boasting of her role, but eventually pleaded guilty to spying. In October 2002, Ana Montes was sentenced to twenty-five years in prison for espionage.

Montes has shown no remorse and refuses to apologise. She claimed that her treachery was justified, because the United States 'has done some things that are terribly cruel and unfair' to the Cuban government. 'I owe allegiance to principles and not to any one country or government or person,' Montes wrote in one letter to a nephew. 'I don't owe allegiance to the US or to Cuba or to Obama or to the Castro brothers or even to God.'

Did she work with other American spies? Her arresting officer alleged that a good proportion of the US intelligence community believed that Montes' penetration of the DIA was but one of many, and that the Cuban intelligence services still had a network of spies and moles within US intelligence agencies.

What is clear is that Montes' spying had major consequences. At a Congressional hearing, the woman in charge of the damage assessment testified that Montes was 'one of the most damaging spies in US history'.

Former National Counter-intelligence Executive Michelle Van Cleave told Congress that Montes 'compromised all Cuban-focused collection programmes' used to eavesdrop on high-ranking Cubans, and it 'is also likely that the information she passed contributed to the death and injury of American and pro-American forces in Latin America'.

Like so many ideological spies, Ana Montes has blood on her hands.

The One Who Got Away: Melita Norwood

The 'Ancient Briton', Melita Norwood, on the other hand was in her dotage when the truth was uncovered – that the nice little 87-year-old grandmother, busy tending her suburban roses in retirement, had been a Communist spy for nearly fifty years.

A committed leftist herself, and daughter of a Latvian Communist, Norwood had married another convinced Marxist. Despite this, she was given top-secret security clearance and allowed access to some of Britain's most important secrets for years. Thanks to the Mitrokhin files, we now know that Norwood was recruited in 1937 on an 'ideological basis', following a tip from the leadership of the British Communist Party, who were ever ready to talent spot likely recruits for Moscow.

Codenamed 'Hola', Norwood was the most important female agent ever recruited by the Soviet Union. She was employed as a confidential clerk at the British Non-Ferrous Metals Research Association in London. In fact the company, as part of a top-secret national project codenamed 'Tube Alloys,' carried out crucially important metallurgy research for the building of Britain's atomic bomb. In 1945 she was cleared for access to sensitive documents, despite MI5 concerns over her links to Communist groups.

By 1949, her access to secrets was reduced after further worries about her Communist sympathies and, in 1951 and 1962, her security vetting clearance was rejected. The damage was done, however. In 1965 MI5 received new information indicating that Mrs Norwood had been spying for the NKVD and then the KGB since the 1940s. Despite the fact that she openly sipped tea from a Che Guevara mug and read copies of the Communist paper, the *Morning Star*, intelligence officers decided not to interview her or alert her; they wanted to find out just what she knew and to protect other investigations.

British suspicions were irrefutably confirmed in 1992 when former KGB officer Vasili Mitrokhin defected, bringing six trunks of archive information about undercover Russian agents back to the UK. Melita Norwood's spying for the Soviet Union was only revealed publicly when Professor Christopher Andrew published *The Mitrokhin Archive* in 1999, finally revealing that the little old lady, supposedly living a seemingly quiet and uneventful life in Bexleyheath, south-east London, was a long-time traitor and spy.

The Mitrokhin files also revealed that she had been awarded the Order Of The Red Banner of Labour for her service to Soviet Union intelligence, plus a lifetime pension in recognition of her 'many years of excellent work'. To the surprise of many, Norwood was never prosecuted, because the Attorney General deemed it 'inappropriate'. One of Moscow's most important assets (we now know that the KGB prized her above Kim Philby) died in 2005, a classic example of the ideological spy.

How she ever got through any security vetting remains a puzzle to this day. Two obvious theories emerge. First, she was a double agent and that Britain's security services knew of her treachery all along and were using her to send disinformation and chickenfeed to the Soviets. That seems unlikely.

A more cynical view is that she was encouraged to betray her country by fellow Soviet sympathisers, deeply embedded in the fabric of Britain's Establishment during the forties. Because the truth is that there were many on the Left in 1945 who secretly favoured Stalin's Russia. After all, the British people had faced the Germans alone in 1940–41, and it was the Red Army that had broken Hitler's Fascist legions to win the European war. In 1945 'Uncle Joe' and the Red Army were greatly admired by many in Britain. In her passion for the USSR, Communism and the Marxist dream, Melita Norwood got away with it for too long. Logic says that she had friends in high places.

She was not alone. Fellow travellers like James MacGibbon and Alan Nunn May sold the farm to the Soviets in the 1940s and early 50s. MacGibbon's excellent German and pre-war knowledge of Berlin found their natural home in military intelligence and he was posted to the planning staff of the combined chiefs in Washington in 1944. From there, code-named 'Dolly' by his Soviet handlers, he passed military secrets to the Soviets between 1942 and 1945, including details of British war plans, among them the D-Day landings.

The physicist Nunn May told the Russians everything he knew about atomic research and the top-secret 'Manhattan Project'. He even managed to send small samples of uranium 233 and 235 to the Soviets. (The unwitting courier became irradiated and had to spend the rest of his life having regular blood transfusions.)

This combination of betrayal by ideologues like Klaus Fuchs, Maclean, Burgess, Philby, Nunn May, MacGibbon and Melita Norwood – and doubtless many others – meant that America's top secret atomic programme was an open book to Moscow. It enabled the Soviets to develop and build their own atomic weapons in record time and at a fraction of the cost to the West. It also led to a furious US ending the sharing of atomic information and to Britain developing its own bomb.

From our twenty-first-century perch, looking back at the economic and social disaster that was Marxist-Leninism, where Communism is seen as a failed idea, riddled with its own contradictions, it is hard for us to grasp that in the 1930s some of the finest minds in the West fervently believed that Communism, Kremlin-style, was the answer to mankind's problems.

Lenin himself dryly referred to them as 'useful idiots'.

CHAPTER 8

Compromise/Coercion

John Vassall

Not all spies enter into service willingly. An individual can often be threatened into providing secret information to another country.

Coercing someone to act as an agent is by no means difficult. If you threaten to kill someone *and clearly mean it*, people can become very cooperative, as the British found out in 1940. As the threat of a Nazi invasion loomed that summer the Abwehr began to parachute half-trained agents into Britain. As far as we now know, the whole lot fell into the hands of MI5.

The startled German prisoners would be dumped in an interrogation room with a cup of tea, here they were given a simple choice: cooperate with MI5 and Whitehall's 'Double Cross Committee' by sending false radio messages back to the Abwehr in Hamburg from a nice warm cell, with three square meals a day and regular outings, or we will hang you as a spy. It wasn't a tough choice for most. The threat of the gallows worked every time. A genuine fear of death works, without any need for torture.

However one major problem with the use of coercion and compromise as opposed to credible death threats is that because the target has no real loyalty to their blackmailers, once away from the danger they will frequently turn on them when possible. A more reliable and subtle form of coercion is blackmail. Many people have skeletons that are best kept hidden in a cupboard. Many things can be used for blackmail:

sexual peccadilloes; embezzlement; paedophilia; secrets from the past; corruption. The list is long. A classic case of straightforward blackmail was British Foreign Office clerk John Vassall, who was threatened with exposure as a homosexual unless he provided secret information.

Admiralty worker John Vassall was the victim of a classic KGB honeytrap. The Soviets and particularly Markus Wolf, head of the East German Secret Service, the Stasi, were particularly adept at snaring potential spies by compromising them with sexual indiscretions, as many a menopausal NATO secretary found out to her cost.

In 1954, the effete and snobbish Admiralty civil servant with access to top-secret material on Royal Navy nuclear weapons, radar and tactics was posted to Moscow as assistant to the British naval attaché. Unhappy and miserable in the drab grey Moscow of the early fifties, he later said, 'I felt that the general atmosphere in the embassy was an unhappy one, the senior officials mostly seemed pre-occupied with their own private and official duties and in some ways junior staff were left to fend for themselves. If we were cared for as one family I do not think that some of us would have got into these troubles.'

The ever vigilant Soviet talent-spotters quickly noted the potential of this lonely, sensitive bachelor with access to secrets. Vassall was befriended by a Russian interpreter and invited to dinner at a restaurant near the Bolshoi. There he was shown into a private room. He told his interrogators after his arrest:

> We had drinks, a large dinner and I was plied with very strong brandy and, after half an hour, I remember everybody taking off their jackets and somebody assisted me to take off mine. I remember the lighting was very strong, and gradually most of my clothes were removed.
>
> There was a divan in the corner. I remember two or three people getting on the bed with me, all in a state of undress. Then certain compromising sexual actions took place. I remember someone in the party taking photographs.

When he sobered up, the KGB showed a hung-over and panicky Vassall the sexually explicit and compromising photographs taken during the homosexual orgy. He was blackmailed with threats of criminal charges by the police and disclosure of his secret homosexual life to the British Embassy. Humiliated and fearful of losing his job, he agreed to work for the KGB in return for them keeping quiet. That was a mistake and would ruin his life. From then on he passed over embassy secrets and continued to do so after his return to Britain in July 1956.

Back in London the traitor would hide top-secret files in his briefcase and take them home to photograph them with a camera provided by the Russians. Vassall was well paid for his troubles, lived in some style and made little attempt to hide it. The Soviet payments almost equalled his salary and his colleagues at work believed that he had a private income.

Vassall came to grief in September 1962 when he was arrested following a CIA tip-off that there was a spy in the Admiralty. He confessed all and was sentenced to eighteen years in prison, serving ten. Chapman Pincher, one of Britain's best informed journalists, who specialised in intelligence and security stories, described Vassall as 'the classic example of the spy who, while of lowly rank, can inflict enormous damage because of the excellence of his access to secret information'.

Pincher continued: 'I am in no doubt that the recruitment and running of Vassall was a major triumph for the KGB. He provided information of the highest value to the Soviet defence chiefs in their successful drive to expand and modernise the Red Navy.'

Before he died, Vassall said he had never been motivated by 'political bias'. His lame excuse for his treachery was that he had 'felt unloved . . .'

Clinton and Pollard

But not all attempts at compromise are aimed at breaking the little guy with access to secrets. Perhaps the most ambitious, and certainly one of the most remarkable examples of coercion, albeit unsuccessful, was at a very high level indeed: the astonishing attempt by Israel to blackmail Bill Clinton, the President of the most powerful country on earth, the United States.

Bill Clinton's sexual peccadilloes are well documented and they made him extremely vulnerable. His concupiscent shenanigans down the years make even the libidinous Jack Kennedy look like a monk in a cloister. Not content with embarking on a potentially ruinous affair with the statuesque Paula Corbin Jones, an Arkansas state employee who would in 1994 sue the President of the United States for sexual harassment, demanding $750,000 in damages; once in the White House, Clinton unwisely began an affair with a girl half his age. The woman in question was a chubby-faced, dark-haired 21-year-old intern called Monica Lewinsky. Unfortunately for Clinton, the affair was far from secret. Many curious ears were listening to the White House's telephones back in 1995 – and they were not all American.

By 1997 Clinton had had his fun and people were gossiping. Like so many other Clinton *amours*, a tearful Lewinsky accepted that her big affair was over and was quietly moved to another job in Washington on Clinton's orders. On 28 December 1997 Miss Lewinsky made her final visit to the White House, where in a private meeting Clinton warned her to keep her mouth shut: Paula Jones had suddenly called upon Lewinsky as a witness on her behalf to testify against the President in the Arkansas woman's sexual harassment lawsuit.

If Clinton hoped to hush up the affair, he failed miserably. Jones's lawyers were determined to show that Clinton had a pattern of behaviour where he repeatedly became sexually involved with state or government employees. Jones' lawyers subpoenaed women with whom Clinton was suspected of having had affairs, one of whom was Monica Lewinsky. In the words of one, 'with Bill, we were spoiled for choice'.

However, in his deposition for the Jones' lawsuit, Clinton staunchly denied having 'sexual relations' with Monica Lewinsky. Based on testimony provided by Linda Tripp, which identified the existence of a blue dress with Clinton's semen on it, the lawyers closed in for the kill on grounds of perjury.

On 26 January 1998 President Clinton, with his wife alongside him, told a packed White House press conference:

> But I want to say one thing to the American people. I want you to listen to me. I'm going to say this again: I did not have sexual relations with that woman, Miss Lewinsky. I never told anybody to lie, not a single time; never. These allegations are false.

Not for the first time, Clinton lied. Jones's lawyers and, more danger-
ously, his hidden listeners knew that he had lied. The trap closed in
October 1998, when Clinton called the Wye River Summit with
Benjamin Netanyahu (replacing the assassinated Yitzak Rabin) plus
Palestinian leader Yasser Arafat, in an attempt to keep the doomed
Oslo peace process alive.

In the margins of this high-level summitry Netenyahu quietly
dropped his bombshell: he informed a startled Bill Clinton that the
Israelis had hard evidence from White House phone-taps that
the President had had a sexual relationship with Monica Lewinsky.
Despite the President's very public TV denials to the American people
that, 'I did not have sexual relations with that woman,' Netanyahu
knew that Clinton was lying. Moreover, he could prove it, and openly
threatened to expose him with incriminating tapes, which Mossad had
collected. In return for keeping his mouth shut, the Israeli Prime
Minister demanded the release of Jonathan Pollard, an American Jew
who had spied for Israel. This was blackmail and an attempt at compromise at the very highest level.

That Pollard, languishing in an American high security prison was
an Israeli spy, was never in any doubt. In 1977, according to a now
declassified 1987 CIA damage report, the young Jonathan Pollard,
who from an early age was determined to aid Israel, applied for a job
in the CIA. He did not get it. The CIA induction polygraph test indicated that Pollard was a high-risk recruit; he was an obvious security
risk and was a user of illegal drugs. Despite this, the 25-year-old
Pollard was subsequently hired by Naval Intelligence in 1979 as an
Intelligence Research Specialist working for the Field Operational
Intelligence Office in Maryland. Although the Navy asked the CIA
for its findings on Pollard's security vetting the CIA, as ever mired in
the maze of American bureaucracy and inter-agency suspicion, refused
to volunteer its findings about the Navy's flaky new employee. The
result of this agency non-cooperation was that the treacherous Pollard
would work in Naval Intelligence for a total of seven years.

From the start, Jay Pollard was not altogether happy in his new job.
He later claimed that his fellow employees made anti-Semitic jokes or
criticisms of Israel. This was hardly surprising. The US Navy was no

lover of Israel. In 1967, during the Six-Day War, the Israelis had attacked and bombed an American intelligence-gathering ship, the USS *Liberty*, killing thirty-four Americans and causing the US Navy's biggest single loss in peacetime. (See page 453)

After two years on the job Pollard managed to obtain access to high-level classified data including the most sensitive of all, 'Special Compartmented Information' (SCI). SCI is a US designation reserved for especially sensitive classified information, 'the dissemination of which is strictly controlled and limited to selected individuals within the military and intelligence community who have special security clearances'.

To his colleague's surprise, Pollard then went outside the chain of command and approached Admiral Shapiro, Commander, Naval Intelligence Command, claiming that he knew South Africa's chief of military intelligence, Lieutenant General. P. W. van der Westhuizen, and could cultivate him as a friendly source. At the time, Washington was desperate for hard high-level intelligence out of South Africa and Shapiro heard the rookie out. However, after the meeting, an unimpressed Shapiro ordered that Pollard's security clearances be revoked and that he be transferred to a non-sensitive position, dismissing the young analyst as a 'kook', and saying later, 'I wish the hell I'd fired his ass.'

Others were equally unconvinced by Pollard's tall tales of having lived in South Africa while his father was serving as a CIA station chief in the country. This was bunkum and the Navy suspended him as a Walter Mitty character and ordered him to take a polygraph test. The testing officer reported that Pollard, 'began shouting and shaking and making gagging sounds as if he were going to vomit', and was deliberately trying to spoil the test. The Navy promptly suspended Pollard's clearances and sent him to see a psychiatrist. Unfortunately the shrink found Pollard free from mental illness and, under the law, his security clearance had to be restored.

In 1984 Pollard was re-assigned to the Anti-Terrorist Alert Center (ATAC) of the Naval Investigative Service's Threat Analysis Division. His boss was Jerry Agee, a career Navy man and a seasoned professional.

Agee found his new employee competent, but no more. 'He was . . . above average in his analysis of things.' But Agee was troubled by Pollard's fantasising. '[He] made comments that he had worked for Israeli intelligence ... the man was a bullshitter. He was always telling tall tales. It was more or less a joke in the office: "Did you hear the story about Pollard?" There were a lot of Pollard stories.'

Pollard had already broken all the security rules as early as 1982, when he took classified documents home to impress his friends. He also brought his pro-Israeli views into the office by insisting that a photograph of a poison-gas factory being constructed in Iraq should be transmitted to Israel. According to Pollard, his boss merely laughed and said Jews were too sensitive about gas because of their experiences in World War Two.

By 1983, when terrorists bombed the Marine Corps headquarters in Beirut, Pollard finally threw his hand in with Mossad, later claiming that if America could not protect its own interests in the Middle East, then it could not be expected to protect Israel. In early 1974 he approached an Israeli Air Force colonel studying in New York and offered to spy for Israel. Despite some early misgivings that the American might be part of a security sting to entrap them, the Israelis soon found Pollard's information to be gold dust.

Soon he was passing everything he could get: and not just to Israel, either. Navy investigators later discovered that Pollard had sold classified information to South Africa, and attempted, through a third party, to sell classified information to Pakistan on several occasions, as well as giving classified documents to his wife to help promote her business interests in China. A suspicious Australian naval exchange officer reported to Canberra that Pollard had frequently tried to pass him classified documents caveated 'No Foreign Access'.

Pollard's downfall began in 1985 when he was reported for drawing excessive amounts of classified documents from the NIC registry. Many of these were outside his area of responsibility, and the FBI was asked to begin a security investigation. A week later, Pollard was stopped in the lobby and questioned by FBI agents while taking classified documents out of the building. He claimed to be taking them to another agency for a conference, which turned out to be a lie. He was detained for questioning but insisted that he would have to phone his wife and let her know that he would be late. During that conversation he somehow managed to warn her that he was in trouble. She promptly packed all the incriminating material in the house into a suitcase and took it round to a neighbour, an officer in the Navy, asking him if he could look after it for her.

Pollard made a partial admission to investigators but without mentioning Israel and was placed under secret surveillance. The worried Pollards finally cracked and tried to claim asylum at the Israeli embassy on 21 November 1985. The Israelis slammed the gate in the face of their key US agent and watched FBI officers move in to arrest him. His wife fled and managed to warn his Israeli handlers, who left for Israel the next day.

However the Israelis claimed that Pollard was nothing to do with them and worked as a lone wolf. It was over ten years before they finally agreed to cooperate with the investigation, in exchange for immunity for the Israelis involved.

Pollard was subsequently sentenced to life imprisonment for selling thousands of classified US Navy documents to his Israeli handlers. For example, on 23 January 1985, the FBI determined that he had handed over five full suitcases of secret documents.

On 4 March 1987 Pollard was charged on one count of espionage and sentenced to life in prison. The prosecutor complied with the plea agreement and asked for 'only a substantial number of years in prison'. However the judge was not bound by the terms of any deal with the prosecution and instead imposed a life sentence.

The Israelis, who take great pride in always bringing their boys home, lobbied hard for Pollard's release, without result. It took until 1998 for Netanyahu to admit that Pollard was an Israeli agent. Next Netanyahu demanded his release, and followed this up with his threat to blackmail the President.

However, when a worried Clinton quietly brought Israel's demand for Pollard's release to the Director of the CIA, George Tenet, he 'blew his top', angrily pointing out that Pollard had sold classified information to South Africa and Pakistan as well as Israel and threatened to resign on the spot should Clinton cave in and release the convicted traitor.

The entire US intelligence community threatened to rebel if Pollard was released to keep the Israelis and the Jewish lobby happy. The result was that the Lewinsky affair eventually petered out after the story came out anyway and was followed by an attempt to impeach President Clinton for perjury. That failed, thanks to plentiful Jewish bribes on Capitol Hill and dark threats to expose several well-known Republican Senators who, like the randy Bill Clinton, just couldn't keep their flies zipped.

Clinton ultimately declined the Israeli request to release Pollard, since when the government of Israel and their well-funded and numerous mouthpieces in the US have lobbied hard for a pardon, claiming that the convicted spy is really a martyr and a loyal Jew – as if that somehow makes the traitor's crimes against America and betrayal no crime at all.

Joe Cahill

Not all spies are run to betray state secrets. One of the messiest and most dangerous roles in the intelligence world is that played by the agent in place inside a terrorist organisation. One false move and the unfortunate spy can expect little mercy from his erstwhile comrades. Torture, decapitation and death are the normal terrorist responses to the exposure of a traitor in their midst, as organisations like ISIS demonstrate. A swift bullet is a merciful release compared to an agonising decapitation on film. The Provisional Irish Republican Army (PIRA) even specialised in boring holes in offenders' kneecaps with an electric drill before the traditional gunshot to the back of the head. During the long-running anti-terrorist campaign in Northern Ireland from 1970 to 1998 the British security forces relied heavily on intelligence to penetrate the terrorist cells and bring the terrorists to justice.

Perhaps the most spectacular example of this was the blackmailing and recruiting of the Provisional Irish Republican Army's Joe Cahill. Cahill had a long record of Republican terrorism and had been sentenced to death long before for the murder of Police Constable Patrick Murphy – a Roman Catholic and a father of ten – in the 1940s. Cahill was reprieved and served fewer than ten years before his release, but was jailed again during the IRA's Border Campaign of the 1950s.

When the the Troubles started in 1969, Cahill was one of the founding fathers of the new paramilitary Provisional Irish Republican Army, an underground terrorist organisation that targeted and murdered soldiers and civilians in Ulster and England between 1970 and 1998.

Cahill rose to become a member of the PIRA's original governing Army Council and served as an IRA leader throughout PIRA's long campaign. However, Joe Cahill had a secret little vice: he liked sex with under-age girls. The undercover British intelligence units tracking Cahill eventually caught and photographed him in flagrante with a fourteen-year-old girl.

In the tightly-knit Catholic communities of Northern Ireland this was social and political dynamite. An intelligence source revealed in 2014, 'the pictures clearly identified both Cahill and his victim', adding, 'The girl's father would have killed him if he had found out.' Cahill was never prosecuted for his sex abuse and instead the pictures were used by the British to turn him. As a member of the PIRA leadership, Cahill would have had detailed knowledge about its bombing campaigns and was deeply involved in gun running, buying arms and Semtex explosive from Gaddafi's Libya and collecting money from gullible Irish Americans for 'Noraid'.

Intelligence officers then, just like the KGB, blackmailed Cahill to spy for Britain during the Troubles. He was given the choice of exposure as a paedophile and facing the wrath of his PIRA comrades, let alone the abused girl's angry father, or spying for British intelligence on the terrorist organisation he had helped to found.

Hopelessly compromised, like so many others before and since, a broken Cahill agreed to betray his comrades. Interestingly, as the IRA campaign ran out of steam in the 1990s, he was one of the principal advocates for a settlement.

Cahill died in 2004 and was buried with some ceremony at the Republican shrine of Milltown Cemetery, in one of the largest republican funerals in Belfast since the death of Bobby Sands in 1981. His coffin was borne by Gerry Adams and Martin McGuinness, little realising that they were carrying on their shoulders an IRA traitor or 'tout', considered by British intelligence as one of their 'prized assets' in Northern Ireland.

CHAPTER 9

Ego: Robert Hanssen

One of the great puzzles about Robert Hanssen, the traitor responsible for the FBI's worst security breach ever, is whether he was a man who was motivated by money or by ego.

A careful analysis of the case points us firmly in the direction of ego, although money undoubtedly played its part. But it is hard not to agree with his biographer that Hanssen 'had a fractured ego seeking recognition. He wanted to be a player on the world stage and felt overlooked by the Bureau.'

A college friend, Robert Lauren, recalled an incident where Hanssen showed his colours long before he joined the FBI.

> I was leaving his house I think it was 1968 or 1969 and Bob handed me the memoirs of a British traitor who had spied for Moscow over a twenty-year period. The book was *My Silent War* by Kim Philby. He thought the book was terrific. After a few weeks I returned the book and he asked me if I liked it and I said it was very interesting. Bob then said and I've never forgotten it, particularly how he said, 'You know, someday I'd like to pull off a caper like that.'

Hanssen was clearly successful at his dangerous game for a very long time – twenty-two years. There were two basic reasons for him getting away with his crimes for so long: first, unlike most agents, he managed to hide his identity from his Soviet handlers as well as the FBI. For a spy, that was both unusual and clever. He never met the Russians face to face, except on one occasion, and even then they never knew exactly who their mysterious – and prolific – source was. The KGB obviously knew that they had a highly successful mole called 'Ramon' at the heart of American counter-intelligence: but because they never knew who it was, they could never betray their invisible asset.

Second, Hanssen was clever, there is no argument: Hanssen was very bright. Once, at university, a professor noticed Hanssen had taken no notes in a lecture and berated him for his idleness. Hanssen said nothing; but when the professor went back to the lectern the student recounted the lecture so far, verbatim, to the amazement of his fellow students – and the professor.

It was, said a witness, 'like he had a tape recorder inside his brain. Afterwards he told me, "I can remember every conversation I have ever had."'

Hanssen had trouble settling down after high school, where he was remembered as 'a bit of a geek', and obsessed by *Mad* magazine's 'Spy vs. Spy.' He went to nearby Knox College in Galesburg, and got a BSc in chemistry. One of the requirements for graduation was to study a foreign language for two years. Hanssen opted for Russian and became enthralled by the works of masters like Tolstoy and Dostoyevsky.

His undercover career started early. When his hard-nosed father (Howard Hanssen was a career Chicago cop and didn't take any non-sense, even from his own son) retired in 1972, the young Bob Hanssen was ready to keep the family tradition going and joined the Chicago Police Department as a rookie. However, with a good MBA degree, recruit Hanssen was too valuable an asset to waste on becoming a mere patrolman. He was quickly hauled out of his training class and invited to become a member of a new secret squad called C-5 that was being set up to identify cops on the take.

Hanssen quickly made his mark; so much so that his boss, John Clarke, began to have concerns that Hanssen might have really been sent to spy on the new unit and report back to headquarters. 'I always thought he was a spy, a counter-spy, when he worked for us. I thought he was work-ing for the police brass who wanted to know what we were doing.'

Meanwhile, his career in the Chicago Police Department was blos-soming. John Clarke remained uneasy about his bright young rising star and so, when the FBI started recruiting, he encouraged Hanssen to move on and join the Feds. On 12 January 1976, Bob Hanssen was sworn into the FBI. In the words of a later investigator, 'The fox was in place and inside the hen house.'

Hanssen cut his FBI teeth on white-collar crime around Chicago but was soon posted to the Field Office in New York City. Money was tight for the Hanssens, what with a house in Scarsdale and four growing children, but they seem to have coped remarkably well for a household on only £40,000 a year. One clue came at a dinner for the Donovans, the couple who had sold them the house. Bob Hanssen admitted that 'I've wanted to be a spy ever since I was a child.' The Donovans were intrigued; they thought that he was talking about his job with the FBI.

Some time in 1979, Hanssen approached the GRU (the Soviet military intelligence agency) and offered his services. His tradecraft was ingenious. He remained anonymous and just pushed hard-copy classified material to the Soviets via dead letter-boxes, which he alone selected, and at times that he alone selected. It was a clever system, though the need to communicate by hard copy would always be vulnerable to interception if the time and place should ever be compromised, or if Hanssen was ever placed under covert surveillance.

Once the Soviets realised that they had a genuine prime source on their hands, they responded with cash, using the same anonymous dead-drop method to pass the money to their mysterious agent. His material was gold dust to the Soviets. Since his move into FBI counter-intelligence, Hanssen had been given the job of compiling a secret database of Soviet intelligence sources for the Bureau. With access like this, he could pinpoint the Soviets' own traitors and sell their identities. In his enclosures Hanssen identified three Soviet KGB officers – Sergey Motorin, Valeriy Martynov and Boris Yuzhin – who were acting as undercover agents for American intelligence. Two of them would later be executed and Yuzhin escaped with his life after serving six years of a fifteen-year sentence in Perm 35, a Siberian prison.

Hanssen's undercover career very nearly came to grief in 1981. Bonnie Hanssen walked into their basement and confronted her husband while he was writing a letter to the Soviets and counting bundles of cash. Hanssen thought quickly and told his wife that he was just acting as a double agent on the instructions of the Bureau and passing chickenfeed as part of his job. He boasted about the deal, saying he had tricked the Russians and was giving them worthless information in exchange for cash. That Sunday (the Hanssens were devout Catholics) Hanssen took confession from an Opus Dei priest and asked for guidance. The cleric, Father Robert Bucciarelli, told Bob to give any ill-gotten gains to the Mother Teresa charities. After that, the secret of the Confessional remained absolute.

By the time Robert Hanssen was assigned to Washington in 1981 to work on the Bureau's Congressional budget, he had begun to realize that his FBI career was going to be limited. His colleagues regarded him as an oddball. Behind his back he was known as 'Silent Bob', 'the Mortician' and 'Dr Death' because of his fondness for black suits and unwillingness to shoot the breeze with his fellow agents.

'He was different,' his boss, Richard Alu remembered. 'I thought he was an intelligent guy, but he was an introvert. The ideal agent is like a used-car salesman; you've got to be able to sell yourself. Hanssen simply didn't have any interpersonal skills. He was able to see problems, see solutions, and implement them. His solutions were not always easy for his peers to follow. He did not suffer fools gladly.'

If his earlier spying for the GRU was the overture, Hanssen now deliberately moved into the big time. On 4 October 1985, after a trip to Washington, Bob Hanssen mailed an anonymous letter to Viktor Degtyar, a KGB colonel living in Alexandria, Virginia. As an insider, Hanssen knew that the FBI was not conducting surveillance on Degtyar and so the Russian was a safe courier. Hanssen sent a letter to Degtyar. Inside was another envelope with instructions, 'DO NOT OPEN. TAKE THIS LETTER TO VICTOR I. CHERKASHIN.' (Cherkashin was the secret coordinator of Soviet espionage efforts in Washington.)

Hanssen's letter read:

Dear Mr. Cherkashin,

    Soon, I will send a box of documents to Mr. Degtyar. They are from certain of the most sensitive and highly compartmentalized projects of the U.S. Intelligence community. All are originals to aid verifying their authenticity. Please recognize for our long-term interests that there are a limited number of persons with this array of clearances.

As a collection they point to me. I trust that an officer of your experience will handle them appropriately. I believe they are sufficient to justify a $100,000 payment to me.

Hanssen kept his word. One of his key treacheries was identifying a vital CIA agent codenamed Tophat, who had been a major informant for more than twenty years and who had passed massive amounts of information to American intelligence. By naming Tophat, Hanssen betrayed America's most important long-term agent inside Soviet intelligence. The Soviets bided their time and, eventually, Red Army General Dmitry Polyakov, late of the GRU, was arrested and executed in 1988, along with several others, thanks to Hanssen's betrayal.

Tophat was not the only American asset to go off the radar. Several other key American agents mysteriously disappeared around that time.

The Americans were baffled; obviously there was a leak. But where? Suspicion centred on the CIA where, unknown to him (and CIA security) another Soviet agent, Aldrich Ames, was busy betraying his country and colleagues in parallel with Hanssen. The very few CIA and FBI agents who knew Tophat's identity agonised over what mistake they could have made that had given their prime source away. Only later did they learn the truth. When Aldrich Ames, a career CIA officer, was arrested in February 1994, he admitted that he had already sold the identities of many Soviet and East Bloc citizens spying for the CIA to the KGB. At least ten of these people were executed; Polyakov – Tophat – was one of them. The luckless Russian had actually been betrayed by both Hanssen and Ames.

Having proved that he knew what he was talking about, Hanssen then told Cherkashin that he would never reveal his identity to his Soviet handlers or ever meet with them. He also added a simple code for dates that he asked them to follow. By doing this, Hanssen believed he was now running his own case and was master of two worlds.

The Russians were delighted with the haul from their anonymous source, 'Ramon'. For $100,000 they had been able to smoke out and eliminate dozens of traitors in their midst. The Americans, on the other hand, were now profoundly worried. Too many of their best sources were being hauled in and arrested. Washington now knew that they had a serious problem on their hands; but, once again, all investigative eyes turned on the CIA as the most likely source of the leaks – or worse. What muddied the waters even more was that the CIA mole, Aldrich Ames, was, unbeknown to Hanssen, betraying everything he knew to the Soviets at the same time.

Investigators closed in to concentrate on the CIA. The result was that the October 1985 letter to the KGB opened up a long, active period for Hanssen of spying for the Soviets, unsuspected by everybody. To make things worse, he was recalled to Washington in 1987 and given the task of making a study of all possible penetrations of the FBI in order to find the source of the leak that had betrayed Martynov and Motorin. This meant that Hanssen was effectively tasked with looking for himself!

Naturally Hanssen made sure that his study was thorough and comprehensive, including the list of all Soviets who had contacted the FBI about FBI moles. However he made equally sure that the study did not point at him. And, just to be certain, he passed the whole document over to his Soviet handlers.

The Soviets were suitably grateful. A few days later, the KGB responded by dropping off $50,000 in $100 bills at Nottoway Park, across the street from the Hanssens' first house in Northern Virginia.

Over the next five years, Hanssen turned over 6,000 pages of classified documents to his KGB handlers, from nuclear deployment plans to detailed breakdowns of FBI counter-espionage operations, and from satellite positions to the complete contents of classified FBI computers. The Russian take was phenomenal. He downloaded the hard drives on FBI computers onto twenty-six disks and turned them over using his personally chosen dead drops. It was simple, it was elegant; it was safe. It paid well.

Hanssen used some of the KGB's money to put his six children through expensive Catholic private schools. By the 1990s he appears to have believed that he was a soldier engaged in some greater religious war, which would somehow lead to the world that Opus Dei wanted, where abortion, divorce and other evils of the world, including Communism, would be no more.

Hanssen put some of the KGB's money in to a curious relationship with a stripper called Priscilla Sue Galey. They first met in a seedy strip club in Washington in early 1990 where Hanssen sent her a note with his FBI business card, a $10 bill and a request for lunch after watching her act – in which she transformed herself from a bespectacled, strait-laced librarian into a raunchy bump and grinder dropping her panties.

Soon Hanssen was giving his new girlfriend money to get her teeth fixed, buying a Mercedes and jewellery, and even giving her an AMEX card, which he paid off every month. Galey, not surprisingly, couldn't believe her luck, saying that 'I thought he was my personal angel.' Hanssen calculated that he spent at least $80,000 on his sexy strip-club squeeze.

This odd-couple relationship only lasted two years, before Galey returned to her hometown of Columbus, Ohio, to join a former lover. There, she fell apart, becoming addicted to crack cocaine and turning to prostitution. Years later, after reading of Hanssen's arrest for espionage, Galey said she now suspected that Hanssen may have been grooming her to help his undercover work. 'He had to have wanted me for something,' she said. 'I trusted him completely, and if he had asked me to do anything, I probably would have.'

Hanssen's Catholicism became a greater pre-occupation as time went by. The intelligence author James Bamford, himself a Catholic, wrote this in the *New York Times* about Hanssen's obsession with Opus Dei:

> Hanssen squeezed religion into most conversations and hung a silver crucifix above his desk. Occasionally he would leave work to take part in anti-abortion rallies. He was forever trying to get me to go with him to meetings of Opus Dei.

Hanssen's obsessions gradually began to manifest themselves in ever more deviant ways. By the early 1990s he was spending hours in his basement cruising Internet porn sites, and posting masturbatory fantasies online, using the real names of his wife and friends. He even set up a secret camera in the main bedroom and invited an old friend Jack Hoschuer to watch downstairs as the Hanssens had sex.

On one occasion in 1993 he called Kim Lichtenberg, his blonde, 21-year-old administrative assistant into his office without warning for a trivial meeting about office rumours. The meeting dragged on until Litchenberg suddenly left the meeting to catch her transport home. Hanssen came up behind her and threw her to the floor.

The FBI kept the assault in-house. Hanssen was disciplined and suspended for five days without pay for the attack. Lichtenberg was awarded $16,000 for damage to her arm after filing a worker's compensation claim.

At the time, Hanssen seems to have been taking a break from spying. Worried about the chaotic break-up of the Soviet Union in 1990–91 and the uncertainties of the new intelligence mayhem that split the old KGB into the FSB and SVR, for the next seven years he stopped supplying intelligence, although he stayed on at the FBI, specialising in computer security.

By the time the former KGB officer Vladimir Putin rose to power in 1999, Hanssen felt more confident and that it was safe to re-establish contact with the Russians. In an extraordinarily risky move he broke cover for the first and only time and openly visited the Russian embassy in Washington DC, where he went up to a known GRU officer in the car park. He told the officer that he was a 'disaffected FBI agent', and 'you knew me as "Ramon Garcia"', adding that he now wanted to spy for the new Russian Federation.

The startled Russian fled, thinking that he was being set up by the Americans; and the Russian Embassy subsequently filed a formal protest with the US State Department for a 'diplomatic provocation'. Incredibly, despite having revealed his face, used his previous code name and revealed that he was an FBI agent, neither the Russians, nor the FBI investigation, ever identified Hanssen as 'Ramon'.

But the clues were now starting to mount up that Ames at the CIA was not the only source of American secrets haemorrhaging to Moscow. The investigators cast their net wider but without result. This was surprising, because Hanssen was becoming over-confident and sloppy.

He installed a password-cracking program on his own computer without clearance. A member of the FBI IT security unit investigated the unauthorised installation and Hanssen was questioned. A routine security violation report was issued but no further action was taken as his reputation shielded him from suspicion: his explanation was accepted. Later, Hanssen was caught actually hacking into a fellow agent's computer, which he smoothly explained away by claiming that was only demonstrating the security flaws in the FBI computer system.

Hanssen's security dossier had grown thicker, when in 1990, his brother-in-law, Mark Wauck, who was also an FBI agent, told his superiors that he had discovered that Hanssen was 'hiding thousands of dollars in cash', and 'was spending far too much money for someone on an FBI salary'. The FBI 'evaluated the episode' but found no evidence of wrongdoing. Hanssen made another serious mistake in 1993 when he hacked into the computer of Ray Mislock, a fellow FBI agent, and printed out a classified document. The FBI launched a security investigation but accepted Hanssen's story that, once again, he was merely demonstrating flaws in the FBI's security system.

Suspicions should again have been aroused a year later when, in 1994, Hanssen asked if he could be transferred to the new National Counterintelligence Center, which had been set up to coordinate all US counter-intelligence activities. However, when his boss told him that a routine lie detector test was a requirement for the new post, Hansen abruptly withdrew his request. It later turned out that Hanssen had somehow managed to avoid taking any polygraph test since joining the Bureau.

By 2000, the FBI investigators had exhausted all lines of enquiry into the mole. In desperation they turned to the simplest, most direct and most expensive solution of all. They decided to try and buy the answer from the Russians. They found a former KGB agent and offered him a whopping $7 million to reveal the identity of the mole for whom they had been searching for so long. The delighted Russian promptly came up with the goods and sold the FBI 'a suitcase full of evidence', including a voice recording of the mole talking to his Russian handler, as well as files passed over by 'Ramon', plus the plastic bags in which they were delivered. They didn't identify the mole by name: but Robert Hanssen's fingerprints were on these bags.

The voice on the tape was immediately recognised by a fellow agent. The FBI at last had their man. Now they moved in for the endgame. Hanssen was placed under surveillance and videotaped taking documents marked 'secret' from the FBI office. The Bureau bugged his office, car and house and bought a house across the street from the Hanssen home, in Vienna, Virginia to give twenty-four-hour surveillance.

Hanssen's office was bugged by the simple action of promoting him to a new job supervising all FBI computer security where, coincidentally, he would have no legitimate access to ongoing operations. His new job also included an office assistant, Eric O'Neill, who was in fact a young FBI undercover officer with a brief to spy on his suspect boss. O'Neill soon spotted that Hanssen was recording a lot of information on a small Palm PDA, an early hand-held digital data storage system. Hanssen was lured out of his office on a pretext and O'Neill and a special team of data specialists were able to download the contents of the PDA. Hanssen's guilt was no longer in doubt. The investigating team moved in for the kill.

On 18 February 2001, Hanssen went to church and then dropped off his friend Jack Hoschuer at Dulles Airport in Virginia. He then drove to Foxstone Park, got out of his car and walked over to the footbridge, placed a white sticky tape on a road sign, then climbed down and tucked a plastic bag containing documents he had stolen from his office and a computer disk under the bridge. Inside was a goodbye letter to the Russians.

> Dear Friends,
>
> I thank you for your assistance these many years. It seems, however, that my greatest utility to you has come to an end, and it is time to seclude myself from active service ... Life is full of its ups and downs ... I will be in contact next year, same time, same place.

As he walked away from the dead drop, ten armed FBI agents converged upon him, placing him under arrest. Arrogant to the last, Hanssen first words were: 'What took you so long?'

Hanssen's spying days were over. He was now facing certain execution as the Justice Department demanded the death penalty for a man who had been responsible for untold deaths of others. On July 6, 2001, Robert Hanssen pleaded guilty to fifteen counts of espionage; eleven months later he was sentenced to life in prison without the possibility of parole. He escaped execution by agreeing to be debriefed by FBI interrogators as part of a comprehensive damage assessment. Even then, the arrogant, slippery traitor managed to muddy the waters.

Despite being interviewed for 215 hours over seventy-six different days and undergoing two polygraph tests by America's most skilled interrogators, the government was largely unsatisfied by his answers. Suddenly the great brain and owner of a 'tape recorder memory' lost his tongue. An embittered FBI inquisitor complained, 'His claim of a poor memory was an excuse for not engaging fully in the debriefing or was a means to hide facets of his activity.'

Hanssen, the ego-maniac spy who inflicted incalculable damage to American intelligence, will one day die in jail as Federal Bureau of Prisons' prisoner #48551-083. He is serving his sentence at the ADX Florence, a Federal Supermax prison in Florence, Colorado He remains in solitary confinement twenty-three hours a day. At least he has his monstrous ego to keep him company . . .

CHAPTER 10

The Grievance: Penkovsky

The most experienced agent handler at Britain's MI6 used to start his lecture on agent running by spelling out the M.I.C.E. acronym on an agent's motivation, but then adding, 'But the powerful motive of all is the Grievance.' He may have been right. Psychiatrists and care workers often note that the last thing that a dementia sufferer really remembers is some long-held grievance against a relative, a neighbour – or their boss.

The Penkovsky case from the early sixties is an example of a spy with a grievance. Penkovsky was a colonel in the GRU – Soviet military intelligence – and became the most senior Soviet officer to spy for the United States or Great Britain up to that time. During his time in the military, Penkovsky grew disillusioned with the Soviet regime. He felt that Nikita Krushchev's relentless pursuit of spreading Communism throughout the world was leading the Soviet Union down the path to destruction. Penkovsky claimed that he wanted to help prevent a nuclear war between the superpowers, so he volunteered to spy for the United States and the United Kingdom.

In April 1961, Penkovsky established contact with Greville Wynne – a British businessman working for MI6. A few days later, Penkovsky met with two British and two American intelligence officers to pass on information about the Soviet Union during a trip to London. Penkovsky travelled frequently to Britain and France as a representative of a Soviet scientific research delegation and continued to meet his CIA and MI6 handlers there for extensive debriefing sessions. In

Moscow he delivered documentary material in meetings using the wife of an MI6 officer posted to the British Embassy.

During the brief period that Penkovsky passed information to the United States and Great Britain, he was a prolific agent. Over a period of fourteen months he was debriefed face to face for 140 hours and passed photographs of 5,000 secret papers to the CIA and MI6. The take was so big that CIA and MI6 had around thirty translators and analysts working it full-time. His information was immensely valuable. He passed on the technical secrets for the radar guidance systems of the USSR's new – and highly dangerous – SA-2 Guideline missile, which was causing great concern to Germany's BND (*Bundesnachrichtendienst* – Germany's secret intelligence service) and Israel. Operations Caligula and Cerberus, designed to uncover Soviet radar development, had lasted for nearly ten years: Penkovsky provided the answers overnight. He also helped dispel concerns about Soviet strategic superiority, showing that Khrushchev was bluffing: the United States had the advantage in missile systems.

His real contribution came during the autumn of 1962 as the Cuban Missile Crisis terrified the world. The Soviets believed that the United States would not detect the Cuban missiles until it was too late to take action. It was Penkovsky who first alerted Washington that the Soviet Union was deploying nuclear missiles to Cuba by providing detailed plans and descriptions of the launch sites.

Penkovsky's information gave the Kennedy administration the vital technical knowledge that enabled Kennedy to know that he had three days to negotiate a diplomatic solution before the Soviet missiles were fully operational. Penkovsky is rightly credited with altering the course of the Cold War.

Penkovsky, described by one intelligence officer as the 'best spy in history', was considered so important that a meeting was arranged between him and Sir Dick White, the head of MI6. According to Joe Bulik, his CIA handler:

> during the second meetings with Oleg Penkovsky in London in the autumn of 1961, Oleg told us that he wanted to have military rank in both the British and American armies. So we went about and I'd

gotten the uniform about his size from the US military attaché, whom I happened to know, in London and we took photographs of him, first in the British uniform, then in the American uniform. He was very proud and he felt that he was a symbol, that he was with us.

And another story I must tell you. When the Soviet cosmonaut, Gagarin, was there, Oleg said Gagarin met the Queen, why can't I meet the Queen? And this was where Shergold really sweated crocodile drops. There was no way he could really satisfy Penkovsky on this part. He could have gotten Lord Mountbatten, which would have done the trick, instead he sent Sir Dick White, who was head of MI6, for a meeting with Penkovsky and Penkovsky was clearly not impressed.

That Penkovsky did nurse a grievance of some sort against his masters in Moscow was confirmed by Bulik. Oleg was at the time a senior colonel in the Red Army, and according to Bulik, 'he resented particularly the way Khrushchev treated the military and Marshal Zhukov, who really won the war militarily for the Soviets, Penkovsky felt that Zhukov had been thrown aside and it made it very difficult for Soviet officers who had retired to live on their pensions . . . And so he had very low regard for Khrushchev, it was a hate actually.' He is supposed to have admired himself in his British uniform in a mirror and said, 'If only those ******* in Moscow could see me now.'

According to Bulik:

Well, one always wonders why a traitor, in this case in the eyes of the KGB, turned to the West and you have to examine that motivation very, very thoroughly and carefully. Besides that, he was sour on the Soviet Union because there's one point I should mention, Oleg's father was a White Russian and the KGB had been investigating apparently all of Oleg's life, whatever happened to him, and the view is that his father probably died during the Civil War when the Soviet Union was young. But they never let Penkovsky forget about the fact that his father was a White Russian and they never could find out what happened to him and this soured him even further. And there are many spies who work for money. Well, he never asked for a heck of a lot of money; all he wanted was to buy gifts for his family, his friends and also to butter up the Soviet leadership.

Bulik has produced photographs of the GRU man and his CIA handlers in a London hotel room examining Polaroid photographs of Soviet operators in their various embassies and trade missions throughout the world, so that he could identify KGB and GRU officers. Bulik added, 'After the case was blown, I'm told that about three hundred to six hundred of the KGB officers were recalled back to the Soviet Union.'

Penkovsky was arrested in Moscow by the KGB on 22 October 1962 at the height of the Cuban Missile Crisis. We now know that his real motivation was his deep sense of grievance. It was only when the KGB, long-time rivals to the military's GRU, had blocked Penkovsky's promotion to major general, citing security concerns because his father had fought for the Whites long ago, that he seems to have snapped and offered to spy for the British and American secret services. It is still not clear how he was betrayed. Many suspect that George Blake was somehow responsible. Later it emerged that Penkovsky had been under surveillance for some time on suspicion of treason.

After a public trial in May 1963, Penkovsky was sentenced to death. He was executed in the Lubyanka Prison in Moscow on 16 May 1963. Spying is a dangerous occupation.

CHAPTER 11

HUMINT in action: Werther and the Battle of Kursk

The Battle of Kursk started in April 1943 as 'Operation Citadel', the Germans' great plan for an offensive to pinch out the Kursk pocket and once more to drive the Russians back in headlong retreat. After the fall of Stalingrad in February 1943, the Germans had two strategic options: attack or go on the defensive. Hitler elected to go for the former against the advice of many of his senior military advisers, although the Führer admitted 'it made me sick to my stomach to think about it'.

We now know from the now uncovered KGB archives that, from 1941 onwards, there was a senior Soviet spy at the very top of the Nazi war machine. His code name was 'Werther'. Via a network of radio operators and couriers based in Switzerland, the spy Werther betrayed every German operation in Eastern Europe, sending battle plans, details of the Nazi military strategy, tank positions, endless sets of numbers, plus details of the weaknesses of German army positions.

This Swiss spy network, called the 'Lucy Ring', sent over 2,300 messages to Moscow between 1941 and 1945, of which a fifth came from Werther. The CIA has managed to decrypt all or some of 332 messages in all. The information supplied by Werther was so important that it was marked 'VYRDO', meaning 'Extremely Urgent', and went immediately to Stalin personally. Though he never knew who Werther was, Stalin eventually trusted him completely, basing his battle plans on the information he received.

Werther was prolific, answering (sometimes on the same day) detailed lists of questions from the Russians, and giving away the most sensitive secrets of the Third Reich. His intelligence was crucial to the outcome of the war in the East: despite their better tanks, better generals and better soldiers, from late 1942 onwards the Wehrmacht was outmanoeuvred every time. In Hitler's own words, 'It was almost as if they knew we were coming.'

They did.

Astonishingly, current thinking points to Werther having either been a very clever British front for passing on deciphered SIGINT to Moscow, or a spy in the Führer's entourage. The former seems unlikely because the ULTRA decrypts took time to decode and disseminate and, whoever Werther was, he had much faster turnaround times. The British official historian of intelligence in World War Two writes, 'there is no truth in the much-publicised claim that the British authorities made use of the "Lucy" ring . . . to forward intelligence to Moscow.'

Whoever he was, Werther's clandestine work for the Soviet regime changed the course of history and defines the world we live in today. Without his treachery, the Germans would – almost certainly – have defeated the Russians by 1942–43 and the final outcome of the war would have been very different.

After Rudolph Hess's defection on a fool's errand to Scotland in May 1941 in a futile attempt to negotiate a pre-Barbarossa peace with Britain, Martin Bormann became more powerful than any of the other Nazi Satraps surrounding Adolf Hitler, primarily through his role as the trusted Personal Secretary to the Führer. As the war went on and Hitler became more deranged (largely through Parkinson's disease and the bizarre concoctions of drugs given to him by his doctors) he began to rely increasingly on his trusted aide. Bormann alone controlled access to the Führer, and Bormann was the only one allowed to issue orders in his name.

No-one knows how Werther first made contact with the Lucy ring in Switzerland but the radio material began to flow in 1941. The spy's warnings about Operation Barbarossa were certainly included among the 103 separate reports given to Stalin of Hitler's plans to invade Russia: warnings which the Soviet leader so stubbornly ignored.

He was not to make the same mistake again. The flow of top-grade intelligence from the heart of the German war machine continued and it was so good that initially Stalin believed it must be a German trap. By the late summer of 1942 it was clear that the reports coming from Werther were pure gold. Instead of fighting the Wehrmacht at every opportunity – and losing – by summer 1942 Stalin had opted for his own strategic trap, one that would eventually help to win the war. The Red Army was ordered to give ground and retreat to lure the Germans deep into Russian territory, starting at Stalingrad.

The mysterious spy's career might all have ended there in 1942. A message from Moscow Centre to Rachel Dubenborfer ('"Werther" is to state clearly how many replacement divisions in all are being formed from recruits by 1 January. Reply urgent') was intercepted by German intelligence, who now knew they had a major spy called Werther in their midst. But, as Hitler's triumphant German divisions had swept all before them deep into the USSR by the autumn of 1942, one spy seemed an irrelevance in the euphoria of victory. Even with the disaster of Stalingrad looming over them, the German High Command ignored the warning. The alarm bells went unheard.

Werther's task was made easier by Ober Kommand Wehrmacht's (OKW) new daily procedures to ensure that no detail or decision was missed at the daily Führer conference. Stenographers should in future attend every such meeting and keep detailed notes so that Hitler's brilliance could be recorded for posterity. The moment the new secretaries started work (often producing 500 typewritten pages a day) the level of detail given to the Lucy group soared.

Suddenly Stalin was receiving intelligence from Werther of who said what in the Führer's daily war conferences *on the very day they took place*: and long before the orders had been sent out in Enigma code to the front-line German commanders (and the waiting code breakers of Bletchley Park). We now know that there were only two recipients of these stenographers' draft transcripts: Martin Bormann, Hitler's closest day-to-day confidant and General Erich Fellgiebel, the senior communications officer in the OKW. As his confidence grew, Stalin grew bolder, often sending Werther dozens of highly detailed questions.

Kursk was Werther's most dramatic success. The 'greatest tank battle in history' was one which, (all things being equal) the Germans had expected to win. But, with the precise and detailed German operational orders in their hands, the Red Army laid 400,000 mines to channel their attackers into a lethal crossfire from pre-placed anti-tank guns. An astonishing 40 per cent of the Red Army was moved into place to ambush the German onslaught when it came. Thanks to Werther's intelligence, the Red Army's deadly trap destroyed a year's production of German tanks, guns and planes. Kursk broke the Wehrmacht in the East once and for all and opened the door to the Soviet drive through Eastern Europe that would end two years later amid the ruins of Berlin.

The Germans had been defeated, not by Russian brilliance, but by the determined treachery of the greatest spy or provider of intelligence of modern times. Only one man in Hitler's headquarters appears to have had the opportunity to access all the intelligence reported to Stalin over the period in question: the faithful Martin Bormann. He seems to have taken the Socialist part of National Socialist to heart.

The circumstantial evidence appears to be overwhelming. According to researchers, 'All the suspicions concerning Bormann by the spymasters over the years were valid. The pieces of the puzzle fit together. In Martin Bormann we have found Werther.'

Bormann was last seen amid the burning ruins of the Führer Bunker in Berlin as the vengeful soldiers of the Red Army closed in for the kill on 1 May 1945. At the end of the war, Bormann disappeared. Neither he – nor his body – have ever been found. After the war Albert Speer from his prison cell sardonically stated that he believed that Bormann should have been declared a 'hero of the Soviet Union'.

Sometimes there is no substitute for a really good spy. Even SIGNINT, with all its wartime triumphs, can never be steered to tell you exactly what you want to know. For all its risks and fallibility, HUMINT is absolutely necessary and has been at all times and in all ages.

CHAPTER 12

On Interrogation

The purpose of interrogation is to gain intelligence. Interrogation is one of the major sources of human intelligence. Unlike police interrogations (which are primarily aimed at acquiring evidence for a criminal conviction) interrogation for intelligence purposes exists purely to obtain accurate information that can be combined with other sources to provide intelligence.

Unfortunately 'interrogation' both as a word and as a source was seriously tainted in both the United States and Britain by a number of scandals – involving torture, illegal methods and even murders – following al Qaeda's 2001 attack on the World Trade Center and the subsequent invasion of Saddam Hussein's Iraq in 2003.

A shocked and frightened America reacted strongly to this attack on their country and declared war on terrorists everywhere. The secret American interrogation centre and military prison within the Guantanamo Bay naval base in Eastern Cuba was established in 2002 as part of the 'War on Terror', according to the US Defense Department, to detain 'extraordinarily dangerous persons, to interrogate "detainees" in an optimal setting, and to prosecute detainees for war crimes'. Detainees captured in the continuing US War on Terror that dominated much of the first decade of the twenty-first century mainly came from Pakistan, the Yemen, Saudia Arabia and Afghanistan, with smaller numbers coming later from Iraq, the Horn of Africa and South Asia.

Controversy very quickly arose over four main issues swirling around the prisoners of this curious 'war'. First, the legality in international law of scooping up suspects across the globe. Second, disquiet about what the *New York Times* called '... a chain of shadowy detention camps that includes Abu Ghraib in Iraq, the military prison at Bagram Air Base in Afghanistan and other secret locations run by the intelligence agencies that are part of a tightly linked global detention system with no accountability in law'.

There was also widespread concern about the movement of the detainees and prisoners. The CIA captured alleged terrorists all over the world and, in a black programme euphemised as 'extraordinary rendition', flew its captives in secret flights to secret locations. Calls for *Habeas corpus*, or even just basic information on the identities and locations of the disappeared detainees were widely ignored. Lawyers and the liberal press had a field day.

However, the fourth and final issue, arousing the fiercest criticism of all, was over the treatment of the detainees as they were interrogated at Guantanamo and the other secret camps. Allegations of ill treatment, torture and even death came from a wide variety of sources.

The US attempted to 'legalise' its string of secret interrogation camps through two main initiatives designed to justify its actions. As early as November 2001, in the heat of the emotion and outrage following the attacks of 9/11, the American Bar Association announced that: 'In response to the unprecedented attacks of September 11, on November 13, 2001, the President announced that certain non-citizens [of the USA] would be subject to detention and trial by military authorities.'

Capitol Hill reacted to the storm of criticism, even from its friends, by passing the 'Military Commissions Act 2006', a highly controversial bill giving the US President the power to designate certain people with the status of 'unlawful enemy combatants', thereby making them subject to US military commissions, where they had fewer civil rights than in regular criminal trials.

In one respect Washington was right. Some response to what was a genuine problem was undoubtedly needed. The US War on Terror had taken into custody a number of non-US citizens who, when apprehended, had no real legal status. Were the detainees subject to American justice? Were they prisoners of war? POWs have well defined legal rights under the various Geneva Conventions. Or were they just common criminals? If so, the USA had a perfectly sound legal criminal justice system based on a network of law.

The truth was that the Guantanamo detainees were simultaneously none and all of these things.

All were understood to be jihadis; all appeared to have been associated with Islamic terrorism; all their cases lacked hard evidence that would stand up in a criminal court. Not protected by either the rules concerning the police or the military on questioning of suspects, let alone the Geneva Conventions, the detainees were treated to what Washington called 'enhanced interrogation'.

The whole issue of Guantanamo and the CIA's secret programme of detention without trial, as well as allegations of torture under 'enhanced interrogation' began to dominate the media. Following his election in 2008 President Obama promised to close the camps. He did not. At the time of writing he is yet to succeed.

On 12 December 2013, even retired US Marine Major General Michael R. Lehnert, (the very officer who oversaw the construction of the first Guantanamo detention facility) broke cover and denounced Guantanamo as 'our nation's most notorious prison – a prison that should never have been opened', and provided a succinct summary of its history and significance:

> Our nation created Guantanamo because we were legitimately angry and frightened by an unprovoked attack on our soil on September 11, 2001. We thought that the detainees would provide a treasure trove of information and intelligence.
>
> Even in the earliest days of Guantanamo, I became more and more convinced that many of the detainees should never have been sent in the first place. They had little intelligence value, and there was insufficient evidence linking them to war crimes. That remains the case today for many, if not most, of the detainees.

The whole issue of the detention, interrogation and the treatment of the Guantanamo detainees came to a head at the end of 2014, when the US Senate Intelligence Committee chairman, Dianne Feinstein, released a damning report criticising the CIA's mishandling of the

Guantanamo detainees and specifically of the regime of interrogation and torture. She wrote, 'The CIA ... decided to initiate a program of indefinite secret detention and the use of brutal interrogation techniques in violation of U.S. law, treaty obligations, and our values.'

The report went on to make a number of extremely damaging charges against the CIA, summarised as:

1. The CIA's interrogation techniques were much more brutal and employed more extensively than the agency had admitted. The report described extensive waterboarding as a 'series of near drownings' and suggests that more prisoners were subjected to waterboarding than the three prisoners the CIA has acknowledged in the past.

2. The CIA interrogation program was mismanaged and was not subject to adequate Congressional oversight.

3. The CIA misled members of Congress and the White House about the effectiveness and extent of its brutal interrogation techniques.

4. Interrogators in the field who tried to stop the brutal interrogation techniques were repeatedly overruled by senior CIA officials.

5. The CIA repeatedly under-reported the number of people it detained and subjected to harsh interrogation techniques under the programme.

6. At least twenty-six detainees were wrongfully held and did not meet the government's standard for detention.

7. The CIA leaked classified information to journalists, exaggerating the success of interrogation methods in an effort to gain public support.

The Feinstein report pointed the finger at the whole US policy on dealing with the detainees, with the implicit suggestion that the US had knowingly engaged in illegal acts and broken international and domestic law for a decade. Above all, with its detailed descriptions of the use of torture, specifically water boarding, in interrogations, the controversy brought the whole business of interrogation into the spotlight. This was surprising – and unnecessary – because experienced interrogators have known for centuries that torture was a very unreliable method of interrogation. Under duress most people will say something if only to (literally) save their skin. That is the danger of intelligence obtained under in this way. People can be induced to say anything, true or false, to stop the fear or the pain. But the interrogator wants truth.

Even historic uses of torture to gain intelligence, certainly in Britain, were unusual. For example, after Guy Fawkes was arrested for his role in the Gunpowder Plot of 1605, it required a special Royal Warrant from King James I to authorise his torture in an effort to discover the names of his fellow conspirators. And later, following the assassination of George Villiers, 1st Duke of Buckingham in 1628, the Privy Council's application to torture John Felton was rejected by the High Court. The judges ruled unanimously its use, 'to be contrary to the laws of England', a view confirmed four centuries later by the unanimous Law Lords judgement on 2005 that ruled that, under English law tradition, 'torture and its fruits' could not be used in court.

However the judges caveated this by adding that information thus obtained could be used by the British police and security services as: 'it would be ludicrous for them to disregard information about a ticking bomb because it had been procured by torture'.

Even during the total war of 1939–45 interrogation methods tended broadly to avoid the use of torture, instead concentrating on debriefing the subject. This was for very practical reasons, best summed up by the interrogator's maxim: 'I don't want him to talk: I want the truth!'

But not always. One of the most successful uses of interrogation during World War Two was the so-called London Cage, the Combined Services Detailed Interrogation Centre in Kensington. There is little doubt that torture (in its mildest form) was a deliberate policy. The Cage was run by MI9, the War Office section responsible for gleaning information from enemy prisoners of war. The interrogation methods at The Cage were not pretty. Petty brutality was the norm and a secret

1950 assessment by MI5 pointed out that the commanding officer of the London Cage, Lieutenant Colonel Alexander Scotland, who was then trying to publish a book about his wartime experiences, had revealed repeated breaches of the Geneva Conventions. The book's manuscript described how prisoners had been forced to kneel while being beaten about the head; forced to stand to attention for up to twenty-six hours; threatened with execution; humiliated; soaked, and starved. Life was anything but easy for the inmates of the London Cage. In one complaint lodged in the British National Archives, a 27-year-old German journalist who went through The Cage said he had spent two years as a prisoner of the Gestapo. And not once, he said, did they treat him as badly as the British . . .

These damning revelations stand in stark contrast to MI5's Latchmere House, Richmond, better known as Camp 20, where captured spies were confronted by Lieutenant Colonel 'Tin Eye' Robert Stephens, (so called because of his monocle) an experienced and painstaking interrogator. Life at Camp 20 was never a holiday camp and the regime could be harsh and the preliminary interrogations very hostile indeed. Stephens picked the captured spy's legend and life history apart then, if judged acceptable, he handed them over to his number two, Major Thomas Argyll Robertson (usually called 'Tar,' from his initials), whose task was to turn the frightened spies and use them to send fake messages back to their handlers in Germany.

In autumn 1940 they got their first breakthrough. Gösta Caroli and Wulf Schmidt had landed via parachute and been captured. The two had trained together and were friends. The interrogators pulled an old trick. In return for Schmidt's life being spared, a broken Caroli was coerced into turning double. Schmidt was told that Caroli had sold him out. Furious at what he believed to be his friend's betrayal, Schmidt offered to change sides and work as a double agent for the British. The double agent game was afoot, thanks to clever management and skilful interrogation.

By January 1941 the system had been institutionalised into a long-term operation controlled by the 'Double Cross Committee', under the chairmanship of an Oxford don, Sir John Masterman, and the number of double agents began to expand. MI5 established a secret detection centre at Ham Common in which suspects could be isolated and interrogated. In all, while thirteen German agents were executed in Britain during the war, more than three times that number actively chose to cooperate with their MI5 handlers. By the end of the war the Double Cross Committee concluded that it had effectively taken control of the Abwehr's entire spying organisation in Britain.

The agents were expecting to be tortured or abused by the British if they fell into their hands. However, once the prisoner had been conditioned to understand that his life depended on his cooperation, he was generally treated with kindness and patience by his captors. The resident MI5 psychiatrist, Dr Harold Dearden, went to considerable lengths to ensure that there was no ill treatment. In the sole recorded instance of a beating by an over-enthusiastic visiting interrogator, the misguided MI5 officer was given a formal reprimand by Colonel Scotland and sent packing, posted overseas. Dr Dearden even went so far as to go to the victim's cell afterwards and share a bottle of whisky with him by way of apology.

The point, looking back on this life or death game of interrogation, is that the calm, kind debriefing proved, in the end, to be more efficient in terms of gleaning accurate intelligence, and was frequently quicker at securing results, than any harsher regime. Leaving the question of morality aside, the debriefing system actually proves more effective – provided that the interrogator has the time.

The truth of this is borne out by the work of a man fighting for the other side.

One of the most successful interrogators during the Second World War was the Luftwaffe's Hanns-Joachim Gottlob Scharff. A mere *Obergefreiter* (the equivalent of a senior lance corporal), the 'Master Interrogator' of the Luftwaffe was responsible for interrogating captured American fighter pilots during the last years of the war.

Scharff's technique was simple: he would overwhelm the shocked and frightened downed POW with his encyclopaedic knowledge of the downed aircrew's airfield, his local villages, the squadron organisation, aeroplane numbers, colleagues and mess mates, and even the pubs he went to with his English girlfriend. Scharff achieved this by constructing an ever-growing database of snippets, which he assembled and collated to look like a comprehensive intelligence brief. Astounded aircrew were shocked into believing that there was no point in not talking, because obviously Scharff knew everything already.

He gained a reputation for getting the answers he needed from the prisoners of war, without them realising that even the most seemingly insignificant chit-chat could provide an important new piece of the wider intelligence picture. Scharff always treated his prisoners with respect and dignity and, by using psychological rather than physical techniques, he was able to make them drop their guard and converse with him, even though they were trained to remain silent. One embittered POW commented that, 'Hanns Scharff could probably get a confession of infidelity from a nun.'

The experience of the Second World War proved conclusively that the best methods of interrogation were still the time-honoured standard techniques: exploit the shock of capture; let the prisoner become so frightened through the isolation and fear of solitary confinement as to 'condition himself'. If that was not enough, then the four classic techniques of softening the prisoner up were still valid as part of the interrogations: the harsh, shouting and banging approach; the relentless, silent hostile stare accompanied by unemotional threats; the stupid interrogator with the wrong file, who even needed help from the prisoner; the kind, 'sympathetic' debrief. In the final analysis, all of them led to the real facts, which is what interrogation is all about.

However, the whole business of interrogation received a seismic shock in the Korean War of the early 1950s, where the world encountered the Communists' brainwashing techniques for the first time. Allied POWs suffered the most appalling physical treatment in an attempt to get them to confess and admit to imaginary war crimes. For the American prisoners, brutal torture, lack of food, absence of medical aid and subhuman treatment became a daily way of life. Many of the young GIs found that their training had not prepared them for this new psychological battlefield. In the cold and misery of the North Korean camps, the unfortunate American prisoners died like flies. Out of 7,000 US prisoners, 40 per cent died in captivity and, in far too many cases, collaborated with their captors.

After the war, many former US prisoners came back to their home-land only to be criminally charged and tried for offences that 'amounted to treason, desertion to the enemy, mistreatment of fellow prisoners of war, and similar crimes'.

More than a thousand British servicemen fell into enemy hands in Korea. Many were subjected to the same brutal treatment and 'political re-education' and eighty-two British prisoners died. At the end of the war, twenty-two Americans opted to stay behind, and one British Royal Marine chose to remain in China. Only the stern, strictly hier-archical Turks lost no soldiers to either brainwashing or to ill treatment. Brainwashing and brutal interrogation were obviously something to be guarded against in future.

The upshot of the post-war Western analyses and studies of the Korean POW experience was that special training was clearly required in *resistance* to interrogation, especially those troops such as special forces, stay-behind parties and aircrew, who were particularly vulnera-ble to capture. From 1958 onwards, military interrogation units spent a lot of their time on exercises practising on SAS and Green Beret personnel, preparing them for what might happen should they fall into hostile hands. This approach inevitably seeped into their own approach to interrogation. Techniques such as hooding, sleep deprivation and extremes of temperature were no longer simply examples of what a captured soldier could expect at the hands of the KGB or GRU, but accepted as part of the interrogator's toolkit.

Matters came to a head in 1971 when the British Joint Service Interrogation Wing was ordered to deploy to Northern Ireland where internment without trial had become government policy. Due mainly to faulty intelligence from the Royal Ulster Constabulary, many of those arrested were Catholics or Irish nationalists who had no links whatsoever with the IRA, but whose names, through administrative incompetence, appeared on the list of those to be arrested.

Much later, in 1977, the Home Secretary Merlyn Rees wrote to the British Prime Minister James Callaghan secretly confirming that a policy of 'torture' had in fact been quietly authorised by the British Government's ministers in 1971. The letter states: 'It is my view (con-firmed by Brian Faulkner before his death) that the decision to use methods of torture in Northern Ireland in 1971/72 was taken by ministers – in particular Lord Carrington, then Secretary of State for Defence.'

The interrogation techniques used on the IRA internees were taken straight out of the resistance to interrogation training course. Fourteen 'hooded men' were selected by the interrogators as targets for five highly controversial techniques. The European Court of Human Rights (ECHR), in the 1978 case of Ireland v. United Kingdom, defined them as follows:

1. Wall-standing: forcing the detainees to remain for periods of some hours in a 'stress position'.

2. Hooding: putting a black- or navy-coloured bag over the detainees' heads and, at least initially, keeping it there all the time except during interrogation.

3. Subjection to noise: pending their interrogations, holding the detainees in a room where there was a continuous loud and hissing noise.

4. Deprivation of sleep: pending their interrogations, depriving the detainees of sleep.

5. Deprivation of food and drink: subjecting the detainees to a reduced diet during their stay at the centre and pending interrogations.

In every case the subject broke down and talked openly and truthfully about what he knew. But the disappointment for the British was that, instead of a flood of hard intelligence on the Provisional IRA, most of the internees questioned knew very little. Interrogation success resulted in minimal intelligence.

The ECHR decided that official use of the five techniques in unison did constitute inhuman and degrading treatment, and therefore violated the European Convention and customary international law. Six years earlier, the Parker Report 'on the authorised procedures for the interrogation of persons suspected of terrorism into interrogation in

Northern Ireland, 1972' exonerated the interrogators, but in its dissenting voice, defined the problem very accurately:

> The blame for this sorry story, if blame there be, must lie with those who, many years ago, decided that in emergency conditions in Colonial-type situations we should abandon our legal, well-tried and highly successful wartime interrogation methods and replace them by procedures which were secret, illegal, not morally justifiable and alien to the traditions of what I believe still to be the greatest democracy in the world.

The Russians suffered from no such inhibitions. When they arrested Greville Wynn, Penkovsky's courier, his KGB interrogators quickly detected that the British businessman was a fastidious soul. In order to break him they put him in a 'bottle dungeon', where he was forced to stand upright for over a week, deep in his own filth. Degrading and inhuman it may have been; but it worked. Greville Wynn told all, a broken man.

While the British Establishment was agonising about whether their interrogators had behaved with excessive force towards a tiny handful of old dissidents and rebels, America was suffering similar problems in Vietnam in the sixties and early seventies, but on a much greater scale. America was involved in a brutal war in Vietnam that covered the whole spectrum of violence, from backstreet terrorist murders to full-scale battles with tanks and aircraft involving whole divisions. Inevitably there were widespread atrocities and excesses.

From the evidence presented at the 1968 Russell Tribunal into American war crimes in Vietnam it is clear that prisoners of war captured by the armed forces of the United States had been routinely subjected to treatment prohibited by the laws of war.

Looking at the testimony of Peter Martinsen of the 541st Military Intelligence Detachment, who served as a front-line tactical prisoner of war interrogator during the great battles of 1966 and 1967, it is hard to disagree with this conclusion. From his own words a clear picture of what was accepted as routine interrogation practice among US forces in Vietnam emerges.

I started to question him and he kept saying that he was not a Việt Cộng. I was quite sure he was lying. I decided to beat him. This did not help . . . and then – as was often the case – another interrogator took my place, an interrogation officer. The lieutenant had an army field telephone, which runs on batteries and generator. You crank it and it gives a nasty shock, a very nasty shock, quite painful. The interrogation commenced with the prisoner being tortured by field telephone. The telephones were first placed on his hands and then the field telephone wires were placed on his sexual organs . . .

Martinsen agreed that brutality and ill treatment was common practice during his time in Vietnam, although:

Yes, it was stressed in the [interrogation] school that torture was not permitted in the army, but that was before the Vietnam war got very large. They didn't teach us about the Geneva Conventions. They taught that war crimes must not be committed, that prisoners must not be tortured nor mishandled, nor harassed, coerced or forced into doing anything. The instructors say privately, 'Yes, I know they do it in Vietnam, but we don't officially admit it.'

When asked if he had ever come across any examples among the hundreds of interrogators, where people had insisted on interrogating *without* beating or torture? He replied:

No, I don't know of a single case . . . but what is torture? Is torture electrical torture or is torture beating? I don't know. Personally, I had a lot of success once I learned to speak Vietnamese. I had a lot of success with pure coercion, because I'm a fairly large person. I was able to intimidate the rather small Vietnamese, specially when I learned to speak their language.

The Vietnam experience of interrogation, as in so many other fields, left a deep scar on the American military psyche. However, any misgivings about how to interrogate enemy prisoners were swept away in the anger following the World Trade Center attacks in 2001. In the national desire for revenge many taboos were discarded. In 2003 and 2004 the US government at Cabinet level officially sanctioned the routine use of 'stress and duress' methods as part of their War on Terror.

In conjunction with this confused idea of what really constituted 'acceptable interrogation', particularly by the military, the Second Iraq war from 2003 onwards eventually became the catalyst for the debate that was to tear America in half. As the scandal of the ill-treatment of prisoners at the Abu Ghraib prison in Iraq unfolded, from 2004 onwards it became clear that the interrogators of the United States Military and the CIA had once again committed a series of human rights violations against detainees. It was a disturbingly familiar story. The violations included torture, rape, sodomy, and murder as well as the familiar litany of lack of sleep, use of strobe lights and loud music, shackling prisoners in awkward positions for long hours, ritual humiliation, use of barking dogs to terrify the Muslim prisoners, and manipulating the levels of pain medication the prisoners received.

While the US moved to court-martial those responsible, and the commander in charge of military jails in Iraq swore that it was an aberration and would never happen again, sceptical civilian critics and the media began to investigate the story in more detail to discover who had authorised the brutalities. A nonpartisan, independent review of interrogation and detention programmes in the years after the 11 September 2001 terrorist attacks concluded that, 'it is indisputable that the United States engaged in the practice of torture' and that the nation's highest officials bore ultimate responsibility for it. Lawyers became involved and lawsuits alleging abuses against prisoners by the British and American governments brought reaction in both London and Washington.

The death of an innocent Iraqi civilian, Baha Mousa, who had been in the custody of the British Army in Basra became yet another major legal challenge. The result was that judges supported the rights of the prisoners. British judges found that an interrogator who 'held the hand of the captured person', was in 'a breach of the prohibition on physical contact'; and an interrogator who 'slammed the desk with his hand', or who 'slammed the wall with his hand', were guilty of breaking the law. Judges also found other violations, including a soldier who used 'insulting words throughout an interview' and threw 'vulgar abuse' at a captive. They said the 'most striking example' of a breach of the policy was when an interrogator 'suddenly moved forward from a crouching position so that his face was right in front of the captured person's. This was physically intimidating.' The whole point was that from the interrogator's point of view, it was meant to be. Nonetheless, the traditional methods had to be scrapped. The upshot by 2015 was that military interrogation became so circumscribed by laws and regulations as to be almost impossible.

In Britain there was growing disquiet that the latest guidelines were so stringent that interrogation was either impossible or pointless. Professional soldiers pointed out that the rules on interrogations have been tightened up, because of the lawyers, to the extent that the military were no longer able to carry out tactical questioning of prisoners. Colonel Tim Collins, a decorated Iraqi war veteran, summed up the problem facing Western interrogators:

> The effect of the ambulance-chasing lawyers and the play-it-safe judges is that we have got to the point where we have lost our operational capability to do tactical questioning. That in itself brings risks to the lives of the people we deploy. These insurgents are not nice people. These are criminals. They behead people; they keep sex slaves. They are not normal people.

While the previous 'harsh' policy gave soldiers the right to 'shout as loud as possible [with] uncontrolled fury', as well as aim personal abuse, taunt and goad a captive, and if necessary resort to 'psychotic tendencies', Britain's new rules on interrogation effectively prevent military intelligence officers from shouting at a terrorist suspect for more than a few seconds, banging their fists on tables or walls and using insulting words, and that 'there must be no intimidation of any kind'.

The tragedy of this neutering of interrogation, particularly in Britain and the US means that the only people to benefit will be the terrorists and the lawyers.

The problem confronting Western interrogators intent on gathering HUMINT is that the guidelines are now either too strict or plain unworkable. Any sensible person understands that there is a wide spectrum between fright and discomfort at the one end and deliberate physical violence or mental torture at the other. Discomfort and force-ful questioning are clearly highly subjective matters, which any persons suspected of crime, under ordinary conditions, expects to suffer and society accepts as permissible. Equally, everyone would agree that deliberate torture, whether physical or mental, is not justified under any conditions. Where, however, does hardship and discomfort end and humiliating treatment begin? Where does the latter end and tor-ture begin?

This is the dilemma facing interrogators in the West in the twen-ty-first century. Most other nations, from Israel to Indonesia, ignore such legalistic niceties and concentrate instead on the aim: to extract accurate, timely intelligence from an unwilling captive . . .

CHAPTER 13

How Soviet HUMINT
Changed the World

The Soviet espionage offensive was not just concerned with Japan, Nazi Germany and the 'Great Patriotic War'. To the Cheka-GPU-NKVD-MGB-KGB, collecting intelligence was a seamless affair, serving the Soviet Union in war and peace alike. They had not given up any of their pre-war targets just because they were now allies against Hitler: Western capitalism was still capitalism and a foe to be fought. By 1942–43 their intelligence networks in Britain and the USA were already reporting a mysterious American project to build a giant bomb that would unsettle any post-war balance of power once Germany was defeated. The Soviet spy rings were tasked to find out the secrets of the Atom bomb from their allies.

Soviets penetrated the 'Manhattan Project' almost from its very beginning. American writers tend to blame the leaks on 'foreign scientists' working on the project. This is untrue. The Soviets were first tipped-off by one of the Cambridge spies, John Cairncross, now acknowledged as the fifth man, as early as 1941. There is little doubt that the Manhattan Project was penetrated at all levels.

Whatever the truth is, it's beyond doubt that that the Soviets made a massive effort to glean the secrets of the Atomic Bomb. Not for nothing did they code name the Manhattan Project 'ENORMOZ'.

From scientists like Klaus Fuchs at Los Alamos, to researchers like Alan Nunn May and Bruno Pontecorvo in Canada, the whole Project was as insecure and as full of holes, certainly as far as Moscow was concerned, as a Swiss cheese. If that were not enough, another Cambridge spy, Donald Maclean, was in Washington as the Anglo-American atomic weapons programme coordinator. All reported back direct to Lavrenty Beria, chief of the NKVD, coordinator of the intelligence war against the West.

If the Cold War started anywhere, it started well before the Potsdam Conference of 1945, or Churchill's 'Iron Curtain' speech of 1946. The Cold War was alive and kicking from midsummer 1944 onwards, and nuclear weapons were the battlefield on which it would be fought. Details of the Soviet's spying did much to poison the already deep wells of distrust between the war-time allies after the war. As cooperation broke down and 'an iron curtain descended from Stettin in the north, to Trieste in the south', in Churchill's words, more evidence surfaced of the Soviets' wartime espionage against Great Britain and the United States. A defector called Gouzenko fled the Soviet Embassy in Ottawa (where he was the NKVD's cipher clerk) in 1946. His revelations to the Royal Canadian Mounted Police (RCMP) and the decrypts of the 'Venona' SIGINT traffic between Soviet spies in the West and their NKVD masters began a trail that would eventually lead to a round-up of many of the key players in the NKVD's great spy apparatus. The damage they had done, however, really was '*enormoz*'.

Any doubts about the Soviet's post-war intentions had been clarified by their 1948 blockade of the Western Allies' half of Berlin. The world realised that the wartime allies now stood bitterly opposed to each other. Everywhere political, ideological, economic and military differences divided East and West deeply. A new world war seemed highly likely, if not inevitable. From the airlift that circumvented the Berlin Blockade onwards, both sides began to prepare for a final clash of arms. The world re-formed into ideological power blocs and new antagonistic alliances. Both sides set out to spy on each other by every means possible.

Thanks mainly to HUMINT and its ubiquitous spies and traitors, the Cold War became an intelligence war. A war that would be dominated by technical intelligence.

PART FIVE

TECHNOLOGY TAKES OVER

CHAPTER 14

On SIGINT

Reading other people's correspondence is as old as human literacy.

Attempts to disguise text by using codes and ciphers have been used since time immemorial, and by the discreet practitioners of Venus just as much as by those of Mars. Purists point out (correctly) that a code is different to a cipher. A code can be anything from symbols and dots, to modern strings of zeroes and ones.

A cipher, on the other hand, is the substitution of one letter for another. Traditionally secret writing (for example, invisible ink) and simple substitution codes were the staple of the ancients.

The word cryptography, meaning the science of codes, comes from the Greek words *kryptos* (secret) and *graphos* (writing). In 405 BC the Spartan admiral Lysander was sent a servant's belt that had a curious sequence of letters inside. However, when Lysander wrapped the belt around a wooden pole he found that he could read a coded message warning him that Persia was about to attack Greece. The Spartan fleet set sail and defeated the Persians.

Julius Caesar is credited with inventing the schoolboy system of using one letter of the alphabet to represent another according to some pre-arranged agreement: the so-called substitution code.

Byzantium and Islam's mathematicians soon improved on such unsophisticated practices. The Arabs in particular began to record various methods of cryptanalysis (the science of finding weaknesses in crypto systems) around the ninth century. An Arab mathematician called Al-Kindi, actually wrote a book on cryptography entitled

'Risalah fi Istikhraj al-Mu'amma' ('A Manuscript on Deciphering Cryptographic Messages'), explaining frequency analysis for the first time (The English language has twenty-six letters, of which the letter 'E' appears most often. So, if you look for the most frequent ciphered letter, you've found your 'E' . . . 'A' is the second most frequent letter, and so on.)

For the next five centuries, ciphers generally remained vulnerable to frequency analysis. However, in 1468 the Italian Renaissance polymath Leon Battista Alberti invented the polyalphabetic cipher, employing double and even multiple encryption, thereby earning himself the title, 'the father of Western cryptology'.

By the late fourteenth century, the Florentines were seeking new and even more secure methods of 'secret writing' to protect their covert correspondence. By 1500 even the use of Alberti's double alphabets to muddle the frequency of letters had been superseded by a new toy, the 'cipher disc' – an early coding machine.

'Code Machines' rely on hardware, which can be incredibly simple. Alberti's cipher disc was simply two flat copper discs, one outside the other, like a wheel and its tyre. Each had an alphabet inscribed on its rim. The letter on the outer ring could be aligned to coincide with any letter on the inner ring. However, by changing the setting of the discs in relation to each other, say, every ten letters, the message could only be deciphered by someone who had access to – or had cracked – the secret list of settings.

Alberti's disc was followed, in about 1580, by 'Vigenère's Square'. The method was first explained by Bellaso in his 1553 book *On Secret Writing* (*La cifra del. Sig. Giovan Battista Bellaso*). The Vigenère cipher is a method of encrypting alphabetic text by using a series of different ciphers based on the letters of a secret keyword. It is essentially a simple form of polyalphabetic substitution that operates on several levels. Though the Vigenère cipher is deceptively simple to understand, for three centuries it resisted all attempts to break it. Vigenère, whose *Treatise on Ciphers* was printed in 1586 proudly dubbed his invention, *'le Chiffre undéchiffrable'* and indeed, for nearly three centuries, until the advent of Babbage's primitive computer in the 1840s, the 'Vigènere Square' remained the standard for high-security ciphers.

Despite Vigenère's boast, his device was never truly unbreakable. To crack these increasingly sophisticated ciphers, in the 1650s Cromwell's spymaster, John Thurloe and his 'black chamber', had relied on the skills of code breakers to keep both Royalist plotters and England's foreign foes permanently neutralised. As fast as a plan was hatched, it was uncovered. Thurloe's cryptanalysts ensured that Oliver Cromwell could read most of his enemies' secret intentions like an open book. This led Ambassador Segedo of Venice to say, with grudging admiration: 'There is no government on earth that divulges affairs less than England, or is more punctually informed of those of others.'

By the middle of the nineteenth century, communications intelligence began to develop systems that were more than just case-by-case attempts to crack code by cryptanalysis.

During the Crimean War in the 1850s, Charles Babbage cracked the Russian's Vigenère autokey cipher, using cryptanalysis of polyalphabetic ciphers, although the British government wisely kept quiet about this for fear of 'losing the intelligence advantage'.

Babbage's major scientific breakthrough had come in 1834, when he started work on what he called it his 'Analytical Engine', a steam-powered machine intended to perform an infinite variety of programmable operations. Although never fully completed, it is recognisably the first modern computer. Like Alan Turing's subsequent designs for an 'Automatic Computing Engine', at Britain's Bletchley Park code-breaking centre over a century later, Babbage's primitive computer used vast banks of rotating drums allowing it to store numbers, and even had what can be described as a processor and memory bank. In these early attempts at code breaking by computer he was aided by the mathematical genius Ada Lovelace, who worked on algorithms. Indeed, it is fair to describe Babbage as the first hardware designer and Lovelace as the first ever computer programmer.

Interest in code breaking accelerated. In 1863 a retired Prussian colonel, Friedrich Kasiski, published his *Die GeheimSchriften* (On Secret Writing), with its analysis of frequencies of the actual encryptions themselves. And, in 1883, Auguste Kerckhoffs went further, publishing some key principles of cryptography that are still relevant today:

1   Any code system must be practically, if not mathematically, indecipherable.

2   It should not require secrecy, and it should not be a problem if it falls into enemy hands.

3   It must be possible to communicate and remember the key without using written notes, and correspondents must be able to change or modify it at will.

4   It must be applicable to telegraph communications.

His central point was that the *key* was the essential element of security and not the system itself.

From the very start, it was obvious that the Great War was going to be a wireless war. Wires and cables, though they couldn't be physically intercepted, were still highly vulnerable. For example, on 5 August 1914, the British cable ship *Telconia* winched up the Germans' submarine cable, which linked the Kaiser's Reich to the rest of the world, and cut it. From now on, Germany would have to rely on the wireless or neutral friends to talk to the outside world. Britain's Naval Intelligence Division, soon joined by a dedicated group of private radio enthusiasts, listened to Berlin and Bremen's increasing radio traffic with bewilderment. It was all in code.

The British then had a stroke of good luck. In rapid succession they acquired *all* three of the key German naval codebooks. The full story of this remarkable series of coincidences has never been fully explained and many doubts still surround the official account.

By a combination of hard work, recruiting clever academics from civilian life and ensuring that the First Sea Lord (Churchill) was kept 'onside', the Naval Intelligence Division's intercept and code-breaking staff now became a war winner. Its director, Admiral 'Blinker' Hall (so called because he blinked a lot) put his growing team of code breakers into Room 40 of the Old Admiralty Building – and 'Room 40' was the name that stuck.

Room 40 was remarkably successful. For the rest of the war, the Naval siginters kept the German High Seas Fleet under close surveillance at all times. In this they were aided, in the early days, by the

Germans' assumption that their low-powered sets could not be intercepted from a range of more than eighty kilometres. The German operators chattered away, often not even in code, and, across the North Sea, 'Room 40' hoovered it all up. As a result, British Naval Intelligence was nearly always one step ahead of the opposition and provided the Fleet with accurate and timely intelligence.

Unfortunately, the rigid caste distinction between 'Ops' and 'Int' sometimes led to some very basic blunders, the most notorious being before the potentially decisive clash at Jutland. The senior operations officer asked Room 40 where the High Seas Fleet's commander's radio call sign was located. Not knowing why the information was needed, Room 40 reported quite correctly, 'DK [the German commander's call sign] is at Wilhelmshaven.'

However, they did not inform the ops room that the call sign had been transferred ashore, as was routine when the flagship sailed. The question that the ops room really wanted to ask was, 'Where is the flagship of the German *High Seas Fleet*?' As a result, and thinking that the High Seas Fleet was still in port, the Admiralty ops room failed to get the Grand Fleet to sea in time to cut off Scheer at Jutland and misled both Jellicoe and Beatty, once they had sailed.

Partly as a result of this sort of nonsense, the Navy changed its staff intelligence procedures. Originally it had been felt that comprehending and assessing raw intelligence on ships was a matter for experienced sea-going Royal Naval officers alone, not for a bunch of long-haired civilian academics. In May 1917, Room 40 was reorganised into 'Naval Intelligence Division 25' and encouraged to send *full* intelligence reports in future; complete with context, interpretation and assessments to the naval ops staff.

Room 40 and its SIGINT made a notable, even world-changing intervention in early 1917. When the German submarine cable had been cut in 1914, Sweden let Berlin use its cable to send its diplomatic telegrams out to its embassies worldwide. But this cable route went through the UK and the British code breakers could soon read the Swedish – and German – signals. The so-called 'Swedish roundabout' suddenly hit paydirt on 17 January 1917, when the Room 40 code breakers intercepted a German telegram that contained a set of instructions from the German

Foreign Minister Zimmermann to the German ambassador in Mexico City informing him that Germany was about to resume unrestricted submarine warfare. More significantly, it also instructed the ambassador to offer Mexico an alliance with Germany on the promise that Berlin could offer 'an understanding ... that Mexico is to reconquer the lost territory in Texas, New Mexico and Arizona'.

The British sat on this explosive document for over two weeks, in the hope that America might be provoked into declaring war without any action on London's part. The Germans began their submarine campaign, while the British obtained a second copy of the offending message in the shape of the actual telegram that had been delivered to the Germans in Mexico City.

The problem now was how to tell the world of the Germans' plans without letting them know how they had been discovered. That would compromise the true source and the Germans would swiftly change their codes. London's 'insurance' copy of the Mexican version of the telegram provided the solution. When the Americans were handed the formal copy of the Zimmermann telegram, on 24 February, an outraged Washington and the American press were told that it had been obtained by 'an agent in Mexico'. To British astonishment, Germany confirmed this deceit. Zimmermann admitted that the telegram was no forgery. Berlin ordered Mexico to burn all compromising material as 'indications suggest that the treachery was committed in Mexico'.

Even when confronted with this open evidence of hostile German intentions, President Wilson still hesitated to call for war. He only briefed his Cabinet on 20 March, nearly a month after he had first seen the telegram. By then, the U-boats' sinkings of American merchant and passenger ships, plus the explosive content of the 'Zimmermann Telegram', had completely changed American public opinion.

On 2 April an indignant President briefed the House and Senate, calling for a declaration of war. In true idealistic style he sold the enterprise as a great moral crusade: 'The world,' Wilson declared, 'must be made safe for democracy.' On 6 April 1917 the USA declared war on an unrepentant Germany.

After the end of World War One, Washington committed an egregious (and self-inflicted) intelligence blunder. 'MI-8', the code and cipher branch of America's fledgling military intelligence unit had been especially successful during the war and into the twenties. Its head was a Captain Herbert Yardley who, by 1921, was cracking and reading Japanese diplomatic codes. In peacetime, the majority of these were of interest to the State Department. In May 1929, Henry Stimson, the new Secretary of State, saw his first decoded intercepts of Japanese secret signals. He demanded that it must cease immediately. Stimson added, in a famous line: 'Gentlemen do not read each other's mail.' Yardley was out of a job.

There was no 'Official Secrets Act' in America at the time, so Yardley decided to do what every publisher and literary agent advises: 'Write about what you know.' Herbert Yardley sat down and did just that, writing a book called, *The American Black Chamber*, revealing just how American SIGINT worked and how cleverly he had broken the Japanese codes. The book was a best-seller, particularly in Japan. The Japanese promptly changed their codes – which should have surprised no-one – and an embarrassed US government rushed a secrecy law through Congress. It was not American intelligence's finest hour.

SIGINT was to change dramatically during the 1920s when the Germans brought the supposedly unbreakable Enigma machine into service for all their classified signals. This new electromechanical technology transformed the original Alberti disks into genuinely random rotor machines in which an encrypting sequence with an extremely long period of substitutions could be generated, by rotating a supposedly infinite sequence of rotors.

However, in 1931 the French managed to recruit a German cipher officer, Hans-Thilo Schmidt, who worked in the Germans' most secret cryptographic office. He opened up the secrets of the new coding machine. He also handed over operating manuals, keying instructions, old key settings and explained how the whole system worked. This was useful, but only if you possessed an Enigma machine to check them against – which the French did not.

The Poles however, had managed to build their own, and had been forging ahead for a decade, using an impressive mixture of theft, 'reverse engineering', mathematical logic, commercial purchases and sheer brain power to unravel the secrets of the 'unbreakable' Enigma code. By 1938, Polish intelligence had discovered exactly how to recreate Enigma's key settings on its three electrical rotors. It was an amazing breakthrough. But, in September 1938, the Germans began to reset their security codes daily, by using a self-selected random key of any three letters. It would take months to crack the new system.

In desperation, the Poles turned to the French and British for help. With war imminent, and Poland at risk from Hitler's Germany, two key members of Britain's Government Code and Cypher School (GC & CS), who had been moved to the rural safety of Bletchley Park, flew to Warsaw to meet the anxious Poles. On 24 July 1939 Major Gwido Langer, chief of the Polish Cipher Bureau revealed everything the doomed Poles knew and handed over working copies of the latest Enigma machines they had manufactured for themselves, offering one each to London and to Paris.

On 16 August 1939, just three weeks before Hitler invaded Poland, the British received a working Enigma set with extra plug-board settings and Polish 'cribs' on how to make it work. For the first time the British – and later their American allies – would be able to read the mind of the German High Command. Thanks to the Poles, intelligence had provided a war winner.

SIGINT is actually a number of separate activities: it involves intercepting radio signals; 'direction finding' to identify their location; technical analysis of the transmitter concerned; traffic analysis to establish the identities of who is talking to whom, as well as their communication patterns; and reading the signal. Or, if you can't read the message, trying to decipher and break the enemy's code.

The final thing (often forgotten by over-simplified TV dramas) is actually using the stuff; which means getting the intelligence, in conditions of maximum secrecy, to the individual decision maker who has to act on what they have learnt in time to make a difference. Given the sensitivity of the source (if the enemy knows you are reading his signals, he will change his codes) signals intelligence is often very hard to use without compromise. The code breakers, clever and important though they undoubtedly are, are only one small cog in a very large intelligence machine. More basic signals intelligence such as 'Traffic Analysis' or 'Direction finding' is instantly usable without risk;

after all, 'transmission is treason'. Every time you transmit you risk compromise.

For example, those charged with the air defence of the Third Reich *always* knew when a big air raid was on its way, from the chatter as the USAAF and RAF aircrews tested their radios before taking off: simple stuff, but vital intelligence. Code breaking, however, tends to get all the glory. It is customary to portray the British as pre-eminent in this field during the Second War. Indeed they were, but the British were not the only 'master code breakers' of the time – not by a long way. The activities of the Americans and Germans are worthy of note, too. German skill and code-breaking success between 1939 and 1944 cost many Allied lives.

German code breakers had an extraordinary coup in the autumn of 1940. Reading the British Armed Merchant Shipping (BAMS) code, the German code breakers, the *Bundesnachrichtendienst* discovered that the MV *Automedon* had been routed to the Far East on a special secret mission. In November 1940 the disguised German surface raider *Atlantis* intercepted and captured the *Automedon* deep in the Indian Ocean.

The unlucky vessel was carrying a treasure trove of British secret documents, including a new set of BAMS codes, courier mail and classified 'Most Secret' Cabinet correspondence. It was a triumph for the *Bundesnachrichtendienst* and a disaster for British interests in the Far East. The Germans promptly turned over this potentially campaign-winning haul of British correspondence to their allies, the Japanese, who were already turning a speculative eye to Malaya and the Dutch East Indies.

But SIGINT still had an even greater role to play in what was to become one of the turning points of the war, because America had broken the Imperial Japanese Navy's most secret codes . . .

CHAPTER 15

The Triumph of SIGINT: Midway

Every intelligence coup is by definition a failure for the other side. This immutable law of conflict lies at the heart of the Yin and Yang of the intelligence world. Perhaps no better example exists than the Battle of Midway in the high summer of 1942. America's intelligence triumph at Midway was inevitably a Japanese intelligence disaster.

In June 1942 the Imperial Japanese Navy was on the rampage. As the Royal Navy's official history of the war with Japan puts it:

> Vice Admiral Nagumo's striking fleet had operated across one-third of the globe from Hawaii to Ceylon, conducting effective air strikes against ships and shore installations at every important Allied base out of reach of shore-based aircraft . . . they had destroyed the United States' battle fleet and driven the British out of the Indian ocean.

However, within a few short weeks, Nagumo's all-conquering Carrier Striking Task Force would be crushed and its battered survivors running for cover. In a matter of hours, four Japanese aircraft carriers were sunk, hundreds of their best aircrew killed and Japanese expansion stopped dead in its tracks. Midway completely altered the course of the war in the Pacific and marks the beginning of America's growth into a true world power. Midway is also a prime example of the power of intelligence, because it was accurate, timely intelligence that enabled Admirals Spruance and Fletcher to win one of the most decisive battles in maritime history.

It was a SIGINT coup that enabled America to trap the Japanese fleet off Midway. Following their victory at Pearl Harbor, Tokyo considered its options. The whole point of going to war had been to seize the economic assets of the Dutch East Indies and British-controlled Malaya. Japanese success had, paradoxically, complicated their strategic picture. Admiral Yamamoto was acutely aware that the American aircraft carriers had escaped destruction at Pearl Harbor. If he could find and sink the US carriers, then America would have to go on the defensive. However, with Japan's Combined Striking Fleet now outnumbering the US in the Pacific, he reasoned that the Americans would not dare risk a major fleet engagement for anything other than the defence of a vital target.

The isolated island of Midway, 1,000 miles west of Hawaii, fitted the bill perfectly. It had an American garrison, an airfield and was the base for long range scouting planes and bombers. Whoever controlled Midway could threaten Hawaii. It could also be the springboard for any attacks on America's west coast. Any attempt to capture Midway would force the Americans to defend it and draw their carriers into battle.

Midway was nothing less than the vital ground for the Central Pacific War. Yamamoto's aim was therefore to seal a gap in his defensive ring of Pacific islands, which acted as 'unsinkable aircraft carriers', by capturing Midway and luring the remaining US carriers into a trap. From the start, the Japanese plan was hampered by poor intelligence. Yamamoto's intelligence staff assessed that the US had only two carriers remaining, the USS *Enterprise* and *Hornet*, because the USS *Lexington* had been sunk at the Battle of the Coral Sea in May and the USS *Yorktown* damaged so severely in the same engagement that she would be unable to sail for months. They were wrong. In fact, *Yorktown* limped into Pearl on 27 May and, despite her battle damage (estimated at '90 days in the dockyard'), was made ready for sea by the Pearl Harbor dockyard in two-days-flat by 1,400 men working round the clock. So the US Navy had *three* carriers available, not two. The Battle of the Coral Sea had another crucial impact on Midway: the two Japanese carriers lost or damaged there were not available for Yamamoto's planned showdown with the American carriers off Midway.

The US Navy faced its own serious problems, however. Admiral Nimitz's only option therefore was to concentrate his forces in the right place at the right time: and for that he needed accurate, timely intelligence. Fortunately, help was at hand. The Americans had been reading the Japanese Naval code JN-25 since the start of the war. Good intelligence was to prove the battle winner.

In March 1939, the Japanese introduced their own version of an Enigma encoding machine and began to use a new high-level enciphering system called 'Purple'. Within eighteen months, the US Army's Signals Intelligence Service (SIS – not to be confused with the British MI6/Secret Intelligence Service) had broken the Purple code with a team under their top code-breaker William Friedman. It was staffed by highly talented and very dedicated cipher staff. Friedman called his team 'Magicians' and the name stuck. Appropriately enough 'Magic' became the code word for intelligence gleaned from the Purple coded messages.

The key was on Hawaii in the US Navy's OP-20-G Navy Radio Intelligence Section, now led by Lieutenant Commander Joseph Rochefort, one of the US Navy's most experienced cryptographers. Joe Rochefort was a fluent Japanese speaker who had spent nine years of his naval career intercepting and cracking Japanese codes.

One of the most important attributes of an intelligence officer is that he or she enjoys the confidence of his commander. Admiral Nimitz, the new Commander-in-Chief, United States Pacific Fleet, had been impressed by OP-20-G's successful reporting of Japanese naval movements prior to the Battle of the Coral Sea, so Rochefort's reputation was riding high with his boss as he and his team took on the crucial task of working out just what the Japanese were up to in May 1942.

As early as 9 May, US Navy SIGINT translated the Japanese Top Secret '1st Air Fleet Striking Force Order No. 6,' confirming that a new carrier strike force was assembling, with orders to sail on 21 May. On 20 May 1942 they deciphered orders for a powerful Japanese carrier strike force to attack an unidentified target. The real problem, as always, was knowing where it was headed. Part of the difficulty lay in the fact that the Japanese used coded references for specific locations. Rochefort and his team knew that 'AF' was a prime target: but what the hell did 'AF' stand for?

Captain Jasper Holmes, one of OP-20-G's cryptologists, had an inkling it might be the Midway Atoll in the middle of the Pacific, which lacked fresh water and relied on a desalination plant to provide its meagre garrison with potable water. He baited a simple communications trap to get the Japanese to reveal their real target.

The wily code breakers therefore sent a message by secure undersea cable to Midway's commanding officer in Hawaii, telling him to: '... send a plain language radio message to Com 14 [Commandant 14th Naval District] stating that the distillation plant had suffered a serious casualty and that fresh water was urgently needed.' Com 14 was briefed to acknowledge and reply, also in plain language, 'that water barges would be sent, under tow, soonest'.

Soon after that message was sent, a Japanese message was intercepted. The code breakers read it on 22 May, noting that, 'AF is short of water.' So 'AF' *was* Midway: OP-20-G was able to identify the Japanese objective for Admiral Nimitz.

Armed with this information, Nimitz made his dispositions accordingly. It's always useful in cards – or in war – to see the other fellow's hand ...

A screen of over twenty US submarines was ordered to Midway, with the USS *Gudgeon* patrolling the northwest, the most likely approach route. The island's garrison was reinforced and two separate carrier task

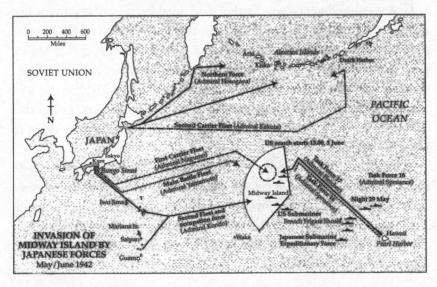

forces readied to sail. Nimitz was just in time. The Aleutian invasion force had sailed on 26 May to attack Dutch Harbor. The next day, Nagumo's First Mobile Force, consisting of the four large fleet carriers *Akagi*, *Kaga*, *Soryu* and *Hiryu* with 230 aircraft left for Midway, followed a day later by the Japanese First Fleet with Yamamoto on board his flagship, the huge battleship *Yamoto*.

Nimitz ordered the carriers *Hornet* and *Enterprise* to a holding position at 'Point Luck' about 350 miles northeast of Midway. As Admiral Halsey was ill, Rear Admiral Raymond A. Spruance took over as commander of Task Force 16. As soon as *Yorktown* was repaired on 30 May she put to sea under the command of Rear Admiral Frank Jack Fletcher, as part of Task Force 17, and sailed to rendezvous with Spruance's carriers. By 2 June, the three American carriers had joined forces. The total force had 230 carrier aircraft available, plus the 110 land-based fighters, bombers, and patrol planes at Midway.

The Japanese were well aware that the Americans were at sea. Increased radio traffic and direction finding alerted them that the US ships were on the move. However, Yamamoto's insistence on strict radio silence meant that this vital intelligence was not passed on to the rest of the fleet. Yamamoto assumed that Nagumo's carriers had picked up the same radio warnings about American movements from Tokyo, not realising that Nagumo had been unable to monitor that particular traffic.

Japanese intelligence was further degraded because the Americans had sent light forces to cover the all-important French Frigate Shoals, five hundred miles northwest of Hawaii. The Japanese had planned to use the deserted atolls as a secret base. The idea was for one of their submarines to refuel long-range Emily flying boats to let them reconnoitre Pearl Harbor. The snag was that they had pulled that trick at the shoals once before, so the US Navy had despatched a ship to prevent it happening again.

During the night of 3 June, Fletcher moved his two task forces 200 miles north of Midway. Admiral Nimitz warned the task force commanders that the Japanese attack group was about 570 miles west of Midway. However, just after dawn a patrol plane spotted two Japanese carriers and their escorts, reporting: 'Many planes heading Midway from 320 degrees distant 150 miles!' The Battle of Midway was on.

At dawn Midway had launched an anti-carrier strike of ten torpe-do-bombers. Shortly after they had taken off, Midway was attacked by over 100 Japanese planes, which targeted the power plants and oil installations. Damage on the ground was serious; but more serious still were the catastrophic losses to the defensive screen of Midway-based Marine fighters, who lost sixteen planes, though they managed to shoot down four Vals and three Zeros. Only two of Midway's fighters were left airworthy.

But the Midway attack had hit the Japanese air wing hard as well. Of the 108 Japanese carrier aircraft launched for the attack, eleven were destroyed, fourteen were heavily damaged, and twenty-nine needed repair before they could fly again. Moreover, the initial Japanese attack had not knocked out the runway. Returning Japanese pilots reported to Nagumo that another aerial attack to soften Midway's defences would be necessary if troops were to go ashore by 7 June.

Nagumo was in a quandary. The attack against his carriers by the Midway-based strike failed to achieve its objective. He had a strike force coming in from Midway, most of his fighters were still in the sky, and he needed to prepare for a second strike on Midway. The returning strike force needed to land promptly or it would have to ditch into the sea.

As the strike force touched down to be refuelled and rearmed, at 0715 Nagumo ordered them to be loaded with ground bombs. Just as this frantic activity was underway he received the first reports that American carriers were in range. Nagumo now ordered the aircraft to change their ground attack bombs for torpedoes and to prepare for an anti-shipping strike to attack the US carriers.

But Nagumo and his carriers were now the target. At 0700 Spruance had launched a mixed force of sixty-seven Dauntless dive-bombers, twenty-nine Devastator torpedo-bombers and twenty Wildcat fight-ers. The aircraft had taken off piecemeal and the US attack plan was hasty and uncoordinated.

The torpedo squadrons, flying low over the water, found the Japanese carriers – but they had no fighter cover for their attack. Nevertheless Lieutenant Commander Waldron bravely led his torpedo-bombers from *Hornet* and *Enterprise* on what amounted to a suicide run.

Without fighter escort, all fifteen Devastators of VT-8 Squadron were shot down without being able to inflict any damage. Of the thirty VT-8 aircrew from *Hornet* which took off, Ensign George Gay was the only survivor, spending thirty hours in the water after his plane was shot down.

Only four torpedo-bombers made it back to *Enterprise* and two to *Yorktown*, none returned to *Hornet*. The torpedo-bombers had, however, made a significant contribution to the battle, albeit indirectly. Their attacks had forced the Japanese carriers to scatter and spread out from their tight defensive box.

The Americans' suicidal torpedo attacks had not resulted in a single hit. It was just as well; with their packed flight decks and hangars, the Japanese carriers were now extraordinarily vulnerable to attack. Avgas fuel lines were open, and bombs and torpedoes scattered all over the hangar decks as mechanics worked desperately to refuel and rearm their planes. The carriers were saved by the intervention of their Zero CAP fighters, which swooped down on the luckless Devastators and shot them into the sea. As the last American torpedo-bomber splashed down, Nagumo and his staff congratulated themselves on a job well done. They had beaten off a series of attacks without loss, the attackers had been slaughtered and the Imperial Japanese Navy was on the verge of launching a massive strike of ninety-seven planes against the American carriers. All it needed was a few more minutes. The battle could be won.

They could not have been more wrong.

Because, high overhead, fifty Dauntless dive-bombers finally appeared. They hadn't been detected, because in mid-1942 the Imperial Japanese Navy did not have radar aboard its carriers. This was yet another serious gap in Japanese intelligence gathering capabilities. The undetected US bombers were led by Lieutenant Commander Wade McClusky, who had spotted the white wake of a Japanese destroyer steaming at full speed to rejoin the carriers. McClusky decided to follow and the destroyer obligingly led his force straight to Nagumo. With no fighter cover and their decks packed with refuelling planes, torpedoes and bombs, the Japanese carriers were helpless. Afterwards Admiral Nimitz said that McClusky's decision, 'decided the fate of our carrier task force and our forces at Midway'.

His dive-bombers certainly made sure of that. At 1022, diving from 14,000 feet, twenty-five of McClusky's SBD Dauntless dive-bombers from *Enterprise* hit *Kaga* with four bombs. The wounds were mortal: the explosions ruptured the ship's avgas lines, damaged fire mains and fire pumps, and knocked out the fire suppression system. The burning avgas flowed across the deck setting off hundreds of tons of bombs and torpedoes in a series of catastrophic explosions.

Kaga's agony was then transferred to the carriers *Sōryū* and *Akagi*. Attacked at almost the same time as *Kaga*, *Sōryū* was hit by thirteen Dauntlesses from *Yorktown*'s VB-3 Squadron. The carrier received three direct hits from 1,000 bombs. Within a very short time, the ship was without power and most of the crew taken off. Unfortunately for her, she ran into the USS *Nautilus*, one of Nimitz's submarine screen, which had been playing a lethal game of hide and seek with Japanese destroyers all morning. *Nautilus* moved into a firing position and put three torpedoes into the stricken carrier at close range. *Sōryū* broke in half and sank.

The flagship *Akagi* was next; a 1,000-pound bomb exploded in the upper hangar, setting off more explosions among the fully armed and fuelled B5N torpedo bombers. Like her sisters, *Akagi* was soon a blazing inferno and had to be abandoned.

The sole surviving Japanese aircraft carrier now was the *Hiryū*, who wasted no time in counter-attacking with a wave of eighteen dive-bombers plus a small fighter escort. The Japanese pilots found *Yorktown* by the simple expedient of following the retreating US planes back to their carrier. *Yorktown* was hit by three bombs, blowing a hole in the deck, and temporarily putting out her boilers. Despite the damage, repair teams were able to plank over the flight deck and restore power to several boilers and resume air operations within an hour.

That was just as well, as a second Japanese strike from *Hiryū* turned up about an hour later, with ten torpedo bombers and six escorting Zeros. *Yorktown* was struck by two torpedoes, which put her out of action and forced Admiral Fletcher to shift his flag to the cruiser *Astoria*, leaving damage-control parties to try and save the stricken flat top.

What no-one realised was that, when the second *Hiryū* strike had arrived over *Yorktown*, they *assumed it was a different carrier*. The pilots could see what appeared to be an undamaged vessel making twenty knots; there were no obvious holes in the flight deck and the ship was not on fire. This time *Yorktown* really was out of action. But the upshot was that the Japanese pilots now reported back that they had knocked out *two* carriers. The Japanese battle staff now believed that, despite the heavy losses, they could scrape together enough aircraft for one more strike against what was believed to be the only remaining American carrier.

They were sorely mistaken.

By late afternoon, a scouting aircraft from *Yorktown* finally located *Hiryū*. Admiral Spruance, now in overall command on board *Enterprise*, ordered a final strike of dive bombers. *Hiryū* was hit by four 1,000-pound bombs, three on the forward flight deck and one on the forward elevator. The story of the other carriers was repeated. As night fell at Midway on 4 June 1942 it was obvious that the US Navy had won a stunning victory. The question now for both sides was, what to do next?

Spruance retreated to the east to avoid any clash in the dark. Yamamoto did a sweep to the east, ordered a bombardment of Midway and then pulled back to the west. With no air cover left, the Japanese invasion force and the follow-up battleships had abandoned any idea of landing on Midway and headed for home.

The crippled *Yorktown* was the last to go. Although damage-control parties had actually managed to get the damaged carrier under control by the morning of 6 June, the Japanese submarine I-68 was close and launched a spread of four torpedoes. By dawn the following day, the wounded carrier capsized, turned turtle and sank.

They were the last major casualties of the Battle of Midway.

Midway was a disaster for Japan. The Imperial Japanese Navy would never recover their losses: four fleet aircraft carriers, one heavy cruiser, over 250 aircraft and 3,000 men, including many irreplaceable naval aircrew. Midway changed the balance of power in the Pacific overnight. Intelligence had changed the course of world history.

Despite this, what followed was not exactly one of the US Navy's finest hours and tells us much about what often goes on behind the bureaucratic scenes in the sneaky-beaky world of intelligence.

Although Rochefort was recommended for the Distinguished

Service Medal for his part in the victory by Nimitz himself, Navy politics intervened. A vicious bureaucratic battle broke out over who was really responsible for the intelligence success at Midway and, more importantly, who would control SIGINT in the future. It was the classic SIGINT problem which continues to this day: who owns the SIGINT operation: the communicators and signallers – or the intelligence people?

The US Navy communicators in Washington claimed that all the intercepts were due to their good work. This was because Captain Joseph Redman and the naval communicators in Washington were determined to centralise command of all radio intelligence work done by OP-20-G in their hands. This classic piece of empire building manifested itself into a fight over who really deserved the credit for breaking JN-25 and correctly anticipating the Japanese plans for Midway.

On 20 June, just a few weeks after Midway, Commander John Redman (Nimitz's Fleet Communications Officer) sent a memorandum to the Vice Chief of Naval Operations stating that 'experience has indicated that units in combat areas cannot be relied upon to accomplish more than the business of merely reading enemy messages and performing routine work necessary to keep abreast of minor changes in the cryptographic systems involved'.

Simultaneously, his older brother, Captain Joseph R. Redman, now Director of Naval Communications in Washington, was complaining that Station Hypo (Hawaii) was, 'by virtue of seniority, in the hands of an ex-Japanese language student' who was 'not technically trained in Naval Communications', adding that, 'Rochefort should be replaced with a senior officer trained in radio intelligence rather than one whose background is in Japanese language.' It was the perennial battle for primacy between signallers and intelligence.

Washington now moved with considerable spite against the hapless Rochefort. In October he was summoned to the Navy Department in Washington DC for 'temporary additional duty'. Nimitz protested against the move but was assured that Washington simply needed Rochefort's expert advice. Rochefort read the runes differently and bade farewell to his team, adding sadly, 'I won't be coming back.'

He was right. A month later Nimitz received a letter informing him that Rochefort had been permanently assigned Stateside. The US Navy's best Japanese code breaker ended up in command of a floating dry dock in San Francisco and never worked on codes again. A furious Nimitz refused to talk to his own Fleet Communications Officer.

Captain Edward C. Dyer, a USMC communications specialist who witnessed the whole ugly bureaucratic turf war, observed before his death in 1985, 'I have given a great deal of thought to the Rochefort affair, and I have been unwillingly forced to the conclusion that Rochefort committed one unforgivable sin. To certain individuals of small mind and overweening ambition, there is no greater insult than to be proved wrong.'

Two of the Hawaii Station naval SIGINT team, Dyer and Holmes, were awarded the Distinguished Service Medal after the war.

Rochefort, the true victor of Midway, finally got his medal from a grateful nation, too – in 1985, nine years after his death. Despite this shabby treatment Rochefort's achievement lives on, and he will be long remembered as the architect of what is arguably SIGINT's greatest triumph – victory at Midway.

The Death of Yamamoto

SIGINT was also responsible for one of the most significant operations in the Pacific theatre: the interception, on 18 April 1943, and shooting down of Admiral Isoroku Yamamoto, the architect of Japan's naval strategy in the Pacific and the attack on Pearl Harbor. When American code breakers found out that he was flying to Bougainville Island to conduct a front-line inspection, sixteen P-38G Lightnings were sent on a long-range fighter-intercept mission, flying 435 miles from Guadalcanal at wave-top height to avoid detection. The Lightnings met Yamamoto's two Mitsubishi G4M 'Betty' bomber transports and six escorting Zeros just as they arrived. The first Betty crashed in the jungle and the second ditched near the coast.

Japanese search parties found Yamamoto's body at the jungle crash site the next day. Once again SIGINT had delivered a silent but lethal wartime blow.

CHAPTER 16

On Surveillance

It is hard to know where communications intelligence ends and mass surveillance begins. One of the greatest problems facing communications intelligence in the twenty-first century is technology's ever-increasing reach. The digital revolution of the last two decades of the twentieth century had given communications companies and governments alike unparalleled access to literally billions of what had always been private exchanges. Thus was born the surveillance state, a world where the Internet, the telephone and social media like Facebook and its rivals was accessible to all.

Under the circumstances it was always improbable that national security services would agree to a self-denying ordinance. Emboldened by the universally agreed need to track terrorists after the 2001 attack on the World Trade Center, security and intelligence services the world over embarked on policies aimed at intercepting and reading as many of their citizens' private communications as they could get away with – and all in the name of 'security'.

The extent of this mass surveillance now risks altering what Rousseau called the social contract between the citizen-taxpayer and the state, because the new technology of the digital age has placed undreamt of monitoring devices in the hands of governments worldwide.

Microchip implants are now routinely placed under the skin of animals by vets. The chips, about the size of a large grain of rice, use passive RFID (radio frequency identification) technology, and are also known as PIT TAGs (for passive integrated transponder). These can be totally passive until electronically interrogated by the monitoring agency – just like an aeroplane's transponder. The idea has now spread to humans. In 2015 it was revealed that corporate tenants of the Epicentre high-tech office complex in Sweden are having RFID-PIT chips implanted in their hands, enabling access through security doors, as well as services such as copy machines, all without pin codes or swipe cards. The possibilities – and the dangers – are obvious.

PowerPoint slides of the US National Security Agency's PRISM clandestine surveillance programme that were leaked by Edward Snowden show the wide range of methods to detect and track any individual or vehicle, the companies identified as participants, and that much of the world's electronic communications flow through the US and are therefore vulnerable to interception.

After the London and Madrid bombings, the slaughter of 132 school children by fundamentalist jihadis in Pakistan and the murder of the editor and cartoonists of *Charlie Hebdo*, a satirical Parisian magazine, ministers and the public have been only too ready to let the organs of state wipe out, in a few short years, individual liberties that had been centuries in the winning. But the electronic monitoring went much further than that. In 2013 a leaked US National Security Agency memo revealed that such surveillance extended not just to suspected terrorists, but to routinely bugging and monitoring world leaders.

According to a classified document provided by an NSA whis-tle-blower called Edward Snowden, it emerged that the agency monitored the phone conversations of thirty-five world leaders after being given the numbers by an official in another US government department.

The confidential memo, dated October 2006, was issued to staff in the agency's Signals Intelligence Directorate (SID), entitled 'Customers Can Help SID Obtain Targetable Phone Numbers.'

'In one recent case,' the memo notes, 'a US official provided NSA with 200 phone numbers to 35 world leaders . . . Despite the fact that the majority is probably available via open source, the PCs [intelligence production centres] have noted 43 previously unknown phone numbers. These numbers plus several others have been tasked.'

Unsurprisingly the revelations sparked a furious diplomatic row between the US and its allies, after the German chancellor Angela Merkel accused the US of tapping her mobile phone.

Merkel had suspected the surveillance for some time after seeing her mobile phone number written on a US document. She accused the US of a breach of faith. 'We need to have trust in our allies and partners, and this must now be established once again. I repeat that spying among friends is not at all acceptable against anyone, and that goes for every citizen in Germany.'

Although the White House rushed to calm the situation by reassuring the world that the US 'is not monitoring and will not monitor' the German Chancellor's communications, it failed to end the row because, as Berlin quickly pointed out, the US did not deny monitoring the phones in the past.

As the row escalated, the full extent of the US monitoring of the EU emerged. President Obama was forced to call the French President François Hollande in response to reports in *Le Monde* that the NSA accessed more than seventy million phone records of French citizens in a single thirty-day period, while earlier reports in the German magazine *Der Spiegel* uncovered NSA activity against the offices and communications of senior officials of the European Union.

As a result, the European Commission backed proposals that could require US tech companies to seek permission before handing over EU citizens' data to US intelligence agencies, while the European Parliament voted in favour of suspending a transatlantic bank data sharing agreement after *Der Spiegel* revealed the agency was monitoring the international bank transfer system Swift.

What the whole row revealed was just how extensive and wide-ranging technical surveillance had become in modern society. From CCTV cameras on the street, to reading every citizen's private emails, the state had become a voyeur of the individual. SIGINT had morphed into a new form of social control – the surveillance state.

CHAPTER 17

On Technical Intelligence

After the Second World War, a number of forces combined to develop national security policies based primarily on intelligence.

As the 1940s drew to a close, the primary worry for America and her Western allies was the avoidance of strategic surprise by a now nuclear USSR. For the US, the memory of Pearl Harbor cast a long shadow. This was the event which Washington was determined would never be repeated. Intelligence was, rightly, seen as the key.

The second factor was the need for greater cooperation at the national level and control among the various intelligence agencies involved in the Cold War's undercover struggle over foreign, diplomatic, military, and economic events and policy.

Walter Bedell Smith, President Harry S. Truman's executive director of the National Security Council, found this state of affairs to be unsatisfactory. Particularly troubling was the failure of the US intelligence agencies (AFSA) during the Korean War when they were unable to break the Chinese and North Korean codes. His view was shared by General James van Fleet, commander of the US Eighth Army, who complained that '[W]e have lost, through neglect, disinterest and possibly jealousy, much of the effectiveness in intelligence work we acquired so painfully in World War II.'

This necessity for greater intelligence effort was supported by the experience of successful cooperation between the armed forces, the intelligence agencies, and the British and American partnership during the Second World War. Both London and Washington, and indeed

Moscow, realised that intelligence, in all its forms needed to be unified at a national level. In America this was recognised by the 1947 National Security Act, which created the Central Intelligence Agency (CIA), the National Security Council (NSC), and attempted to unify the squabbling single-service military intelligence organisations in the US Army, Navy, and Air Force. All were to be united under a Secretary of Defense in a national defence establishment that soon became the Department of Defense (DoD). Along with the newly created CIA, the other founding member was the Bureau of Intelligence and Research (INR) in the State Department.

In Britain the MI6 and MI5 were joined by Government Communications Headquarters (GCHQ) and the Joint Air Reconnaissance Intelligence Centre (JARIC), all reporting with a Defence Intelligence Service to the Cabinet's Joint Intelligence Committee.

This was accompanied by the recognition that, in the modern age, technical intelligence was just as important as the traditional diplomatic and HUMINT sources. This in turn has led to the establishment of what is now known as the intelligence community; still disunited in all too many cases but all united in one goal: to work together to prevent another surprise attack like Pearl Harbor. And the potential enemy back in 1950 was clearly the Soviet Union. For Washington and London this identifiable adversary could only be dealt with by a policy of containment backed by intelligence – from all sources. Thus were born what we can call the technical intelligence agencies. Technical intelligence can best be summarised as collecting information across the known electromagnetic spectrum, from ultra-low frequency radio

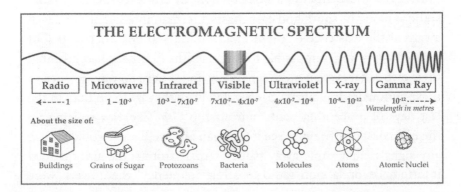

THE ELECTROMAGNETIC SPECTRUM

Radio	Microwave	Infrared	Visible	Ultraviolet	X-ray	Gamma Ray
◄ - - - - -1	$1 - 10^{-3}$	$10^{-3} - 7\times10^{-7}$	$7\times10^{-7} - 4\times10^{-7}$	$4\times10^{-7} - 10^{-8}$	$10^{-8} - 10^{-12}$	10^{-12} - - - - -►

Wavelength in metres

About the size of:

| Buildings | Grains of Sugar | Protozoans | Bacteria | Molecules | Atoms | Atomic Nuclei |

waves to incredibly high-frequency receptors: from detecting a football field or a submarine, to exploring the radiation particle characteristics inside a nuclear bomb. Sensors aboard modern platforms such as satellites or UAVs can collect all these wavelengths, and in most cases relay them back in near real time to their controlling agencies.

The visible light spectrum occupies a surprisingly small proportion of the known electromagnetic spectrum. From the nineteenth century scientists have been aware that there were more wavelengths than those that humans could actually see. For example, it had been long known that bats find their way by echo-location, relying on very high frequency squeaks to navigate in the dark.

As early as 1887 Heinrich Herz noted that radio waves could also reflect and bounce off solid objects; and by 1922 Marconi was outlining a system that could be 'applied to lighthouses and lightships, so as to enable vessels in foggy weather to locate dangerous points around the coasts . . .'

In 1904, the German Christian Hülsmeyer gave public demonstrations using radio echoes to detect ships, showing how collisions could be avoided in fog. He even managed to test his patented device on German canal bridges.

By the mid-1930s the French were experimenting with an 'anti-iceberg radio detection beam' for their new liner *Normandie,* and by the outbreak of war in Europe in 1939, both the British and the Germans had developed viable military systems of 'radio location', or radar, as the Americans eventually named the new technology.

By 1939 the British had built a chain of crude air-defence radar stations along its south and east coasts. German intelligence was well aware of the existence of these 'chain home' stations; their 200-foot lattice towers were impossible to disguise. The Germans had invented their own radar system quite separately and it bore no resemblance to these curious 'radio towers'. So puzzled were they by them that, in the last days of peace, they sent their airship *Graf Zeppelin* cruising up the east coast of Britain to see if German air intelligence could collect any signals. They came away baffled. Apart from some 'unexplained interference on a non-radio-locating frequency' the towers were apparently silent. The truth was that the cunning British had switched them off.

What was going on was the birth of a completely new kind of intelligence: 'ELINT', or electronic intelligence. As the war progressed it would begin to dominate the battle as the combatants struggled to maintain technical superiority over their enemy's weapons, especially in the air. Air combat, particularly at night, was becoming a competition between machines and their technical aids. Not for nothing was radar sometimes called an 'instrument of darkness'. Technical superiority was the key to success in this new battlefield and collecting the enemy's transmissions became a vital intelligence task.

Knowledge of a radar's exact wavelength, pulse repetion frequency, and power became essential intelligence to both locate and to combat enemy radars.

One particularly notorious example, demonstrating both the strength and weakness of this new technical struggle, was a British 'radar detector' device called Monica. it was designed to sweep the area behind RAF bombers, searching for the presence of prowling night fighters sneaking up on the bombers. The problem was that Monica was an active radar. It *transmitted* radar beams, proving once again, for the hapless RAF crews, the old adage that 'transmission is treason'. Monica was in fact highly dangerous to Bomber Command. German intelligence had checked the new mysterious rearward-looking radar devices on shot-down RAF bombers and identified the new radar's frequency. It was child's play then to fit a simple receiver tuned to Monica's characteristics to the front of the Luftwaffe's night-fighters. From then on, using Monica was the equivalent of shining a bright pointing backwards in the darkness to guide the delighted German night-fighter crews towards their lumbering targets, plump with high explosive and high-octane petrol. Bomber Command losses rose dramatically until a captured German night-fighter was tested. The boffins discovered to their horror that, while flying over London, they could 'see' an RAF Monica transmitting from a bomber flying over fifty miles away, near Bristol. Monica was removed – rapidly – from the RAF's inventory, just another victim on the new battlefield of technical intelligence.

However, while TECHINT and ELINT have now evolved to dominate our new technical age, photography and intelligence taking in the visible light spectrum still remain the oldest and clearest source of imagery intelligence or IMINT.

CHAPTER 18

Photographic Reconnaissance

Soldiers have always tried to seize high ground for the very simple reason that you can see further from up there. That way you have a better chance of checking on what the enemy is up to. So, the minute that man first took to the air, it was inevitable that the military would quickly follow.

Sure enough, at the Battle of Fleurus in 1794, the French employment of a balloon called *l'Entreprenant* (the enterprising one) marked the first real military use of aerial reconnaissance. Observers used their bird's eye view from above to keep track of Austrian deployments and drop the information to the ground, where the French Revolutionary commanders adjusted their dispositions accordingly to force an Austrian retreat.

Balloons were used during the American Civil War in 1861 by the Army of the Potomac to map out terrain and even to direct fire from a hidden artillery battery onto a Confederate encampment by using flag signals.

The Union used balloons from the start. In 1861 a Mr Thaddeus Lowe had demonstrated that, at 1,000 feet, a man in a balloon could see deep into rebel territory. Unfortunately, this first balloon could only use Washington's town gas supply, which restricted its mobility – it had to be tethered near its gasometer. The idea caught on however, and, in 1862, balloon intelligence was an important factor at the Battle of Fair Oaks, with Lowe's balloons providing regular, accurate, intelligence reports to the Union commanders on the Confederates' dispositions, forcing them to adopt early camouflage measures.

The enterprising Lowe even invented the first aircraft carrier by converting a coal barge to tow a balloon aloft. His great ballooning rival, John LaMountain, went one better: he used a converted tug to launch untethered hydrogen-fuelled balloons over the rebel lines. The Prussian observers of 'this amateur war' were so impressed with these technical developments that they sent an observer out to America to report on the military potential of balloons. His name was Count Ferdinand von Zeppelin.

Surprisingly, despite the Frenchman Gaspard Tournachon's first aerial photographs in 1858, there is no evidence of photography from balloons during the Civil War. However, British Army engineers were quick to see the military possibilities of the eye in the sky. By the 1880s, the British had established a military balloon squadron and their 1896 training manual covered aerial photography and even how to interpret the photographs.

The invention of the aeroplane accelerated the growing technology and its applications. By 1911 both the Italians and the US were using aerial photography to find out what their adversaries were up to: the former against the Turkish lines in Libya and the Americans in secret flights over Mexico, hunting for the elusive Pancho Villa.

In 1912 the British Royal Flying Corps was formed and was immediately used for reconnaissance and photography from the air. Lieutenant General Sir James Grierson recorded after the 1912 manoeuvres on Salisbury Plain (which he won, thanks to aerial reconnaissance): 'There is no doubt that before land fighting takes place we shall have to fight and destroy the enemy's aircraft . . . warfare will be impossible until we have mastery of the air.'

The following year, more combat reconnaissance flights were mounted by the Italians in Libya and by Bulgarian aircraft over Turkish lines during the Balkan war. And, by the summer of 1913, the Royal Flying Corps was photographing Southampton docks from the air and even developing the photographs in flight.

France and Germany were equally well aware of the value of aerial reconnaissance. German optics were the best in the world and the German air force fitted a specialist Goerz camera onto a Rumpler Taube for aerial reconnaissance as early as 1913. By 1914, the French followed suit and had equipped several observation planes with cameras. They had also developed procedures for getting prints into the hands of field commanders as quickly as possible.

The outbreak of the First World War in 1914 confirmed the importance of aerial reconnaissance. The first British aerial reconnaissance of the war revealed massed German columns marching southwest from Brussels. Although the British Commander-in-Chief expressed polite interest to the youthful aircrew, he then found it hard to believe the critical intelligence they had brought him ('It must be very confusing for you up there, my boy,' said Sir John French.) His more intellectually agile staff officers were quick to see the value of this new 'scouting cavalry of the air'.

The advent of static trench warfare by the December of that year further reinforced the importance of this vital new source of information. Enemy positions could be photographed and mapped accurately from the air, artillery batteries identified, logistic dumps plotted, and even the movements of reinforcements monitored well behind the lines.

The first real use of aerial photography was to improve mapping for the troops and for the artillery. Every soldier – and especially every gunner – knows that, without an accurate map, life becomes very difficult, if not impossible. With artillery well dug-in on the Western Front, photographic reconnaissance could not only pinpoint the enemy gun positions but, even more important, tell both sides precisely where their own guns were; and that was vital to the development of indirect artillery fire. 'Shooting off the map' always presupposes that you have a decent map that lets you know here you are as well as where the target is. With their ability to pinpoint the enemy's precise locations, aerial reconnaissance and aerial photography had arrived as an invaluable intelligence tool for all the armies.

The new intelligence collection capability broke neatly into two quite distinct areas: collection and interpretation. For the first, reliable, stable aircraft were important as collection platforms, but without a decent camera even the best aeroplane was pointless. At first the British used hand-held 'A type' cameras that had to be pointed over the side of the aeroplane, with the observer trying to load and unload each glass plate by hand in the freezing cold at eighty miles an hour.

Despite this, they gave excellent results and the British swiftly moved on to fixed cameras with longer focal lengths.

Having got the aerial photographs, the next stage was to work out what they meant. Fortunately, the discovery of stereoscopic photography in 1838 by Charles Wheatstone, which offered three-dimensional images, would revolutionise photographic interpretation. By 1918, the British alone had processed over half a million aerial photographs on the Western Front, and the arrival of the Americans in 1917 completed the process for the Allies. The American Eugene Ives summed up the combined results in 1920 as:

> The task of harmonizing the photographic practice as taught in America, following English lines, with French practice as followed in the theater of war, and of adapting planes built on English designs so that they could carry French apparatus, was a formidable one, not likely to be soon forgotten by any who had a part in it.

Unfortunately, as with so many other First World War innovations, British aerial photography, like the tank, withered and died between the wars at the hands of a parsimonious Whitehall Treasury. So much so that, when Victor Laws returned to the RAF in 1933 as a group captain, he discovered that RAF photography 'was at a dead end'.

Not so in the United States. George W. Goddard, late of the US Army Signals Corps Air Service (which became the US Army Air Corps in 1926), was a young Army captain who admitted to being an average pilot, but who had an avid interest in photography. Encouraged by his superiors, he was posted to McCook Field, Ohio as the officer in charge of aerial photographic research, where he started developments in specialised aerial cameras, photographic aircraft, high-level long-range photography and even experimented in the infra-red spectrum. He also pioneered the development of portable field laboratory equipment, which later went on to become the nucleus of the photographic laboratory at Wright-Patterson Air Force Base, Ohio.

By 1925, Goddard was experimenting with aerial photography at night and, on 20 November 1925, woke up the good citizens of Rochester NY by detonating an 80-pound 'flare bomb' above the town, which lit up the night sky for miles and allowed the very first night aerial-photograph to be taken. Goddard was a real pioneer. He even transmitted photographs of Fort Leavenworth from the air in near real time by telephoto transmission.

Goddard was not alone in the US. In 1928, Captains Stevens and St Clair Street took clear photographs from 37,800 feet (a world record) and in 1935 two other airmen went up in a balloon and took pin-sharp photographs from 72,400 feet – the same height as the notorious U-2 photographs of thirty years later.

It took the rise of Nazism to jolt the British out of their pacifist post-war torpor. The realisation that Hitler's Germany really was intent on tearing up the Treaty of Versailles and thus threatening the peace of Europe led to a panicked re-arming in the late thirties – it was too little, too late. One of the results was Whitehall had to race to play catch-up: British intelligence suddenly had to find out exactly what was going on inside Nazi Germany. HUMINT, spies and diplomacy could help, certainly, but what Whitehall needed was hard photographic evidence, if only to ram it under ministers' noses. To do this they had to mobilise all their resources.

Desperate times need desperate remedies. In the feverish atmosphere of 1939, one individual changed aerial photographic reconnaissance for ever: Sidney Cotton, an Australian, today recognised as the father of modern photographic reconnaissance. Cotton was a remarkable man, a buccaneering wartime 'larger than life' character more akin to a swashbuckling sixteenth-century privateer than a normal businessman. He loved flying, women and money. He volunteered to join the RFC in 1915 and learned to fly, but his career as a combat pilot in 1916–17 was cut short when he resigned his commission after a row with his senior officers, a pattern that was to be repeated. However, during his time in the RFC he designed and marketed a warm high-altitude flying suit, which he marketed (with typical modesty) as the 'Sidcot Suit'.

Between the wars he ran an aerial photographic business and had flown seal-spotting operations in Newfoundland as well as developing a new colour film process. Cotton was well connected, counting James Bond's creator Ian Fleming and Kodak boss George Eastman, as well as Winston Churchill, as personal friends. He was also on good terms with a number of high-ranking Nazis.

In late 1938 Cotton was approached discreetly by MI6 and recruited to fly his business trips to Germany over certain targets of interest, especially the growing Luftwaffe, by now a major British intelligence priority. His Lockheed 12A six-seater was rigged out with French cameras and flew a number of missions along the Franco-German border on behalf of the Deuxième Bureau, France's external intelligence agency, as well.

Cotton was disappointed with the French results. As a result, MI6 bought him a new twin-engine Lockheed and had the aircraft modified to hide bigger F24 cameras in the floor, plus two oblique cameras set at a 45-degree angle, which were designed to take photographs from the side. At 20,000 feet these cameras could cover an area sixteen kilometres wide. Cotton solved the problem of frozen condensation by bleeding warm air from the engines to flow over the camera lenses. A hidden button under the pilot's seat activated the cameras.

Armed with this pale-blue 'private plane', Cotton made several trips to Germany, posing as a businessman or a film producer looking for locations. On MI6's instructions, many of his routes passed over or near targets of intelligence interest such as the Luftwaffe test centre or troop concentrations, factories and airfields. The take was phenomenal. He even managed to take Luftwaffe General Albert Kesselring as a passenger on a flight along the Rhine, claiming that he had a maiden aunt who lived there – all the while taking spy photographs, literally under the German's nose.

With the outbreak of war, his work for MI6 led to Cotton being re-commissioned as a squadron leader in the RAF and ordered to form his own secret photographic unit, with a budget to hire civilians or military members. The unit was based at a private flying-club airfield at Heston and equipped with modified Bristol Blenheims. These twin-engine light bombers were too slow and could not fly high enough for aerial reconnaissance. Worse, they were taking serious losses from the German fighters. A memorandum from the period spells out the requirement for a less vulnerable aerial photographic platform:

The best method appears to be the use of a single small machine relying on speed, climb and ceiling to avoid destruction. A machine such as a single-seat fighter could fly high enough to be well above ack-ack fire and could rely on sheer speed and height to get away from enemy fighters. It would have no use for armament or radio and these could be removed to provide room for extra fuel to get the necessary range. It would be a very small machine painted so as to reduce its visibility against the sky.

Armed with this requirement, Cotton managed to obtain two Spitfires, stripped them down, polished their skins, and fitted them with cameras and long-range fuel tanks instead of guns. These were successful from the start, roaming high and fast over Germany and photographing everything they could in a way that the even the Luftwaffe's specialist high-flying Junkers Ju 86P photo-recce planes could not match over Britain.

Cotton also contracted the only Swiss stereoscopic plotting machine in Britain, belonging to the Aircraft Operating Company, to turn his photographs taken from 35,000 feet into 1:25,000 scale maps. This combination of good aircraft, good cameras and skilful interpretation meant that Cotton's 'private' photo reconaissance unit was making a major and unique contribution to Britain's national intelligence effort.

Cotton's undoing came with the Fall of France. In June 1940 he was tasked to fly his Lockheed to Paris to evacuate British agents and secret papers. But, when he arrived, he found Marcel Boussac, the head of Christian Dior who, with many of his countrymen, was desperate to get out of France. Boussac offered Cotton handfuls of thousand-franc notes to fly him to England. Cotton, the businessman, accepted.

This was too much for the strait-laced British authorities. Cotton was summarily dismissed from the RAF. His Photographic Development Unit was incorporated into the regular RAF with a regular RAF wing commander in charge. Cotton received a formal letter from the Air Ministry thanking him for the 'great gifts of imagination and inventive thought which he had brought to bear on the development of aerial photography' and was sent packing. Despite his efforts to be reinstated, even involving Churchill himself, Cotton was forced to resign his commission, although he was eventually rewarded with an OBE. Sidney Cotton's aerial photographs were far ahead of their time, but a brilliant mind with an imaginative flair for aerial photography was lost to the British war effort.

To accompany Cotton's revolutionary new reconnaissance methods and capabilities in the air, the equally important aspect of strategic photographic *interpretation* was being developed in the village of Medmenham, where a requisitioned stately home became the headquarters of the British Military Intelligence (MI-4) and its Central Interpretation Unit (CIU).

When the United States entered the European war in 1942–3 the US Army Air Force quickly saw the value of photo reconnaissance, both for targeting and bomb damage assessment. They based their air photo interpretation doctrine on RAF techniques and tactics.

Some of their initial experience had been gained in the Pacific theatre by Colonel Karl Polifka, who pioneered many of the operating procedures that would later become standard. Operating from Port Moresby, Papua New Guinea, to overfly the Japanese base at Rabaul, he discovered that the US F-4 recce aircraft (a modified P-38 Lightning) was not ideal for the mission, a view confirmed in England, where the USAAF initially procured British Spitfires and Mosquitoes for their aerial reconnaissance squadrons over Europe.

Lacking an aircraft designed specifically for aerial reconnaissance, the USAAF quickly acknowledged the need for speed, altitude and range to reach out into Germany while avoiding enemy fighters. The initial American specialist aircraft, the F-4, despite its four high-quality reconnaissance and mapping cameras was never ideal for the role. However, by 1944, the superlative P-51 Mustang became available. Its performance was comparable to the Photo Reconaissance Spitfires, but with much longer range. Its variant, the F6, eventually became the primary reconnaissance aircraft for the USAAF in Europe.

In the Pacific the USAAF eventually introduced the F-13, a modified Boeing B-29 Superfortress designed specifically to conduct long-range aerial reconnaissance from over 30,000 feet. On 1 November 1944, an F-13 flew a fourteen-hour mission from Saipan to Tokyo at an altitude of 32,000 feet, the first US aircraft to fly over

Tokyo since the Doolittle raid of April 1942. From then on, F-13s flew literally hundreds of missions over the Japanese mainland, plotting every significant target in Japan.

In Europe, RAF Medmenham, with its unique ability to look at thousands of aerial photographs and analyse their significance (otherwise known as 'third phase deep interpretation') and provide prompt service to all its 'customers', had evolved into a major strategic national intelligence agency that offered as great a contribution to winning the war as SIGINT. For example, it was Medmenham that confirmed the existence of the German V weapons at Peenemünde. Although there had been numerous HUMINT and SIGINT reports that the Germans were experimenting with new and potentially dangerous weapons, it was the photographic interpreters who finally spotted and confirmed the existence of the tiny V1 flying bomb, the V2 long-range missile and the Messerschmitt 163 rocket fighter.

By the end of the Second World War, Cotton's embryonic Photographic Development Unit had grown into the Allied Photographic Reconnaissance Unit and the Allied Central Interpretation Unit. By 1945, *daily* intake of material averaged 25,000 negatives and 60,000 prints – over thirty-six million prints had been produced during the war. The ACIU print library documented and stored images from across the world: it held five million prints from which 40,000 reports had been produced. By the war's close, RAF Medmenham employed more than 5,000 pilots, ground crew, photographers and photographic interpreters. It was an intelligence epic of industrial proportions.

After the usual over-hasty and ill-considered post-war demobilisation and run-down, within eighteen months of the war's end it was obvious that photo reconnaissance was needed again – badly. As early as 1946 the United States Army Air Forces was mounting aerial reconnaissance flights along the borders of the Soviet Union and other Eastern Bloc states in order to determine the size, composition, and disposition of Soviet forces.

By 1947 the first aerial missions to spy on the Soviets' capabilities inside Eastern Europe were mounted, using a variety of aircraft. By 1950 the new British twin-engine Canberra jet revolutionised the task: at 50,000 feet and with good cameras it could even overfly parts of the Soviet Union. The US procured their own variant, the Martin B-57 for high-altitude photographic reconnaissance.

The need for aerial reconnaissance flights was reinforced after the Korea War started in 1950. President Truman authorised overflights of the Soviet Union and, in 1952, a modified USAF B-47B Stratojet bomber made the first deep-penetration US overflight of Soviet territory to photograph Soviet bombers in Siberia. This was always a dangerous game – at times the Cold War became very hot.

By 1954, the US was becoming ever more concerned. Alarming rumours of new Soviet high-performance bombers under construction prompted a highly risky flight over Archangel and Murmansk to see and photograph what was on the runways of the Soviet Air Force's main bases in the north, especially any long-range bombers. The aircraft selected was one of the new Stratojets, capable of flying too high for the Russian MiG-15s. The Stratojet entered Soviet territory over Murmansk in the North Cape, collected masses of radar data and good photographs as it flew southeast towards Archangel, then headed west for the Finnish border and safety.

The reconnaissance jet had been over Soviet airspace for about fifteen minutes when the first MiG-15s appeared, well below the B-47, cruising at over 40,000 feet. They quickly fell behind. However, as it turned west and put its nose down to head for home, the B-47 crew got a nasty shock. Coming up at them was a flight of the new MiG-17s, which bore in to attack from astern at 38,000 feet. The Stratojet's tail gun kept them partly at bay but the Stratojet was damaged in the MiG-17s' firing passes. Leaking fuel and losing height, the USAF (after 1947 the airforce became a separate arm of the separate arm of the defence establishment and changed their name from USAAF to USAF) aircraft was only saved by crossing into Finnish airspace, at which point the MiGs broke for home. The Stratojet staggered back to RAF Fairford with the help of a 'wet tow' – semi-permanently plugged into one of the tankers waiting to see them home. It had been a close-run thing; but at least the USAF now had first-hand experience of the characteristics and deployment of the Soviets' new fighter as well as the mass of other intelligence they had collected.

As a result of these dangerous overflights, and driven by a critical need to acquire intelligence on the Soviet's latest weapon developments, in 1955 President Eisenhower actually proposed a joint 'open skies' policy for the USA and USSR in a bid to lower the international tension. A year later the Soviet Union rejected the idea out of hand.

This grim undeclared war continued for the next twenty years. Aircraft progressed from carrying just cameras for photographic reconnaissance to electronic intelligence gathering as well as monitoring and collecting SIGINT. It was risky work and the aerial attacks on the flights continued. In 1958 a CIA C-118 Liftmaster transport was shot down over Soviet Armenia. The crews parachuted to safety and were released by the Soviets a week later. Later that year, the crew of a probing USAF C-130A Hercules transport modified for signals intelligence was not so lucky; the plane was shot down, seventeen men were killed and their bodies repatriated eventually by the Soviets.

On 1 July 1960, a USAF Stratojet flying over the Barents Sea was shot down by a Soviet MiG-19. Two of the crew survived and were captured and held for six months by the KGB. All sides recognised that aerial reconnaissance, even in 'peacetime', could be a hazardous occupation.

After the seizure of the US Navy's SIGINT ship the USS *Pueblo* (see page 451) the Pentagon ordered increased intelligence collection. One of the US Navy's intelligence flights came to grief on 15 April 1969, when a modified Constellation EC-121 was shot down by Korean jets in the worst loss in the history of American aerial reconnaissance. The doomed aircraft was flying its last mission with a double crew, thirty-one men in all, for training purposes, and was under orders not to come closer than fifty miles to the coast. Apart from some floating debris, no trace of the aircraft, or its crew, was ever found.

The vital Western overflights would have to continue, but this time the USA decided to build a special intelligence-collection aeroplane.

The U-2, designed by Kelly Johnson and built at Lockheed's secret Skunk works in California, was essentially a motorised jet-powered glider able to float high above the earth on the edge of the atmosphere, carrying a payload of high resolution cameras and electronic warfare sensors. Its strange mixture of metal, balsa-wood and plastic construction meant that it was remarkably light and its powerful J79 engine meant that it could climb like a lift on take-off. At 65,000 feet and more, floating high above the Soviet Union from 1956 onwards the U-2, or 'Black Lady', could collect intelligence out of the reach of the Soviet PVO-Strany air defence organisation. Despite furious Soviet protests, the intelligence overflights continued and the U-2s earned their money. Although the U-2 was only ever intended as a short-term solution for finding out what the USSR was up to at the height of the Cold War, the intelligence was incredibly valuable and the U-2s were seemingly invulnerable, for all that they infuriated the Soviets.

The British were involved too. One of Britain's most closely guarded secrets of the Cold War was that at least four RAF pilots were decorated for their part in the CIA's U-2 spy plane missions over the Soviet Union. The leader of the RAF U-2 detachment, Wing Commander Robert Robinson, spoke of his role before he died. 'In 1958 this was the most secret operation in the world and the British involvement most secret of all.'

In order to emphasise American denials of the operation, the U-2 planes were formally transferred on paper to the British government. President Eisenhower wrote a top-secret letter to Harold Macmillan stating: 'British missions are carried out on your authority and are your responsibility.'

And the flights remained a secret in Britain, too. The pilots were no longer paid by the RAF, but 'off the books' by MI6, and the press was told the men were helping the Americans with 'high-altitude weather-sampling missions'.

The number of U-2 overflights by the British remains a secret, but it is probably four – all personally approved by the Prime Minister. The first mission was flown by Robinson on 6 December 1959, over the Kapustin Yar missile test range and a squadron of long-range bombers in the Ukraine.

It was a huge success and proved the Soviets did not have as many bombers as they claimed – a vital piece of intelligence at the height of the Cold War. The head of the CIA called Robinson's bomber picture 'a million-dollar photo'. The U-2s proved their value yet again a year later when they photographed the SS-6, a monster Soviet missile which, despite American fears over its capability as an inter-continental ballistic missile (ICBM), was obviously liquid-fuelled and therefore merely a slow, clumsy rocket.

All that ended on 1 May 1960 when Major Gary Powers of the USAF (who had been 'sheep dipped' – in the jargon, to have ostensibly retired from the USAF to become a 'civilian contractor' for the CIA) was tasked to fly a CIA-controlled U-2 from Peshawar in Pakistan heading northwest over the Soviet Union to Bodo in Norway. On the way he would overfly the possible new ICBM bases at Plesetsk and Tyuratam.

Something went horribly wrong. The U-2 has a very narrow operating envelope at altitude. Ten knots too fast and the plane's delicate structure begins to break up; ten knots too slow and it will stall and fall out of the sky. For safety at 70,000 feet, pilots *have* to rely on the autopilot. Boredom is the biggest problem for a pilot on a nine-hour flight in a nice warm cockpit, on the dark edge of a black stratosphere with only the hiss of his breathing in his ears. It was not unknown for U-2 pilots to read a book or sing to keep awake.

The Russians had detected Powers' Black Lady as soon as it crossed their border and were tracking it on their radar screens as the U-2 cruised northwest, east of the Urals. MiG interceptors struggled for height and, frustrated, fell away far below. The U-2 sailed on serenely. What happened next remains a mystery. According to Powers, near Sverdlovsk a SA-2 Guideline missile suddenly detonated nearby and blew off part of the U-2's tail. The U-2 began to fall out of the sky.

Powers made three serious mistakes on his intelligence flight across Russia. He had failed to operate the U-2's self-destruct mechanism, thereby giving the USSR a present – albeit as a monster jigsaw – of a top-secret aeroplane and all its equipment. Secondly, his failure to kill himself with the poison needle so thoughtfully provided by his CIA handlers meant that the KGB interrogators could roll their sleeves up and get to work. And last, but no means least, his failure wrecked the 1960 Four Powers Summit in Paris. Khrushchev confronted an embarrassed Eisenhower, proved that the American President was lying and then walked out. Photographic Reconnaissance – gone wrong – had ruined any chance of an historic US–USSR rapprochement in the Cold War.

The usual well-publicised Soviet show trial followed. Powers 'confessed all' in the dock at Moscow and got three years of imprisonment plus seven of hard labour. Two years later he was exchanged for the imprisoned Soviets' illegal KGB '*rezident*' in North America, Colonel Rudolf Abel. There were no more U-2 overflights after Powers'. It was the twenty-fourth, and last, illegal U-2 flight over the USSR. From then on the USA relied on their newly developed programme of spy satellites flying in space, well above any one country, to peer down Soviet chimneys.

The US and UK were not the only ones to try and snoop on their neighbours. The French, Swedes and Germans all attempted to collect aerial photographs of Soviet targets. The USSR preferred using civil airliners to conduct secret Cold War spying missions over Europe. Aeroflot planes would regularly switch off their transponders (which helped air traffic controllers to identify their position) and then wander way off their filed flight plans to carry out aerial intelligence-gathering missions over sensitive targets.

In a memorandum marked 'Secret UK-US Eyes Only', in December 1981, Secretary of State for Defence John Nott informed Prime Minister Margaret Thatcher that the RAF was monitoring the hundreds of monthly flights through UK airspace by Warsaw Pact airliners.

One incident of particular interest took place on 9 November 1981, when an Aeroflot IL62 made an unauthorised and unannounced descent from 35,000 feet to 10,000 feet, just below cloud level, to fly over RAF Boulmer, a radar station currently being modernised. It subsequently climbed back to 37,000 feet.

During this manoeuvre its secondary surveillance radar, which automatically broadcasts the aircraft's height, was switched off, though it was on before and after the incident. It must, therefore, be assumed that it was switched off intentionally to conceal a deliberate and premeditated manoeuvre.

Our investigations have now revealed it was the same aircraft which overflew the USN base at Groton when the first Trident submarine was being launched. You will recall that as a result of this incident the President banned Aeroflot flights over the USA for a short period.

CHAPTER 19

Photographic Reconnaissance in Action – The Cuban Missile Crisis

Photographic Reconnaissance's finest moment arguably came in 1962 when it revealed the existence of Soviet nuclear missiles in Cuba, sparking off the Cuban Missile Crisis. There had been several HUMINT reports of a mysterious Soviet build-up in Cuba and Colonel Oleg Penkovsky, the double agent in the GRU, working for the CIA and MI6, (see page 112) reported details of some planned missile placements. But it was technical intelligence – aerial photography – that provided the conclusive proof needed by the Kennedy administration. On 14 October 1962 a U-2 overflight brought back 928 pictures confirming an SS-4 Soviet nuclear missile site under construction at San Cristóbal, in western Cuba.

This Cold War bombshell unleashed what can only be described as a full-scale photo-recce blitz. The Navy and Marine Corps pilots flying the fast RF-8A Crusader, with its five cameras, and USAF pilots flying the RF-101 reconnaissance version of the Voodoo fighter, blasted low over Cuba and brought back spectacular photography.

As soon as each low-level mission landed and delivered its film to the squadron and wing photo labs, it was developed and flown to Washington and to other photographic analysis centres. The nerve centre for the US reconnaissance effort at the time was the Joint Reconnaissance Center (JRC) in the Pentagon, which provided the President and his war cabinet committee with daily large-scale photographic documentation of the Soviet build-up. On 25 October the US used these images as photographic evidence in briefing America's formal case to the UN Security Council. The photographs were confirmed by images of Soviet freighters lumbering towards Cuba with what were obviously missiles under wraps on their decks.

The regular photo recce missions that provided these images were extremely dangerous and risked escalating the crisis beyond the control of either side, should anyone open fire. Sure enough, on 27 October, a U-2 piloted by USAF Major Rudolf Anderson was shot down by an SA-2 Guideline SAM missile launched from Cuba and Anderson was killed. Later that day, several US Navy RF-8A Crusader aircraft on low-level photo reconnaissance missions were fired upon. This was the high spot of the crisis. The USAF's cigar-chomping General Curtis LeMay recommended an all-out attack on Cuba. President Kennedy declined and instead ordered overflights every two hours to update the intelligence picture and to bring pressure to bear for a solution.

Fortunately for the world, saner counsels than Curtis LeMay's Dr. Strangelove-like views on how to prosecute the Cold War prevailed. We now know that, behind the scenes, the Soviets had indicated they were happy to do a deal: if the US removed its Jupiter nuclear missiles from Turkey, then the Kremlin would remove its missiles from Cuba. Both sides backed away from war, although Kennedy, ever conscious of his political image, insisted that no public mention should be made of his promise to the Soviet premier that the US would withdraw America's missiles from Turkey. After all, with an election coming up, he didn't want it to get out to the voters that the hero of the hour had blinked and backed down over Cuba just as Khrushchev had ...

The crisis of 1962 changed the emphasis in modern intelligence from human to technical intelligence collection. The reasons were clear to all. Classical HUMINT could only offer so much and the successes of photographic reconnaissance showed that it could fill in the vital intelligence gaps.

There is, however, one aspect of intelligence in which the increased prominence of technical intelligence, be it photographic images, radar, or electronic surveillance, can never guarantee success: and that is the interpretation of the capabilities it has identified. TECHINT will show us what the adversary has and where it is; but the key question is always, what does he intend to do with it? Intentions are still best tracked by HUMINT and Communications Intelligence (COMINT).

The demise of the U-2 as a high-altitude collector of photographic intelligence was paralleled by two complementary developments: the SR-71 Blackbird and the coming of age of satellites. Kelly Johnson, Lockheed's brilliant designer, and the brains behind the U-2, began research into an aircraft that could fly at an unheard of speed and height and would also be virtually invisible to radar. By 1966 he and his Skunk Works team succeeded. The extraordinary SR-71 Blackbird made its first mission. Built of titanium, with radar-reflecting composite material, and a shape that reflected radar signals, the SR-71 was like no other aircraft.

At 80,000 feet and 2,000 miles per hour it was effectively invulnerable. Its six high-definition optical cameras could photograph a hundred-thousand-square miles in an hour with a resolution that could identify a hole on a golf course. The SR-71 also carried infrared imagery systems; sideways-looking airborne radar (SLAR); plus electronic intelligence gathering systems as well as a Fairchild tracking camera and an HRB Singer infrared camera.

The most advanced camera systems were located either in the wing chines or the interchangeable nose. Wide-area imaging was provided by two operational objective cameras (OOCs), which provided stereo imagery across the width of the flight track, or an optical bar camera (OBC), which gave continuous horizon-to-horizon coverage. In later years the radar was replaced by an advanced synthetic-aperture radar system (ASARS-1) and a specialist electronic intelligence called the electromagnetic reconnaissance system (EMR), which could collect and analyse every electronic signal the plane flew through and was pre-programmed to identify items of interest. By the time the SR71 finished its operational life it could download its intelligence data in real time. A digital data-link system could send ASARS-1 and ELINT data from about 2,000 miles of track coverage to the photo interpreter sitting in a suitably equipped ground station as the flight progressed.

The Blackbird was quite simply a world-beater and stood as the ultimate photo and electronic reconnaissance aircraft of its day. But, remarkable as it was, even the Blackbird was starting to become obsolescent by the 1980s. Satellites could provide better information, using high-resolution electro-optical scanners, millimetric wavelength radar, and infrared thermal images. Nowadays, advanced cameras can see through clouds and even work at night. Moreover, the process of interpreting images has been digitised. Photos from space are now in real time. Satellites can film with infrared high-tech software that lets analysts zoom in, enhance the quality and make other adjustments. Lockheed Martin's Skunk Works has confirmed that it hopes to develop an SR-72 spy plane. The SR-72 will be a hypersonic unmanned aircraft capable of Mach 6, or just over 4,500 miles per hour using scramjet engines. At hypersonic speeds, the SR-72 will be able to traverse any continent in around an hour. At an operational altitude of over 80,000 feet and at Mach 6, the SR-72 will be almost impossible to shoot down. A missile climbing at Mach 2 will take at least two minutes to reach 80,000 feet and, in that time, the SR 72 will already be fifty miles away.

It is all a long way from the simple photographic cameras of the first two world wars. In the digital age, the electronic equipment inside a modern reconnaissance aircraft now costs more than the plane itself. Modern hi-tech intelligence does not come cheap.

Photographic Reconnaisance provided invaluable information of Soviet developments throughout the latter years of the Cold War as well as collecting intelligence on a wealth of other US intelligence targets all over the globe. It also rammed home the point that aeroplanes have at least two major advantages over satellites: in a crisis they can be placed over the target more quickly and a lot more cheaply.

However, the fact that aerial reconnaissance still remains a dangerous business was demonstrated when, in April 2001, a Lockheed EP-3E ARIES II was forced to make an emergency landing in China after a J-8II interceptor fighter collided with the Navy plane. The Chinese pilot, conducting foolishly aggressive manoeuvres to intimidate the US aircrew, managed to collide with the EP-3E and was killed. The crew survived, thanks to the skill of the pilot, who managed to make an emergency landing of the damaged Lockheed on Hainan

Island. The twenty-four crewmembers were detained and interrogated by the Chinese authorities until a statement was delivered by the United States government regarding the incident.

The Lockheed four-engined EP-3E, along with the British Nimrod and the French Atlantique, was a workhorse of maritime reconnaissance and able, as a Maritime Patrol Aircraft (MPA), to accomplish missions that even the SR 71 could not. With its ability to loiter over the sea for hours and make low passes, it could spot and hunt submarines as well as taking pin-sharp oblique photographs of possible enemy ships, revealing their weapons and radars, for photographic interpreters ashore to study in detail.

Its land-based counterpart, the latest version of the sixty-year-old English Electric Canberra, now completely redesigned and rebuilt for the digital age as the 'WB 57', has a different mission and can operate from up to 80,000 feet. This remarkable aircraft is configured to conduct reconnaissance missions with equipment that includes interferometric synthetic-aperture radar, magnetic-field mapping, gravity-field mapping and hyperspectral imaging. This combination of cheaper aerial platforms that can be deployed quickly and very high-tech imaging equipment, now allied to reconnaissance satellites, meant that photographic reconnaissance's time had come.

CHAPTER 20

On Satellites

As early as 1946, more than eleven years before *Sputnik 1*, history's first artificial space satellite, went into orbit the US Project RAND released a remarkably prescient report: Preliminary Design of an Experimental World-Circling Spaceship (SM-11827).

Although it was the US Navy that first mooted the idea of space satellites, the then Major General Curtis E. LeMay USAF insisted that space operations were just an extension of air operations and tasked Project RAND to undertake a wider feasibility study. The resulting reports noted:

> Since mastery of the elements is a reliable index of material progress, the nation which first makes significant achievements in space travel will be acknowledged as the world leader in both military and scientific techniques ... A satellite vehicle with appropriate instrumentation can be expected to be one of the most potent scientific tools of the twentieth century. The achievement of a satellite craft would produce repercussions comparable to the explosion of the atomic bomb ...

Thus the space race was born.

Little could the science fiction writer Arthur C. Clarke, often quoted as having come up with the concept of the communications satellite, have realised that his 1945 article titled 'Extra-terrestrial Relays' in the British magazine *Wireless World* would spawn a revolution in global communications, intelligence, and mapping. Clarke's article described the fundamentals behind the deployment of artificial satellites in geostationary orbits to relay radio signals.

Despite the optimistic RAND report little progress was made in the following decade. For a long time the USAF did not believe that the satellite could be a military weapon. They only saw its potential as a tool for communications, and science. In 1954, the US Secretary of Defense stated publicly, 'I know of no American satellite program.'

It was only in 1955, as part of American plans for the International Geophysical Year 1957–58 that the White House publicly announced that the US intended to launch satellites by the spring of 1958. This became known as Project Vanguard. Shortly afterwards the Soviet Union countered by announcing that they intended to launch a satellite by the autumn of 1957.

After that the pace of satellite development accelerated. In early 1956 President Eisenhower established an Intelligence Advisory Board, who urged the development of a reconnaissance satellite. The Air Force's WS-117L project showed promise as it offered multipurpose technical reconnaissance capabilities. The planned satellite included a SIGINT payload, an imagery intelligence (IMINT) payload in which film from onboard cameras could be scanned and transmitted to ground stations, and a hard-copy camera system by which film would be returned to earth via a re-entry capsule. Hard-copy photographs were important because their resolution would be pin-sharp, unlike the fuzzy electronically transmitted images, which were comparable to 425-line black-and-white television at best.

The Advisory Board was, however, concerned about the pace of the satellite programme, which they believed was too slow to meet the threat presented by the Soviets. They directed that priority be given to the USAF WS-117L project and concentrated on the technology of hard-copy film recovery.

The Americans were right to be worried about the Soviets' progress. On 4 October 1957, to the world's amazement, the USSR launched a football-sized satellite called *Sputnik 1* into orbit. The global propaganda impact was enormous as the 22-inch diametre sphere, weighing 190.5 pounds, passed overhead making electronic beeping noises. The

Soviets followed up their scientific triumph when, a month later, TASS, the Russian news agency announced the launch of *Sputnik 2*.

This second satellite was a 507 kg, 1.2 metres-long cone. In addition to the scientific measuring instruments, it carried a live dog called Laika inside a pressurised cabin. Laika was the first animal to reach the upper layers of the atmosphere. The message was clear; if a dog could do it, then so could a man. Sadly, the good-natured mongrel bitch only made a one-way journey. Her planned launch was never designed to be followed by a recovery from orbit.

However, the launch of *Sputnik* and its display of Soviet technical power caused serious concern in the United States. Any rocket capable of launching such a payload into earth orbit was equally capable of carrying a nuclear weapon and acting as an ICBM. America was shocked by the sudden turn of events, and the Cold War ratcheted up another notch.

Desperate to catch up, the United States managed to launch their first satellite, *Explorer 1*, on 31 January 1958. The programme was driven by the need to be able to detect any Soviet nuclear build-up and, more important still, to give any warning of a Soviet missile launch.

The First IMINT Satellite started under the name Discoverer as part of the follow-on work on the USAF's 1956 WS-117L satellite reconnaissance and protection programme, soon to be renamed Corona.

The Discoverer/Corona programme carried out thirty-eight public launches and achieved many technological breakthroughs. *Discoverer 1*, launched in February 1959, was the world's first polar-orbiting satellite. The first mission returned with 3,000 feet of film (more than the entire U-2 program up to then), covering 1.65 million square miles of Soviet territory. *Discoverer II*, launched in April of 1959, was the first satellite able to be:

Stabilised in orbit in all three axes

Manoeuvered on command from the earth

Separate a re-entry vehicle on command

Send its re-entry vehicle back to earth

These characteristics meant that the US now had the potential for a new technical intelligence collection source, parked overhead in space. *Discoverer 8*, launched in August of 1960, ejected a capsule that was subsequently recovered from the Pacific Ocean, the first successful recovery of a man-made object ejected from an orbiting satellite. It was *Discoverer 9* that inaugurated the age of satellite reconnaissance when its discharged film capsule was recovered in the air over the Pacific by a specially-modified JC-130 aircraft, making it the first successful aerial recovery of an object returned from orbit. Satellite reconnaissance was now filling a crucial strategic intelligence gap because, after the Gary Powers U-2 debacle, President Eisenhower had suspended all overflights of the USSR.

The Corona programme continued in secret until 1972 (the date of the last film recovery), with 144 launches. The growing importance of the satellite reconnaissance and intelligence was recognised in 1961 when the White House ordered that all satellite reconnaissance programmes would come under a new intelligence agency, the National Reconnaissance Office (NRO).

The NRO operated several different versions of Corona during the program's lifetime, introducing different camera systems and making improvements. Eventually these so-called 'Keyhole' (KH) missions could produce imagery with 5–7-foot resolution. It was Keyhole imagery from the Corona series that showed that the Soviets had far fewer strategic missiles and bombers than had been originally thought. For the remainder of the Cold War, technical intelligence from satellite IMINT, combined with SIGINT, consistently gave US officials accurate estimates of how many missiles, bombers, and submarines the Soviet Union really had.

The second satellite programme to evolve from WS 117L was called SAMOS, and was intended to carry a heavier reconnaissance payload. Four of the eleven SAMOS launches failed and the image quality was poor. As a result, the programme was stopped in 1962. SAMOS was accompanied by MIDAS early warning surveillance satellites stationed in geosynchronous orbit over Soviet missile sites. However by 1974 the Department of Defense had developed a new system called GAMBIT, with a '77-inch focal length camera for providing specific information on scientific and technical capabilities that threatened the nation', according to the NRO.

Later GAMBITs carried a state-of-the-art reconnaissance pack, including a 175-inch focal length camera with a resolution of less than two feet, and the ability to process, transmit, and receive electronic signals while on mission, thus allowing dissemination of near real-time digital imagery for targeting and strategic threat.

As the Cold War turned even more dangerous in the mid 1960s, American planners conceived a new and highly advanced satellite codenamed 'Hexagon'. Hexagon was an extraordinarily ambitious project to place a huge spy satellite into space to look into the very backyards of the Soviet Union and Communist China. At the time (1967), it was the most classified project in America. It was also the most unlikely. Joseph Prusak, who had worked as an engineer on earlier civilian space projects, spent six months waiting for his security clearance, working in what the hirees called the 'Mushroom Tank' (because they were kept in the dark about what their new jobs were to be). When he was finally cleared and briefed on Hexagon, Prusak wondered if he had made the biggest mistake of his life.

The massive KH-9 Hexagon spy satellite was the largest satellite up to that time. 'I thought they were crazy,' Prusak said. 'They envisaged a satellite that was 60-foot (18-metres) long and 30,000 pounds (13,600 kilograms) and supplying film at speeds of 200 inches (500 centimetres) per second. The precision and complexity blew my mind.' Not for nothing was the Hexagon dubbed, 'Big Bird'. The plan to fire something weighing fifteen tons and the length of two busses into space was, in 1970, almost beyond belief. The project suffered a serious setback on its first launch when the delivery rocket blew up on the pan. Undaunted, the American intelligence agencies persisted. They knew that, potentially, they had a game changer on their hands.

Earlier space spy satellites such as Corona and Gambit were at least a whole generation – if not two – behind the plans for Hexagon. But neither offered the resolution nor sophistication of Hexagon, which was intended to take thousands of high-resolution pictures of Soviet missiles, submarine pens and air bases, even of individual bombers, missile silos and army units on exercise.

Later launches were more successful. Early Hexagons could stay up for 124 days but, as the satellites became more sophisticated, follow-on missions were extended to last for up to five months in space. The key to the missions' success was the satellites' revolutionary imagery package. The so-called 'Key Hole' system was built around a suite of new cameras with a panoramic 'optical bar' designed by Phil Pressel. Much later, Pressel explained his motivation to work on the Hexagon. 'I never wanted to work on an offensive weapon system, something that would kill people. I am happy that I always worked on reconnaissance or intelligence projects, projects that secured our country.' The result of his lifelong secret, one of the United States' most closely guarded intelligence assets, was a behemoth larger than a London bus: the now declassified KH 9 spy satellite.

One of his revolutionary rotating cameras looked forward of the long thin satellite as the other looked aft, thus capturing detailed imagery in stereo, with a *declared* resolution of about two to three feet. (Insiders hinted that it could spot and photograph much smaller objects.) The Hexagon's twin optical-bar panoramic-mirror cameras rotated as they swept back and forth while the satellite flew over earth, a process that intelligence officials referred to as 'mowing the lawn'. The results were astonishing. According to the National Reconnaissance Office, one *single* Hexagon frame could cover a swathe of 370 nautical miles (680 kilometres) – about the distance from London to Köln, or Washington to Cincinnati.

The film was recovered by dropping film return-capsules for recovery. A specially equipped aircraft would try and catch the return capsule in mid-air by snagging its parachute as it floated to earth after the film canister's re-entry. However, the very first recovery of the 'film bucket' from a KH-9 Hexagon in spring 1972 went badly wrong. The Air Force recovery aircraft failed to snag the parachute and the capsule, with its vital load of high-resolution photographs of the Soviet Union's submarine bases and missile silos, plunged into the sea to sink to the bottom of the Pacific Ocean.

The Americans were undaunted by the failure. In a remarkable feat of Cold War clandestine ingenuity, the US Navy's deep submergence vehicle *Trieste II* managed to locate and recover the film bucket and its priceless cargo at a depth of nearly 16,000 feet.

After that the Keyhole success rate increased and the KH Series satellites became a vital part of the US intelligence effort, as the Cold War went into its increasingly expensive end game and America ratcheted up the price of staying in the fight. The Soviets were increasingly falling behind in the race for eyes in the sky. By the early 1980s they were unable to invest enough to keep up with burgeoning American technology, especially as the NRO developed the Keyhole programme to operate the KH-8 Gambit 3 and KH-9 Hexagon in tandem, teaming up to photograph areas of military significance in both the Soviet Union and China. The KH-9 would make the first pass, imaging a wide swathe of terrain, to be scrutinised by imagery intelligence analysts on the ground looking for so-called 'targets of opportunity'. Once these potential targets were identified, a KH-8 would then be manoeuvred over the target to photograph the precise location in much higher resolution.

The Hexagon's final launch in April 1986 met with disaster just like the very first launch, as the spy satellite's Titan 34D booster erupted into a massive fireball just seconds after lift-off, crippling the NRO's orbital reconnaissance capabilities for many months. However, by then, the Hexagon satellites' early warning job was nearly over as the USSR slid into economic and eventually political ruin.

NASA's Rob Landis was unequivocal about the contribution satellites made to US and Allied intelligence during the Cold War: 'You have to give credit to leaders like President Eisenhower who had the vision to initiate reconnaissance spacecraft, beginning with the Corona and Discoverer programs,' Landis said. 'He was of the generation who wanted no more surprises, no more Pearl Harbors. Frankly, I think that Gambit and Hexagon helped prevent World War Three.'

Few would disagree. The 1970s programme of Rhyolite/Aquacade satellites were designed specifically to intercept Soviet and Chinese microwave relay signals traffic, much of which missed the receiving dish and, because of the curvature of the Earth, carried on into space. By placing a satellite in a geosynchronous orbit at a position in the sky where it could intercept and catch the beam, the US government was able to listen in on Soviet telephone calls and telex cables during the Cold War. Even the Kremlin's car-phone system was vulnerable.

It was not just SIGINT. Jimmy Carter was astonished, on coming into the White House in 1977, to be presented by the CIA with a series of pin-sharp photographs of the movement of tanks in Poland in real time. The images had been taken by the latest KH 11 satellite. Carter was delighted at the intelligence that satellites could now provide to him as Commander-in-Chief. From then on the US satellite budget has always been safe.

In 1991, the role of intelligence was revolutionised by the Gulf War. Satellite intelligence was used to provide warning of Scud attacks, to target Patriot anti-missile rockets, to provide weather data, aid with land navigation and aerial bombardment, and serve as a communication channel. The growing struggle against Islamic jihadi terrorists has also seen a heavy reliance upon satellite imagery and electronic intelligence in efforts to trace the movements of key terrorist leaders and identify targets.

This switch from strategic to tactical intelligence has brought with it enhanced capabilities for reconnaissance satellites. For example, the US government's hunt for, and elimination of, the al Qaeda leader Osama bin Laden could only have been accomplished with real-time satellite surveillance.

And where the US led, other countries have followed; every nation with the technical prowess and financial resources now has satellites in space, from communications satellites to GPS navigation systems, as well as the numerous intelligence platforms. Foremost among them is Israel, which, unwilling to rely on the US for its satellite images, launched its first reconnaissance satellite in April 1995. Japan has also acted on its own regional security concerns and launched reconnaissance satellites; its first launch was in 2003, specifically to keep an eye on China and North Korea. Germany, France, Italy, Spain, India, and Pakistan have all become owners of the most expensive intelligence-collection assets in history.

Inevitably, much of the work and technology of the satellite intelligence programmes has been highly classified and we can only guess at the very latest intelligence collection systems. One satellite intelligence programme, however, has been well aired in the world's press: the US-controlled ECHELON system.

ECHELON first made the news in 1988 when a Lockheed employee, Margaret Newsham, admitted to a US Congressman that the telephone calls of a US senator were being collected by the NSA. Congressional investigators determined that 'targeting of U.S. political figures would not occur by accident, but was designed into the system from the start'. Later that year, British investigative journalist Duncan Campbell wrote an article for the *New Statesman* called 'Somebody's listening', outlining the signals intelligence gathering activities of ECHELON. By 1996 the cat was truly out of the bag. Nick Hager, a New Zealand journalist provided specific details about the ECHELON satellite surveillance system, claiming that it was a joint UK–US–Canadian–Australian system that could eavesdrop on any telephonic communication.

In 2000 a former Director of the CIA confirmed that US intelligence uses interception systems and keyword searches to monitor European businesses. This prompted the European Parliament to investigate the ECHELON surveillance network. The US refused to meet the members of a European investigating committee, and the BBC reported that, 'The US Government still refuses to admit that Echelon even exists.'

According to the whistle blowers – or traitors, depending on your point of view – ECHELON and its follow-on systems such as PRISM, DISHFIRE, TURBULENCE and MYSTIC still exist, now with enhanced capabilities to monitor, intercept, and record telephonic and email transmissions, as well as any other communications in the electronic sphere. If ECHELON's intelligence collection capabilities in 2001 were described as 'awesome', then there is hard evidence that that Big Brother's electronic ear is today even more powerful: a conclusion that raises serious questions for the citizen's right to privacy, democratic politicians and lawyers.

That the post-ECHELON systems exist is not in doubt. In 2012 a Royal Canadian Navy intelligence officer, Sub Lieutenant Jeffrey Delisle, was sentenced to twenty years after pleading guilty to having downloaded and sold information from the Codeword (the security level above top secret) STONEGHOST communications interception system to the GRU, Russia's military intelligence agency.

TYPES OF RECONNAISANCE SATELLITE

Along with the all-important communications and GPS navigation satellites, there are four other types of military reconnaissance satellites.

1. Optical-imaging satellites that have light sensors in the visible light, infra-red and ultra violet spectrum that can 'photograph' objects and weapon systems down to the size of a tennis ball. They can identify targets, make maps and also spot dangerous events like enemy missile launches.

2. Radar-imaging satellites aimed at the same targets that can observe the Earth using different radar wavelengths, even through cloud cover, to cover targets invisible to visible light, infra-red and ultra violet spectrum imagery.

3. Signals-intelligence, or ELINT-ferret, satellites to collect the radio, microwave and electronic transmissions emitted from any country on Earth.

4. Relay satellites that speed military satellite communications around the globe by transmitting data from spy satellites to ground stations on Earth. Most military satellites can now transmit intelligence in real time.

All these satellites can be launched into a regular movable orbit, or can be positioned to hover above a single target on the globe's surface in what is known as a geosynchronous (geostationary)orbit

The digital age and modern communications systems have taken satellite and intelligence collection to new heights, in every sense. Until its retirement in 2011, modern intelligence satellites were intercepted and refuelled in space using the Space Shuttle, whose design was specifically tailored to include a cargo bay big enough to recover and repair America's intelligence collectors in space. Intelligence agencies and decision makers now rely almost entirely on satellites for their technical intelligence.

Today's satellites still have five major roles as intelligence collection sources: early warning, to provide warning of an attack by detecting ballistic missile launches; detecting nuclear explosions on the ground and in space; photo surveillance, (IMINT) to provide images from space using a variety of sensors that can see through cloud using synthetic aperture radar and millimetric radar as well as spectral imaging; intercepting electronic-reconnaissance radio waves across all frequencies (SIGINT); and radar imaging to identify and measure any particular equipment or systems of interest, (MASINT).

Inevitably, the market place has recognised the potential profitability of satellites. Literally thousands of commercial satellites now surround the earth, competing for commercial reconnaissance as well as communications. This broader role for reconnaissance satellites was recognised in 2005 when America's National Geospatial Intelligence Agency used information from US government satellites, commercial satellites, and airborne reconnaissance platforms to support hurricane-relief efforts and provide information to the Federal Emergency Management Agency.

With the end of the Cold War, private companies even began to sell declassified imagery as the distinction between government military satellites and commercial satellites disappeared. Since the 1990s, commercial vendors have entered the market and their modern, relatively high-resolution imagery from satellites offer an invaluable tool to commercial enterprises such as oil prospecting, geologists, weather forecasting, or crop production, as well as many other applications. And, since the advent of 'Google Earth' in 2005, we can now all gain access to free satellite imagery. Google's systems are capable of excellent resolution — down to less than half a metre; and even that is rumoured to be limited only by US government restrictions to prevent the image quality from getting *too* good.

Today the NRO and its fellow intelligence agencies operate ground stations around the world that collect and distribute intelligence gathered from reconnaissance satellites, both imagery and electronic. Along with the National Geospatial-Intelligence Agency (NGA), with its primary mission of collecting, analysing, and distributing geospatial intelligence (GEOINT) in support of national security requirements,

US hi-tech satellite intelligence has reached a new level, providing comprehensive GEOINT for US military and intelligence efforts, as well as assistance during natural and man-made disasters, and even security planning for major events such as the Olympic Games. It was the NGA that was credited by the White House and Pentagon with providing critical intelligence for Operation Neptune's Spear in 2011, when United States SEALS raided a secret compound in Abbottabad, Pakistan, and killed Osama Bin Laden.

However, just as satellites seemed poised to take over the role of image collectors entirely, there was a significant development in the field of reconnaissance *aircraft*. In the last twenty years new Unmanned Aerial Vehicles (UAVs) have been developed for imagery and signals intelligence. These drones are significant because they give the decision maker and the battlefield commander an 'eye in the sky' without, crucially, risking an expensive and vulnerable pilot. Moreover, modern UAVs are relatively cheap, they are flexible, they can stay aloft for hours and they provide a remarkable cost-effective force multiplier for commanders at all levels.

For example, at the time of writing (2015) the USAF's RQ-4A Global Hawk is a high-altitude, long-endurance, unmanned aerial reconnaissance system which can give field commanders high resolution, near real-time imagery of large geographic areas from thousands of miles away. It can carry out reconnaissance missions in support of all types of operations. With its 14,000 nautical-mile range and forty-two-hour endurance, combined with satellite and line-of-sight communication links to ground forces, the Global Hawk can operate anywhere in the world. High-resolution sensors, including visible and infrared electro-optical systems and synthetic aperture radar, will conduct surveillance over an area of 40,000 square nautical miles to an altitude of 65,000 feet in twenty-four hours.

Global Hawk is high-tech, big and expensive; but it is still a great deal cheaper and more flexible than rocket-launched satellites. Its smaller cousins are much cheaper still, and these smaller UAVs have the added advantage of being very hard to detect, and even more difficult to shoot down. Some are even expendable, designed to be abandoned once the mission is completed; others are small enough to be shaped like birds. But all have the capability of relaying intelligence images in real time to a commander at any level from a reconnaissance patrol to defence ministers.

Even Britain's cash strapped austerity MoD has confirmed that the most cost-effective way ahead for aerial reconnaissance is the UAV, announcing at the end of 2014 that Britain was adding extra Reaper remotely-piloted aircraft to its forces deployed to fight Islamic State militants.

In the twenty-first century, IMINT has come to dominate our lives and the battlefield, from space and from drones, whether we like it or not. Unless it is undercover, tucked away in a hangar, or out of sight, nowadays nothing is secret from the eye in the sky that is aerial reconnaissance.

PART SIX

INFORMATION INTO INTELLIGENCE

CHAPTER 21

On Collation: Vietnam and Tet Offensive

If Pearl Harbor in December 1941 represented a salutary example of the low point of a great nation failing to value intelligence properly (see page 245) and suffering grievously as a result, then it must be said that America learned rapidly from its mistakes. A formal national intelligence assessment staff was activated with the prime task of ensuring that the president and his advisers would always have access to the best and most timely information, whatever the cost. With the astonishing energy and sense of purpose that characterises the very best qualities of its people, the USA set about making sure that Washington would never be taken by surprise again by constructing a national intelligence service second to none.

The results were spectacular. By 1945 America had a fully developed worldwide signals intelligence capability, an international secret intelligence service, an effective clandestine operations capability and the best equipped aerial reconnaissance capability in the world. These assets were reflected in the increased priority given to intelligence within the individual armed services and were backed by a formidable array of expensive technical aids and highly trained specialists to make the whole thing work. It was a staggering achievement.

Theoretically, by the early 1960s, only twenty years after Pearl Harbor, the US authorities were masters of the most sophisticated, and certainly the best resourced, intelligence service in the world.

New and powerful intelligence agencies attracted new and powerful budgets. The consequence was that, by the 1960s, the competition for primacy between the US intelligence agencies had become the new US intelligence problem.

The problem of having too little intelligence scattered around became the problem of having too *much* intelligence from competing organisations and the struggle for its control. Each agency clung jealously to its own particular monopoly and kept it tightly 'compartmentalised', with the CIA trying, unsuccessfully, to become the overall master of US intelligence. A kind of competitive market economy had begun to dominate.

Ideally, a strong executive would direct such matters without argument. However, the US Constitution is specifically designed to make central authoritative control of just about anything very difficult to achieve. Add to this the irresistible lure of big defence contractors' dollars, systematised inducements ('lobbying') for elected politicians, regional demands for a share of the pork barrel of taxpayers' money, plus the competing demands of the armed services, and the internal battles over US intelligence become just another reflection of how Washington does business. Eisenhower's warning over the greed and influence of the 'military industrial lobby' was only too true.

The Vietnam War illustrated the problems only too clearly. By 1967 the Americans were on the road to victory. By massive use of force they had driven the Việt Cộng and North Vietnamese Liberation Army (NVA) headquarters out of South Vietnam and were bringing Hanoi to its knees. But the Americans were fighting a war on two fronts: the enemy in Vietnam and sceptical domestic opinion at home. It was in this atmosphere of impending defeat that the Communist cadres in North Vietnam met in July 1967 to plan one last major attack 'to mobilise the masses in South Vietnam'. The North Vietnamese leadership had been stunned by both the scale and success of the US intervention in Vietnam. Thus the Tet Offensive was born.

US intelligence was well aware of the coming storm. Indeed, in early January 1968 Military Assistance Command Vietnam's (MACV) Public Affairs Officer in Saigon actually issued a press release which amounted to the operation order for the Tet Offensive, based on a document captured by the US 101st Airborne Division in November 1967. The document included phrases like:

> Use very strong military attacks in conjunction with the local people to take over towns and cities. Troops should flood the lowlands ... and move towards liberating SAIGON, seize power and rally 'puppet' units to our side ...

It seems incomprehensible that, given this quality of intelligence, the US could have been taken by surprise by the Tet Offensive. Yet, with certain exceptions, General Giáp and Hanoi achieved complete *strategic* surprise.

The US Intelligence machine had one huge advantage in Vietnam. The US military had an almost limitless supply of knowledgeable, articulate, well-informed and highly cooperative 'country experts' on Vietnam: the South Vietnamese. Every document could be translated; every prisoner interrogated without delay; and the linguistic nuances, the Communist jargon and the regional prejudices of the country were completely transparent to US analysts – provided they consulted their allies. This was a remarkable trump card for any army fighting on foreign soil against an enemy with a difficult language and an alien culture.

A dizzying amount of intelligence flooded through this labyrinth of Vietnam intelligence organisations. The Combined Document Exploitation Centre (CDEC) – which, given the language problem, was an Army of the Republic of Vietnam (ARVN) fiefdom – was dealing with *half a million* pages of captured NVA material *every month*. But every blood-or faeces-smeared page had to be handled and read. The workload was huge.

The US problem was not that they lacked intelligence in Vietnam; they quite simply had too much.

Hanoi's desperate, last-ditch offensive took the American leadership by surprise. The principal reason was the nature of the US intelligence organisation: it was too compartmentalised, too big and slow, and went down at least ten different chains of command from the armed services, the CIA, DIA, the diplomats as well as the South Vietnamese. So, although the US knew every detail of the Tet Offensive

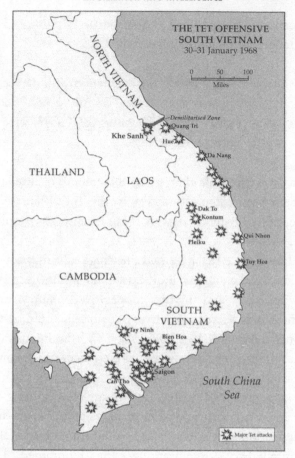

before it broke, it was unable to collate and disseminate a coherent warning in time.

The Tet Offensive was in fact a serious *military* defeat for the Communists, who lost 30,000 dead across Vietnam: but it was a complete PR disaster for the American administration. Their breezily confident predictions that the Việt Cộng were defeated and that 'the war was nearly won' blew up in their faces, with TV images of house-to-house fighting in Saigon and Hue as well as a series of country-wide attacks on US and South Vietnamese forces. Even the fortified US Embassy in Saigon was assaulted, although the attackers were cut down by the well armed defenders. For the NVA the Tet Offensive was nothing less than a bloody defeat: *but it didn't look like one on TV.*

And intelligence was to blame.

CHAPTER 22

On Interpretation: Yom Kippur

If a defeat caused by a catastrophic failure of intelligence such as Pearl Harbor can catapult a nation into creating a better organisation for ordering its affairs, then paradoxically a great victory assisted by brilliant intelligence can lead to complacency and an intelligence disaster further down the line. Thus, it proved for the small state of Israel in their mauling at the hands of the Arabs in October 1973.

On the Day of Atonement, 'Yom Kippur', 6 October 1973, the Syrians and Egyptians fell on the extended borders of 'greater Israel' and inflicted grievous losses on the surprised and shocked Israel Defense Forces (IDF). After a bitter struggle lasting eighty days, the invaders were flung back having suffered heavy losses, and Israeli territory recaptured, but the damage was done.

The myth of Israeli invincibility and intelligence omniscience, so carefully nurtured after the brilliant military successes of the Six-Day War in 1967, had been shattered for ever. The gallant little state that always triumphed over the odds, despite struggling for its very existence surrounded by hostile Arab neighbours, emerged as just another country caught by its adversaries with its trousers down because of intelligence blunders.

Often billed as a triumph of Arab deception, the Yom Kippur War is actually an example of a serious intelligence failure, because the Israelis were not really deceived by Syria and Egypt. The IDF and the Israeli elite deceived themselves. Israeli intelligence chose to insist on allowing its own narrative of what was going on to over-ride the evidence of their eyes. Israel's failure was essentially one of *interpretation.*

On 14 May 1948, the State of Israel was formally declared. On 15 May 1948, the armed forces of the Arab states of Egypt, Syria and Transjordan, Lebanon and Iraq fell on the new nation simultaneously in an all-out bid to destroy it at birth by pushing the cuckoo in the Middle East nest, as they saw Israel, straight back into the Mediterranean Sea.

They failed. With the courage of desperation and the moral fervour of their centuries-old crusade, the new Israelis flung back their Arab enemies at every point, despite being outnumbered many times over. Battered, defeated and licking their wounds, the Arab invaders retreated, astonished by the ferocity and fighting power of the Jewish state. So Israel was born in bloodshed and straight away tempered in the fire of victory on the battlefield. But the Arab nations never accepted this new state of affairs. Israel's very right to exist and its dispossession of the Palestinian people from their land became the irreconcilable poles of a dispute that has continued to this day.

Yet another war exploded in 1956, when the Israelis conspired with the French and British to attack Nasser's Egypt after he nationalised the Suez Canal. The result was the same as 1948: Arab humiliation, Israeli triumph. The sore festered on. In 1967, desperately outnumbered and surrounded by threatening Arab armies preparing to attack yet again, Israel struck first in one of the most dramatic pre-emptive strikes in the whole history of the bloody twentieth century. At dawn on 5 June 1967 the Israeli Air Force destroyed their Egyptian and Syrian counterparts on the ground and then, with total air superiority, threw the Syrians off the Golan Heights on Israel's northern border, captured Jerusalem from the Jordanians in the east, and seized the Gaza Strip plus the whole of the Sinai Peninsula from a soundly beaten and fleeing Egyptian Army in the south. 'Greater Israel' was born.

By 1968, for the first time since it came into being, Israel could feel territorially safe behind defensible borders. But, confronted by unwavering Arab hostility, these extended frontiers had to be manned and protected, like so many soldiers ranged along the battlements of a medieval castle. This was a heavy manpower and economic burden for a small country. It also obscured the fact that, especially in the south, Israel had lost her 'no man's land' or warning zone. Before 1967, Egyptian forces had to traverse 150 miles of Sinai desert to get at their Jewish opponents. Now all they had to do was cross 150 metres of the Suez Canal. This was to prove a crucial difference in 1973.

Israel realised that some real defensive barrier was now needed. Lieutenant General Haim Bar-Lev, the Chief of General Staff of the Israeli army, gave his name to what was to become a line of fixed fortifications along the length of the Suez Canal. The Bar Lev line eventually became a hundred-mile chain of sand-covered mutually supporting forts with deep shelters, minefields and weapon firing pits, backed by a maze of trenches, covered roads, water storage tanks and dug-in tanks and artillery. With the Bar Lev line, Israel had exchanged the flexible sweep of mobile armoured forces for her own desert version of the Maginot line. All this cost money. One estimate for the expenditure on defence infrastructure for Sinai in 1971 is half a billion US dollars at 1970s prices.

On 28 September 1970 President Nasser of Egypt died. At a stroke the mouthpiece of Arab Socialism, Pan-Arab Nationalism and the Soviet Union's principal client in the Arab World – the self-professed hammer of the Jewish State – was no more. His successor was Anwar Sadat.

Sadat was one of Nasser's original group of nationalist Egyptian officers who had led the revolution. A devout Muslim, he was more patient and thoughtful than the flamboyant and excitable Nasser. From the start he said quite openly that he realised that, for Egypt to achieve her goals, Egypt would have to fight.

Sadat's 'Year of Decision' started badly. The new President had funked his big battle in the 'Year of Destiny', claimed his detractors. However, while Sadat may not have attacked the Israelis, this was merely common prudence, not lack of resolution. Weeks turned into months as 1971 dragged on inconclusively.

Sadat realised that time was running out. In fact we can trace his frustration and his thinking very clearly in an address to the leaders of serious student riots in Cairo on 25 January 1972, just before he flew to Moscow for his inconclusive meeting with Brezhnev: '[the decision] to go to war against Israel has already been taken ... this is no mere words; it is a fact'.

The Soviets stalled. Arms supplies would be 'difficult'. Sadat emphasised the need for military action against the Israelis. The appalled Soviets, keen to encourage a policy of detente and anxious to avoid any further stand-offs between the superpowers, could not tolerate any resumption of fighting.

Sadat struck. The USSR had built up a massive military presence in Egypt by summer 1972. The air defence of Cairo was supplied by 200 Soviet jet fighters complete with Russian air and groundcrews. The SAM umbrella over the canal was manned by an estimated 12,000

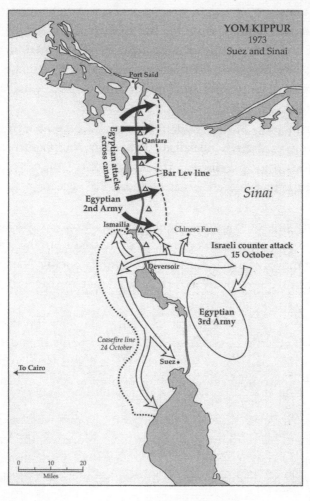

Soviet experts. In addition, there were five thousand other military advisers. 'The Soviets,' avowed one Egyptian officer, 'were everywhere'.

On 8 July 1972, Sadat summoned the Soviet Ambassador and told him that all, repeat all, Soviet personnel must be out of Egypt within ten days. With the Soviet Ambassador, Vinogradov, visibly palpitating with shock, Sadat left the meeting. Later he said, 'I felt that we all needed some kind of electric shock . . .' Sadat meant what he said. On 17 July, the Soviets began to pack their bags and leave.

The Soviet expulsions strengthened Sadat's domestic standing enormously. The army was glad to be rid of their patronising advisers, and the mosques were openly delighted to see the back of a pack of godless foreign atheists.

However, once the euphoria and sense of liberation had worn off, Sadat's concerns grew again. The gesture had not solved Egypt's real problems. Hoped-for peace feelers from the US and Israel failed to materialise. The Egyptian economy continued to be squeezed to near suffocation by the need to maintain the country as an armed camp. And social unrest (always a powerful attention-getter for Egyptian rulers) became an ever more serious threat.

Sadat had to do something to break the logjam before it was too late. Some time in late 1972, he made the fateful decision to attack Israel.

The first evidence of his resolution probably came at a closed meeting of the Arab Socialist Union Central Committee on 14 November 1972. From that moment, President Sadat's Egypt began planning to resume the long-running war with Israel by launching a full-scale surprise attack across the Suez Canal to seize limited chunks of occupied Sinai from the Israelis. The goals were mainly political. Israel would be given a 'short, sharp shock'.

Sadat realised that, alongside allies, he needed three things for his enterprise: money, guns and a diversion. The money came from the oil-rich Arab states, especially Saudi Arabia, who welcomed Sadat as a conservative bastion against the potential excesses of radical leaders like the wild-eyed Colonel Q'addafi of Libya. The guns and other arms could be acquired from the long-suffering Soviet Union. And the diversion would be provided by Egypt's partner in the humiliating defeat of 1967, Syria. In the last months of 1972, President Sadat of Egypt and President Assad of Syria began to build a secret military coalition to strike Israel with a surprise attack on two fronts simultaneously.

From the point of view of the Egyptian general staff planners, the Israel Defense Forces had five great advantages, only one of which could not be discounted. These were guaranteed arms supplies from the USA; a high preponderance of technological weapons systems; Western standards of training; and air superiority. Egypt could do little about Israel's fifth and final advantage. General Ismail, who had been charged with planning the assault, was realistic enough to accept that the Israeli people believed that if they were defeated in a war their country could not survive, and so would fight to the bitter end. The Egyptian commander therefore made sure that any plan of attack would be for limited objectives only. They would make no attempt to push Israel back into the sea. Instead the Egyptian battle plan called for a limited assault across the canal to seize ground and inflict a humiliating reverse on the Israelis. The political reverberations of this would then rumble around the world, which was all Sadat wanted; a political blow caused by a clear military success.

It is an irony of history that both sides tend to draw different lessons from the same war. The victors invariably tell themselves (and anyone else who will listen) that their success was entirely due to their brilliant generals, superb tactics, superior equipment and the matchless courage of their soldiers. The defeated tend to brood on their mistakes, note their enemy's strengths, try to work out just how their conquerors actually did it, and usually resolve to do their best to ensure that it will be their turn to get it right next time.

Thus, reasoned Ismail, would it be for the ever-victorious Israelis, revelling in the hubris of their 1967 successes and declaring triumphantly in a succession of media interviews, 'the Israeli Army is the best in the world . . . the Israeli Air Force has the most practised fighter pilots in the World . . .' This well-justified pride, amounting to arrogance, in the myth of Israeli martial superiority was founded on the very real triumphs and achievements of their armed forces.

Unfortunately it was also founded on one of the less attractive Zionist beliefs: that the Jews were in some way intrinsically superior to Arabs. Many leading Zionists viewed the Arabs as 'feudal, backward and pre-nationalistic people', This was a core belief of many pillars of Radical Socialist Zionism, like Weizmann and Jacobinsky. No-one dared to use the word '*untermenschen*', but the germ of that idea infected some elitist Israeli thinking.

But the Israelis also had other, more measurable weaknesses. To their perennial inability to sustain a long war or heavy casualties was added a new dimension: long lines of communication.

The Egyptian staff analysed Israel's strengths and weaknesses before coming up with an operational concept for the coming assault. The plan capitalised on the seven main conclusions of the Egyptian intelligence assessment:

1. Strike first by surprise to pre-empt the Israelis.

2. Use massive force on as wide a front as possible to disperse any attempt at a counter-attack.

3. Keep an air-defence umbrella over the ground troops at all times to protect them from the Israeli Air Force.

4. Force Israel to split and disperse resources between widely separated geographical combat areas.

5. Blunt any Israeli counter-attacks by emphasising defensive weapons and fighting from defensive positions.

6. Force Israel to incur heavy casualties.

7. Ensure that Egyptian forces had the most up-to-date and technologically superior weaponry to match Israeli systems.

The last requirement, for technologically advanced weapons, sent the Egyptians speeding back to Moscow, demanding either the latest MiG-23 fighter-bombers or SCUD missiles. It took time, but by autumn 1973, Sadat's troops had the hi-tech weapons called for by what had now been called Operation Badr.

Whatever key intelligence was collected by the Israelis was also distorted by a number of self-imposed misunderstandings of what was transpiring. These misconceptions had the effect of rendering those responsible for the interpretation of intelligence blind to the significance of the facts being presented to them. Chaim Herzog sardonically observed of the Israeli intelligence establishment of 1972–73 that 'eyes they have but they see not'. It was a perceptive summary of the failure of Israel's much vaunted intelligence system in the run-up to Yom Kippur, and one that the Agranat Commission made much of in its analysis of Israel's failure to anticipate the war.

The roots of the problem lay deep inside Israel's recent history and political organisation. Israel is a small country and intensely politicised, partly because her governments are elected by proportional representation. This made every cabinet an uncomfortable alliance of differing views and differing agendas. Coalition was a fact of government; but it was a much smaller 'kitchen cabinet', led by Golda Meir, the Prime Minister, that really ran the country.

In 1973 the only organisation that saw all the information that was collected, as well as processing and interpreting it ahead of briefing ministers was the army or, more accurately, Military Intelligence. Mossad ran overseas intelligence operations; Shin Beth, the equivalent of Britain's MI5, was limited to internal security; and the Foreign Ministry's Research and Evaluation Staff evaluated diplomatic traffic. All other intelligence – SIGINT, TECHINT, order of battle, logistics intelligence, foreign liaison sources, targeting, overhead reconnaissance and foreign country assessments – was either carried out by the military or controlled by their staff.

This unique situation had arisen because of Israel's growth as a warrior nation from the very start. In a nation under arms every crisis was, by definition, a military crisis. Representatives from Military Intelligence had always been dragged into the smoke-filled inner councils of Israeli prime ministers to say their piece. Even when briefing the cabinet, the minister of defence was always accompanied, not just by the chief of the armed forces, but also the head of Military Intelligence.

Somewhere between 1967 and 1973 the rigid line between

intelligence and policy in Israel became blurred. Some commentators claim it never really existed.

The situation was made worse by Golda Meir's working arrangements with Israeli intelligence. Members of the Agranat Commission were astonished to learn after the war that there was no direct contact between the Prime Minister and the head of Military Intelligence, except via the defence minister.

The Mossad and the armed services gathered data, and Military Intelligence screened and analysed it in conjunction with information from other sources, in order to make its assessments. However, the Mossad chief had been instructed to convey to Meir directly – immediately and without any intermediaries – any especially important material. Only those in the innermost counsels within Golda Meir's kitchen cabinet really knew what was going on. It was a small, highly secure, but potentially dangerous organisation.

With this dangerous arrangement institutionalised at the heart of its national affairs, Israel began to evaluate the first indications of an Egyptian build-up during 1973. From the start the whole process was bedevilled by political considerations imposed by Golda Meir's inner circle.

The first of these was a classic example of 'group think', supported by politicians and military alike. Israel in the early 1970s was awash with national pride and hubris, particularly the politicians and the soldiers. The Arab armies and air forces had received such a thrashing in 1967, ran the thinking, that they would never dare to take on the Israelis again unless two conditions were fulfilled. Egypt needed to be able to overcome Israeli air superiority before she would dare to attack, and only a joint Syrian and Egyptian attack could succeed. As neither condition was anywhere near to being fulfilled, reasoned the Israeli *bien pensants*, then Israel was safe from any serious threat. Certainly the Arabs would try to attack again. But not now. They were just not strong enough. These political judgements became Israeli national policy, overriding any contrary views culled from intelligence.

This astonishingly arrogant view of their adversaries actually had a name; in the offices of senior defence planners it was known as the 'Concept'. This 'Concept' was even peddled as a serious political deterrence policy when combined with Israel's new extended borders. By holding on to the 1967 gains, both territorial and psychological, Israel was in fact guaranteeing peace in the region. Or so it was argued.

This was a bold claim. Military Intelligence had crossed an invisible line and were now firmly cast in the role of 'policy advocates and not information assessors', in Edward Luttwak's phrase. But, as every thinking soldier knows, any enemy worth their salt is unlikely to have the good grace to conform to one's own cherished hopes and plans.

Other factors were working against Israeli Military Intelligence in the spring and summer of 1973. The first of these was the cost of mobilisation. For example, in May 1973 the Israeli Chief of Staff, David 'Dado' Elazar ordered a partial mobilisation, in response to a rising incidence of Egyptian attack indicators and the heightened regional tensions resulting from a PLO uprising in Lebanon and a civil war that looked like spilling over into northern Israel. But the May 1973 attack did not materialise. The partial mobilisation cost Israel $20 million, which the economy could ill afford. Caution, the 'Concept' and the high cost of any mobilisation began to corrupt the kind of answers that Israeli intelligence supplied.

Another factor that blunted intelligence assessments was the frequency of Egyptian mobilisations. Since Sadat had taken over three years before, there had been several major Egyptian escalations of tension leading to call-ups and serious troop redeployments in Egypt, all spotted and monitored by the ever vigilant collectors of Israel intelligence. In 1971, to calls from the Cairo press that 'war was inevitable', the Egyptians had mobilised, deployed their Army headquarters into the desert, called up reservists and civilian vehicles, and marched tanks and floating bridges towards the canal. Nothing happened. Like the Grand Old Duke of York, Sadat marched his legions back down again.

During the second major alert (in 1972) the interested Israelis watched the same thing unfold again, but this time without civilian mobilisation or bridges moving to the canal. Again, nothing happened. There were two more mobilisations in 1973. One in May, following the outbreak of fighting in Lebanon – to which Israel's General Elezar reacted so strongly; and the final one in October 1973 for Yom Kippur.

This drumbeat of regular mobilisation has an effect on intelligence observers. It de-sensitises them and conditions them to accept abnormal activity. Added to the constraining girdle of the 'Concept', plus a reluctance to be seen to cry wolf again – and be the cause of unnecessary expenditure – it is perhaps not surprising that the Israeli Military Intelligence were muffled and muzzled, falling into hypnotised inactivity when Sadat's final mobilisation was identified in early October 1973.

The Egyptians played on this in their deception plan for Operation Badr. They had three real secrets to conceal: their secret agreement with the Syrians for a simultaneous onslaught; their technical and other preparations for war; and the exact date and time of their attack. The last was relatively easy to do, for even the Egyptian commanders did not know. During 1973, Sadat kept changing his mind and post-poning 'Y-Day'.

So, even though the final broad arrangements were secretly agreed by the general staffs of Egypt and Syria on 1 April 1973, a senior Egyptian general was glumly playing up the problems by stating on 22 April that 'political and military problems [still] inhibit any joint action'.

In the middle of 1973, as the Egyptian secret build-up began to gather pace, the US State Department's INR (Intelligence and Research Bureau) produced an internal analysis of the Middle East situation. Unusually, it was a predictive document.

Intelligence agencies are frequently reluctant to engage in the haz-ardous business of making predictions (although one might think that is their prime task). The INR in Washington was different. It had been proved right in the long-running internecine battle between US intel-ligence agencies that had accompanied the Vietnam War, about which it had been determinedly pessimistic. 'I told you so,' is never popular, but it does attract a certain grudging respect for an organisation's or an individual's reliability. So it was with the INR's paper of June–July 1973 on the Middle East.

Although the document did not have the status of an NIE (national intelligence estimate) it drew broad support from the CIA, the INR's ally against the Panglossian assessments made by the military and the DIA regarding Vietnam. Both the CIA and the INR forecast a war in the Middle East by autumn 1973. Henry Kissinger, a man who generally believed he knew better than his own intelligence agencies and experts, disagreed. He not only ignored his own department's findings but joined Israeli intelligence and Golda Meir in misinterpreting the intelligence evidence. They believed that the Egyptians were building up their *defences*.

General Ismail's planning staff realised that the Israelis were bound to counter-attack any assault across the Suez Canal. This was established IDF doctrine and practice, and had almost always been successful in the past. These quick counter-attacks relied on two hammers to smash the Arab troops: air superiority overhead and a scythe of tanks and armour on the ground.

The Egyptians needed a defensive umbrella of surface-to-air missiles (SAMs) over the Suez Canal and extending into the Sinai desert, to cover their army as it crossed the canal.

On the ground the Israeli tanks could be relied upon to hurl themselves forward in furious counter-attacks against the Egyptian invaders. To blunt their effectiveness, the General Staff called for as many of the new Soviet anti-tank weapons as possible, especially the newest model of anti-tank guided missile (ATGM), known by its NATO identification as the Sagger. The small suitcase-sized wire-guided weapon could be carried by two men and worked by one. With a range in flat desert of 1,500–2,000 metres, a man hiding behind a rock could, by the early 1970s, track and kill a moving tank from over a mile distant. The ATGM was a formidable weapon. Suddenly every infantryman, suitably equipped, could become a long-range tank destroyer.

Although the intelligence analysts identified no fewer than one thousand of the secret Soviet SAM 6 missiles in Egypt and Syria, backed by dense belts of the SAM 3 and the older SAM 2, they were not unduly concerned. Let the stupid Arabs waste their money on defensive junk; Israel had no intention of attacking.

The third and final great secret the Egyptians strove to hide was the date and time of their attack. If, in Chaim Herzog's words, they were to fall on the Israelis like a 'wolf on the fold', then they had an absolute need for total security.

The date of the attack was the subject of considerable debate within the Arabs' general staff secret planning cell. The final decision was taken surprisingly late (in August 1973) only two months before Y-Day. The so-called 'Federal' (Syrian and Egyptian commanders) high command planning staff eventually decided on 6 October. The reasons were complex and a mixture of the practical and psychological.

October 6 would be a moonlit night, which offered many obvious practical benefits. The less tangible psychological reason had a massive significance for the Islamic World; 6 October that year was the tenth day of Ramadan and the anniversary of the Prophet Mohammed's victory at the Battle of Badr near Medina in AD 624, which established him as both a political and religious leader. The symbolism was obvious.

Egyptian junior officers and men only learned of the attack on the morning of 6 October, Y-Day itself, and even then, many of them thought that it was just the start of another day's exercises. In one case, an Egyptian assault engineer platoon only realised it was not an exercise when they were told to unload their rubber boats and put them in the canal, 'So we won't be going back to barracks tonight then, sir?' one soldier is supposed to have enquired of his commander as they began to paddle across the canal. In Chaim Herzog's words, 'The Egyptian planners had succeeded in misleading not only the Israel Defense Forces and practically all the intelligence services in the West, but the bulk of the Egyptian Army as well!'

As September 1973 rolled on, the final preparations for war were made. This should have been the most dangerous time for the Egyptians.

But their unsuspecting enemies believed that they had seen it all before. Arrogance and over-familiarity combined to encourage a complete misinterpretation of what was going on. There had already been over twenty separate mobilisations of Egyptian reservists for training since the beginning of 1973. It was yet another example of the strategy of deception by repetition that worked so well to dull Israeli intelligence's reactions.

Everything else proceeded as usual. There was no call-up of civilian transport, no civil defence preparations. The political and diplomatic round continued as normal, too. The repercussions from the shooting down of thirteen Syrian warplanes by the Israeli Air Force in an aerial battle following Syrian provocations in mid-September still rumbled on, but were slowly dying down. In the circumstances it seemed hardly surprising that Syria had mobilised some extra troops and was apparently hastily trying to fortify its southern border opposite the Golan Heights. This was clearly a defensive move following Israel's recent aggressive aerial ambush. The Soviet Moscow radio seemed to confirm this by broadcasting to the Middle East that an *Israeli* attack was imminent and that Syria should 'prepare to defend itself'.

As September turned into October the dam of security and deception sprang a leak.

It is rare for there to be a hero in intelligence matters. In the Sinai, a young Israeli intelligence officer in General Shmuel Gonen's Southern Command intelligence staff had been conscientiously 'ticking the boxes' as he filled in a standard 'indicators and warning collection plan'. He cared little for preconceived 'concepts', 'political pre-requisites' or the national assessment. Lieutenant Benjamin Siman-Tov just methodically followed the intelligence cycle in his office at Southern Command and, by 1 October 1973, he did not like what he could see. Nearly all the attack indicators showed a build-up, and many of the indicators were red for danger, not green, 'confirmed safe'.

And too many indicators were still showing 'black', meaning 'unknown – no answer yet from the collection agency'. Accordingly, he drafted a short paper to his boss, Lieutenant Colonel Gedalia, pointing out that the Egyptian 'Combined Arms Exercise' on the other side of the canal was, in his opinion (based on an objective analysis and interpretation of the available evidence) nothing less than a sophisticated deception plan to mask an imminent Egyptian attack.

History does not record what Lieutenant Colonel Gedalia, the Chief Intelligence Officer, Israeli Southern Command, said to his alert young officer when Siman-Tov produced his warning memorandum. What it does tell us is what he did with the 1 October paper and another follow-up paper, which Siman-Tov submitted on 3 October.

Gedalia did something unforgiveable, which was to cost him dear: he deliberately suppressed the lieutenant's report because he didn't agree with it. The Director of Military Intelligence, General Zeira, eventually did see the report, but not until March 1974. To his eternal credit, General Zeira promoted the young man on the spot. Unfortunately for Israel he was seven months too late.

With yet another chance missed, the days turned to hours. By dawn on 5 October both Egypt and Syria were on alert on Israel's frontiers. Egypt had 194 artillery batteries in the line and all five of its infantry divisions. Israeli officers in the Bar Lev line warned that it looked as if an attack was imminent. Headquarters demurred: the front-line troops didn't understand the wider picture. This was just another exercise; only they understood the political activity behind this sort of thing . . .

The Israeli high level-intelligence establishment had a clear warning from their highly-placed Egyptian spy Ashraf Marwan, an associate of President Sadat. Lior later testified, 'The same source who told us about the war on Friday [the eve of Yom Kippur], had talked to us three times already,' referring to a secret meeting in London between Zamir and Marwan.

Intelligence chief Zamir's last meeting with Meir was on September 21, two weeks before the war. After that he did not go to her unbidden, and he did not inform her of the fact that he had flown to London to meet and debrief Marwan on the eve of Yom Kippur, following the Egyptian's urgent demand for a crash meeting.

The sensational report from agent Marwan – which was later proved to be mistaken when it came to the exact hour of the Egyptian and Syrian attack, but was otherwise 100 per cent correct, regarding the launching of a joint war – was transmitted to military intelligence, which doubted its reliability and included it, or rather buried it, in a compilation of documents that came to the conclusion that war was unlikely.

On Wednesday 3 October, Golda Meir called an unscheduled meeting of her National Security Committee. The meeting examined all the evidence, and, despite Zamir, the head of the secret service's unease, eventually concluded that the Arab build-up was *defensive*, probably as a reaction to the 'Schönau Incident'.

It is impossible for us to understand the atmosphere in that last week before the 1973 war without taking into account the extent to which politicians and decision makers' eyes were focused on an obscure terrorist attack on the Austrian border. On 28 September two gunmen claiming to be Palestinian revolutionaries seized five Jewish emigrants and an Austrian customs official. Apart from the usual demands for an aeroplane to an Arab country, the incident prompted the Austrian Chancellor Kreisky to agree to close the transit centre that had been established at Schönau Castle for Soviet Jews who were emigrating to Israel. The Israelis were horrified.

The Schönau incident became a cause célèbre and a major focus of Israeli political activity. Schönau was a remarkably timely coincidence, if one believes in timely coincidences that just happen to divert Israeli attention immediately before a major Syrian attack. The gunmen claimed to be from an unknown group of Palestinians, but were recruited from al-Saika, the guerrilla group run by the Syrian army and its secret services. There is no direct proof, but one likely conclusion must be that the Schönau incident was a deliberate Syrian deception ploy to divert attention away from the coming attack.

It worked. There was public indignation inside Israel at the release of the Palestinian terrorists. Would Israel retaliate? Combined with the shooting down of the thirteen Syrian jets in September, the atmosphere of political crisis deepened. No wonder the Syrians were reinforcing their border, concluded Mrs Meir and her kitchen cabinet on 3 October, they must be running scared. One piece of evidence supporting this version of events is the fact that Golda Meir spoke for over two hours at that meeting – on Schönau.

On 4 October Soviet families were evacuated from Syria and Egypt and further confirmation of the massive build-up on Israel's borders poured in. By Friday morning, 5 October the alarmed Israeli generals reported to Golda Meir, but (following a meeting at the office of the Minister of Defence, Dayan) advised her that the general staff's and Military Intelligence's assessment was that the likelihood of war remained 'low'. General Zeira, the head of Military Intelligence, emphasised several times that the Arab troop concentrations revealed by Israeli photo reconnaissance flights could be for either attack or defence – which was true. However, as an insurance policy the meeting decided to place the regular Israeli army on the highest stage of peacetime warning: a 'C' alert. (The next step in the alert process would be the call-up of reservists for war.) To ensure that that would be possible,

Mrs Meir confirmed that reservist mobilisation centres should remain open and manned during the Jewish Day of Atonement (Yom Kippur) holiday on 6 October.

There is in intelligence a well-known situation known as 'circular intelligence' or 'the daisy-chain syndrome'. What happens is that one agency reports an unconfirmed fact or assessment. This is subsequently picked up and repeated in a second agency's assessment as a straight-forward report. But the first agency sees it in someone else's report and then seizes on it as independent proof that their initial information has now been confirmed by another source! This is dangerous stuff and mechanisms exist inside the professional analytical intelligence process to stop it happening.

No such mechanism existed inside Israel and Washington's intelligence exchange in 1973. The CIA and State Department had reduced their previously high assessment of the probability of war only because the *Israelis* had not been concerned by the Arab build-up. After all, if the Israelis – who had most to lose and possessed the best sources – were not alarmed, then that was an important intelligence fact. The US downgraded their assessments accordingly. Tel Aviv never bothered to check exactly why Washington had downgraded their threat assessment. If Washington was unruffled, concluded Mrs Meir and her inner circle on 5 October, then why should they be? To deception and mis-interpretation was now added lazy, unprofessional intelligence bungling.

Each side was reporting the other as a good source ...

Everyone left the 5 October meetings uneasy. General Ismail's deception plan had, against all the odds, succeeded. Israel's interpreta-tion of the intelligence to hand was spectacularly wrong.

When the telephone rang before dawn on 6 October 1973, General Zeira, the head of Israeli Military Intelligence, 'just knew it was bad news'. It was. An unidentified source – almost certainly Marwan – telephoned him at home with absolute confirmation that Israel would be attacked that day on two fronts 'probably 1800 hours'. An appalled Zeira immediately telephone his boss, General Elazar.

The telephone call was wrong in one important respect: the Arab attack *had* originally been planned for 6 p.m. but, two days before, the

Egyptians and Syrians had compromised for practical reasons and agreed that the attack would now be brought forward to 1400 hours local time. The Israelis now had less than seven hours to react to the telephone warning.

On the question of mobilisation, the former general Dayan, the hero of the '56 and '67 wars, dismissed General Elazar's demands for full mobilisation with the airy assurance that 'his [Dayan's] measures – to call up a few key commanders and tank reservists – would be sufficient'. A furious Elazar was directed only to implement this *partial* mobilisation. (Elazar disobeyed this order and was vindicated at 1300 hours, when a now thoroughly alarmed Israeli Cabinet ordered full mobilisation.) Dayan later took much of the blame for the debacle.

At 1400 hours, the door burst open on a Cabinet meeting in Golda Meir's office where, yet again, the normal spirited Israeli disagreement was in full voice (over whether the attack would begin at 6 p.m.) and her military secretary silenced the meeting by announcing baldly, 'The war's begun, Prime Minister.'

The startled Cabinet recalled later that the distant wailing of an air raid siren broke the silence that followed.

The Yom Kippur war went exactly as Sadat had intended – at first. As planned, Egypt and Syria struck in unison at 1400 hours and achieved both strategic and tactical surprise in the south and north. At 1400 on 6 October the Egyptians and Syrians advanced in broad daylight. In the north, 700 Syrian tanks fell upon the Israeli defences on the Golan Heights as heliborne commandos seized key positions on Mount Hermon in a daring *coup de main*. Surprise was total. In the south the Egyptians attacked on a broad front across the Suez Canal.

On the Suez Canal the lookouts in the Bar Lev forts gradually became aware that the usual crowd of cheerful civilians and soldiers strolling around on the far bank had quietly disappeared. The next thing they knew was a devastating artillery barrage crashing down on the roof and, ominously, laying down a curtain of fire behind them to cut off any retreat. Through the smoke and dust the startled defenders saw thousands of rubber boats crossing the canal, packed full of Egyptian assault infantry.

The Bar Lev line was only half manned. In the gaps the Egyptians now deployed their secret weapon: Magirus Deutz high-pressure water pumps. Blasting canal water at hundreds of pounds per square inch the water jets cut through the Israelis' carefully constructed sand ramparts like so many laser knives as the attackers sliced through the supposedly impregnable Bar Lev line with contemptuous ease. The horrified defenders saw their defences opened up with surgical skill and the very latest Soviet floating bridges swung out across the canal to allow a flood of tanks, personnel carriers and guns to race into the Sinai and take up positions well to their rear. The whole operation took less than twelve hours. Piecemeal counter-attacks by Israel's 252 Division were easily brushed aside and they retreated, taking as many of the shaken survivors of the Bar Lev strongpoints as they could carry.

The Egyptian attack across the canal shook the Israelis and demonstrated the soundness of Ismail's planning. By 8 October, the Egyptian Army occupied the whole east bank of the Suez Canal to a depth of about ten miles and awaited the inevitable counter-attack. Sure enough, the Israeli armour obliged. Tanks on the ground and aircraft overhead hurled themselves against the attackers to eject the invaders from Sinai. Both ran into Egypt's new defensive weapons. The air defence SAM umbrella hacked Israel pilots from the sky. In the desert the Israeli tanks were stopped dead by the new anti-tank missile screen, and suffered appalling casualties from 'little men with suitcases'.

By day three of the war Israel needed help and badly: in particular, new missiles, new intelligence and a lot more ammunition and equipment. On 9 October the USA, alarmed at a nuclear-armed Israel facing disaster, duly obliged. In an effort to even the odds for their client state against the massive Soviet support that had made Operation Badr a possibility for Egypt, President Nixon ordered 'Operation Nickel Grass', the complete military re-supply of the Israeli Defense Forces. Huge USAF C5 Galaxy and C141 transports began to land round the clock, bringing in new electronic warfare systems to counter the Soviet SAMs, new anti-radar missiles and anything else that the IDF wanted.

In the Golan, despite being outnumbered ten to one, a heroic defence by the 150 tanks of Israel's 7 and 188 Brigades fought off a

Syrian onslaught by over 1,000 tanks and fighting vehicles. The bat-tered Israelis held their attackers off long enough for fresh units to arrive from the south to join the desperate fight. Israeli casualties were the worst in their history: Syrian losses were even heavier. At critical moments the Golan defenders were minutes away from defeat and down to their last five rounds of tank ammunition. From their new positions on the heights the Syrians could see tantalising glimpses of the Mediterranean and victory. Had they broken through, Israel would have been doomed. But the defence held and, by 10 October, the Syrian advance faltered, then finally stopped, exhausted.

In the south the Egyptians now became the architects of their own defeat. In a fruitless and foolish bid to divert Israeli attention from the Syrian front, Sadat personally ordered an advance into Sinai 'for politi-cal reasons'. The reluctant front commander, General Shazly, obeyed orders and on 14 October watched his armoured brigades shot to rib-bons as they advanced outside the protection of the SAM belt and made a frontal attack against well prepared IDF defensive positions. In the centre, Egypt's 1st Mechanised Brigade lost ninety-three tanks. It was a massacre all along the line and two hours of fighting cost Egypt nearly 300 tanks and the war. To compound their problems, the Egyptians' 4th and 21st Brigades, despite pleas by Shazly to pull back to the west bank of the canal as a reserve, were left exposed and trapped in Sinai.

It was the chance the Israelis had been waiting for. After the usual furious row with the high command, General Ariel Sharon, recalled to the colours by Dayan at the outbreak of war, planned a remarkably bold counter-stroke to cross the canal in the south. If successful, it would cut off the Egyptians in Sinai and blast a ground corridor for the IAF through the troublesome SAM belt.

Between 15–17 October, Operation Gazelle sliced through the Egyptian southern defences near a disused Japanese agricultural site known as 'Chinese Farm'. In confused night battles both sides inflicted heavy casualties as the Israelis probed forward in the dark seeking a clear route to the canal, before finally breaking through at Deversoir on the north of the Great Bitter Lake.

Around 0135 hours on 15 October, the Israeli assault engineers finally cut through the barbed wire on the canal. By dawn the following day, Sharon's leading tanks were in Africa. Once across, the plan was for them to fan out and blow a hole in the Egyptian defensive SAM belt. By 18 October the Israelis had two armoured brigades on the western bank. Once across, their tanks dashed around with impunity, shooting up everything in sight and sowing chaos and confusion in the Egyptian rear areas.

Running out of targets, two tank brigades then turned north and south respectively. By 21 October Israeli paratroopers were fighting in the north on the outskirts of Ismaïlia on the road to Cairo, and in the south Israeli armour had reached the Red Sea at Suez, actually sinking two Egyptian torpedo boats with tank fire as they fled.

More important, the Israelis had cut the umbilical cord for the Egyptian 3rd Army in Sinai. An entire Egyptian army was now completely separated from Egypt and trapped in the desert without food, ammunition, water or hope. The USSR, seeing their client state in serious trouble, began to make threatening noises. As the UN desperately sought to mediate a ceasefire, the fighting surged to a final frenzy.

By 24 October, the war was over. The Soviet Union and the United States began to go to nuclear alert. No-one was willing to risk a nuclear exchange over the Arabs and Israelis fighting – again. The UN Security Council saved the Egyptians from further humiliation and Israel from more casualties, and negotiated a final ceasefire.

Both sides claimed their own version of victory. The Egyptians, despite being driven back, had hurt Israel badly and shown the Arab and Islamic world that the IDF was far from invincible. Contemplating nearly 3,000 dead – half of them tank crews – and over 7,000 wounded, Israel's final military victory, however complete, had been as costly as any defeat. Over 100 Israeli combat aircraft had been downed against 270 Egyptian. The cost of the war was astronomic. In 1973 the US taxpayers gave $492 million to Israel. In 1974 (after the war) the figure leapt to $2.65 billion of which $2.48 billion was free military aid. With Israel's own costs the true cost of the Yom Kippur was therefore in the region of $3 billion at 1973 prices – which in today's values is worth at least $18 billion. No-one knows the full costs to Egypt and Syria. Syria had sustained 8,000 casualties, lost almost all her effective tank strength and a whole year's Gross Domestic Product. The Yom Kippur war had been ruinous for everyone involved. Only courage and pride remained.

The biggest casualty was Israeli confidence. In the aftermath, Golda Meir set up a special inquiry to investigate the causes of failure. When it finally reported in 1975 the Agranat Commission was scathing. Intelligence, discipline and mobilisation of reserves were all found to be wanting. Complacency and arrogance had eroded the IDF at the highest levels. Israeli intelligence had allowed itself to be deceived and had misinterpreted the evidence.

The euphoria and hubris of the 1967 Six Day War was gone for ever. Israel had to find an accommodation with her aggressive neighbours. Within four years, Egypt and Israel signed a peace treaty at Camp David. Two years later, Sadat himself was gone, assassinated by Islamic fanatics bent on even more radical solutions to Israel's military dominance whose echoes still ring down to us today. For Israel the new war of terrorism that followed meant that, for the forseeable future, the Jewish homeland would now face a continuous low-intensity war waged by implacable Arab foes.

The intelligence lessons of Yom Kippur are very different from other wars. There can really be no excuse for the Israeli failure. Pearl Harbor was bad organisation; Tet was poor dissemination. Yom Kippur was neither of these things. By a savage irony, the Israeli failure in 1973 can be traced directly to their triumphant and emphatic victory in 1967.

The first failure was the cardinal sin of any intelligence officer, organisation or commander. The Israelis, flushed with success, discounted the Arabs' ability to learn from past mistakes. They discounted the Arabs' new weapon systems. Above all, they failed to take the revitalised Egyptian staff planning, Egyptian training and Egyptian bravery into account. It was the classic mistake. At every level Israel under-estimated her enemy.

When the war was over, the Israelis captured vast amounts of Egyptian maps, code books and plans. To their horror, the Israelis discovered ample evidence that Egyptian intelligence was more than ready for the battle. Most shocking of all was the discovery of an Arab translation of Israel's pre-war and top-secret code map of Sinai, including all the secret codes and nicknames for every location. As was usual in the stress of battle, Israeli radio operators had further compromised security by arguing in open speech. As a result, for the first week, many of Israel's moves in Sinai had been an open book to the Russian-trained Egyptian SIGINT Service.

Israeli technical intelligence also contributed to the debacle. In 1973 Soviet ATGMs such as SAGGER, and SAMs such as the SAM 6 were seen as new and deadly battlefield threats – certainly by NATO, who gave them their codenames and probably passed Israel a lot of intelligence material under the counter through the US Defense Intelligence Agency. One startled reservist Israeli Intelligence Corps warrant officer discovered pages and pages of information on the new Soviet missiles tucked away in an office drawer. He recalled:

> We could hear on the radio what was going on in Southern Command. We were awed and struck by the clear sense of helplessness that tank crews were expressing facing SAGGER missiles in the hundreds ... One afternoon I browsed through piles of old intelligence reports. Among them I found a technical manual published by the IDF Military Intelligence Corps, dated two years earlier and dedicated to the technical specifications of the SAGGER missile! I rubbed my eyes ... I wondered how, if the missile was so well known as to generate a fully detailed manual, that the fighting forces had no idea of its existence ...

No proper evaluation of the Saggers' battlefield impact appears to have been done by Israeli operational research, let alone passing it on to the Israeli Armoured Corps. Perhaps the Israelis thought that the simple peasant conscript Arab soldier would be unable to operate an anti-tank missile under fire for thirty seconds. Both on the ground in Sinai and in the air over the Golan many Israelis were to die learning the real truth about the new weapon's capabilities and the capabilities of their adversaries.

The final big mistake by Israeli intelligence was ossification. When Israel was young and 'everybody knew each other', genuine all-source debates took place among decision makers with the intelligence experts chipping in their views. It worked. But as the years passed, Military Intelligence pulled all the strings into their hands. Military Intelligence became powerful, highly political and sometimes plain inefficient.

As a result, the intelligence capabilities that had kept Israel informed and a step ahead were forced into becoming just another intelligence bureaucracy. However, unlike its American and British counterparts, in the small incestuous village of the Israeli political and military elite the Israeli Military Intelligence had a national monopoly of all-source intelligence. No bureaucratic rival existed to challenge its assessments; and perhaps worst of all, the unrivalled access to – even an official 'membership' of – national policy committees and the inner political councils of state ate away at any pretence of objectivity.

In the ultimate test, Israeli Military Intelligence failed the nation in 1973. Despite having all the intelligence in its hands, it was misinterpreted and corroded from within by the acid of sheer prejudice, domestic politics, personal cronyism and just plain bad analysis. When we consider the sheer quality, expertise and range of Israeli intelligence resources, which had served the nation so well from the start, it is tempting with respect to Yom Kippur to reverse Boulay de la Meurthe's scathing dictum: 'It was worse than a blunder – it was a crime.'

CHAPTER 23

Telling the User: Barbarossa and Stalin

'Don't worry; Comrade Stalin knows what he's about . . .'
(The standard response by Stalin's staff in 1941 to any expression of
concern about an impending German attack.)

One of the most delicate tasks of any intelligence organisation is disseminating the finished product. The job seems quite straightforward: just get the answer into the hands of the decision maker who called for it, plus anyone else with a legitimate need to know, securely and in good time.

The truth is that it all depends on the boss; it all depends on whether he or she agrees (or not); and it all depends on if it's what the leader wants to hear . . .

No better example of clear intelligence warnings being distorted, hidden away, or just plain ignored because of the personality and temper of the boss, can be found than the performance of the Soviet intelligence services during 1941.

At 0145 on the morning of 22 June 1941, a Soviet train steamed up to the frontier post on the Russian-German border at Brest-Litovsk, loaded with 1,500 tons of grain. The trucks were part of the 200,000 tons of grain and 100,000 tons of petroleum products delivered to the west *every month* for the German war economy by Stalin, keeping his word to Adolf Hitler as part of the Nazi-Soviet Non-Aggression Pact's 'cooperative economic ventures' clause. The scene at the border was of routine, calm and order. The Union of Soviet Socialist Republics and the Nazi Party's Greater Germanic Reich of the German Nation were allies, by solemn treaty.

An hour and a half later, the all-conquering Wehrmacht burst across that same bridge to the east in another ferocious blitzkrieg, to begin the invasion of Communist Russia. 'We have only to kick in the door,' the boastful Führer told his inner circle, 'And the whole rotten structure will come crashing down.' The Nazi leadership, in a phrase that has eerie echoes, genuinely believed that it would all be over by the autumn, let by alone by Christmas.

By 1941, the Soviet Union had the largest, most efficient and best-informed intelligence service on the planet. Using a vast network of agents and sympathisers, little went on in the rest of the world that did not find its way back to the seat of the Communist revolution in Moscow. Comrade Stalin, First Secretary of the Communist Party of the Soviet Union was determined that, in the historic clash of ideologies between Capitalism and Communism, the heirs of Marx and Lenin would not be found unprepared or wanting.

Yet over three million men and 3,350 tanks of the armies of the Reich had invaded the Soviet Union and took its unprepared western border defences almost completely by surprise. How on earth could such a catastrophic failure of intelligence, which led to the most destructive war in human history, have happened – apparently without warning?

The answer is very simple – Stalin's personal failure to acknowledge a truth that was presented to him over and over again: Nazi Germany was going to invade the Soviet Union.

The roots of the intelligence disaster that befell Russia in 1941 all have one common source: Stalin. The Soviet dictator's obsession with avoiding a war with Hitler, and his persistent refusal to acknowledge clear intelligence that the Germans were about to invade, ensured the USSR suffered catastrophically as Operation Barbarossa pushed the Russians back to the gates of Moscow itself.

Stalin's motives were complex, but seem to stem from an overriding desire to buy time. He knew, better than anyone, just how unprepared the Red Army was for war, and he seems to have been prepared to ignore the most accurate reports of trouble in a vain attempt to convince himself that, 'it can't happen to me'.

Stalin expected war. Indeed, in the historical analysis beloved of Marxist-Leninists, a final clash between Communism and Capitalism was 'an historic inevitability'. Stalin's problem was that he was not yet ready for this particular stage in the unfolding of the great dialectic process. For just three years before, he had wrecked – deliberately – his army.

In the spring of 1937, as part of what become known as 'The Great Terror', Stalin had moved to 'purge' the Red Army of 'internal enemies'. During the next three years he executed most of his senior military commanders on trumped up charges. The cull was horrific: seventy-five of the eighty members of the Military Soviet were killed; every commander of every military district: two thirds of the divisional commanders, half the brigade commanders and over 400 of 456 staff colonels. Stalin effectively sliced the head off the Red Army.

Hardly surprisingly, the Red Army's invasion of neighbouring Finland in the winter of 1939 turned into a military debacle. Little Finland's 200,000 defenders carved the million-strong Red Army invaders to pieces, inflicting nearly a quarter of a million casualties on the Russians before finally being ground down by superior numbers.

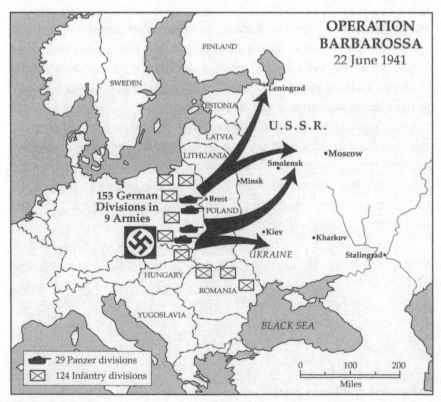

David had not only thrashed Goliath, but shown him to be a blundering, sluggish incompetent, a fact of which Stalin was only too well aware.

For example, at the Battle of Raate Road in December 1939 the Soviet 44th and parts of the 163rd Rifle Divisions were cut off and trapped by a Finnish ambush as they advanced along a narrow forest road. With no chance of retreat and spread out over twenty miles in the dead of winter, the static Soviet column was an easy target for the marauding Finnish ski troopers who attacked out of the frozen forest and cut the enemy force into smaller fragments. Both divisions were effectively destroyed. It cost the Red Army 9,000 casualties; the Finns lost just 400 men. An angry and embarrassed Stalin ordered both divisional commanders shot. But by then the weakness of the Red Army had been revealed to the world.

So it is to the inner recesses of Stalin's secretive, fearful and cunning psyche that we must turn for the truth behind the surprise attack known as Barbarossa. Stalin may have wielded supreme authority in the USSR, but at heart the Russian dictator was terrified – paranoiac even – of losing power. While he could master events in the Soviet Union by killing off his enemies, real or imagined, one man, Adolf Hitler and his all-conquering army, posed a potentially mortal threat to the Communist regime and its leader.

Stalin's genuine fear of the threat from Germany makes many of this actions become, not only understandable, but also strangely rational. By the bizarre standards of suspicion-crazed dictators, Stalin's behaviour makes a kind of curious sense. He felt he had at all costs to prevent a war that could destroy him until he, Stalin, was ready for the final historic combat between the great ideologies.

If we understand this '*Weltanschauung*', or world view, then Stalin's attempts to ignore the unequivocal intelligence warnings of an attack, in order to keep the USSR out of the war seem, at best, almost logical. At worst they offer the ultimate nightmare for the intelligence officer: a commander who chooses to suppress the very best intelligence, handed to him on a plate, because he has his own agenda, and is prepared to go to any lengths to prevent the truth becoming known, much less acted upon. Stalin was not the first – or the last – commander to utter the immortal words, 'I am my own intelligence officer!' He just wasn't a very good one, as events proved.

The facts speak for themselves: between late July 1940 and 22 June 1941, no fewer than 103 separate, unequivocal warnings of an impending attack on the Soviet Union were passed to Stalin. In every case they were professionally collated, evaluated, interpreted and briefed to Stalin alone. As far as we know, none of them was disseminated further. As a direct consequence of this intelligence failure, the USSR lost four million soldiers – including an astounding three million prisoners of war – 14,000 aircraft, 20,000 guns and 17,000 tanks in the battles that occurred between the frontiers and the outskirts of Moscow from June to December 1941.

In 1939, all was friendly between the two great totalitarian dictatorships, who had just signed a non-aggression pact. To understand how this came about, we have to go back to Munich and 'appeasement'. The Munich Agreement of 1938 had come as a great shock to the Soviet Union. Convinced by Marxist dogma of the historic inevitability of another Franco-German capitalist war, (from which there could only be one beneficiary – the Soviet Union) and still trusting in the international system of 'collective security' to contain Hitler's resurgent Germany, for the Soviets, Munich spelled a new and dangerous Europe. The Soviet Ambassador in London, Maisky, warned Moscow that, 'International relations are now entering an era of brute force, savagery and the policy of the mailed fist.'

Further Soviet analysis of the USSR's position in the post-Munich world spelled out British and French policy in brutally stark terms: '[British] Foreign Office policy now has only two aims: peace at any cost, and secondly, collusion with aggressors at the expense of third countries to grant the aggressor concessions . . .'

Such a policy of colluding with Hitler was seen by Stalin and his advisors as both fundamentally anti-Communist and anti-Russian, and therefore a serious threat to the USSR. For, looming ever larger in Soviet official thinking, was the belief that Britain and France would be only too happy to use a conflict between Germany and the Soviet Union to divert Hitler's ever more rapacious attention away from themselves.

The problem of deciding what was reality in Moscow was further hindered by Stalin's decision to kill as many of his intelligence analysts as he could. Like the Red Army, the NIO (the foreign intelligence service) and the NKVD/NKGB had both been ruthlessly purged between 1937 and 1939. Litvinov, the architect of the Soviets' failed 'collective security' foreign policy was removed and replaced by a Stalin-led committee early in 1939 after Munich. Although, surprisingly, Litvinov survived, his staff did not. Many diplomats and foreign service officers tainted by association with 'counter-revolutionary elements' (which simply meant that they had had long and meaningful conversations with foreign nationals) disappeared overnight, 'liquidated' in the Great Purge that reached into every aspect of Soviet life in the years immediately before the Second World War.

In these circumstances, it is hardly surprising that Stalin lacked sound, informed and experienced foreign policy advice in the months after Munich. Most of those who understood what the British and French might do were dead, or in the slave camps of the Gulag, enjoying the delights of 'honest proletarian labour'. Those who survived were keeping their heads well down, following a survival policy based on the well-known Soviet adage, 'sniff out, suck up, survive . . .' Only a brave man or a fool was going to gainsay Comrade Stalin's interpretation of events in 1939–40.

The irony was that the post-Munich period really marked the end of appeasement by the French and British.

Hitler's cynical invasion of the rump of Czechoslovakia in March 1939 had in fact strengthened Allied resolve and convinced the hitherto timid Western politicians that a war between the Anglo-French entente and Germany was inevitable. The Soviets read it differently. From Stalin's perspective, the USSR now had a hungry Fascist wolf loose on her unprotected western border, aided and abetted by gutless and perfidious Capitalist democracies. An accommodation with Germany had therefore to be sought: Stalin believed he had to buy Hitler off at all costs.

The Soviet leadership believed the USSR was now isolated and alone in a dangerous world. Almost in desperation Stalin tried the Western Allies one last time, although he believed that neither Britain nor France was in any position to protect their new eastern 'clients', Poland and Romania. In April 1939 Stalin proposed a new triple treaty based on a collective defensive alliance against Hitler, consisting of Britain, France and the USSR, to protect Eastern Europe and, by definition, the USSR. Simultanously, Stalin ordered Molotov to seek an alliance that would bind their potential enemy, Germany, into a non-aggression pact. Hitler's peremptory rupture of the Munich Agreement in March 1939 merely accelerated the process.

Whether this was to put pressure on Hitler, buy time or, most likely, merely to keep Stalin's options open, the French and British response to this proposal was both lukewarm and ambiguous. They counter-proposed a military pact where Russia would come to Britain and France's aid if Poland was attacked. As every intelligent observer in Europe knew that Poland was next on Hitler's territorial shopping list, and that neither France nor Britain was capable of protecting that isolated and encircled nation in the event of a Nazi attack, this looked to Stalin like just another cynical ploy to suck the USSR into war with Hitler: the very thing he was determined to avoid.

The negotiations for the triple alliance dragged on through the summer of 1939. Unfortunately, the French and British saw the talks as a political exercise designed to frighten Hitler and apply pressure on Berlin. The British in particular dragged their diplomatic feet and played for time, rather as they were to try to do, equally unsuccessfully, with Galtieri's Argentina over forty years later. The French, correctly, feared that if the talks were unsuccessful, Stalin might feel that he had no choice but to get into bed with Hitler. Stalin himself viewed the discussions differently: the Soviet dictator needed – urgently – a guarantee of peace.

Exasperated by the lack of progress in the triple alliance talks, and receptive to German counter-approaches for a pact designed to give Hitler the free hand he needed to deal with Poland, in August 1939 Stalin decided to make a pact with his potential arch-enemy. In an astonishing volte-face, he authorised face-to-face negotiations between Molotov and Ribbentrop.

On 23 August, to the surprise of diplomatic observers, Ribbentrop flew to Moscow. The Soviet-Nazi non-aggression pact was signed the

very next day, on 24 August; eight days before Hitler's invasion of
Poland. At a stroke, Hitler was given a free hand to attack Poland; and
for his part, Stalin had his cherished guarantee of peace and a long
awaited opportunity to gobble up the three weak Baltic republics.

As the German delegates left, a relieved Stalin announced; 'The
Soviet Government takes [this] new pact very seriously . . . The Soviet
Union will never betray its partner . . .' He meant it.

Stalin kept his promise. He knew the state of his weakened army.
Over the next eighteen months, he steadfastly chose to ignore the
mass of indications that his partner was about to betray him. Whether
this was calculation, wishful thinking or just fear, we will never know.
The seeds of the Barbarossa disaster were sown.

The most striking feature of the Soviet leader's appeasement of
Germany was a series of political and economic gestures designed to
conciliate Hitler. For example, as late as 8 May 1941, the Russian news
agency, Tass, denied the existence of any German troop concentrations
on the Soviet border. This was despite a mass of evidence to the contrary, as the German Barbarossa build-up gathered pace.

Even German photo-reconnaissance overflights were studiously
'overlooked', despite the crash at Rovno on 15 April 1941 of a Luftwaffe
photo reconnaissance flight laden with incriminating exposed intelli-
gence-films in the wreckage. Soviet anti-aircraft defences were
specifically ordered not to open fire on German aircraft, even if they
strayed into Soviet airspace. Apparently no humiliation was too much
for Stalin in his desire to avoid provoking the Germans.

According to Churchill, the Soviet leader later claimed ruefully, 'I
thought I could gain another six months or so,' and there is a mass of
evidence that indicated that Stalin's aim was to delay war until the Soviet
Union was prepared, perhaps in 1942. Wrongly, the Russian believed that
he alone could do this. The last thing Stalin wanted was objective and
honest reporting that would compel him to take action. So, any adviser
bringing a contrary view was dangerous: not just to Stalin's perceived –
and obsessive – beliefs, but also to 'peace'. The task of being one of Stalin's
intelligence officers in the spring of 1941 was fraught with danger.

There was no shortage of intelligence warnings. As early as the end
of June 1940, there is evidence that some information about Hitler's

future intentions had already been passed to Moscow. Where this came from is obscure, but it was subsequently reinforced by ninety hard, factual reports; accurate, credible, and in many cases confirmed by other sources, between July 1940 and 22 June 1941.

As early as 22 July 1940 (before the Battle of Britain had reached its peak) the German Army Chief of Staff Halder noted that Hitler wanted to 'begin planning for an attack on Russia'. A week later, Jodl and Hitler are both on record as saying Russia must be smashed. On 9 August 1940, the German High Command issued the Directive for 'Otto', the preliminary planning for an attack in the east in spring 1941. And on 8 September 1940, the new Wehrmacht quartermaster general at Zossen took over a draft operation order for the invasion of Russia in his safe. There is ample evidence that Stalin was made aware of German intentions.

For example, on 1 July 1940, Churchill wrote personally to the Soviet dictator to warn him. Churchill was the wrong man to alert Stalin and, considering Britain's post-Dunkirk plight, it was the wrong time. Stalin read it merely as a feeble attempt to involve the USSR in Britain's lost war and, coming as it did from the arch anti-Bolshevik Churchill, as just another clumsy provocation. Amazingly, he passed the message directly to the German ambassador, von Schulenburg, as yet another example of perfidious Albion. No-one was going to accuse Comrade Stalin of breaking faith with his valued ally, Herr Hitler.

On 25 December 1940, the Soviet attaché in Berlin passed a résumé of Hitler's 18 December 1940 Führer Directive 21, the operation order for Barbarossa; and on 1 March 1941 Sumner Welles, the US Undersecretary of State, formally summoned and briefed the Soviet ambassador to Washington with the full details of a forthcoming German attack. His source was the junior US commercial attaché in Berlin, Sam E. Woods. Woods had been briefed by a disgruntled anti-Nazi official in the Berlin Trade Ministry on detailed German plans for an invasion of the USSR in spring 1941.

Welles gravely informed the astonished Soviet Ambassador that the evidence was 'so overwhelming it should be passed to Foreign Minister Molotov immediately'. Urmansky, the Ambassador, went 'white with shock', according to the US officials. Stalin's reaction on being told was different. He ignored the US reports, and in the Russian phrase, 'safed it in the wall'. And 'safed' the intelligence stayed. When Churchill (armed with hard Enigma decrypts that key Nazi divisions were in Cracow, Poland, and not in the Balkans) decided again to try to alert Stalin with a personal message from 'a trusted agent' in April 1941, Stalin is alleged to have scrawled 'Another English provocation!' in the margin before filing it and taking no action.

The reason Stalin could do this was simple: like many dictators and supreme commanders, he allowed an intelligence organisation to grow up around him that was literally 'politically correct'. Only the 'right' intelligence could be passed to the Great Man, if intelligence officers wanted to survive. Being human, General Gorlikov, his chief intelligence officer, who had no reputation as an intelligence analyst but commendable political loyalty, made sure that any intelligence reports reaching his master were carefully sorted into two piles, 'reliable' and 'not confirmed'. As the Kremlin definition of 'reliable' in early 1941 seems to have been 'any information that agrees with Comrade Stalin's analysis of the present politico-military situation', Stalin's propensity for self-delusion was powerfully reinforced.

Golikov was certainly in Stalin's confidence; in December 1940, on Stalin's direct orders, he had secretly briefed the twenty-five most senior officers of the GRU, 'that the Nazi-Soviet Pact – which was a product solely of the political genius of Comrade Stalin – was no more than a temporary expedient', and 'that Hitler would never dare to attack Russia as he was not unbalanced, and to a realist such a course would be suicide'.

Stalin had chosen Gorlikov – who, unlike his two executed predecessors, died in his bed – to bear the poisoned chalice of the GRU in July 1940, precisely because he trusted his slavish devotion to the Party and to Stalin personally, and could rely on him to follow his orders without question.

The result was that, with Timoshenko and Zhukov, Gorlikov conspired with Stalin to ensure the total inaction of the Soviet Intelligence apparatus before 22 June 1941. On 20 April 1941 he had brandished Churchill's warnings of the impending German invasion in front of a group of GRU officers and parroted the very words Stalin had just screamed at him; 'This cannot be true. It is an English provocation! Investigate!'

Golikov was not alone in this. His counterparts, Merkulov, the Georgian head of the NKGB and Fitin, the head of the International Department, the INU, adopted a similar survival strategy. Even when Fitin took his life in his hands and bravely suggested they sign a joint warning report to Stalin, a frightened Merkulov flatly refused, saying; 'No – up there at the top [Comrade Stalin] knows far more about intelligence than we do.' For the head of a national intelligence service this is a remarkable statement.

Faced with frightened intelligence advisers like these, Stalin was easily able to delude himself about German intentions.

To add to this catalogue of ignored warnings from other governments, Stalin's intelligence service was feeding him with high-grade information from a number of trusted Communist agents deep within the combatants' war machines. Oleg Gordievsky, the KGB defector claims that there were literally 'tons of documents' in the Moscow archives from the Soviet spy John Cairncross once the Briton was recruited by Soviet intelligence in September 1940.

This British intelligence was backed and confirmed by other reports: the Schulze-Boysen spy network based on the German Air Ministry, Leopold Trepper's 'Red Orchestra' and the German traitor von Scheliha in the Warsaw Embassy all contributed to the flow of 'alarmist' reports landing on Golikov's desk in Moscow. They all confirmed one clear and constant trend: Hitler and his generals were planning an attack on the USSR in spring 1941. Stalin even ignored the detailed intelligence on Barbarossa from Richard Sorge, the NKGB's prized agent in Japan, to such an extent that Sorge was reduced to weeping, 'Moscow doesn't believe me . . .' in his mistress's arms, after Stalin had rejected his warning of 19 May 1941 that nine armies with 150 divisions were massing against the USSR.

In all fairness, Barbarossa, like any thorough military operation planned by the German General Staff had a substantial deception plan. The major thrust of the deception effort was the pretence that Hitler coveted the Balkans, (where Mussolini's army was deep in trouble fighting the Greeks and Albanians) and secondly, that the movement of troops to the east in winter 1940–41 was a ruse to delude the British into thinking that Operation Sea Lion, the German invasion of England, had been cancelled. The massive Operation Barbarossa troop redeployments were represented as a deception plan for an invasion of Britain.

The overall deception plan worked, despite the numerous accurate and precise warnings. The reason was that Stalin's ears were sealed and his eyes were blind. A modern counsellor would say that he was 'in denial'.

However much evidence he was given, Stalin just ignored it. Across the years, he appears only to have believed reports that coincided with his own perception. Anything else that did not fit the party line was dismissed as provocation or disinformation.

For example, even when early in June 1941, the German Ambassador to Moscow, the ever sympathetic von Schulenburg, briefed the new head of the Soviet International Affairs Department, Dekanozov, that, 'perhaps this has not ever occurred in the history of diplomacy, as I am about to disclose to you the state secret number one ... Hitler has decided to launch an attack against the Soviet Union on 22 June ...', Stalin later indignantly reported to the Politburo, 'We must consider that disinformation has reached the level of ambassadors!'

Stalin also chose to overlook news of Luftwaffe and Panzer units re-locating to Poland, a personal statement by Hitler to his ally Prince Paul of Yugoslavia that 'he would invade the USSR in mid-June', a genuine copy of the outline Barbarossa operation order from an agent, massive German railway traffic to the east, German general staff requests for thousands of copies of maps of the Baltic States and the western USSR, Wehrmacht defectors giving precise details of their targets and objectives and, last but not least, on 9 June 1941, precise details of the German Ambassador's instructions to 'burn all documents' and prepare to leave Moscow. The number and detail of the Soviet reports read like an intelligence officer's indications and warning textbook, and cover every available intelligence source and agency.

Some of the warnings were positively bizarre. At a diplomatic reception on 15 May, Professor Karl Bömer, the head of Dr Goebbel's Foreign Press Department, 'waving a glass', announced to the astonished throng of diplomats and journalists that; 'he would soon be leaving his post as he was being promoted to become Gauleiter of the Crimea after the invasion of Russia on 22 June'.

Another more serious report was of a discussion at the farewell party of Patterson, the American Embassy's First Secretary, at the end of April in Berlin. Patterson introduced Berezhkov, his Soviet diplomatic counterpart, to a Luftwaffe major in uniform, who revealed that his squadron had just been secretly redeployed from Rommel's command in North Africa to Lodz in Poland. 'I know I shouldn't be telling you this,' the German added, 'But I'd hate anything to happen between our two countries.' The startled Berezhkov duly transmitted this to Moscow, where it was doubtless duly passed to Stalin as 'another provocation'.

Stalin ignored all these reports. Worse, he suppressed them, to such an extent that, in the final days before war, he even ordered German deserters coming across the border bringing precise details of their units' Barbarossa objectives to be shot as 'provocateurs'. Not a word reached his generals. Neither Timoshenko, at the Defence Commissariat, or Zhukov at the general staff saw any hard intelligence of the impending German attack.

To compound their difficulties, by spring 1941, the Russian generals' own subordinates in the frontier military districts were warning them from below. German troop and aircraft movements on the scale of Barbarossa could not be entirely concealed. Pleas for contingency plans to relocate forward Soviet units to better defensive positions began to flood into Moscow in late May and June 1941. In desperation, the Soviet marshals turned to their intelligence staffs for accurate assessments.

The fact that they did not get them can be attributed in part to Stalin's suppression of the truth – which had the side-effect of ensuring the success of the arrangements made by the Germans to disguise the Barbarossa attack (although they were both professional and comprehensive, it is doubtful whether they would have worked as well as they did without the dead hand of Stalin's massive self-deception).

But also, for reasons we find hard to credit today, Stalin believed there could be no war without an *ultimatum*. This pre-Pearl Harbor outlook coloured all intelligence assessments, and not just in the Kremlin. As a result, the whole thrust of Stalin's policy of naked appeasement towards the Nazi regime in 1941 seems to have been designed to prevent any situation that could lead to a German ultimatum.

If we accept the fact that no pretext for war was to be offered under any circumstances, Stalin's deliberate suppression of 'provocative' intelligence makes sense. On no account must Hitler be given any grounds for a complaint. Therefore, the more accurate and more forceful the 'bad' intelligence report, the more danger it posed to the Soviet policy of the pre-emptive cringe. Like a dog fearing a beating, Stalin was rolling on his back, determined to avoid provoking Hitler.

In its final days, the prelude to Barbarossa saw perhaps one of the most bizarre events of World War II and one that muddied the waters hopelessly against any Russian perception of British good faith. On the night of 10 May 1941, Hitler's deputy, Rudolf Hess, unexpectedly flew to Scotland in a Messerschmitt Bf 110 long-range fighter. Hess appears to have been making a desperate last-minute bid to negotiate peace with Britain to avoid Germany's long-standing nightmare of becoming involved in a war on two fronts.

Whatever Hess's motives, Soviet suspicion of both the flight itself and the British government's reaction fatally skewed their reactions to the subsequent British warnings over Barbarossa, however accurate and urgent. Stalin's greatest fear – an Anglo-German negotiated peace, enabling the British to do a separate deal with Hitler to save their own skins, thus freeing the Führer to turn his victorious legions east – suddenly looked frighteningly possible.

Every British action over the next month was weighed in the Kremlin against the belief that their aim was to do everything in their power to provoke a Soviet-German clash. Even Anthony Eden's personal warnings (2–13 June 1941) of the impending Nazi onslaught were dismissed by the Soviet Ambassador to London as merely part of Hitler's 'war of nerves to wring concessions from the USSR without a fight'.

The stage was set for Barbarossa.

So it was that, on the night of 21–22 June, trains full of wheat and oil were still being despatched west by the Soviets. The grain shipment at the bridge across the River Bug at Brest-Litovsk was the last one. Nazi customs officials solemnly cleared the train and its cargo, which then steamed slowly across the bridge over the River Bug into the Reich, to add to the thousands of tons of Soviet food and petrol with which Hitler, with calculated effrontery, would use to supply his invasion of the USSR.

As it crossed west onto Polish soil, the train snaked between batteries of German artillery massed in the darkness, where sweating gunners stock-piled shells in the short, humid night. An hour and a half later they were part of the huge barrage that flamed into action at 0315 along the 1,250 miles of the whole Eastern Front, from the Baltic to the Black Sea, to launch the biggest invasion in history, and the bloodiest campaign of the Second World War. Barbarossa had begun.

Its first casualty was a German Communist, Private Alfred Liskow, who deserted on 21 June to alert the Russians. He was shot immediately on Stalin's orders.

The surprise – and shock – of the attack in Moscow was total. Comrade Stalin had the equivalent of a nervous collapse. The Great Leader disappeared to his villa at Kuntsevo, leaving a shaken Molotov to go on the radio and break the news to the 'Soviet People'. Stalin was stunned and panicky, telling his family to 'flee to the Urals with all their children . . .' and ordering his personal train to get steam up and wait for him.

It was to be several confused days before he regained his composure and authority. Everything for which he had deceived, killed and suppressed apparently lay in ruins. We can even speculate that he may have felt his own position was at risk as a result of his policy of denial and misreading of intelligence vital to the state. Fortunately for the Russian dictator, the Kremlin had more pressing concerns than politburo leadership squabbles in the last week of June 1941.

Across the years we can ask ourselves how could such an obvious build-up be ignored? How could seasoned intelligence professionals allow such an intelligence disaster to happen?

In all fairness, many of the warnings were *not* ignored. They were misread and interpreted wrongly: as political pressure; as re-locations of units for other purposes; as part of Hitler's wider ambitions in the Balkans and Eastern Mediterranean. Stalin was not alone in his misinterpretation of the available intelligence. Even the British JIC was ambivalent in its conclusions until the end of May 1941, and only confirmed the Germans' final intention to invade early in June.

But, in the final analysis, Barbarossa must stand as one of the greatest intelligence failures in history. And there can be no doubt that the blame must be laid squarely at Stalin's door. American diplomat Harrison Salisbury, who was in Moscow at the time, sums up the Soviet dictator's intelligence failure thus in his book *900 Days*:

> Neither quantity nor quality of intelligence reporting determines whether national leaderships act in a timely and resolute fashion. It is the ability of that leadership to comprehend what is reported, to assimilate the findings of spies and the warnings of diplomats. Unless there is a clear channel from lower to top levels, unless the leadership insists on honest and objective reporting, and is prepared to act on such reports, regardless of preconceptions, prejudices . . . then the best intelligence in the world goes to waste – or even worse, is turned into an agency of self-deceit. This was clearly the case with Stalin. Nothing in the Bolshevik experience so plainly exposed the defects of the Soviet power monopoly as when the man who held that power was ruled by his own internal obsessions.

Stalin's obsession, and his fatal misinterpretation of the clear intelligence he was given was to cost the Soviet Union twenty-five million dead, six million houses, six thousand hospitals, seventy thousand cities, towns and villages laid waste, and changed the map of the world for ever.

With potentially the best intelligence service in the world at his beck and call, Stalin blew it. There can be no other judgement. Stalin was indeed 'his own intelligence officer' – and a thoroughly bad one at that. We are still paying the price for his mistakes today.

CHAPTER 24

On Dissemination: Pearl Harbor

If D-Day (see page 341) was a triumph of deception operations over an efficient intelligence service, and Barbarossa (see page 229) the neutralisation of an outstanding intelligence service by a dictator's stupidity, then Pearl Harbor represents the catastrophic consequences of a nation not having a proper intelligence service at all.

For the intelligence analyst, Pearl Harbor deserves particular attention because it was the classic case of a nation actually having nearly all the key intelligence indicators of an impending attack, but failing to recognise them or act upon the warning. As a result of bad intelligence the course of world history was altered irreversibly, and the new dominance of the USA confirmed four years later in the world's first atomic bomb. That mushroom cloud over Hiroshima has cast a shadow over world affairs to this day and yet, without Pearl Harbor, the US would have been reluctant to become involved in Japan's war in the Pacific.

The disaster at Pearl Harbor on Sunday 7 December 1941, when eighteen major fighting ships were sunk, (including four out of eight battleships) 188 aircraft destroyed, and 2,403 Americans killed by the Japanese Imperial Navy in a surprise dawn air attack, came as a huge shock to the American people. Every American of that generation could 'remember where they were the day war broke out . . .' President Roosevelt called it 'a day that will be remembered in infamy'.

The USA of 1939 was a world power; economically, politically and in terms of sheer size. But, with the exception of her navy, she exhibited few of the trappings of a major global force. Her army was tiny,

she was not even a member of the League of Nations, and both government policy and public mood were fiercely isolationist. Not only
did America not have any integrated intelligence organisation, she
steadfastly refused to organise one. Secure behind her ocean barriers,
continental USA wanted nothing more than peace and a return to
prosperity after the Great Depression.

The advent of yet another European war was in many ways an
unmitigated blessing for the United States. Provided the country could
stay out of the conflict, rich economic pickings could be made out of
the miseries of other peoples' battlefields. For example, unemployment
plunged by nearly three-quarters of a million in the autumn of 1939 as
the value of the great 'defence stocks' of chemicals, aircraft, steel, ship-
building and auto manufacturing soared following Hitler's invasion of
Poland. Industry and the economy boomed; in the words of the old
Depression song: 'Happy Days are here again!'

In this atmosphere there was little incentive for the US political
authorities to do anything that might endanger the USA's domestic
prosperity. While President Franklin Delano Roosevelt's enemies
claimed that he was trying to drag the US into an unwanted war, the
facts seem to indicate that FDR, although not unaware of the threats
posed by both triumphant Fascism and Communism in the long term,
wanted nothing more than to keep the US economic recovery going.

To the professional intelligence analyst, the factors that led to the
failure at Pearl Harbor are fairly clear:

1. There was no national intelligence organisation.

2. Total under-estimation of the Japanese as potential enemies.

3. No single analysis of all the evidence.

4. Under-resourcing of the various intelligence providers.

5. Failure to understand the significance of intelligence
   provided.

6. Competition between intelligence agencies.

7. Ignorance of senior officers.

8. Lack of any warning system.

9. Inter-service rivalry for political-military power and influence.

10. Lack of trained intelligence analysts.

11. No sense of urgency.

Alarming as this list of intelligence mistakes (compiled from the various inquiries after the disaster) is, it could be longer. But it makes the point: in December 1941, the USA was not taking the possibility of a war with Japan seriously, and was certainly not organising her intelligence services – such as they were – to provide advance warning of war.

One unusual feature of the Pearl Harbor story is that we can identify almost precisely the catalyst for the saga that triggered the Japanese attack on the sleeping US fleet. The story of the slippery slide to war really begins with an *American* action.

By July 1941, Imperial Japan's continuing policies of militarism and expansion, and the invasion of her neighbours had finally caused the exasperated Allied powers to act. After the brutal invasions of China and Manchuria, the 1941 Japanese seizure of southern Indo-China was the final straw. In retaliation, the United States, followed by Britain and the Netherlands' colonial government in the East Indies, imposed a strategic embargo on any exports of oil or steel to Japan in a policy move designed to force the Japanese government to come to the negotiating table.

Japan's ability to make war – indeed to survive economically – depended on oil and other crucial raw materials such as rubber from the Dutch East Indies and British Malaya. Surely, reasoned the far-off politicians in their committee rooms, surely this would bring aggressive Japan to its senses; and if not, then it would force Japan to its knees?

In fact, for Prime Minister Hideki Tojo's Japan, there was another policy option. As any knowledgeable adviser on Japanese culture and thought processes at the time could have explained, the American diplomatic pressure left only one real choice open to the proud, fiercely independent and irredeemably martial heirs to the samurai: to fight, and to seize what Japan needed, and which was now to be denied to them by the Americans and their friends. From July 1941, the die was cast, certainly in Japanese minds. Force was the only real option.

It was even possible to work out the timing of any likely attack. In the summer, American planners had calculated, correctly, that Japan had stockpiles of aviation spirit for only another six months. Surely then, reasoned the policy makers in Washington, by December 1941 the Japanese would be forced to come cap in hand to the Allies? Would not the Japanese have no choice but to agree to demands for a withdrawal from their illegal conquests in South East Asia, if they wanted to get their hands on the precious stocks of oil and strategic materials they needed if they were to survive? Not for the first time in intelligence matters, two opposing sets of planners looked at identical information and came up with diametrically opposed conclusions. Therein lay the real roots of the blunder – and the fascination – of the disaster at Pearl Harbor.

However, despite having made a naïve miscalculation as to the probable Japanese intentions, the US administration was not completely unaware of Japanese policy and military thinking. By 1941 the US could read Japan's most secret codes and ciphers. Every high-level Japanese diplomatic message could, theoretically, be 'unbuttoned' and made available to defence planners from the president downward. The code name of this priceless intelligence advantage was appropriately enough, MAGIC, and covered the ability to intercept and decipher the Japanese government's top-level codes and radio traffic. Through the labyrinth of the secret code-breaking world many of the secrets of Pearl Harbor were to be revealed in advance.

The Army's Signal Intelligence Service (SIS) under William F. Friedmann, a dedicated and scientific figure, now took on the task of deciphering the Japanese diplomatic codes.

To further complicate the picture, yet another American SIGINT organisation was successfully reading the Japanese radio traffic. In Washington, the US Navy had established its own highly secret code-breaking organisation, known as 'OP-20-G'. Under a quiet and untidy naval Lieutenant, Laurence Safford, the Navy embarked on its own secret programme to intercept the Japanese Navy's most secret messages. There is no evidence that any of these signal intelligence organisations' activities were coordinated.

Neither the Army nor the Navy agency fully trusted the other or shared its information. Therein lay yet another seed of disaster ahead of 7 December. The inter-service deal struck between OP-20-G and SIS late in 1940 almost beggars belief. Safford, the head of OP-20-G recorded: 'We agreed [with SIS] to divide all Japanese diplomatic processing on a daily basis, the navy taking the odd days' traffic and the army the even days' traffic ... later Naval Intelligence and Army G2 arranged for dissemination of the Japanese diplomatic (take) to the White House and State Department on a monthly basis, Navy taking the odd months and Army the even months ...'

By December 1941, the US intelligence services had between them managed to read the key Japanese naval operations code, JN 25, and to read the Japanese government's high-level diplomatic traffic, MAGIC. They therefore possessed the capability to decipher and read the Japanese intentions before Pearl Harbor. But this information was not shared.

But there is much more to the 'mystery of Pearl Harbor' than a confused and incompetent misuse of SIGINT. The American authorities had access to plenty of other evidence from a variety of other sources.

One of MI5's prize double agents, was Dusko Popov, a Yugoslav, code-named 'Tricycle' (a reference to his alleged preference for entertaining two ladies at a time), who was dispatched by the British to brief the Americans. Tricycle had received one of the German's new microdots with clear instructions from his official Abwehr masters on their collection priorities. Tricycle had a long questionnaire that revealed the Germans were asking questions of behalf of the Japanese.

One whole section was devoted to Pearl Harbor, its layout, dispositions and defences. The Director of the FBI, J. Edgar Hoover, interviewed Popov and was not impressed. Even the significance of such pearls in the long German questionnaire as, 'What is the progress of the dredger at the entrance to [Pearl Harbor's] East and South East Loch?' were ignored or overlooked by Hoover. The FBI was

responsible for security and counter-intelligence on Hawaii and, since
the Japanese Consul General was using a similar questionnaire to
Popov's, it might have been expected they would pay closer attention.
But Tricycle (whose private life was, admittedly, somewhat louche)
was dismissed out of hand by the apparently sexually fastidious – and
certainly xenophobic – Hoover.

But in 1941 no-one in Washington coordinated intelligence, no-one
assessed all source material, and there was no way that J. Edgar Hoover
was going to cooperate with the armed forces and share his
information.

Even Stalin's Russia helped, unwittingly, to build the picture of
Japanese preparedness. As part of the Soviet dictator's desperate
attempts to avert a war on two fronts, Stalin signed a Japanese-Soviet
neutrality pact on 13 April 1941. This freed the Soviets to concentrate
on their western border and the looming Nazi threat; but the pact
obviously released Japanese forces for deployment elsewhere than
Siberia.

As the year progressed, further confirmation of Japan's warlike
intentions came with the so-called 'Canton' signal intercepted in
mid-summer 1941, which spelled out the precise target list for what
was later to become notorious as 'The Greater East Asia Co-Prosperity
Sphere'. While not denying its provenance, the US Office of Naval
Intelligence (ONI) dismissed its contents as a mere Japanese 'wish
list', an 'expression of Tokyo's wishful thinking', and not as a possible
warning of targets for attack – which in fact it was.

Reviewing the evidence, we must ask ourselves two key questions.
First, did the available intelligence up to 6 December 1941 identify
Pearl Harbor as a definite target? Secondly, was Pearl Harbor prepared
– and if not, why not?

It is important to remember that Pearl Harbor was, especially to the
Japanese strategic planners, merely a sideshow. It was intended as
nothing more than a surprise aerial blitzkrieg, designed to neutralise
the American fleet on the flank of the real Japanese attack. The prime
strike was designed to seize Japan's key economic objectives in South
East Asia. Hard though it is to accept, Pearl Harbor was not the main
Japanese target on 7 December 1941.

This balance of strategic priorities was strongly felt in the Japanese councils of war. For example, the Japanese naval staff in particular was initially highly sceptical of Yamamoto's plan for Pearl Harbor. Admiral Nagano, the chief of Japanese naval staff, only authorised the attack on condition that it could be cancelled at any time and would not interfere with or jeopardise other, more important, strategic operations. So, while there was a wealth of evidence that Japan was going to assault the Far East, the signals for any activity at Pearl Harbor were essentially secondary to the main assaults being planned.

The key fact about the intelligence disaster at Pearl Harbor is that most of the evidence was hidden by a positive blizzard of other information at the time. This masking of vital indicators amidst a welter of other signals is called 'noise' by professional intelligence officers. Quite simply, the clamour of other voices drowned out the Pearl Harbor material. After any surprise attack it is relatively easy to go back over the evidence and pick out the key indicators; and thus it proves with Pearl Harbor. But at the time they were competing for attention with other, more likely events.

By the end of November 1941, almost every informed commentator had realised that the diplomatic pressure and policy of bringing Japan to her knees was failing and that the Japanese were preparing to go to war. The problem was that although everyone recognised the gravity of the looming international crisis, every informed commentator was focused on Thailand, Malaya, Burma and the Dutch East Indies as the most likely targets and area of operations for any Japanese onslaught. But there can be no doubt that the US took the situation very seriously. Secretary of War Stimson, acting for Roosevelt while the President was on holiday in the last week of November 1941, actually signed a 'war alert' signal to all US commands on 27 November. The US Navy's OPNAV version of this signal of 27 November, sent by the Chief of Naval Operations to his fleet commanders in both the Atlantic and Pacific theatres, could not be clearer or more specific:

This despatch is to be considered a war warning ... an aggressive move by Japan is expected within the next few days.

Crucially, the signal goes on:

> The ... organisation of naval task forces indicates an amphibious expedition against either the Philippines or Kra Peninsula [Thailand] or possibly Borneo ...

There was no mention of Pearl Harbor.

So, of the two key questions, the first is clearly answered: by December 1941 the balance of evidence is that everyone who counted knew that war was imminent with Japan, but, and the 'but' is crucial, there was little unambiguous intelligence available to commanders that Pearl Harbor was a definite objective, even though it was acknowledged that US territories might be a target.

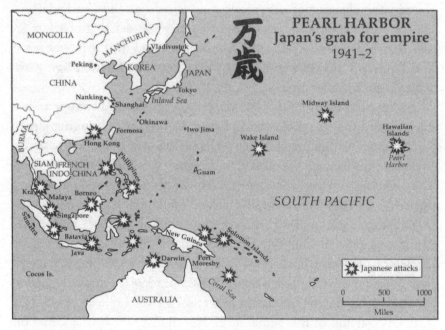

The focus of our investigation now homes in on the second question about Pearl Harbor; were the US commands on Hawaii prepared? And if not, why not? More ink has been spilled on this issue than almost any other. Nowadays Pearl Harbor stands as a model of the surprise attack, with innocent sailors preparing to go to church on a Sunday morning being slaughtered by a perfidious hail of bombs and high-explosive raining from a clear blue sky. No fewer than six separate inquiries have examined the disaster at Pearl Harbor, although only one appears to have been privy to all the available intelligence.

Roosevelt and his advisers knew that something was going to happen; but they didn't know what that was until it was almost too late to save Pearl Harbor.

Churchill and the British signals intelligence service (GCCS), particularly their Far East Communications Bureau, shared the bulk of their relevant vital operation intelligence with their American counterparts. They passed across much more than any belligerent nation would normally pass to a neutral country. No-one disputes Churchill's relief at the involvement of the US in the conflict or his delight at Hitler's ill-judged declaration of war on the USA. But there is no evidence that Churchill deliberately misled his American colleagues or knew more about the Pearl Harbor attack than Roosevelt. Both parties knew a great deal of what was going on in Japanese official thinking.

The reasons for the detailed operational and tactical failures at Pearl Harbor on the ground on the morning of 7 December 1941 are therefore neither political, nor strategic. The intelligence failures before Pearl Harbor were undoubtedly failures at national, governmental, level. But the issue of commanders' 'preparedness' in Hawaii on the day cannot be laid at Roosevelt's or Churchill's door, or any other Machiavellian conspirator; the failure at Pearl Harbor lies squarely at the feet of the respective commanders at Pearl Harbor and their immediate supervisors.

To understand this we have to be clear about the status of the US Hawaii commands in 1941, and see the world as it was then, and not as we see it now in a world of 'unified commands', 'joint service organisations' and the like.

The first, and most striking fact, is the plural, 'commands'. Hawaii was a divided responsibility: the US Navy, under the Commander-in-Chief of the Pacific Fleet, Admiral Kimmel was responsible for the fleet, its operations in the Pacific and its fleet anchorage at Pearl Harbor. On the other hand, the US Army under Lieutenant General Short was responsible for ground and air security (the US Air Force did not exist as a discrete branch of the military until 1947) of all the

Hawaiian islands, defence against invasion and counter-sabotage. The sad fact is that the US Army and the US Navy did not work together in 1941. They were two entirely separate, competing organisations.

Relationships between the two commanders and their staffs were distant. The US Navy regarded itself as the premier service and saw Short as little more than a high-ranking garrison commander for their naval base. There were no joint staffs, and no effective liaison between the Navy's intelligence assets on the islands and the Army.

Another factor intrudes, hard for us to judge across the years, but one that is instantly understandable. Rather like Cyprus for the British and Tahiti for the French armed forces, Hawaii was the classic 'cushy billet' or soft posting. The islands' reputation for sun, sand and the other obvious recreational delights of a semi-tropical paradise were as strong in 1941 as they are today. For the Navy, 'Pearl' was where you came back to from tough sea duty to go ashore and relax while the ships were refitted. For the Army, Hawaii was, in the words of Colonel Henry Clausen, the lawyer appointed to carry out the definitive secret US Department of Defense investigation into the debacle, 'a perpetual happy hour ...'

This view of the state of affairs in Hawaii before Pearl Harbor is reinforced by a damning and little known report by a Colonel H. S. Burwell into the Hawaiian command, dated July 1941.

> A dangerous lack of awareness of the possibility of a surprise enemy attack in the event of 'an abrupt conflict with Japan'.
>
> Complacency at all levels based on 'the ingrained habits of peacetime'.
>
> Lack of 'aggressive attitiude' and 'unconcern for the future'.
>
> Inattention accorded in peacetime to intelligence functions.
>
> Failure to implement joint planning sufficiently with other services.

Lieutenant General Short was not alone in his problems. The US Navy, under Admiral Kimmell, almost deliberately cut off the Army from the deliberations of the fleet and its staff. For example, there was, according to the subsequent inquiries:

No joint planning staff on the islands.

No joint air or radar surveillance of the waters around Hawaii.

No official liaison staff between Navy and Army.

A deliberate Pacific Fleet policy to withhold key signals intelligence from the Army (especially a key decision not to pass on the final Japanese alert for war, or the so-called 'Winds Code' messages).

Squabbles between Navy and Army over who should be in command of the 'outlying islands' such as Guam and Wake.

Faced with a divided command, no real liaison, a reluctance to share vital intelligence plus a peacetime 'in barracks' ethos at all levels in the islands, it is hardly surprising that the US forces on Hawaii were unprepared.

As the final days before the tragedy unfolded the US and Allied intelligence staffs went into overdrive. Early in December traffic analysis correctly spotted the build-up of the Japanese attack fleets for Batavia, Thailand and Malaya. The timing of any attack then became the key requirement. The 'essential element of information' or prime intelligence requirement came down in the end to one simple question: when?

On 19 November, Tokyo issued a specific warning to its Washington Embassy to listen out for a special radio broadcast 'in case of an emergency [cutting off diplomatic relations] and the cutting off of international communications'. This would be done by inserting a coded personal message into the daily Japanese international short-wave news broadcast. The messages were to be disguised as 'meteorological reports' (hence the 'Winds Code') with 'EAST WIND RAIN' standing for a breach with the USA, and 'WEST WIND CLEAR' for a break with the British Empire. This 19 November instruction went on to order all low-level secret diplomatic codes and ciphers to be destroyed and for the diplomatic staffs to prepare for war. The message was duly intercepted, and read, by all the Allied intelligence staffs.

Needless to say, from that moment on, the number one priority of all US and Allied intelligence staffs was to listen out for the 'Winds' messages. It was to become the great intelligence obsession of the Pearl Harbor story, and the mystery as to whether it was ever sent endures to this day.

On 3 December the Washington Navy Bureau alerted Admiral Kimmell in Hawaii with two crucial signals:

> Highly reliable information has been received that categoric priority instructions were sent yesterday to Japanese diplomatic posts at Hong Kong, Singapore, Batavia, Manila, Washington and London to destroy most of their codes and ciphers at once and to burn all other confidential and secret documents.

The second message from Washington to Kimmell on Hawaii should have rung even more alarm bells.

> ...Tokyo One December ordered London, Hong Kong, Singapore, Batavia and Manila to destroy 'machine'. Batavia 'machine' already sent back to Tokyo. December second Washington also directed to destroy all but one copy of other systems and all secret documents...

When an embassy is ordered to destroy all its codes and ciphers and, more importantly, its code machines, there can only be one explanation: the embassy is about to be withdrawn, and diplomatic relations broken off. Once the code machines have gone, there can be no turning back. Destruction of code and cipher machines is one of the intelligence analysts' ultimate 'warnings of war'.

We know from the record that the Hawaiian naval intelligence staff received this intercept.

Sadly, there is no evidence that Admiral Kimmell passed on this vital information to his Army counterpart, the man responsible for the defence of Hawaii, Lieutenant General Short. Looking back, years later, there seems to be an almost tragic acceleration towards disaster in the last days. The US Navy, aware but not alert, struggled with the problem of what to do. In their barracks ashore, a peacetime garrison army held meetings that decided that there were not enough specialists to man the new surveillance radars for more than three hours a day and to lobby Washington for more specialist manpower to be posted to Hawaii to start up a low-level liaison staff with the Navy. As an interim counter-sabotage measure all the aeroplanes at Hickham Field air base were drawn up wing-tip to wing-tip so that they could be better guarded. The effect was, tragically, to create what a later generation of military planners would call 'a target-enriched environment' for the Japanese planes when they eventually did swoop down.

There was one final chance that Hawaii could be saved from the Japanese combined fleet, which had sailed in secret from northern Japan on 26 November and was now closing in on the Hawaiian islands from the fog-shrouded and empty waters of the northwest Pacific, timing its arrival for Hawaiian dawn, 7 December. If the US could only see clear intentions of the Japanese attack in time, Hawaii could still be warned.

Fortunately for the intelligence specialists, as the crisis deepened, one clear political indicator of the likely course of future events was becoming ever more significant. The Japanese had been given a final set of diplomatic proposals to find a peaceful solution by the US and their reply, when it came, would be crucial. It would only a yes or no: peace or war. All efforts were diverted to listening for and unbuttoning any Japanese reply. Once again the aptly named MAGIC code breakers did not fail.

The US authorities were alerted by their siginters that the Japanese embassy in Washington was to receive a long fourteen-part top-secret message from the Japanese Foreign Ministry on or about 6 December 1941. The message was to be handed formally to the US authorities as 'the Japanese answer'. The timing for precise delivery of the message to the US was to be sent in a separate message. The US codebreakers, using their MAGIC access to Japanese diplomatic codes, could intercept and read this vital message as soon as it came into the Japanese Embassy in Washington. American foreknowledge of its contents might buy a few vital hours of warning.

What happened to the 'fourteen-part message' was the final link in the chain of mismanagement, bad organisation, bureaucratic wrangling and chronic understaffing that characterised the whole saga of Pearl Harbor.

Some time about 2200 hours on 6 December Washington time, a Navy courier took the first thirteen parts of the Japanese reply to President Roosevelt, who read it with his aide, Harry Hopkins. Both men read the English text carefully, and Roosevelt commented, 'This means war ...'

The naval courier, Lieutenant Commander Kramer, then carried the highly sensitive signal by hand around late-night Washington to a number of other indoctrinated senior naval officers, and then, seeing no sign of the fourteenth part of the signal on his return to the Navy SIGINT office, went home to his bed at about 0100 hours, Sunday 7 December, after a twelve-hour working day.

Across at the Army's intelligence the same message was getting the Army treatment. This time the signal was unbuttoned and the two watch officers, Colonel Rufus Bratton, chief of the Far Eastern Section and his deputy, Lieutenant Colonel Carlisle C. Dusenbury waited impatiently for the full text to arrive. By 2130 hours, like the Navy, the crucial fourteenth piece was slow in arriving. But, unlike his naval counterpart, the Army intelligence chief Bratton was not prepared to wait to drive around the Washington dinner circuit late on a Saturday night. Bored and tired, (for he had been working long hours as the Japanese crisis developed) Bratton went home to bed, enjoining his deputy to, 'make sure he showed the whole signal to General Marshall,' (the Army Chief of Staff).

Some time around midnight on 6–7 December 1941, Dusenbury received the final, fourteenth, part of Tokyo's secret instructions to their Washington embassy. It ordered the Japanese Ambassador to break off relations with Washington at precisely 1300 hours Eastern Standard Time (Hawaii is six hours behind EST: 1300 Washington is dawn at Pearl Harbor).

Having, at last, received the final part of the long awaited message, Dusenbury tried to contact General Marshall. He could not be located and so a weary Dusenbury decided to go to bed at about 0130 hours.

He decided that the full message could be delivered to the interested parties on Sunday morning. While Washington slept, nine precious hours of warning time were lost.

Early on Sunday morning the truth dawned on the key players. President Roosevelt read the fourteenth section, given to him by the navy, and said, 'so it looks as if the Japanese are going to break off negotiations . . .'

It read: 'The Imperial Japanese government regrets to have to notify hereby the American Government that in view of the attitude of the American Government it cannot but consider that it is impossible to reach an agreement through normal negotiations . . .'

Fortunately, the President's service chiefs were not as casual about the message as their subordinates. The significance of the Washington deadline was immediately obvious both to Admiral Stark and General Marshall, who drafted a warning to be sent urgently to Hawaii as well as all other Pacific commands. The agreed text read: 'The Japanese are presenting at 1 pm [1300] Eastern Standard Time, today, what amounts to an ultimatum. Also they are under orders to destroy their code machine immediately. Just what significance the hour set may have we do not know, but be on alert accordingly . . .'

A message like this from a national command authority is not just an umbrella against any future board of inquiry. A regional commander-in-chief can use a signal like this to take whatever steps he deems appropriate, particularly at a time when even the press are headlining a war as imminent. The message from Washington effectively devolved a massive freedom on them to act as they saw fit: 'be on alert accordingly'. The fleet could have been prepared for sea; the Army and Army Air Force could have gone on red alert and issued ammunition. Professional officers ever since have claimed that that is precisely what they would have done on receipt of such a message from the head of the Army or Navy, given the international tension at the time, and their existing knowledge of events.

Unfortunately, the message was never sent in time.

Marshall released the signal at about 1130 hours Washington time, but the War Department message centre could not raise Hawaii on their secure radio. As a result, Marshall's crucial warning had to be sent, suitably encoded as a Western Union cable to San Francisco and thence by RCA commercial radio to Honolulu. The message was logged at 1201 hours Washington (0601 Hawaii). By the time Marshall's final warning reached Hawaii, delivered by a motor cycle messenger to General Short's headquarters at 1745 hours Washington time (1145 Hawaii), the air raids had already started Apparently the RCA courier apologised for taking longer to deliver a cable than was normal, but said he had had to 'take shelter from an air raid'.

The chain of intelligence warnings had failed completely and, despite futile last-minute attempts to alert Hawaii, the Japanese fell onto unprepared US fleet and land bases.

As the seismic shock waves of the Japanese attack reverberated around the Pacific, some other fairly obvious indicators suddenly assumed a new significance. Why they were ignored at the time remains a mystery to this day. What happened to some of those warnings remains an even bigger mystery.

On 2 and 3 December, a liner, the Matson shipping company's SS *Lurline*, had been routinely monitoring the radio frequencies in the empty northern Pacific as she ploughed a lonely passage to the west towards Honolulu, outbound from San Francisco. Suddenly, on 2 December her radio operator had been blasted by powerful signals in Japanese naval code on the lower maritime frequency. The ship's radio operator was able to identify the Japanese Navy's headquarters call sign ('JCS') and to take bearings on them over the next two days. The radio operator plotted the signals as coming along on a bearing that placed a powerful Japanese naval force transmitting somewhere northwest of Hawaii and transmitting slowly *eastwards*.

When the liner docked at Hawaii two days later, the two merchant marine radio operators went immediately to the US Navy's intelligence office at Admiral Kimmell's Pacific Fleet headquarters, turned over their original logs directly to the duty naval intelligence officer and briefed him on what they had heard. The logs have never been seen since and there is no record of the warning ever having being received by the US Navy.

Another curiosity is the saga of the long awaited 'Winds' messages, which everyone in the know was looking out for. Usually, as the bombs rain down and the fighting erupts, *all* the lights on a modern electronic indicators and warnings board are flashing red. Ironically, as the Japanese Navy's aircraft hurled themselves at Pearl Harbor, the most sought-for indicator of all remained stubbornly *green*.

That is odd, because on 4 December a US Navy radioman, Ralph Briggs, a qualified Japanese-speaking radio intercept operator working at the Hawaii intercept station, picked up the Japanese telegraphic code for 'EAST WIND, RAIN' (*Higashi no kaze ame*) in a routine Japanese official naval weather broadcast. He dutifully logged it down, and promptly transmitted it down the secure TWX circuit to Commander Safford's Fleet Intelligence Office at Pearl Harbor. Briggs was subsequently given four days leave by the US Navy, as the official reward for 'the first man to intercept the Winds Message'. This fact is confirmed by the fact that Briggs was at home in Cleveland Ohio, when the Japanese attacked. Briggs is also on record as saying on 7 December 'that the Japanese must have received a terrific surprise, as Pearl Harbor knew that they were coming'.

Both Safford and Briggs were adamant that they had received and reported the vital 'Winds Message', indicating that the US was the target. But in that dreadful week after the Japanese attack, some unknown agency, (probably on the orders of the Director of Naval Intelligence) destroyed a significant number of key signals and documents in a panicky attempt to deny any foreknowledge. An unknown number of highly classified documents were mysteriously removed in silent hours from safes on the 'second deck' of the Navy Building.

It is possible, indeed likely, that Safford's copy to Washington of the 'Winds Message' message from Hawaii found itself there, among those sensitive documents, but got no further. It could have been one of the embarrassing messages sitting in the safe of a naval intelligence officer. We shall never know. The official Washington inquiries forever denied any evidence of a 'Winds Message.' However Briggs undoubtedly got his four days 'special reward' home leave; if not for the 'Winds Message' coup, then for what?

One other curious mystery about Pearl Harbor has never been satisfactorily resolved. As the prospect of war loomed ever closer, the Allied intelligence services around the Pacific began to forge ever closer informal links with each other, for obvious reasons. With the Netherlands overrun by the Germans in May 1940, the Dutch East Indies kept an independent colonial and effective administration up and running. More importantly, it had diplomatic accreditation as representatives of the Dutch government in exile, who were now based in London.

One of its officers was a captain of the Royal Netherlands Navy, Johann Ranneft. The US Navy afforded Ranneft all the easy, informal access that attachés strive so hard to achieve, but so rarely obtain. For Ranneft was not only a valued friend, he was also, in the eyes of the US Naval officers based in Washington, a colleague, a senior naval officer, no threat to US interests (quite the reverse) and recognised as a 'regular guy'. As a result, Ranneft often saw much more than would be normal for a foreigner. The Dutchman also kept an official diary. His record is interesting.

On 6 December Captain Ranneft called at the Office of Naval Intelligence, on the 'second deck' of the US Navy headquarters. Several days before, during an earlier routine visit to the 'Second Deck', Ranneft had been shown the track of a Japanese carrier force in the northern Pacific by two relatively junior intelligence officers. To his surprise, the plot showed them east of Japan and heading towards Alaska and the Aleutian Islands. Ranneft was startled, and noted in his official office diary, '. . . ONI. They show me on the map the position of two Japanese carriers. They left Japan on a easterly course . . .'

Now, two days later, he rounded on Admiral Wilkinson, the head of US Naval Intelligence and his SIGINT bureau translation chief, Lieutenant Commander Kramer, 'What about those two carriers? Where are those fellows?' Someone, (Ranneft didn't remember who) pointed at a position on the chart about 400 nautical miles north of the Hawaiian Islands. Ranneft was stunned, but assumed that, in the words of his official diary entry for 6 December 1941, 'I myself do not consider it, because I believe that everyone in Honolulu is 100% on the alert just as everyone is at ONI.'

Ranneft left the Navy headquarters and the Office of Naval Intelligence and reported on the same day by official cable what he had learned to the Dutch government in exile in London. At no point was

Ranneft's testimony ever read at any of the subsequent official US inquiries into the disaster at Pearl Harbor. The Office of Naval Intelligence in Washington resolutely denied it ever knew where the Japanese carriers were and certainly there is no record that they ever informed Admiral Kimmell at Hawaii that they had a powerful carrier force plotted 400 nautical miles to the north of the Pacific Fleet's main base and anchorage.

What makes this story all the more tragic is that Kimmell, a highly professional two-star admiral, who had only recently been promoted to acting four-star admiral, (a remarkable jump) actually discussed the location of the Japanese carriers with his staff on 2 December. On being informed that the Hawaiian based Fleet Naval Intelligence Staff had no idea of the carriers' location, Kimmell dryly observed, 'so they could be rounding Diamond Head (the entrance to Pearl Harbor) at any moment?' A member of his somewhat embarrassed staff is on record as replying that, 'they hoped that they would locate them before that, Admiral.' In the circumstances, this exchange takes on a particular poignancy.

Years later, in 1960, the now Admiral Ranneft attempted to raise the subject with Admiral Stark (the senior US naval officer in Washington during Ranneft's 1941 tour of duty) while on a valedictory visit to Washington from NATO. When Stark realised why Ranneft wanted to see him, he abruptly cancelled the meeting and refused to see the Dutch officer.

To round off this catalogue of mysteries about Pearl Harbor, finally we have the curious testimony of a newspaper boy. Early on Sunday 7 December 1941, sixteen-year-old Tom Nichols dropped off a copy of the Sunday *Washington Times Herald* to one of his regular customers, the Japanese naval attaché, on the top floor of 3601 Connecticut Avenue, Washington, DC. To his surprise, two burly uniformed US Marines were standing guard on the attaché's door and took the newspaper from him. No-one has ever explained who ordered a special US Marines guard on the Japanese naval attaché at dawn, Washington time, Sunday 7 December 1941; or, perhaps more significantly, *why* a guard was ordered. Even the President hadn't been shown the fourteenth part of the 'end diplomatic negotiations' signal at the time the youngster delivered his papers. However, US Marines are routinely tasked by the US Department of the Navy. No explanation has ever been offered for this curious side-tale to the events of 7 December 1941.

To the intelligence analyst, Pearl Harbor is unique. It presents a story of opportunities missed, intelligence ignored and bureaucratic bungling across a broad and tragic canvas. The whole mystery is also spiced by a slim, but persistent, possibility of conspiracy or cover-up. No fewer than six major national inquiries crawled over nearly every detail of the tragedy for the US authorities, all with a broadly similar aim: who knew what, and when?

Of these, only the top-secret MAGIC inquiry by the lawyer Colonel Clausen, had access to all the facts and, most important of all, to the surviving SIGINT traffic. It is hardly surprising therefore that Clausen's conclusion differed radically in a few key areas from the thrust of the earlier service and political inquiries, which seem to have been primarily designed to assign blame or find scapegoats. Unfortunately, as with so much of the Second World War's signals intelligence, the real facts remained highly classified until Clausen broke his fifty-year silence in 1992.

By meticulously piecing together the story in 1945, mainly by flying all over the world and by shoving top-secret SIGINT intercepts under the noses of the startled 1941 staff members, Clausen discovered that many more people had known much more than they admitted to the various official enquiries, most of whom had not been cleared to read the highly classified SIGINT material, which was held on a very tight 'need to know' basis.

One of the biggest dangers in the world of intelligence is excessive secrecy. The principle of need to know or 'special compartmentalisation', designed to keep access to delicate information very tightly controlled, while a vital part of security, can also be a highly dangerous policy, for two main reasons.

First of all, key decision makers are sometimes denied access to the information on the grounds that they have 'no need to know'. So it was with Lieutenant General Short on Hawaii in 1941, who was not cleared for all available SIGINT and certainly did not know that the Navy was reading Japanese intentions. This ignorance *must* have affected his decisions before 7 December 1941. Equally, Admiral Kimmell's refusal to show his own intelligence to his co-commander on the island becomes almost understandable: Short was not cleared for the Navy's most sensitive secrets. When this is allied to the fact that Kimmell himself wasn't seeing everything that the Navy was intercepting (because his personal MAGIC code reading machine had been removed earlier in 1941 as part of a highly secret intelligence exchange deal with the British), it is clear that both senior commanders on Hawaii were blindsided to a significant degree. The problem was compounded by the uncoordinated organisation of US national intelligence in 1941. There was no national intelligence assessment staff reporting to the President. No single agency saw everything or reported the significance of the intelligence.

Secondly, and much more serious, the secret squirrel mentality can sometimes be used to conceal errors. There seems to be little doubt that in the aftermath of Pearl Harbor, for both good and bad reasons, secrecy prevented an honest and thorough evaluation of the facts. Whatever Clausen's judgements, it is clear that the responsibility cannot be laid solely at the door of the wretched Hawaiian commanders. So the question is, was 'national security' used as a cloak to hide war-winning secrets (that the US was reading Japanese code messages) from an enemy or as an excuse to conceal embarrassing, and politically explosive mistakes?

There is another, perhaps psychological, reason for the disaster. In 1941 every expert *knew* that Pearl Harbor could not be attacked. The US Pacific Fleet base was simply too far from Japan or any other likely enemy, it was too secure and well-guarded, and the surrounding hills and shallow anchorage made any torpedo attack a technical impossibility. The received wisdom of the day was that Pearl Harbor was invulnerable.

Unfortunately, what had been true in 1939 was no longer valid in 1941. On 11 November 1941 the British Royal Navy, in what was one of the most successful and least acknowledged attacks of the Second World War, had caught the Italian Mediterranean battle fleet at anchor at Taranto in Southern Italy. Eleven special torpedoes from obsolescent Swordfish biplanes sank three Italian battleships, two heavy cruisers and effectively neutralised Mussolini's navy in a daring night attack launched from British carriers off the coast.

An abiding American trait, often remarked upon by friends and enemies alike, is the 'not invented here' syndrome. Americans tend only to trust American ideas and developments and tend to ignore – or resent – others' achievements, be they weapons, consumer goods or even TV shows. The US Navy virtually ignored the lessons of Taranto. The Imperial Japanese Navy, on the other hand, recognised it as the remarkable strategic victory it undoubtedly was, and set out to recreate the British success. In the words of the Japanese naval staff, 'Taranto made Pearl Harbor feasible.'

In particular, the Japanese naval aviators were curious as to just how the Royal Navy had been able to launch torpedoes from the air to run in such a shallow anchorage. By trial and error the Japanese discovered that aerial torpedoes could be modified to surface immediately, and not 'dig deep' after dropping, provided they were rigged with special hydrofoils or fins. The superlative Japanese torpedoes, already the best in the world, were rigged with special fins for air dropping in late 1941 and tested for shallow launch. They worked, and suddenly the attack on the anchored fleet in the shallow waters of Pearl Harbor became a practical possibility. This was one piece of TECHINT that the US did not discover until it was too late, although, ironically, it was freely available from the Royal Navy had they only been asked. But then, in the complacency and insularity of Pearl Harbor in 1941, the US Navy felt that it had little to learn. Not so the Japanese.

Whatever the psychology of technical surprise in 1941, it is possible to dissect the attack on Pearl Harbor by straightforward reference to the intelligence cycle. Analysis of this basic intelligence planning system shows clearly the deficiencies and failings of the US intelligence and warning system in 1941.

Was there an overall US national intelligence requirement?

No; although all the key players knew that war with Japan was either a possibility or imminent, and each organisation appears to have been busy collecting intelligence on its own, there is no evidence of any coordinated national collection requirement.

Was there a collection plan?

Again, no. Within the single service agencies there was obviously planned and tasked collection (e.g. Naval Intelligence was interested in the Japanese fleet, the FBI was looking out for Japanese spies, etc.). But it was never integrated and assets were duplicated or wasted.

Were collection assets coordinated and tasked?

No. Each service or agency did its own thing, without reference to others. For example, in 1941 the FBI agent in charge on Honolulu was one Robert L. Shivers. Shivers' primary interest was security: spies, sabotage and subversion. With a large Japanese population on the Hawaiian Islands this was a task the FBI took very seriously, despite Hoover's disregard for 'Tricycle's' Abwehr questionnaire. To ensure smooth working arrangements, Shivers established weekly liaison with his service counterparts on the Islands, Commander Joe Rochefort of the US Navy and Lieutenant Colonel George Bicknell of Army G2 (Intelligence). Shivers was particularly interested in the Japanese Consul General in Hawaii and so he was excited to learn that US Navy Intelligence had been secretly tapping the Japanese office phone for over a year. Wiretaps were officially an FBI domestic speciality, and so Shivers decided to add his own line into the Japanese Consul General as well. Unfortunately, the phone company immediately informed the original 'bugger', Captain Mayfield of the US Navy that another federal agency wanted to get in on the act. Worried about the breach of security and concerned for the political repercussions if the Japanese found out they were being bugged, on 2 December 1941 Mayfield decided to bail out and ordered an immediate halt to any US Navy taps on the Japanese Consul General's telephone. However no-one told Shivers and so he did not proceed with the FBI wiretap. As a result, in the critical last week before the attack, no US agency was bugging the Japanese diplomats on Hawaii: and no-one realised it had stopped.

Was intelligence collated in an accessible and ready format?

Again, no. Single services and agencies squirrelled away their own precious nuggets with no regard for the wider picture and reported independently, if at all, to their masters. There was no single, in the modern jargon of intelligence, 'integrated database' on the Japanese.

Was the available intelligence interpreted correctly?

The answer to this is both yes *and* no. For example, the MAGIC SIGINT take was correctly assessed and interpreted as leading to war with Japan. However, the location of the Japanese combined carrier striking fleet was either ignored or misunderstood by the Office of Naval Intelligence. But the majority of the intelligence received appears to have been understood correctly. The problem appears to have been that, although its meaning was understood, its *implications* were ignored or overlooked. The whole institutional psychology at the time must also have been influenced by the complete contempt for the Asiatic Japanese. The American interpreters of intelligence – at all levels, from the President downwards – completely under-estimated the Japanese both as fighters and technologically.

Was the interpreted intelligence disseminated to decision makers in a timely fashion?

The answer to this must be an emphatic, 'No', from top to bottom. Thus the President and decision-taking Washington were not alerted to the final instalment of the Japanese fourteen-part message in time to act upon it; Admiral Kimmell and Hawaii were left unwarned at the last minute; vital naval operational indicators disappeared between Hawaii and the Navy Department; and the unfortunate Army commander in Hawaii seems to have been kept in the dark throughout. The dissemination of intelligence before Pearl Harbor was not just a sorry tale: it was appalling. There was no integration of all-source material and no 'all-source assessment' and no briefing to those with a 'need to know'.

If there is any single factor that links all these failures of US intelligence in 1941, it lies in the phrase 'all-source integration'. Nowadays it is axiomatic that a single assessment and tasking staff must coordinate and integrate a nation's intelligence effort at the highest level like any other scarce resource.

This principle is easy to state, but desperately difficult to achieve. Every agency has its own monopoly on particular secrets, and equally, every agency is notoriously reluctant to tell its colleagues, for two reasons, one very good and one very bad. The laudable reason is invariably security. A secret shared with another agency, without the strictest 'need to know' is usually viewed as a potential loss of control of a vital source and thus of secrecy; far better 'not to risk a compromise of our best assets . . .'

The second reason is less edifying but understandable. Any bureaucratic agency holding a monopoly on a secret source can invariably guarantee for itself access to politicians, influence, power and resources, usually expressed in the agency's expanding budget. In the constant bureaucratic battle for political advantage, agencies are reluctant to share their victories with others, and only too keen to seize more offices in the corridors of power.

This puts an enormous responsibility on the ultimate decision makers, who are invariably the politicians, elected or otherwise, for they are the only people with the authority and control of national resources to order the agencies to work together. Even if this means a specialist assessment staff (like the UK's 'Joint Intelligence Committee' or JIC) above the agencies, someone has to integrate the effort. In the final analysis, politicians have to knock civil servants' heads together.

In December 1941, the one clear omission in Washington was of a national intelligence assessment and briefing staff, with access to all available intelligence from every source. With the lunacy of the navy briefing on odd days and the army on even days, FDR was effectively cast as his own coordinator and tasker of political-military intelligence. It is a job he did very badly, which, given his other vast responsibilities and lack of understanding of the Japanese, is hardly surprising. He was not equipped as an analyst of the Japanese military mind and nor did he know what questions to ask, or who to ask them of. Broadly speaking, he didn't know what he didn't know. His service chiefs failed him. And in their turn, the service chiefs' specialist intelligence staffs failed their masters too. The truth is that they, and the nation as a whole, consistently under-estimated both the capabilities and intentions of the Japanese as a potential adversary.

Whatever the excuses, and whatever the failings of subordinates at all levels, the brutal fact remains that, by any professional and objective measure, the USA had ample and timely intelligence of a Japanese surprise attack somewhere in the Pacific and probably on Pearl Harbor from a wide variety of indicators and sources. Because the nation's chief executive failed to establish an integrated national intelligence organisation in time, and to control the Washington bureaucracy, over two thousand US servicemen died and America was plunged into a World War, which might have been avoided.

Pearl Harbor stands as an awful warning of the ultimate intelligence 'cock-up' perpetrated by a badly organised and uncoordinated group of parochial intelligence providers who had the tools but didn't know how to do the job properly. In the final analysis they failed to disseminate the vital intelligence to the people who needed to know.

PART SEVEN

ON SECURITY

Security is the handmaiden of intelligence. Secrets that are no longer secret make much intelligence pointless, as any card player who has shown his hand will agree. Security should accompany intelligence at all times.

Sadly, total, absolute security is an unobtainable dream. Human fallibility usually makes sure of that. But security – and intelligence – officers must strive all the time to protect their secrets from the three main attacks: espionage, sabotage and subversion.

The weakest link is invariably the human one. Many of the cases of spies in Part Two are just as much breaches of, or lax, security as outright espionage. That is why personnel security, starting at the lowest level, will always remain vital to protecting a nation's secrets. Because when security fails to detect a weak link the results can be catastrophic, as the case of Aldrich Ames reveals. This was not just a case of espionage; Ames was a case of a dreadful failure of security.

CHAPTER 25

One Who Slipped Through The Net: Aldrich Hazen Ames

According to the US Congressional report on the case, Aldrich Hazen Ames caused more damage to the national security of the United States than any spy in the history of the CIA. While that is probably true, of perhaps greater significance is that Ames was really a walking breach of security and, through sheer inefficiency and incompetence on the part of the CIA and FBI security authorities, was not picked up until he had done huge damage to US intelligence.

Ames started work for the CIA in 1957 as a low-level records analyst, marking classified documents for filing. After college he returned to the Washington area, and took full-time employment at the CIA doing menial clerical tasks. After graduating, Ames was accepted into the agency's career trainee programme.

During his 1962 'entrance on duty' polygraph examination, Ames passed the lie detector examination, and his initial background investigation, completed in May 1962, revealed no negative information from police or credit bureau records.

Upon his graduation from the trainee programme in October 1968, Ames was promoted to the rank of GS-10 and, in October 1969, was given his first overseas assignment to Ankara, Turkey, where he targeted Russian intelligence officers for recruitment. By now Ames was a trained CIA case officer.

By the end of his third year, Ames's superiors considered him unsuited for field work and expressed the view that perhaps he should spend the remainder of his career at the CIA headquarters in Langley – a damaging assessment for a mainstream CIA operations officer. Ames was deeply upset by this critical evaluation of his job performance.

In 1972, he returned to CIA headquarters where he spent the next four years in the Soviet-East European (SE) Division of the Directorate of Operations (DO). In 1973, he was given Russian language training, and specialised in the Russian intelligence services, including the KGB.

He was then assigned to a position where he supported CIA operations against Soviet officials in the US. From the start he appears to have been a security risk. Evidence of Ames's drinking problem surfaced during this period. At a Christmas party on 20 December 1973 Ames became so drunk that he had to be helped to his home by employees from the CIA's Office of Security.

The following Christmas, Ames got insensibly drunk once again and was discovered by an agency security officer in a compromising position with a female CIA employee. Each incident resulted in an Office of Security memorandum being placed in his agency security file, but it does not appear that his operational supervisors were made aware of these incidents.

Ames was reported for another two significant breaches of security during this period. In 1976 he left a briefcase on a subway train when on his way to meet an official Soviet contact. The briefcase contained classified operational materials, which could have compromised the Soviet asset concerned. The FBI managed to retrieve the case but it was unclear if the information had been compromised. Ames received only a verbal reprimand for what was a serious security breach. Several years later, in October 1980, Ames was cited for leaving top-secret communications equipment unsecured in his office, but this, too, did not result in any formal reprimand.

By now Ames' marriage was in trouble and he accepted an assignment in September 1981 to go to Mexico while his wife remained in New York. During the Mexico assignment, Ames acquired a reputation for 'regularly going out with a group of people, taking long lunches, and having too much to drink'. At a diplomatic reception at the

American Embassy in Mexico City, he got drunk and became involved in an aggressive argument with a Cuban official. On another occasion he was involved in a traffic accident in Mexico City and was so drunk he could not answer police questions or recognise the US Embassy officer sent to rescue him.

This episode with the Cuban official worried his superiors. He was counselled by one of his bosses, and another supervisor sent a message to CIA headquarters recommending that Ames undergo an assessment for alcohol abuse when he returned to the United States.

On Ames's return from Mexico, he had one counselling session but there was no follow-up programme or treatment. Ames' blood tests proved normal, and he denied to the counsellor that he had a serious drinking problem. Information about Ames's drinking habits was not passed on to either the Office of Security or the DO.

Ames said in an interview after his arrest that there were 'many much more serious problems of alcohol abuse' within the CIA. He said that his alcohol problem had 'slopped over' only once during a formal occasion (at the embassy reception in Mexico City), and only on 'a couple of less formal occasions'.

In February 1983, the CIA Office of Security conducted a routine background investigation of Ames. The investigative report noted that Ames was a social drinker who was inclined to become a bit enthusiastic when he overindulged in alcohol. But, surprisingly, no serious alcohol problem was identified. His new branch chiefs in the sensitive Soviet East European Division were never made aware of this growing drinking problem.

In April 1983, Ames was assigned to a position in the SE Division after his tour in Mexico. Despite his poor performance and known alcohol problem, Ames's Mexico City supervisors raised no objections to his new assignment, which placed him in the most sensitive element of the DO – responsible for the agency's Soviet counter-intelligence activities.

In the summer of 1984 or 1985, Ames got drunk in public once again. After drinking heavily at a meeting with his official Soviet contact, Ames continued to drink at a CIA–FBI softball game until he became drunk and incapable. The CIA man had to be driven home that night and 'left behind at the field his badge, cryptic notes, a wallet which included alias identification documents, and his jacket'. Some recall that senior SE Division managers were either present or later made aware of this incident; amazingly, Ames security record does not reflect any action being taken as a result.

Ames was involved in yet another breach of security in late 1984, this time involving Rosario, his new woman. Ames showed up with Rosario at a CIA safe house. One of the other officers complained that Ames' girlfriend's presence in the agency housing compromised the cover of the other CIA officers, as well as their activities. When he returned to Washington Ames was warned that he 'had exercised bad judgment'.

In October 1983, Ames formally separated from his first wife, who by this time had found new employment and continued to live in New York. Ames agreed as part of the separation agreement to pay all the outstanding credit card and other miscellaneous debts, which totalled nearly $50,000.

Ames believed this 1984 divorce settlement could bankrupt him, especially as Rosario had added a few new financial burdens to the hard-drinking and near-broke CIA officer. He faced a new car loan, a signature loan, and mounting credit-card payments. Ames later admitted that it was these financial difficulties that led him to first contemplate espionage between December 1984 and February 1985:

> I felt a great deal of financial pressure, which, in retrospect, I was clearly overreacting to. The previous two years that I had spent in Washington, I had incurred a certain amount of personal debt . . . [it] somehow really placed a great deal of pressure on me . . . Rosario was living with me at the time . . . I was I was thinking in the longer term . . .

It was these pressures, said Ames, which in April 1985, led him to conceive of 'a scam to get money from the KGB'. On 16 April 1985 Ames entered the Soviet Embassy in Washington, DC and handed an envelope to the duty officer at the reception desk asking for a KGB officer called Chuvakhin, who he knew to be the most senior KGB officer at the embassy. The duty officer informed Chuvakhin, and Ames had a private meeting with the KGB man. Inside the envelope Ames left with the Soviet Embassy was a note, which identified at least two major CIA cases naming Soviets who had offered their services to the CIA.

To further establish his bona fides, Ames included a page from an internal SE Division directory with his true name highlighted. He also listed an alias he had assumed when meeting Soviet officials earlier in his career. Finally, he requested a payment of $50,000.

Several weeks later, Chuvakhin agreed to a lunch with Ames. According to Ames, he went to the Soviet Embassy on 15 May 1985 and asked for Chuvakhin. The KGB agreed to pay him $50,000 and said that they would use Chuvakhin as the go-between. On 17 May, he received a payment of $50,000.

Ames later admitted later that his motivation to commit treason changed as a result of his initial success. He claimed that he had originally planned a one-time only 'con game' to provide the Soviets with the identities of their own double agents, in return for a one-off payment of $50,000 to cover his debts. He believed that the KGB would pay him $50,000 and this would solve his outstanding financial problems. However he realised he was onto a good thing. Ames got greedy. So did his Soviet controllers.

> I'm still puzzled as to what took me to the next steps. The main factor, on balance I think, was a realization after I had received the $50,000, was a sense of the enormity of what I had done. But certainly underlying it was the conviction that there was as much money as I could ever use. If I chose to do that.

After the KGB paid him the $50,000, Ames 'decided that he wasn't going to stop at that point'.

Ames's next step dealt a crippling blow to the CIA's Soviet operations. Without any prompting or direction by the KGB, or any promise of additional money, he met Chuvakhin again on 13 June 1985, and handed over copies of documents which identified the ten top Soviet agents who were then reporting to the CIA and FBI. This was explosive stuff.

Ames provided the 'largest amount of sensitive documents and critical information, that we know anyway, that have ever been passed to the KGB in one particular meeting ...' according to the US Senate report, Ames wrapped up five to seven pounds of message traffic in plastic bags and openly carried them by hand out of the CIA headquarters building for delivery to the KGB, knowing that the CIA no longer security-checked packages carried out of the building by agency employees. Ames would use this simple and straightforward method at both CIA headquarters and during his Rome assignment to provide information to the KGB.

Shortly thereafter, the KGB paid him another $50,000. During the summer of 1985, Ames met a Russian intelligence officer posing as a diplomat several times. He passed over classified information about CIA and FBI human sources and operations.

In July 1986, Ames was transferred to Rome, Italy. At the conclusion of language training and before leaving, Ames was required to take a routine security polygraph examination on 2 May 1986. He was tested on a series of standard questions to do with unauthorised contacts with a foreign intelligence service, unauthorised disclosure of classified information, and financial irresponsibility.

Ames gave consistently 'deceptive' responses to issues related to whether he had been 'pitched' (i.e. asked to work for) by a foreign intelligence service. The CIA examiner noted Ames's reaction to the 'pitch' issue but believed that this was normal, as Ames' job required him to meet Soviet intelligence officers as part of his routine CIA duties. When Ames was challenged about his nervous reaction during the session, he explained that he was indeed sensitive to the 'pitch' issue because, he stated, 'we know that the Soviets are out there somewhere, and we are worried about that'.

The CIA examiner deemed Ames truthful and concluded the examination, characterising Ames as 'bright [and] direct'. The examiner's supervisors concurred with the assessment that Ames was non-deceptive.

According to the FBI, which examined Ames's polygraph charts in June 1993, the deception indicated in Ames's response to the pitch issue in 1986 was never resolved, even though the CIA examiner

passed Ames on this exam. The FBI also discovered 'significant deceptive responses' by Ames to questions dealing with unauthorised
disclosure of classified material. None of this was recorded or noted in
Ames's polygraph security file.

After completing Italian language training, Ames, now accompanied by Rosario, arrived in Rome in July 1986, where he began his
assignment as chief of a branch that, among other things, dealt with
Soviet operations. As a branch chief, Ames had access to the true identities of CIA agents, the details of planned agent meetings, and copies
of the intelligence reports produced by these agents. He took part in
weekly staff meetings where intelligence assets and potential asset
recruitments were discussed. He coordinated double agent operations
of the US military services and received sensitive intelligence reports
about worldwide events.

While in Rome, Ames continued his meetings with the KGB, and a
Moscow-based KGB officer. He also opened several local bank
accounts, as well as some in his new wife's name, where he would regularly deposit the cash he received from the Soviets. He broke down
these payments from the KGB into smaller cash deposits in sums
under $10,000 in order to avoid bank-reporting requirements that
might have led to enquiries by banking regulators.

Ames also spread a cover story to explain his increased wealth. His
co-workers recalled that Ames encouraged the notion that Rosario
came from a wealthy family in Colombia. Ames explained to several
colleagues that Rosario had a share of the family business, which continued to generate substantial revenue

Nonetheless, some of Ames's colleagues in Rome were uneasy. They
began to suspect that Ames was not reporting all of his meetings with
the Russians. Ames's supervisor knew that Ames was meeting a Soviet
embassy officer, but apparently did not query him about the relationship or ensure that he was documenting all of his contacts. Ames's job
performance was further marred by his fondness for booze, which
resurfaced in Rome and was well known within the office. Once again,
however, there was no official record made of his drinking problems
and it is hard not to feel a little sympathy for someone who enjoys a
good lunch in Rome.

But Ames made a habit of it; not wise in an intelligence officer. In post-arrest debriefings, Ames's former colleagues stated that Ames would go out for long lunches and return to the office mid-afternoon, too drunk to work. One of his Rome supervisors recalled that Ames came back from lunch drunk about three times *a week* between 1986 and 1988. Another colleague commented that in 1987 Ames was very upset when he failed to get promoted, and he began to drink even more heavily. One of Ames's supervisors reportedly once described Ames to a colleague as 'one of the worst drunks in the outfit'.

Back in Langley by the autumn of 1986, frantic agency officials were confronting a holocaust of their best agents. As many as thirty CIA and FBI Soviet operations had been compromised or had developed problems between 1985 and 1986. The inevitable security investigations and mole hunts got underway.

Ames returned to CIA headquarters in September 1989 to find the agency in turmoil. Despite his weak record in Rome and the evidence of flagrant alcohol abuse, no particular suspicion attached to him, even after the special task force involved in the 'mole hunt' had firm information implicating someone based in Rome. His access to classified information remained fully open and at the end of 1993, was even extended as a result of changes in the CIA computer system, which allowed him to download onto floppy disks sensitive CIA operational cables and intelligence reports only marginally related to his office responsibilities.

In June 1992, he wrote a note to his Soviet contacts, which stated, in part:

> My most immediate need, as I pointed out in March, is money. As I have mentioned several times, I do my best to invest a good part of the cash I received, but keep part of it out for ordinary expenses. Now I am faced with the need to cash in investments to meet current needs a very tight and unpleasant situation! I have had to sell a certificate of deposit in Zurich and some stock here to help make up the gap. Therefore, I will need as much cash delivered in Pipe [document drop site] as you think can be accommodated [sic] – it seems to me that it could accommodate [sic] up to $100,000.

Between April 1985 and November 1993 Ames spent at least $1,397,300. In August 1989 Ames paid $540,000 in cash for a house in northern Virginia, claiming that the money came from an inheritance from Rosario Ames's family. Ames also apparently told close friends that Rosario's uncle in Colombia was so pleased at the birth of the Ames's son that he decided to buy the house for them as a gift.

Between April 1985 and November 1993, Ames's total CIA 'take home' salary totalled $336,164. However, the record shows that Ames spent $455,000 on home improvements, furniture, a new Jaguar and Honda automobiles, telephone bills, credit card payments, tuition for his wife's schooling at Georgetown University, and stock and securities purchases, as well as a farm in Colombia, during the same period

From 1990 until the time of his arrest, Ames routinely made large cash deposits into various bank accounts. Ultimately, it was Ames's sudden affluence that made him the focus of investigators.

In November 1989 the CIA received the first information that pointed directly to Ames. A CIA employee, who knew Ames well, reported to the Counterintelligence Center (CIC) that Ames seemed to be living way beyond his means. The employee reported that Ames appeared to have little money when he left for Rome, but now seemed unusually well off.

Based on this report, an Office of Security investigator opened a routine financial inquiry on Ames. The investigator also examined public records and discovered that Ames had purchased his Arlington home for $540,000, but the investigator could find no record of a mortgage. He followed up in January 1990 by asking the Treasury Department for transaction requests and identified three 'hits' involving Ames: a $13,000 cash deposit into a local bank account in 1985; a $15,000 cash deposit into the account in 1986; and, upon his return from Rome, a conversion of Italian lira into $22,107.

However, the investigator assigned to the case then began a two-month training course, and no-one was assigned to perform his duties during his absence. At the end of 1990, the investigator signed off the Ames case with a memorandum to the Office of Security requesting a follow-up background investigation and polygraph.

The memorandum noted that there could be logical explanations for the large dollar transactions, raising the possibility that the money represented the proceeds of his mother's insurance policy, or could have come from his wife's family, who was thought to be well connected in Colombia. It just needed checking.

The Office of Security opened new investigation into Ames in December 1990. Investigators checked Ames's account at the Northwest Federal Credit Union and found nothing unusual. Indeed, it showed that Ames had borrowed $25,000 of the purchase price for the Jaguar, making this circumstance appear less suspicious. In January 1991, the Office of Security sent Ames various forms to complete for the purpose of updating his background investigation. Ames did not return the forms until 4 March, at which time the Office of Security initiated a background investigation.

The Office of Security completed this investigation by 12 April 1991. The investigation was particularly comprehensive. It included background security interviews with many of Ames's past and present co-workers, whose comments included the following:

> Ames was assigned to CIC 'under a cloud'. One individual recalled that SE Division did not trust Ames or his Soviet agents.

> In Rome, Ames seemed to have had far too close contact with his Soviet and Eastern Bloc assets. Ames routinely left his safe open when he was leaving for the day.

> In Rome, Ames could not be expected into the office before 9 or 10 a.m. At least once per week there was evidence that Ames had been drinking heavily during his lunch hour.

> Another of Ames's co-workers said he didn't think Ames was a spy, but wouldn't be surprised if that someday it turned out that he was.

> Ames enjoyed a higher standard of living than most other government employees and that Ames's government salary did not explain his level of spending.

> Another co-worker reported that he understood Ames paid cash for his house, a purchase well into the $500,000 range.

Another colleague stressed that Ames made no attempt to conceal his wealth and observed that Ames had new cars and could afford to employ household help.

According to the CIA background investigation report, '[The investigator] did not consider that the background investigation revealed anything he did not already know. Thus, he did not believe it would be necessary to conduct follow-up interviews with any of the sources, nor did he discuss that possibility with [his supervisors].' According to the CIA security officer who assessed the results of the reinvestigation it 'had no CI [counterintelligence] implications'.

No action was taken with respect to Ames's security clearance on the basis of the investigation.

On 12 April 1991, Ames was given his next routine polygraph examination. The examiners were aware that there was some question about Ames's unexplained wealth, but were not made aware of the questions hanging over Ames. The polygraphers conducted a routine polygraph examination, focusing on routine questions asked of all employees.

Once the polygraph test began, Ames was asked whether he was concealing any financial difficulties from the agency. To this question Ames answered no, showing no signs of deception. Ames showed deception however, when he was asked whether he was concealing contacts with foreign nationals. After several hours of testing, Ames continued to show deception in response to the question. The examiner, as was standard CIA practice, ended the test, called it incomplete, and asked Ames to return again in a few days to try to successfully complete the test.

Four days later Ames returned to finish the polygraph examination. This time there were no deceptive responses, and the polygrapher wrote that Ames had passed the test adding however, 'I don't think he is a spy, but I am not 100% convinced because of the money situation.'

In July 1991, a CIA officer was sent to Bogota to check out the true background on Ames's in-laws. Relying on very limited information, the officer reported on July 31 that the company owned by the family dealt in real estate, import-export, and other business ventures and had had donated land worth several million dollars for a soccer field and sports arena. Overall, the report seemed to corroborate Ames's claims that his wealth came from Rosario's family.

However, the security problem of the serious leaks was still open and in April 1991 the CIA and FBI agreed on a joint investigation to solve the mystery of the 1985–88 compromises of key agents. In the summer of 1991, the joint CIA–FBI unit began to review the failed cases, look for commonalities, determine who had access, and identify suspects for subsequent investigation. The net was closing in on Ames.

By August 1991, the joint unit had identified 198 CIA employees who had access to the 1985–86 compromised cases. However, of these, the joint unit had identified twenty-nine employees, including Ames, for priority attention. Ames made everyone's list; indeed, he was high on several lists because he had access to the information, and there were unresolved questions about his sudden affluence.

The joint unit members decided to interview individuals in an effort to further narrow the list, and to determine who did and did not have access to the compromised cases. Further, the joint unit members agreed to have the Office of Security polygraph everyone on the list of 198 if the individuals were still employees and had not been polygraphed since 1985.

On November 12, 1991, the joint CIA–FBI investigative unit interviewed Ames. According to one of the participants, the interview of Ames, like all of the interviews, essentially concerned 'housekeeping' details: how paper flowed, who did what, who went to which meetings, etc.

Records from the Ames interview indicate that he twice volunteered that he had received a security violation while in SE Division for not closing and locking his safe. He stated the safe contained case chronologies and combinations to other safes. In retrospect, it appears that Ames offered this information as an explanation for the 1985–86 compromises and to detract from any suspicions that he was the mole. It appears to have had the opposite effect. In late 1991, the joint unit conducted a comprehensive computer search of DO records regarding Ames.

Eventually, well into 1992, those FBI officials reviewed the FBI Washington Field Office, as opposed to Washington headquarters records, on the KGB officer Chuvakhin. The Field Office records revealed that Chuvakhin and Ames had numerous contacts during 1985–86 but – significantly – that Ames had never officially reported all his meetings with the KGB man.

By the spring of 1992 the joint CIA–FBI security unit decided to focus more precisely on Ames's finances because of the still unresolved issues about his wealth. It was agreed that the CIA, utilising statutory authorities provided by the Right to Financial Privacy Act, should seek copies of Ames's financial records from banks and credit card companies where Ames was known to have accounts.

In June 1992, the replies came in. They stunned the investigators. Responses from credit card companies indicated that the Ames family charged as much as $20,000 to $30,000 *per month*. The Ames's credit card records also indicated additional overseas travel, which Ames had failed to report as required by CIA regulations.

By August 1992, the CIA enquiries uncovered that, since 1985, hundreds of thousands of dollars had been deposited into Ames's accounts, none of which was attributable to his salary. After careful checking, the investigators managed to find a direct link between the timings of these deposits and Ames's operational meetings with Chuvakhin.

In October 1992, another piece of the puzzle fell into place when the joint unit learned that most of the wire transfers had involved transfers from a bank account held by Ames at Credit Suisse in Zurich, Switzerland.

At that point, in October 1992, the joint unit was relatively certain that Ames was the spy they were looking for. In January 1993, they began briefing the FBI with a view to turning the investigation over to the FBI, the US agency responsible for national security.

In March 1993, the joint unit issued its final report, providing a compelling analysis of the 1985–1986 compromises and of the subsequent efforts by the KGB to divert attention away from the presence of a 'mole' within the CIA. It stated that as many as thirty CIA and FBI Soviet operations had been compromised or discontinued under unusual or suspicious circumstances between 1985 and 1986. The report reached several conclusions that were to prove very close to the mark. All pointed to Ames.

In early 1993 the Foreign Intelligence Surveillance Court issued orders authorising electronic surveillance of Ames's office and residence. Other surveillance techniques used against Ames included monitoring his mail, and a clandestine tracker installed in his car to record his movements.

Over the next ten months FBI special agents and investigative specialists conducted intensive physical and electronic surveillance of Ames. Clandestine searches of Ames's house discovered documents and other information linking Ames directly to the KGB. On 13 October 1993, investigative specialists discovered a chalk mark Ames made on a mailbox confirming to the Russians his intention to meet them in Bogota, Colombia. This was classic KGB tradecraft. On 1 November, special agents observed him and, separately, his Russian handler in Bogota. When Ames, as part of his official duties, planned a trip to Moscow, a plan to arrest him was approved.

Aldrich Hazen Ames was arrested on espionage charges by the FBI in Arlington, Virginia on 24 February 1994.

Following guilty pleas by both Ames and his wife on 28 April 1994, Ames was sentenced to incarceration for life without the possibility of parole. Rosario Ames was sentenced on 20 October 1994 to sixty-three months in prison. Looking back at his record it seems amazing that he managed to evade the security controls of an intelligence agency for so long.

Ames stands as classic case of lax, if not downright appalling, personnel security. From his lack of rigorous security vetting, his long record of security breaches, his inexplicably luxurious lifestyle, and his unreported contacts with the KGB, the rogue CIA man epitomises the profile of a potential security problem.

Even at the time, many of his fellow officers wondered why Ames' performance was never called into question. A subsequent investigation by the Agency's Inspector General showed that Ames struggled professionally. Not only did he suffer from alcoholism, he slept on the job, failed to turn in reports and regularly breached CIA security regulations.

In a memorandum to all the CIA office heads in October 1994, Director R. James Woolsey analysed the CIA's failure to identify Ames as a double agent. According to the director, Ames' 'professional weaknesses were observed by . . . colleagues and supervisors and were tolerated by many who did not consider them highly unusual for directorate of operations officers on the "not going anywhere" promotion track.' Coming from the Director himself, this is a damning indictment of the agency's working practices.

While all intelligence agencies are vulnerable to the mole within, that is precisely why strict security protocols are essential, and why any record of breaches should be investigated ruthlessly.

Even with the problem of having two traitors in the US agencies at the same time (Ames and Robert Hanssen) it is clear that the CIA's security left much to be desired. As a result, the damage Ames' treachery did to Washington's intelligence efforts is, to this day, recognised as being incalculable.

CHAPTER 26

The Avner Smit Case

Sometimes security officers are confronted by threats from unexpected directions. But when you can't even trust your friends, any attempt at security goes out of the window. Nothing better illustrates this than the strange case of Avner Smit of the Royal Netherlands Air Force.

When Israel was founded in 1948 the surrounding Arab armies promptly fell upon the interloper in the region, determined to drive this new Outremer into the sea. They failed. In an astonishing display of military prowess the desperate Israelis drove their attackers off. An uneasy ceasefire settled over the region, policed by observers from the equally new United Nations peacekeeping force, the United Nations Truce Supervision Organisation.

Since then, UNTSO military observers have remained in the Middle East to monitor ceasefires, supervise armistice agreements and, despite the all too frequent wars and clashes in the region, prevent isolated incidents from escalating. These UN observers came from many nations. One of the earliest contributors was the Netherlands, recovering from the nightmare of German occupation during the Second World War and anxious to demonstrate The Hague's commitment to a new, more peaceful, world order.

Most of the earliest observers were idealists, still shocked by the post-war revelations of the Jewish Holocaust in Nazi extermination camps. They tended to be sympathetic to the Zionist settlers building what the Dutch saw as a happy new nation, with its peaceful collective kibbutzim farming in the sunshine, and saw their observer role as protecting Israel from their Arab neighbours.

Unfortunately, many of the earlier Dutch officer-observers were all too easy meat for recruitment by the fledgeling Israeli secret service, Mossad. Not for nothing is Mossad's motto, 'By Way of Deception Thou Shalt Wage War.' As the years rolled by the ruthless Israelis penetrated, and in many cases controlled, large parts of the UN observer forces, especially the idealistic Dutch.

At first very pro-Israeli, many Dutch officers changed their views over the years, based on what they had seen on the ground. During their missions, Dutch officers were eyewitnesses to the various Israeli–Arab conflicts and to the Israelis' routine ill-treatment of the displaced Palestinians. In the words of an expert on the subject, Arthur ten Cate, 'the Dutch officers learned that the Israeli–Arab conflict has two sides instead of one'. Nonetheless, being pro-Palestinian was seen back home in the Netherlands as being somehow anti-semitic. The Dutch public didn't want to know about Israeli ceasefire violations or the petty brutalities of IDF soldiers at checkpoints. Anne Frank's country-men only wanted to hear heroic stories of the 'brave Jewish pioneers', so much so that when a Captain J.C. Mühren told a newspaper about his visit to a Jordanian village in November 1966 (where Israeli forces blew up homes and killed a number of civilians and Jordanian soldiers) the publication was swiftly prohibited by the Dutch Ministry of Defence. Mühren was warned off and told that 'the higher echelons felt that the article did not match with the feelings of the Dutch people about Israel'.

This was ironic because the Dutch officer observer corps was by then riddled with Israeli spies. Mossad took a special interest in recruiting UN observers of the truce between Israel and its neighbours. Mossad's normal approach was a honey trap, where married soldiers far from home would be approached off-duty by attractive Israeli women. Once the inevitable happened, Mossad would blackmail them: they could choose to cooperate or explain to their wives when they got back home exactly what had happened. It was all too easy to go along with Mossad – especially if you were at heart an Israeli sympathiser. Many Dutch were.

In December 1983 the Dutch military police, the Marechaussee, arrested an Israeli 'mole' inside the Foreign Intelligence Service, the IDB. It was one of their own; Major Ijsbrand ('Avner') Smit, who originally came from the Royal Netherlands Air Force Intelligence Service. It turned out that the Netherlands had its own Jonathan Pollard.

Smit was almost certainly recruited during his posting as a UN Observer in Lebanon. He later worked at the Plans Branch of the Intelligence Division at Supreme Headquarters Allied Powers in Europe (SHAPE) in Mons. This department was responsible for the coordination and dissemination of all NATO-intelligence within Allied Command, Europe, including intelligence policy and basic intelligence documents. Mossad could not have wished a better-placed mole.

However, it was at SHAPE in 1981 that Smit first fell under suspicion. His job entailed looking at long-term plans and so it was with some surprise that a young British staff officer responded to Smit's request one Friday afternoon to look at some classified files on new top-secret Soviet tanks.

At the time the request seemed unusual but not suspicious. Both officers had high security clearances and both officers worked inside the top-secret cage. However, when the files had not been returned by the following Tuesday the Brit demanded their return. Smit took them from his safe and handed them over, apologising that he had forgotten he had still got them.

Unfortunately for Smit, the British officer, who worked in Basic Intelligence Branch, had a counterpart in Current Intelligence Branch, down in the SHAPE war bunker. The latter's job was to brief the SACEUR (Supreme Commander Allied Forces Europe) daily on hot intelligence issues as they arose; so he kept a few files on intelligence items of topical interest. Over lunch one day the young major in Basic Branch happened to mention that Smit had been looking at Soviet tank developments and had borrowed some of his Basic Branch 'Secret Close Hold' files over the weekend.

The Current Branch officer was a wily old Lieutenant Colonel called Maurice Maisey, who remarked, 'That's odd. Smit asked to see my tank files in Current Branch last Friday, too. He's always asking to look at my files. And anyway, what is an officer in Air Plans doing looking at our tank files?'

This is when matters took an unfortunate turn for Smit. Both officers knew that Smit was married to a beautiful Jewess called Dalia, and that the Smits were always hanging around the senior officers at SHAPE. The beautiful and charming Dalia was a popular addition to any social gathering and the Smits went to considerable lengths to ingratiate themselves with senior officers at SHAPE. The Smits were popular and regulars on the Command Group party circuit; unusually so for a mere major. Both the British officers were professionals from the Intelligence Corps; and both officers decided to report the matter outside the chain of command, direct to the SHAPE Security Officer, who just happened to be an officer from Britain's Intelligence Corps, too. The multi-national SHAPE security team then took over the investigation with the Dutch national authorities.

Smit was later promoted to head of the Analysis Branch of the Dutch secret service, the IDB, which gave him direct access to sources, top-secret reports and operations, documents from the foreign intelligence community and, what is more important, to Dutch intercepts: the crown jewels of every intelligence organisation, because Smit could now tell his Mossad handlers what the Netherlands code-breaking capabilities and successes were.

In 1983 after a lengthy investigation Smit was finally exposed and arrested. He promptly called on a top Jewish lawyer to defend him; but by now the gloves were off and the unscrupulous and ruthless Marechaussee took the precaution of illegally bugging the supposedly confidential meetings between the Jewish lawyer and his client. What the counter-espionage officers heard shocked them; the lawyer turned out to be the principal undercover Mossad controller for the Netherlands and Smit's wife, the captivating Dalia, turned out to be a career Mossad officer and Smit's designated handler.

Smit's arrest caused an international row because Smit had not only given Israel Dutch secrets but also compromised hundreds of sensitive NATO and other foreign intelligence documents. Smit eventually appeared before a military council behind closed doors. The court accepted his defence – that the cooperation between Israeli and Dutch intelligence was strong and that information would anyway be shared between the two agencies. It is claimed that the Israeli Prime Minister intervened directly with Queen Beatrix and called for Smit's release. Eventually the Dutch Pollard was released due to 'lack of evidence' and fled to Israel, where he started a new life: as a Mossad officer . . .

Against this sort of treachery, even the best security is always at a disadvantage.

CHAPTER 27

The Inadequate – Bradley Manning

One of the worst examples of a major security breach occurred in 2013 when a US Army soldier, Bradley Edward Manning, was convicted of violations of the Espionage Act and other offences, after releasing the largest set of classified documents ever leaked to the public. The Manning case is notorious as a security breach not just because of the sensitivity of the information released, but because of its sheer volume.

Thanks to the computer age and the digital revolution, Manning leaked over 250,000 US diplomatic cables and 500,000 army reports, most of which were published by Julian Assange on WikiLeaks and in the *New York Times*, the *Guardian* and *Der Spiegel*. Collectively the documents became known as the Afghan War logs and the Iraq War logs. Commentators noted that this was a 'watershed moment', and the 'beginning of the information age exploding upon itself'. No-one questioned that the leaks were a catastrophic breach of US national security.

Most damaging of all was the 'Cablegate' leak of 251,287 State Department cables, written by 271 American embassies and consulates in 180 countries, from 1966 to 2010. These exposed the US and its friends to merciless scrutiny and revealed many matters that in normal diplomatic traffic remain unspoken. Suddenly the US was revealed as a very devious and untrustworthy ally. Many friendly nations cut back sharply on exchanges of sensitive information with the US.

Manning enlisted in the army to pay for his education. The young man was a delicate blossom and had a rough ride in the barrack room during basic training. Nonetheless he stuck it out and was eventually trained as an intelligence analyst, a post suited to his shy temperament and bookish habits, and a job that demanded a very high security clearance.

In 2009, Manning was stationed at Forward Operating Base Hammer in Iraq, an isolated site near the Iranian border where his duties as an intelligence analyst gave him access to a great deal of classified information, much of it specially compartmented as well as code word and diplomatic traffic.

As an intelligence analyst in a war zone he discovered that he could access almost anything. Manning later claimed that some of the material he saw horrified him, especially graphic camera-gun footage that showed unarmed civilians being shot at and killed. He began to download classified signals and store them on disk. He said he had downloaded the material onto music CD-RWs, erased the music and replaced it with a compressed split file. According to a transcript of their messages later published on *Wired*'s website, Manning boasted that 'I listened and lip-synced to Lady Gaga's "Telephone" while ex-filtrating possibly the largest data spillage in American history.'

Part of the reason no-one noticed, he said, was that 'the intelligence staff were working fourteen hours a day, seven days a week', and 'people stopped caring after three weeks'.

It appears that Manning first contacted WikiLeaks in November 2009 after having made attempts to speak with the *New York Times* and the *Washington Post*. By then he had downloaded information that included war logs about the Iraq and Afghanistan conflicts, private cables from the State Department and assessments of Guantanamo prisoners. In early 2010, he passed this information – which amounted to hundreds of thousands of documents, many of them classified – direct to WikiLeaks organiser Julian Assange.

The story exploded on 5 April 2010 when Assange released the Baghdad airstrike video 'Collateral Murder' during a press conference at the National Press Club in Washington DC. The video showed two American helicopters firing on a group of ten men in the Amin District of Baghdad. Two were Reuters' employees there to photograph an American Humvee under attack by the Mahdi Army. Pilots mistook their cameras for weapons. The US pilots shot up everything in sight including children. The *Washington Post* wrote that it was this video, viewed by millions, that put WikiLeaks on the map.

Back in Iraq, Manning seemed to be most affected by an incident of corruption in the Iraqi police. He claimed he told his commanding officer who brushed it aside saying, 'he didn't want to hear any of it' and reportedly told Manning that he would be better employed helping the Iraqi police find more detainees.

Manning reacted badly to this. He started behaving oddly, including attempting to attack an officer; he also began to publicly question his identity as a man. As a result of his ill-discipline and increasingly erratic behaviour he was demoted and warned for discharge. In May 2010, a confused and surly Manning made direct contact with Adrian Lamo, a well-known hacker who had been convicted in 2004 of having accessed the *New York Times* computer network. Manning confessed to having passed the classified material to Assange at Wikileaks. Manning told Lamo that what he had seen had made him realise, 'I was actively involved in something that I was completely against ...'

Manning wrote: 'but I'm not a source for you ... I'm talking to you as someone who needs moral and emotional fucking support.' Lamo assured Manning that he was speaking in confidence and replied: 'I told you, none of this is for print.'

However, Lamo was concerned about the story. The enormity of the national security breach worried him and he discussed the information with Timothy Webster, a friend and fellow hacker who had worked in Army counter-intelligence. Webster told Lamo that he believed Manning was endangering lives and advised Lamo to go to the authorities immediately. Webster then reported the conversation to United States Army Counterintelligence who contacted Lamo directly. In May 2010 Bradley Manning was arrested in Iraq.

Manning was charged with leaking classified information in June 2010. In March 2011, additional charges were added. These included the charge of aiding the enemy, as the information Manning had leaked had been accessible to al Qaeda.

Another charge, which Manning's defence called a 'made-up offense' (but of which he was found guilty) read that Manning 'wantonly [caused] to be published on the internet intelligence belonging to the US government, having knowledge that intelligence published on the internet is accessible to the enemy'.

The prosecution presented 300,000 pages of documents in evidence, including chat logs and classified material. The court heard from the head of the Digital Forensics Unit, the Army's Computer Crime Investigative Unit (CCIU) and a digital forensics contractor working for the CCIU, that they had found over 100,000 State Department cables on a workplace computer Manning had used between November 2009 and May 2010; 400,000 military reports from Iraq and 91,000 from Afghanistan on an SD card found in the soldier's basement room in his aunt's home in Potomac, Maryland; and 10,000 cables on his personal MacBook Pro as well as storage devices that they said had not been passed to WikiLeaks because a file was corrupted.

They also recovered fourteen to fifteen pages of encrypted chats, in unallocated space on Manning's MacBook hard drive, between Manning and someone believed to be Julian Assange. Two of the chat handles, which used the Berlin Chaos Computer Club's domain (ccc. de), were associated with the names Julian Assange and Nathaniel Frank.

In February 2013, Manning pleaded guilty to storing and leaking military information. He explained that his actions had been intended to encourage debate, not to harm the United States. He continued to plead not guilty to several other charges, so his court-martial proceeded.

Manning apologised to the court: 'I am sorry that my actions hurt people. I'm sorry that they hurt the United States. I am sorry for the unintended consequences of my actions. When I made these decisions I believed I was going to help people, not hurt people . . . At the time of my decisions I was dealing with a lot of issues.'

Manning was found guilty of twenty counts, including espionage, theft and computer fraud. However, the judge ruled he was not guilty of aiding the enemy, the most serious charge Manning had faced and which could have carried the death penalty.

On 21 August 2013, Manning was sentenced to thirty-five years in prison, dishonourably discharged, reduced in rank and forced to forfeit all pay. Since then Manning's bizarre story has become even stranger.

It emerged during the trial that he had been diagnosed with 'gender identity disorder' while in the Army.

During the court-martial sentencing hearing it turned out that Manning was a personnel security nightmare. A military psychologist who had treated Manning before his arrest testified that Manning had been left isolated in the Army, trying to deal with gender-identity issues in a 'hyper-masculine environment'. A psychiatrist testified that Private Manning had struggled with his gender identity and now wanted to become a woman. In a statement Manning said that 'she' had felt female since childhood, wanted to be known as Chelsea, and wanted to begin hormone replacement therapy to aid his transition into a woman.

'She' is serving her sentence at the maximum-security US Disciplinary Barracks at Fort Leavenworth.

The American government has maintained all along that military and diplomatic sources were seriously endangered by Manning's leak, a view shared by security officers world-wide. Despite this, Manning has emerged as a martyred whistle-blower to some. In 2011, Manning was awarded a '*Whistleblowerpreis*' by the German section of the International Association of Lawyers against Nuclear Arms and nominated for several peace awards, including in 2014 a nomination for the Nobel Peace Prize for 'inspiring change and encouraging public debate and policy changes that contributed to a more stable and peaceful world'.

Whether Bradley Manning did good or ill is a matter for judgement. What is not in doubt however is that a very junior soldier had extraordinary and apparently unsupervised access to a flood of top-level intelligence from a wide variety of sources, and evaded all security controls to tell the world the secrets with which he had been entrusted.

It was a sorry tale of dreadful security with, according to one security analyst, "A combination of: 'Bad security-vetting, weak servers, weak logging, weak physical security, far too much access, non-existent counter-intelligence, inattentive signal analysis, poor supervision ... in fact, a perfect security storm.'

CHAPTER 28

WikiLeaks and the Appalling Assange

The unfortunate Bradley Manning's revelations would not have been seen worldwide without Wikileaks, a website that specialised in publishing sensitive material and embarrassing government documents. Wikileaks was founded in 2006–7 by Julian Assange, an Australian computer nerd with a background in network hacking. Assange started hacking early. In 1987, he and some friends hacked into the Pentagon and other US Department of Defense facilities, MILNET, the US Navy, NASA, and Australia's Overseas Telecommunications Commission; Citibank, Lockheed Martin, Motorola, Panasonic, and Xerox; and the Australian National University, La Trobe University, and Stanford University's SRI International. As a result, in September 1991, Australian Federal Police raided his home and in 1994 charged him with thirty-one counts of hacking and related crimes.

In December 1996, Assange pleaded guilty to twenty-five charges and was ordered to pay reparations of A\$2,100 and released on a good behaviour bond. He avoided a heavier penalty because there was no evidence of malicious or mercenary intent.

In 2006 Assange and his friends established WikiLeaks. Assange is a member of the organisation's advisory board and describes himself as the editor-in-chief.

WikiLeaks posted large amounts of sensitive material exposing government and corporate wrongdoing between 2006 and 2009, attracting various degrees of publicity; but it was the sensational disclosures by the US Army intelligence analyst Bradley Manning that put WikiLeaks – and Assange – in the public eye. The Australian Prime Minister described Assange's activities as 'illegal,' although he had broken no Australian law and US Vice President Joe Biden and many others called him a 'terrorist'. Nobody, however, can deny that Assange had been responsible for one of the greatest breaches of national security in history.

It is hard to define exactly what Assange was. He was never a spy, because he has never spied. Perhaps a better description is a 'fence', an old-fashioned term for a receiver of stolen goods, a criminal act in most countries. In English law and the numerous American statutes that follow the tradition of the English Common Law, Assange is quite clearly guilty of: 'handling stolen goods, knowing or believing them to be stolen goods, and dishonestly receiving the goods ...' Under section 22(1) of the Theft Act 1968, which provides: That property stolen anywhere is a crime and receiving it amounts to dishonestly receiving stolen goods .... ' and that, 'The accused's knowledge or belief as to the stolen nature of the goods is crucial ...' By these standards Assange is certainly guilty of 'receiving goods knowing them to have been stolen'. The information he obtained was stolen without the owner's consent. In law Assange is nothing more than a common criminal, however much he protested his mission to inform the world. Assange himself however was unashamedly proud of his actions, as he showed in a boastful address to Cambridge University in 2011.

Assange acknowledged that the web could allow greater government transparency and better cooperation between activists, but said it gave authorities their best ever opportunity to monitor and catch dissidents. 'While the Internet has in some ways an ability to let us know to an unprecedented level what government is doing, and to let us cooperate with each other to hold repressive governments and repressive corporations to account, it is also the greatest spying machine the world has ever seen.'

He continued: 'It [the web] is not a technology that favours freedom of speech. It is not a technology that favours human rights. It is not a technology that favours civil life. Rather it is a technology that can be used to set up a totalitarian spying regime, the likes of which we have never seen. Or, on the other hand, taken by us, taken by activists, and taken by all those who want a different trajectory for the technological world, it can be something we all hope for.'

Many saw Assange as some kind of harmless geek and a mere gadfly. America and several other nations took his revelations much more seriously and, smarting under his embarrassing disclosures, sought ways of bringing him to trial.

Assange had been under investigation in the United States for some time. After the release of Manning's material on WikiLeaks the US authorities began investigating WikiLeaks and Assange personally with a view to prosecuting them under the Espionage Act of 1917. In November 2010, the US Attorney General confirmed that there was 'an active, ongoing criminal investigation' into WikiLeaks. Assange continued to deny involvement, but the revelation by prosecutors during Manning's court-martial in 2013 of evidence of incriminating chat logs between Manning and an alleged WikiLeaks interlocutor they claimed to be Assange, put pressure on the Australian. If not Assange at WikiLeaks, then who?

Assange had run into further difficulties after a trip to Sweden in 2010 where he bedded two women. Unfortunately the two women later filed complaints alleging rape and, as a result, the Swedish Director of Public Prosecution opened an investigation into sexual offences that Assange is alleged to have committed. Assange was wanted for questioning over one count of unlawful coercion, two counts of sexual molestation, and one count of lesser-degree rape.

The allegations relate to 'non-consensual behaviour within consensual sexual encounters.' Assange denied the allegations and fled Sweden, claiming that it was all a CIA set-up (which, given the track record of the American agency, was not a wholly improbable claim) but was arrested in London by British police on an International Warrant.

On 7 December 2010, Assange was remanded in custody at London's Wandsworth Prison, awaiting his extradition to Sweden for criminal investigation into the sexual assault allegations. A week later he was released on bail after an appeal. Upon his release Assange promptly fled and took refuge at the Embassy of Ecuador in London, where he was granted political asylum.

The UK government has said it will not allow him safe passage out

of the country to fly to Ecuador as it is legally obliged to extradite him
to Sweden. The Swedish Foreign Ministry insisted the sole reason they
want Mr Assange extradited is so the allegations against him can be
properly investigated.

Once in hiding in the Embassy, Assange lost many of his supporters
by refusing to take any responsibility for his publishing of Manning's
revelations on WikiLeaks. He expressed sympathy for Manning with
what many saw as crocodile tears: 'He is in a terrible situation. And if
he is not connected to us, [then] he is there as an innocent . . . and if he
is in some manner connected to our publications, then of course we
have some responsibility.'

However Assange vehemently continued to deny that he was to
blame for Manning's predicament in any way. Responding to a question about the US soldier's imprisonment for passing on classified
information, Assange claimed: 'We had no idea whether he is one of
our sources. All our technology is geared up to make sure we have no
idea.' He went on to make the staggering claim that, 'There is no allegation that he was arrested as the result of anything to do with us. The
allegation is that he was arrested as a result of him speaking to *Wired*
magazine in the United States.'

To his supporters, Julian Assange is a valiant campaigner for truth.
To his critics, he is a publicity-seeker who has endangered lives by
putting a mass of sensitive information into the public domain and left
the prime source of his notoriety to his fate in a US military prison. To
others he is the man who used and then abandoned Bradley Manning's
weakness and insecurity. What Assange clearly is, is a man who has
established a new form of treachery that is neither spying nor breaking
the law: he has become a pedlar of stolen classified information on a
global scale.

In doing so he has redefined security.

CHAPTER 29

Snowden, Security and the Surveillance State

If the security authorities regarded Assange (not unreasonably) as an ego-maniac trouble maker, rather than a spy, then the revelations of his counterpart Edward Snowden are a troubling reminder that there is a very fine line between the crime of spying to steal state secrets and revealing to the tax-paying public exactly what crimes are being committed by their government in their name.

The most dramatic invention of the digital revolution in the closing years of the twentieth century was the spread of the Internet, which brought revolutionary changes to our world. It is extraordinary just what a difference the era of instant personal communications has wrought in the lives of millions over the past few decades. The birth of social media like Facebook and Twitter, networking sites, WIFI, iPads and smart phones have revolutionised the way people live. CCTV cameras to spy on people are now considered perfectly normal in public places.

This also means that no-one is beyond scrutiny most of the time. Nowadays, drones, which used to be the unmanned aerial reconnaissance planes of the military, have become tools and toys for many, and add to the many ways in which we can all be monitored and checked. Big corporations and big governments can watch our activities on the Internet or on the street and, with the help of IP addresses, mobile phone and credit cards, can track your location and every movement.

They can also read your emails, check your shopping and TV viewing preferences and even your politics.

The principal beneficiary of these new technologies has been, inevitably, the market place. Commercial organisations, always quicker to react to new ways of making money, have moved swiftly and nimbly to exploit the surveillance opportunities offered by the digital revolution. Cookies in every computer can track individual wants, likes and preferences; the smart ad-men have been quick to record the information and sell their products to a more precisely tailored customer base.

Instant global Internet access offers some serious military and intelligence applications, too. Intelligence that up to now has only been available on a high-priority basis to senior military communities is available to everyone, everywhere. Intel, pictures, live-video feeds – unprecedented access to mission critical information on the move.

What corporations can do for cash with computers and cookies, governments can do for collecting intelligence. The digital revolution offered the security and intelligence services of every nation the chance to monitor their own citizens – all in the interests of security, of course.

The result of this explosion of intrusion and monitoring of the way people live has changed society. The *New York Times* described what was happening very accurately in 2012:

> The US administration has now lost all credibility on this issue ... the executive branch will use any power it is given and very likely abuse it ... Essentially, the administration is saying that without any individual suspicion of wrongdoing, the government is allowed to know whom Americans are calling every time they make a phone call, for how long they talk and from where.
>
> This sort of tracking can reveal a lot of personal and intimate information about an individual. To casually permit this surveillance – with the American public having no idea that the executive branch is now exercising this power – fundamentally shifts power between the individual and the state, and it repudiates constitutional principles governing search, seizure and privacy.

The message is clear: the world's very best surveillance machine is the Internet.

If Julian Assange and the unfortunate Bradley Manning had alerted the world to what the US government was doing to spy on foreign powers, then in 2014 a computer genius called Edward Snowden revealed how his own government was breaking the law left, right and centre to spy on its own citizens. Hero or villain, whistle-blower or traitor, Edward Snowden tore the lid off the surveillance state to reveal its unconstitutional activities. He also revealed the extent to which private companies had been cooperating with intelligence agencies – especially the NSA.

The National Security Agency, founded in 1952, is the USA's signals intelligence agency, and the biggest of the country's myriad intelligence organisations. However, by law it has a strict focus on overseas, rather than domestic, surveillance. It is the country's phone and Internet interception specialist, and is also responsible for code breaking. After the 2001 attacks on the World Trade Center the NSA suddenly became very interested in monitoring potential terrorists' mobile phone and email communications and turned to the phone companies and the Internet service providers.

The technology companies stressed that they never went beyond what the law demanded when they handed over private material to the government; but other releases indicate that some Internet and telecoms companies went way beyond what was mandatory as they acted as voluntary information collectors for the government.

Edward Snowden was described by his father as 'a sensitive, caring young man' and 'a deep thinker'. He was clever, with an above-average IQ of 145, and computers fascinated him. He even dropped out of high school to study them. Between his stints at community college, Snowden spent four months in the Army Reserves in special-forces training. According to army sources, he did not complete any training; Snowden claims that he was discharged after he broke his legs in an accident.

In 2005 Snowden landed a job with the National Security Agency, initially as a security guard. From there he moved into an information technology job with the CIA and in 2007, the CIA posted him to Geneva. According to colleagues, while in Geneva Snowden was 'considered the top technical and cybersecurity expert in the country' and 'was hand-picked by the CIA to support the President at the 2008

NATO summit in Romania'. A former NSA co-worker said that 'although the NSA was full of smart people, Snowden was a genius among geniuses', who created systems for the NSA that were widely implemented and often pointed out security bugs to the agency. Snowden had full system-administrator privileges, with virtually unlimited access to the NSA's computers and classified NSA data.

Snowden was even offered a position on the NSA's elite team of hackers, 'Tailored Access Operations', but in 2009 he moved on, and left to work for private contractors as a computer systems administrator. His first post was with Dell, who moved him to Japan to work as a subcontractor in an NSA office before he was transferred to their NSA support office in Hawaii. He then moved from Dell to BZH (Booz Allen Hamilton), another NSA subcontractor.

Later Snowden told the *South China Morning Post* that he decided to take a job with a US government contractor for one reason alone – so he could collect proof about the US National Security Agency's secret surveillance programmes ahead of planned leaks to the media. 'My position with Booz Allen Hamilton granted me access to lists of machines all over the world the NSA hacked . . . That is why I accepted that position.'

While working at the NSA's Oahu office, Snowden began noticing government programs involving the NSA spying on American citizens via phone calls and Internet use. In 2013 after only three months, he began copying top-secret NSA documents while at work, building a dossier on NSA domestic surveillance operations that he found invasive and disturbing. The documents contained vast amounts of damning information on the NSA's domestic surveillance practices, including spying on millions of American citizens under the umbrella of programs such as PRISM. After he had compiled a large store of documents, Snowden told his NSA supervisor that he needed a leave of absence to undergo medical treatment.

On 15 March 2013, just three days after what he later called his 'breaking point' of 'seeing the Director of National Intelligence, James Clapper, directly lie under oath to Congress', Snowden quit his job at Dell. Clapper had told the Senate Committee that the US government does 'not wittingly' collect data on millions of Americans.

That answer was shown to have been a downright lie. Later, the London *Guardian* newspaper published a top-secret court order from Snowden that showed the NSA was collecting the phone records of millions of US citizens. Clapper was forced to apologise to the Senate intelligence committee, explaining that he gave the 'least untruthful' answer he could in an unclassified setting. (Clapper later changed his story to say that he had forgotten about an authority claimed by the government under the Patriot Act to collect the records of every phone call sent and received in the US.)

In late 2012 and early 2013 Snowden contacted Glenn Greenwald, an investigative journalist working at the *Guardian* and a documentary filmmaker called Laura Poitras and started giving them classified documents with a view to publication.

Barton Gellman, of the *Washington Post*, later confirmed that Snowden approached Greenwald after the *Post* declined to guarantee publication of forty-one PowerPoint slides that Snowden had showed him. The slides were a classified briefing on the NSA's illegal PRISM electronic data mining program that was tasked to collect real-time information on American citizens. According to Gellman, Snowden knew exactly what he was doing: 'I understand that I will be made to suffer for my actions, and that the return of this information to the public marks my end.' Snowden also told Gellman that until the articles were published, the journalists working with him would also be at risk from retaliatory action by the United States' intelligence community to try and shut them up: 'if they think you are the single point of failure that could stop this disclosure and make them the sole owner of this information'.

Gellman was the first journalist to publish Snowden's documents. He said a worried US government begged him not to specify by name which companies were involved, but Gellman decided that to name them 'would make it real to Americans'. Reports also revealed details of 'Tempora', a British black-ops surveillance program run by the NSA's British partner, GCHQ. The initial reports included details about the NSA's call database, 'Boundless Informant', and of a secret court order requiring Verizon (a cutting-edge major US Internet and technology company) to hand the NSA millions of Americans' phone records daily, the surveillance of French citizens' phone and internet records, and those of 'high-profile individuals from the world of business or politics'.

The NSA was accused of going 'beyond its core mission of national security' when articles were published showing the NSA's intelligence-gathering operations had targeted Brazil's largest oil company, Petrobras. The NSA and the GCHQ were also exposed as monitoring charities including UNICEF and Médecins du Monde, as well as allies such as the EU Presidency and the Israeli Prime Minister.

From then on the disclosures came thick and fast. On 20 May 2013, Snowden took a flight to Hong Kong, China, where he remained during the early stages of the media fallout. On 5 June, the *Guardian* newspaper released secret documents about a demand from the US Foreign Intelligence Surveillance Court insisting that Verizon pass on information 'on a daily basis' culled from its American customers' activities.

The following day, the *Guardian* and the *Washington Post* released Snowden's leaked information on PRISM. A flood of information followed. Within months, documents had been published by media outlets worldwide, in the *Guardian* (Britain), *Der Spiegel* (Germany), the *Washington Post* and the *New York Times* (US), *O Globo* (Brazil), *Le Monde* (France), and similar newspapers in Sweden, Canada, Italy, Netherlands, Norway, Spain, and Australia.

The Snowden files revealed a number of illegal mass-surveillance programs undertaken by the NSA and GCHQ. The NSA got round its legal prohibition on spying on American citizens in continental America by the simple expedient of sub-contracting the job to GCHQ for a paid retainer. The two agencies were able to access information stored by major US technology companies, often without individual warrants, as well as mass-intercepting data from the fibre-optic cables that make up the backbone of global phone and internet networks. The agencies also worked hand in glove to spy on communications and security standards upon which the Internet, commerce and banking rely.

The on-going publication of leaked documents revealed previously unknown details of a global surveillance apparatus run by the NSA, in close cooperation with three of its Five Eyes partners: Australia (ASD), the United Kingdom (GCHQ), and Canada (CSEC). There is no doubt that the revelations were both damning and embarrassing for the Western intelligence agencies. To worry them even more, the *Guardian*'s editor Alan Rusbridger said in November 2013 that only one per cent of the documents had been published. Officials warned that 'the worst is yet to come'.

Snowden's identity was made public by the *Guardian* at his own request in June 2013. He explained his motivation in leaking the documents:

> I have no intention of hiding who I am because I know I have done nothing wrong ... I don't want to live in a society that does these sort of things ... I do not want to live in a world where everything I do and say is recorded ... My sole motive is to inform the public as to that which is done in their name and that which is done against them.

In a later interview Snowden declared:

> The 4th and 5th Amendments to the Constitution of my country, Article 12 of the Universal Declaration of Human Rights, and numerous statutes and treaties forbid such systems of massive, pervasive surveillance. While the US Constitution marks these programs as illegal, my government argues that secret court rulings, which the world is not permitted to see, somehow legitimize an illegal affair ...

Snowden promised that nothing would stop subsequent disclosures. In June 2013, he said, 'All I can say right now is the US government is not going to be able to cover this up by jailing or murdering me. Truth is coming, and it cannot be stopped.'

In a May 2014 interview, Snowden told NBC News that he had tried to alert bureaucrats about his concerns over the legality of the NSA spying programmes while he was employed by the agency, but he was ordered to keep his mouth shut and to stay silent on the matter. Snowden said:

The NSA has records – they have copies of emails right now to their Office of General Counsel, to their oversight and compliance folks from me raising concerns about the NSA's interpretations of its legal authorities. I had raised these complaints not just officially in writing through email, but to my supervisors, to my colleagues, in more than one office. I did it in Fort Meade. I did it in Hawaii. And many, many of these individuals were shocked by these programs. They had never seen them themselves. And the ones who had, went, 'You know, you're right ... But if you say something about this, they're going to destroy you.'

A vengeful US executive closed in to muzzle a man whom they regarded as dangerous traitor, and Snowden fled to avoid the law. In doing so he left a ticking time bomb of American governmental misdeeds against its own citizens. Not all his fellow citizens agreed with the White House. A court order trying to suppress the truth about the Verizon case explained the numerous cryptic public warnings by two US senators, Ron Wyden and Mark Udall, both members of the Senate intelligence committee. They had been prevented from specifying which domestic surveillance programs they found alarming and illegal.

Eventually the two senators confirmed that the NSA, as part of a programme secretly authorised by President Bush in October 2001 after the 9/11 atrocity, had begun a bulk collection program of domestic telephone, Internet and email records. The row erupted in 2006 when the newspaper *USA Today* reported that the NSA had 'been secretly collecting the phone call records of tens of millions of Americans, using data provided by AT&T, Verizon and BellSouth' and was 'using the data to analyze calling patterns in an effort to detect terrorist activity'. On coming into office, President Obama quietly acquiesced to the programme of NSA domestic snooping.

These events reflected how dramatically the NSA's mission had changed over the years, from an agency exclusively devoted to foreign intelligence gathering, into one that focuses increasingly on domestic communications. Many Americans were troubled. William Binney, a thirty-year employee of the NSA, resigned from the agency in protest at this illegal example of mission creep.

In the mid-1970s, Congress, for the first time, had looked into the surveillance activities of the US government as part of its examination of the anti-Vietnam war movement. Back then, it was agreed that the NSA would never direct its surveillance apparatus domestically. Congress spotted the danger of the NSA abusing its powers. At the conclusion of that investigation, Frank Church, the Democratic senator from Idaho who chaired the investigative committee, warned: 'The NSA's capability could at any time be turned around on the American people, and no American would have any privacy left, such is the capability to monitor everything: telephone conversations, telegrams, it doesn't matter.'

Church's words came back to haunt later administrations. Snowden had done his work well, and eventually flew to Moscow via Cuba and was given asylum by the Russian authorities. While many libertarian groups were hailing him as a hero, the unrepentant whistle-blower remained in Russia, with the US government working hard to extradite him. In 2013, United States federal prosecutors filed a criminal complaint against Snowden, charging him with theft of government property, and two counts of violating the US 1917 Espionage Act through 'unauthorized communication of national defense information' and 'willful communication of classified communications intelligence information to an unauthorized person'. Each of the three charges carried a maximum possible prison term of ten years.

Snowden remained unrepentant. 'I told the government I'd volunteer for prison, as long as it served the right purpose ... I care more about the country than what happens to me. But we can't allow the law to become a political weapon or agree to scare people away from standing up for their rights, no matter how good the deal. I'm not going to be part of that.'

There was also a lingering possibility that some of the revelations attributed to Snowden may not all in fact have come from him. There appears to be another leaker spilling secrets under Snowden's name. For example, among the leaked documents the German news magazine *Der Spiegel* printed is a top-secret 'Memorandum of Agreement' between the NSA and the BND from 2002. But 'It is not from

Snowden's material,' the magazine notes. The most likely leak is from the BND inside Germany itself.

The ultimate question – of whether Snowden was pushed by his ego and hunger for fame to steal national secrets, or was genuinely motivated by a desire for truth and justice – still remains unanswered. While there can be little doubt that the whistle-blower's revelations damaged American national security and showed the West's enemies the extent to which they were being spied upon, Snowden also revealed serious law-breaking and illegal practices by government agencies acting out of democratic control.

Above all, the case of Edward Snowden and his treasure trove of classified documents demonstrates that in the new digital age complete security remains not just an illusion but a practical impossibility.

CHAPTER 30

Strategic Security: Insecure from Top to Bottom – Singapore, 1941–2

Security tends to focus on the individual, the potential spy, the leaker of secrets. We can characterise this as micro-security. But sometimes we come across examples of a complete lack of security at the military, corporate and government level. This is a gross failure of macro or national security. Such an example is the appalling story of the British loss of Malaya to the Japanese in 1941–42.

Despite all the other operational and political reasons for the British disaster in Malaya, they were merely consequences of perhaps the most dangerous intelligence vice of all: a complete lack of security and under-estimation of the enemy.

Winston Churchill described the fall of Singapore as 'the greatest disaster ever to befall British arms'. He should know: he was mainly responsible for it.

On 15 February 1942, the British Imperial garrison of the supposedly impregnable bastion of Singapore, on the southernmost tip of Malaya, surrendered to the outnumbered invading Imperial Japanese Forces.

One hundred and thirty thousand well-equipped and well-supplied British, Australian and Indian officers and soldiers capitulated to just 35,000 hungry, exhausted Japanese front-line combat troops, almost out of ammunition and at their last gasp. The Japanese were astonished at the ease of their victory. In the brief but martial history of the British Empire, no greater military humiliation can be found.

In the whole Malayan campaign only 9,000 of the total of 60,000 Japanese soldiers became casualties. The British-led force lost 146,000, of whom over 130,000 surrendered. Many of those Allied prisoners of war died in appalling conditions in Japanese captivity. We have to go back to the Athenian defeat at Syracuse in 415 BC to find any disaster comparable to the great debacle at Singapore: both effectively marked the beginning of the end of a great maritime empire.

The deeply-seated root cause of the British defeat was, like so many defeats, to be found in poor intelligence compounded by security blunders so widespread as to make victory unlikely at best and impossible in the final analysis.

Although we tend to think of security blunders as individual cases such as Blake, Philby, Hanssen and Ames, there is such a thing as strategic security (which is related to wider national issues); and no greater example of bad strategic security can be found in the blundering and smug incompetence of the British Empire in Malaya.

It is no exaggeration that Malaya by 1941 was riddled with spies, traitors and a total disregard for operational security, from the highest to the lowest. Western under-estimation of the Japanese as a potential enemy was combined with the breathtaking complacency on the part of the British colonial regime of the day, who appear to have sleep-walked into a major war in the Far East, sure in the knowledge that, 'it can't possibly happen to us'.

Only on Sunday 15 February 1942 – as the victorious Japanese rounded up the tens of thousands of demoralised British and Indian divisions, ad hoc Royal Naval shore parties, fleeing RAF ground staff and thousands of drunken and mutinous Australian deserters (who had basically 'gone on strike' in the last days), plus the rest of Lieutenant General Percival's humiliated command on Singapore – did it really dawn on the British in Malaya that their world was gone for ever.

For years before the outbreak of the Second World War the British had watched the rise of Imperial Japan's maritime power with mounting unease. In the opening year of the First World War the Japanese had been actually been allies of the British in their long hunt to sweep the Pacific free from German surface raiders.

Yet the Versailles Peace Treaty of 1919 had come as a bitter disappointment to at least one of the supposedly victorious powers. Although Japan was given a mandate over some German colonial territories, the Japanese felt that their contribution to the Great War had not been sufficiently recognised. This resentment at being deprived of the spoils of victory was sharpened after the Washington Naval Conference of 1922, when Japan was theoretically locked into an inferior maritime position, with Britain in favour of a much looser alliance favouring the USA.

Japan had only been opened up to Western influences in the late 1850s. The medieval political mechanisms within the Shogunate state were, by Western democratic standards, primitive and more akin to today's developing world, where the power of the military often permits a disproportionate influence on politics. So it was in Imperial Japan under its divine Emperor. As the global economic stresses of the late 1920s and 1930s swirled round Japan, the military seized political power and began a policy of armed expansion to guarantee Japan access to the economic riches and raw materials of the east. In 1931 the Army engineered an invasion of Manchuria, thus lighting the fuse for the period of military and political expansion that would finally explode at Pearl Harbor and Malaya a decade later, on 7 December 1941.

The British colonies in Malaya were a particularly tempting target for Japanese economic aggrandisement. During the 1930s Japan had managed to secure a plentiful supply of coal by conquest from China, but she still lacked other vital raw materials, in particular iron, tin, oil and rubber. By 1940, in response to Japanese expansion into French Indo China, the USA had slowly begun to apply political pressure to freeze out Japanese imports and other economic activity from the US and its territories. The result was that by mid-1941 the Japanese Economic Planning Board could forecast, fairly accurately, the moment when Japan would no longer be able to function due to lack of raw materials. The Japanese planners also predicted (with a clarity and accuracy unusual among government planners) that, 'it will be impossible to obtain oil . . . by peaceful means'. That should have come as a bit of a clue for Britain's intelligence and the Whitehall establishment.

The obvious targets for the Japanese to lay their hands on that which they so badly sought were the prosperous, ill-defended and peaceful colonies of British Malaya and the Dutch East Indies far to the south. Malaya, with its tin and rubber, was regarded as little more than a dollar 'cash cow' by the British Empire, earning a fortune every year for the City of London and helping to subsidise the war against Hitler in Europe and the Middle East. The defeated rump government of the Netherlands in exile was effectively sustained by the rich outpourings of the Royal Dutch Shell oil wells in the East Indies. Possession of these two colonies would enable Japan to become industrially independent; and neither Britain nor the Dutch seemed to be capable of defending their rich colonies to any marked extent.

To protect their economic empire in the east, after the Great War successive British governments had established a fleet anchorage and naval bastion based on the harbour and island of 'Fortress Singapore'. The theory and intention was clear: to provide a fixed defensive point which could hold out, whatever happened, like some embattled medieval castle until the Royal Navy could send a fleet from Britain to relieve the beleaguered fortress and sweep away the importunate invaders.

In cold print, this Imperial policy looks remarkably suspect as a strategic concept, posing as many questions as it answers. For how long would the naval base have to hold out? And against what? An attack from the land? What size of relieving force would be required? How many days would it take to assemble a fleet and sail it to the Far East?

Armed with these doubts and a cunning Home Civil Service that used the policy of 'no war within the next ten years' as a device for avoiding any government spending, the 'impregnable' fortress of Singapore came into being slowly and inefficiently during the 1920s and 30s at enormous cost and without a single integrated defence plan.

The final product was anything but impregnable, and a remarkably uncoordinated bastion of defence for Britain's economic empire in the east. The main approach, (through the Malayan forests to the north) was virtually ignored by the planners, despite warnings, and airfields had been built all over Malaya by the fledgling RAF in complete defiance of the Army's tactical needs for ground defence. But the illusion of security was there. For illusion it was: Whitehall's plans to defend Malaya were an open book thanks to treachery from the very top.

From the early 1920s the Japanese had made great efforts to recruit spies, concentrating in particular on Britons with access to the secrets of maritime airpower. It was the British, after all, who had fielded the first viable aircraft carriers at the end of the First World War.

The Japanese naval attaché in London was alerted to look out for potential spies and in 1922–23 a likely target swam in to their net. The man was Squadron Leader Frederick Joseph Rutland, a Royal Naval Air Service pilot known as 'Rutland of Jutland' for his exploits in 1916. A genuine pioneer of maritime aviation, Rutland was twice decorated during the Great War. The Japanese made the man with a 'unique knowledge of aircraft carriers and deck landings' an offer he couldn't refuse. In 1923 he resigned his commission and was recruited by Japanese naval intelligence as an agent. He was given the equivalent of £3 million in today's money, plus a handsome yearly salary, and instructions to set to set up a business in America and report on naval affairs on the West Coast and in Honolulu.

Unfortunately for Rutland, Britain's MI5 were on to him from the start as he had been brought to their notice by intercepted communications. Despite this, Rutland worked for the Japanese until 1940, providing technical details that helped the Japanese design their new, fast, fleet aircraft carriers during the 1930s. Following his surprise decision to return to Britain on 5 October 1941 he was put under surveillance and interned on 16 December 1941 for 'hostile associations'.

There can be little doubt that Rutland helped the Imperial Japanese Navy's pre-war build-up enormously. The same source that revealed Rutland had also uncovered a second Japanese agent, this time much closer to Whitehall; a real Establishment figure.

Eton-educated Lord William Forbes-Sempill was apprenticed to Rolls-Royce in 1910 and soon became an enthusiastic aviator, joining the Royal Flying Corps at the beginning of the First World War. He later transferred to the Royal Naval Air Service, where he rose to the rank of commander and was awarded the Air Force Cross. When he retired from the service in 1919, his engineering knowledge led to a life-long involvement with aviation. In 1921 Whitehall even asked him to lead an official British mission to organise the Imperial Japanese Naval Air Service.

During this visit Sempill became a confirmed Japanophile, striking up close and long-standing relationships with the Japanese military. The Japanese were impressed and awarded him several decorations for his service to Japanese aviation during the inter-war years.

Lord Sempill's mission in Japan was officially discontinued after America raised concerns about Tokyo's growing naval strength. However, Sempill carried on providing support to the Japanese by passing classified military and technical information to the Japanese naval attaché in London, Captain Teijirō Toyoda. In 1925 Sempill was questioned about passing on official secrets but, mysteriously, never prosecuted. He continued to receive regular payments from the Japanese government-owned Mitsubishi Corporation and, during the 1930s, openly entertained several high-ranking Nazis.

Despite his track record of passing classified information to foreign powers and his fascist sympathies, Sempill was re-assigned to the Admiralty in 1939 on the outbreak of war with Nazi Germany. His position allowed him access to highly sensitive information about the latest British military hardware and official secrets.

In June 1940 MI5 discovered that Sempill was *still* receiving payments from Mitsubishi and an investigation revealed that he was almost certainly still passing secret information to the Japanese; the Attorney General nevertheless advised against prosecution and Sempill was allowed to keep his position in the Admiralty and his access to sensitive information.

Further suspicions were aroused when, in early 1941, a London-based Japanese businessman, Satoru Makahara, manager of Mitsubishi's London office, was arrested on suspicion of espionage. While he was being held at Paddington police station, Lord Sempill telephoned personally to assure the police of Makahara's innocence and good character. MI5 duly took note, but Sempill somehow retained his Admiralty position.

The problem was that Churchill was a social friend of Sempill. According to revelations in the *New York Post* in 2012, 'When Churchill first learned of this long-time friend's activities in 1941, he was terrified that the world would learn that he had been casually chatting about military secrets with a friend who was then passing them along to their enemy.'

Intelligence historian Professor Richard Aldrich explains Whitehall's reticence over Sempill at the time:

> Sempill goes around for a cup of tea, Churchill's talking about the war, and then Sempill goes to the Japanese Embassy to tell them what Churchill told him. If this comes into court, Churchill's going to be tremendously embarrassed, because he's been blabbing. He drinks a lot, and he's very gregarious. Who knows what he said?

The final straw came in late 1941 when intercepts of Japanese signals showed that Tokyo had been briefed on the top-secret Newfoundland Conference meeting between Churchill and Roosevelt. An investigation concluded that only two men could have leaked the details: Lord Sempill or his aide, a Commander McGrath, who had accompanied Sempill on his various Admiralty missions.

On 9 October 1941 Churchill gave instructions to: 'Clear him out while time remains.' Sempill was shifted to a post in northern Scotland. However, he still continued to assist the Japanese. In early December an MI5 raid on his office found him in possession of classified documents that he had been instructed to return months previously; then around a week later he was caught making phone calls to the Japanese over a week *after* the Japanese invasion of British Malaya and their attack on Pearl Harbor. Sempill was forced to resign, but was never prosecuted for his treasonous relationship with the Japanese.

According to Richard Aldrich, 'This is a classic case of Churchill protecting himself. If Sempill had been revealed as a spy, it would have been politically calamitous for Churchill at a low point in the war.'

Most of the intelligence files on Sempill's activities during the 1930s and 1940s have mysteriously disappeared, but those that remain show that the Japanese had a highly organised spy operation in Britain with at least five British citizens in London providing information to the Japanese. Churchill was almost certainly aware of this. Japan's interest in Malaya was an open secret between the wars. During the 1930s

Japanese businessmen had bought up large amounts of land. Many of these new owners had intelligence briefs or were planted spies. Japan even manged to buy the plans for the Singapore base from a British serviceman called Roberts.

The Australian government was especially wary of Churchill by late 1941. The relationship between the two countries was politically ambiguous and both sides had based their defence needs before the war on a series of highly suspect guarantees and false premises. To Churchill, Australia, as in the First World War, was little more than a potential base in the east and a ready supply of fresh Commonwealth divisions to eke out Britain's small army.

Not all the deceit was on the British side, however. In peacetime it had suited Australian governments nicely to ignore defence and pretend that 'the old country' would pay for Australian security. Military spending was thus kept at less than 1 per cent of the government's budget during the 1930s. Australians were fed on the fiction that the *British* were primarily responsible for their defence and would automatically come to their rescue if the worst happened. Thoughtful Australians could wonder why the British should suddenly be able to send a fleet in war, when they had never been able to despatch one in peacetime. But no-one asked awkward questions like that. It was all too politically convenient to get someone else to pay for your defence, however false the premise.

Churchill, when he finally took over as Prime Minister from Neville Chamberlain in May 1940, eyed events in the Far East and the Japanese threat with growing concern. Fine speeches and rhetoric were no substitute for a credible and well-resourced defence policy. The year of 1941 was to expose his strategic reassurances and final choices as dangerous gambles with the security of Australia and the East at the expense of the Desert War and aid to a beleaguered Soviet Union.

As the year 1941 opened, after their disastrous rebuffs by the Soviets on the Amur River had blocked their expansion north into Siberia, the Japanese played out their strategy of a 'march to the south'. In early summer, Thailand, directly to the north of Malaya, had a brief war with the Vichy French regime (based in Indo China) over a border dispute. By June 1941 the Japanese had established a massive (one estimate is

200,000 troops) military presence in Indo China and was pushing hard for a military presence plus transit rights through Thailand. For the first time, northern Malaya was directly threatened by the Japanese. The Japanese move into the airfields of southern Indo China suddenly brought their bombers well within range of Malaya.

British intelligence had followed these developments closely and with increasing interest and growing alarm. The British were, however, hampered in their intelligence efforts by four fundamental problems: a complete under-estimation of the Japanese armed services as effective fighting forces; fragmentation and lack of any real British intelligence coordination in the Far East; a serious shortage of local resources for collecting intelligence; and lastly, a dangerous lack of any real vocal presence in the war councils of the civil and military staffs in Malaya. Over-shadowing them all was the fact that the British military operation in Malaya was an open book to the Japanese because of Britain's lamentable security: Malaya By 1941 was crawling with Japanese spies and agents from top to bottom.

Of these, without doubt the most dangerous intelligence sin was the first: the under-estimation of the Japanese as a viable, dangerous potential enemy. But bad security ran it a close second.

In many ways it is surprising that the British under-estimated the Japanese, given that Japan was a warrior nation with a good track record of victory – they had trounced the Russians in the Far East in 1904–5 – possessed a large and modern fleet, and had been successfully fighting a major ground war in China and Manchuria since 1931. To understand quite why this came about it is necessary to enter the mindset of the colonial world of 'European Superiority' before the shocks of 1941.

Britain was not alone in this contempt for 'Asiatics' as little more than clever *natives*. The myths of racial superiority were not confined to Hitler's Nazi Germany in the 1930s. The British view was best summed up by the Commander-in-Chief Far East Robert Brooke-Popham on a visit to Hong Kong in December 1940: 'I had a good look at them [the Japanese guards on the frontier] close-up across the barbed wire, of various sub-human species dressed in dirty grey uniform ... If they represent the average of the Japanese army, although the problems of their food and accommodation should be simple enough, I cannot believe that they would form an effective fighting force.'

At the time it was genuinely believed that the Japanese were physically small, bucktoothed, had poor eyesight and were incapable of fighting in the dark or operating sophisticated machinery. White men were inherently superior.

One naval expert even wrote, 'Every observer concurs . . . that the Japanese are daring but incompetent aviators . . . they have as a race defects in the tubes of the inner ear, just as they are generally myopic. This gives them a defective sense of balance.'

These views were widespread. Japanese 'could not fire rifles because they could not close only one eye at a time'. There was even a view that 'the terrified Japanese would flee at the first sight of a white soldier.' For example, the commanding officers of two British infantry battalions in Malaya are on record as saying to their generals that they hoped 'we aren't getting too strong in Malaya . . . as it might deter the Japs from a fight,' and, perhaps most arrogant of all, the remark, 'Don't you think my soldiers are worthier of a better enemy than the Japs?'

This was dangerous nonsense. The reality of operations against Japanese forces came as a profound shock to all the Allied combatants, on the ground, in the air and at sea. The Australian Russell Braddon looked aghast at the first Japanese bodies he came across in Malaya; 'not a specimen under six foot tall, with not a pair of glasses or a bucktooth between them . . .' And as for the Japanese' 'technical deficiencies', while the British did not have a single tank on the Malayan Peninsula, the Japanese, despite their supposed inability to operate machinery effectively, had managed to land armour in the north and used their light tanks to great effect against the static British defensive positions on the main roads.

The Japanese had also developed new 'jungle tactics' (the majority of 1941–2 battles in Malaya were not fought in 'jungle' but in primary forest or rubber plantations with good spaces between the trees and visibility, akin to a European beech wood) that involved thrusting hard and swiftly directly down the lines of the good Malayan roads. Once they were halted, the Japanese infantry deployed quickly into the trees on either side, firing as they went and outflanking the dug-in Allied defensive positions blocking the road.

By using these so-called 'fishbone' tactics they forced a perpetual morale-sapping retreat onto the increasingly exhausted and despondent Australians, British and Indians.

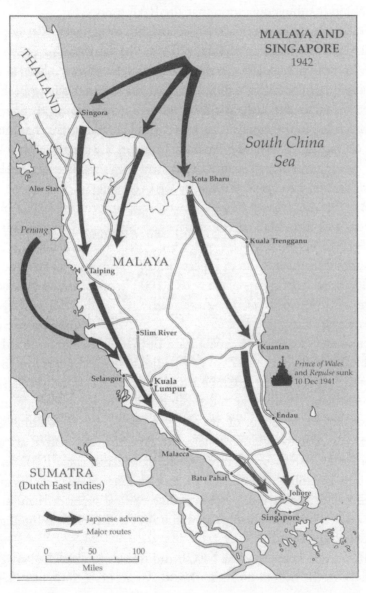

In the air, the same tale of under-estimating the potential enemy unfolded.

As the first bombing raids thundered down on the RAF's airfields the derisive British airmen poured scorn on the Japanese 'diarrhoea' bombing tactics, where tight formations of bombers dropped their loads simultaneously onto an area target. This was not the individual precision bombing operation that the RAF trained for.

But the raids were remarkably successful; using tactics developed in four years of attacks on targets in China the Japanese aircrew proved they knew their business. On the order to release from a master bomber Japanese bombs fell in a broad pattern that turned out to be highly effective tactic for airfield denial, ensuring that some damage was *always* done to the target. And, in a curious development that puzzled the air staff in Malaya, the Japanese bombers always seemed to know just when and what to strike. The answer was simple: every RAF airfield location had been betrayed by Japanese spies.

Another unpleasant surprise in the air, unforeseen by air intelligence, was the high performance capability of Japanese aircraft, especially the Navy Type 0 Carrier Fighter, better known as the 'Zero.' Dismissed by most Western experts as little more than an 'unarmoured, underarmed light sports plane with a 1000 horse power engine on the front', in the words of one American analyst, the Zero's dragonfly manoeuvrability came as a nasty shock to Allied pilots unaware of its phenomenal dogfighting capabilities. But RAF intelligence in Malaya had known all about the Zero and its fighting capabilities long before the war. In May 1941 the Chinese had downed one of the new Japanese fighters near Chongqing and produced a comprehensive air intelligence report warning of its fighting potential. This intelligence eventually got to London where the Air Ministry passed it to the coordinating staff for all intelligence in Malaya, the FECB, or 'Far Eastern Combined Bureau'. In Malaya, despite its clear significance – of all the services, aviation depends on technical superiority more than any other – it was not just ignored: the Air Staff Technical Intelligence report disappeared.

This is not to say that the FECB did not try to alert the services in Malaya to the overall Japanese threat. An accurate and clear General

Staff Malaya Intelligence memorandum from mid-1941 spelled out the Japanese order of battle and weapons capabilities in some detail. The problem was that the information, even when it was supplied, appears to have been largely ignored by the operational staffs and the units. So much so that the day before war broke out, one of the military staff officers on the GHQ staff said publicly that, 'he couldn't understand why the Governor had got the wind up and mobilised the local volunteer forces . . .'

If the British and their intelligence services under-estimated the threat from Japan, then the Japanese did not make the same mistake about the British. Japanese intelligence efforts for their campaign in Malaya before the war were comprehensive, thorough and well resourced. They were also broadly undetected by the British, whose security was lamentable.

The aggressor always has the initiative and for over ten years the Japanese intelligence service had been able to build up a sophisticated organisation inside Singapore and Malaya, largely based on the large numbers of legitimate Japanese companies and business activities trading there, with their seven thousand Japanese residents and travellers. In addition, there was a steady commercial traffic in small boats along the eastern seacoast; many of the Japanese craft included naval officers on reconnaissance missions. It was later claimed that even the official photographer at the Singapore naval base was a serving Japanese intelligence officer, Colonel Nakajima.

This Japanese intelligence activity was widely known about in Malaya. The chief of the Straits Settlement police, writing after the war, claimed that the extent of Japanese espionage had compelled him to recommend to the governor that at least half of any Japanese company's workforce must in future be non-Japanese labour. Nothing was done. The policy from London was to do nothing that might antagonise the Japanese – in case it provoked them to attack.

Sometimes Japanese spying was so blatant that it became farcical. In late 1940 the Japanese press attaché in Singapore, Shinozaki Mamoru, was arrested in flagrante and eventually jailed by the British authorities for three and a half years for openly running espionage agents in Malaysia (including a British Army corporal) and in particular for offering guided tours of British barracks and military installations to Japanese Army officers visiting Malaya.

The most blatant examples of bad security were the unauthorised mooring of two Japanese submarines in the Malayan harbour at Endau, (which was owned by a Japanese mining company) and the remarkable testimony of a Captain Collinge of the Straits Volunteers who, in September or October 1940 saw a Japanese officer, in full Japanese Army uniform, observing a squadron of British armoured cars on exercise before coolly embarking on a motor boat to sail out to sea in the gathering dusk, 'presumably to rendezvous with a Japanese ship offshore'. When he reported this, Collinge was officially told by two British civilians on the Governor's staff not to make an issue of it, 'as the policy of HM Government . . . [at the time] . . . was to appease the Japs and to avoid provoking an incident at all costs . . .' By 1940 British security policy in Malaya was to ignore Tokyo's widespread and blatant spying.

We can only imagine the fury of the intelligence officers in Malaya collating this intelligence and vainly trying to warn the military authorities. It was an Alice in Wonderland situation, made worse by the peaceful languor of colonial life in a humid semi-tropical paradise where the Governor and the white 'tuans' of the Colonial Civil Service and the old Malaya hands ruled supreme.

If the British were unprepared for a war in Malaya, then the Japanese most certainly were not. We are fortunate that the chief operational planner of General Yamashita's victorious 25th Army, Colonel Masanobu Tsuji, Imperial General Staff, has left a full account of the planning for the seizure of Malaya.

Planning for the invasion began on 15 September and was accompanied by an intensive programme of aerial reconnaissance over Malaya. As the date of the invasion drew nearer the busy Japanese pilots flew ever more blatant overflights of RAF airfields and installations, many of which were detected by the British. Not one was intercepted. On one flight on 22 October 1941, Tsuji himself actually went along himself in a Japanese Type 100 'Dinah' reconnaissance aircraft as it flew directly over the sites of the landing beaches at Khota Baru and the RAF base at Alor Star at only 6,000 feet. It is inconceivable that these Japanese flights directly over British RAF airfields went unnoticed.

A second, even more thought-provoking example is the story of Air Technician Peter Shepherd, then eighteen years old, who was serving as an RAF aircraftsman at the forward airfield of Sungei Patani in northern Malaya.

On 4 December 1941 he was ordered to fly as a stand-in crewmember on a Dutch East Indies civilian Lockheed Hudson as the Dutch technician had been taken ill. In his own words,

> To my surprise we landed in Cambodia on a private landing airfield in the south at a place Kampot. As French Indo China was virtually in Japanese hands at the time, this made Cambodia a pretty dangerous place for a Dutch 'plane to land. The French authorities were of course liberally sprinkled with pro-Vichy elements and so no friends of the British in 1941.
>
> Later in the day the pilot took me to a restaurant to eat. There were only the two of us. The pilot went off into the back of the kitchen to do some business, probably about the cargo.
>
> At the restaurant, an Oriental came up to me and offered me some of his Tiger Balm for my mosquito bites, which were pretty bad. He started to talk, but I couldn't understand a word. I gathered from his mixture of pidgin English and sign language that he was a Jap civilian, and some sort of aircraft engineer himself. After all, 'engineer' sounds the same the whole world over. He thought I was a French aircraft engineer. He seemed very pleased about something and kept trying to talk to me. He was pretty drunk, mainly on cognac. We communicated in a weird mixture of sign language and place names and eventually he pulled out his diary and a map and tried to tell me where he had been and what he was doing there.
>
> He indicated that he had sailed on an aircraft carrier from Japan to Hitokappu Bay north of Japan and had seen a huge armada assembled there. On the 24th of November he had been flown south on to Phu Quoc Island to supervise some urgent operational modifications on the bomb racks of the Japanese planes based in Southern Cambodia.

He seemed very proud of what he was doing and what he had seen and indicated that we were the only people who knew about the fleet, and that it had been planning to sail on 26th November to obliterate the US fleet in Pearl Harbor and to launch a simultaneous invasion of Malaya and Singapore. He explained this with lots of signs and 'boom, booms.' When I indicated surprise, he dragged out a kind of diary book and even showed me a few rough sketches of some of the naval ships he said he had seen moored the week before to convince me.

I realised it was important, so when he staggered out to the lavatory, I stole the drawings from his book. He got even more drunk after he came back, and when the pilot told me it was time to go I left my new friend vomiting over the veranda rail.

On returning to Malaya the next day, 5th December 1940, I immediately reported all I had been told to the RAF Station Intelligence Officer. Later that morning I was flown down to Kuala Lumpur where I was interrogated by two civilians who I took to be intelligence officers. I handed over the sketches that the Japanese engineer had drawn and went through all the details yet again. During the course of my interview I said that I believed the Japanese to have been telling the truth as he saw it, and we agreed that if all the details of his story were true, then the time of the supposed attack would probably be in three days on 8 December [7 December Hawaii time, because of the International Date Line]. I flew back north to Sungei Patani that afternoon with strict instructions to keep my mouth shut once I got back to the station.

Nothing happened after I got back. Despite the state of emergency the airfield never even went on full war alert, much to my surprise, and the next thing I knew was when a bomb blew me through the concrete doorway of the aircraftsmans' showers at 7 am on the morning of 8 December during a surprise Japanese air raid. Then I was invalided out of the RAF back in UK in early 1944.

I often wonder what happened to the information I gave to those Intelligence Officers at Kuala Lumpur . . .

Peter Shepherd's story is merely one dramatic example of the mass of intelligence warnings that were flooding into the British intelligence authorities in Malaya in the month before the invasion of Malaya.

To understand this we have to look at the second of the fundamental problems that hampered the British in intelligence in Malaya: poor organisation and rotten security.

The British approach to the management and coordination of intelligence in the Far East seems to have suffered from a remarkably fragmented organisation. It is easy to understand that at the height of a war for survival against a ferocious and dangerous enemy like Nazi Germany the British would inevitably give priority to the most immediate danger on their doorstep and worry less about the Far East. That is logical.

What is less easy to understand is the apparent disorganisation of the intelligence effort in Malaya itself. When this was allied to the other classic British failing, the deliberate starving of taxpayers' funds to essential government activities such as defence, in the supposed interest of economy, then the inevitable conclusion is that the British defeat in Malaya was very much a self-inflicted wound. Some vestigial evidence for this view can be found in the structure of intelligence in Malaya in 1941.

The key coordinating body was the FECB, which was theoretically charged with coordinating intelligence from the three services' SIGINT sources and sometimes secret service reports, providing the 'competent authorities' with up-to-date, accurate summaries of the threat to British interests. In fact its prime role was as an outstation of the Bletchley Park code-breaking operation. In the absence of a full official history of intelligence in Malaya we can only guess at the FECB's real role and influence. But from the contemporary memoirs we do know that the FECB was not a respected voice in the war council of Malaya. If anything, it was *excluded* and because of the requirements of tight security (it was evacuated before the fall of Singapore to prevent its secrets falling into Japanese hands) was unlikely to be heard in the more rarified civil-military committees responsible for the defence of Malaya in 1941. The truth was, no organisation was coordinating intelligence properly in Malaya in 1941.

Part of the fragmentation problem seems to lie with a lack of understanding about just what intelligence could and should do. Military

intelligence was only a small and subordinate staff within the bureaucracies that ran the Malayan colonies and was largely ignored by 'real
intelligence'. This seems to stem from ignorance on the part of the
colonial regime and an out-dated belief that 'intelligence' and 'the
secret services' were one and the same thing in some curious John
Buchan or Bulldog Drummond view of 'the great game'.

The whole of the Far East Command seems to have been permeated
with the belief that MI6 and its secret collection assets was what intelligence was really all about; all the rest of the rather more mundane
intelligence cycle of collection, collation, interpretation and dissemination seems to have been ignored or unknown. Really vital assets like
the services' signals intelligence units, which were breaking Japanese
codes and reading Japanese messages, seem not to have had any real
influence on events before spring 1942, or if they had, intelligence
secrets were not put to work for operations.

Added to this unworldly intelligence unprofessionalism was MI5's
jealously guarded monopoly of Imperial counter-intelligence, through
the Defence Security Officer (DSO). But MI5, as ever, lacked operators. So the fragmentation was increased still further by the 'hands on'
roles of the various secret political police officers (dubbed the 'Special
Branches') from the several colonial police forces, with the result that
intelligence coordination in the Far East was effectively non-existent,
and endless squabbling between agencies was the norm.

To add to the confusion, many of the individuals in charge of the
various fragmented intelligence departments got on so badly on a personal level that cooperation between their offices became impossible.
In just one case, MI5's DSO in Singapore, Colonel Hayley Bell, was
not even on speaking terms with the head of the Japanese Section of
the Singapore Special Police Branch. Relationships were so poisonous
that Major Kenneth Morgan (Retired), late of the Indian Army, the
SB chief, flatly refused to tell the DSO precisely what he knew about
Japanese espionage, citing security concerns!

Eventually the row between the two came to the attention of the
military, and there is a fascinating note in the files of a Colonel A. E.
Percival (who was later to surrender the garrison at Singapore in 1942
as a lieutenant general), when he was the chief staff officer in 1937,

about the secret policeman Morgan, 'It is not possible to feel any confidence in Major Morgan. His statements and views . . . convey a strong impression of an eccentric mentality, ill-balanced judgement, muddled thought and un-called for reticence.'

A sardonic view might be that this is merely the inevitable *déformation professionnelle* and descent into paranoia of any secret policeman anywhere who has spent too long inside the secret world. Percival added 'Morgan is clearly lacking in ability and not fitted for the appointment he holds . . . and this view is supported . . . by his past history and antecedents.'

With men of Morgan's calibre out looking for spies it is no surprise that British counter-intelligence were unable to protect the colony from disaster, which was after all their prime duty. Morgan and his colleagues would have had a pink fit if he had realised that in Malaya in 1940 and 1941 there was a major Japanese military espionage operation being run by a serving British Army officer. The truth was that British security in Malaya was virtually pointless. Not only were British plans betrayed under Churchill's nose in Whitehall, out in Malaya someone was telling the Japanese everything.

Captain Patrick Heenan was probably recruited as a spy by the Japanese Military Intelligence Service during a visit to Japan in the winter of 1938.

He was an unpopular officer with his fellow officers in his battalion, the 16th Punjab Regiment in Malaya; so much so that he was posted out to be an air intelligence liaison officer. This was never going to be a good career move for an infantry officer in any army, but it did provide Heenan with the agent runner's dream: access to joint service military secrets. Heenan could now lay his hands on all the Malaya Command orders of battle, types, dispersal locations and weapon states of every RAF aircraft in Malaya, plus their contingency battle plans.

One of the great mysteries of the Malayan campaign was the uncanny ability of the Japanese to hit RAF airfields so accurately and at a time that guaranteed maximum loss to the British. 'It was almost as if they knew our plans . . .' in the words of one aircraftsman of the time speaking long after the campaign.

They did. Heenan supplied the Japanese with everything he knew, and in particular probably provided accurate detailed plans of RAF Alor Star, the key airfield in the north, that allowed it to be obliterated in a devastating series of air raids early in the campaign, thus virtually guaranteeing the Japanese air superiority for the rest of the campaign. Worse, he almost certainly passed on the top-secret British codes and ciphers which allowed the Japanese SIGINT service to read all the British Army and RAF traffic throughout the battle. British security was not just bypassed in Malaya: it was rendered irrelevant, non-existent.

Heenan was careless. He had attracted attention and suspicion before the war within the military, but nothing was done. However, on 10 December 1941 he was arrested and his quarters searched after what looked like a botched attempt to murder his section head, Major France. He was found to be in possession of unauthorised classified maps, operation orders and codes, plus two disguised transmitters and a code book to encipher transmissions.

In the panic of the retreat a full counter-espionage security enquiry into Heenan's contacts was obviously impossible; but it soon became quite clear that he was heavily implicated not only in his own direct espionage activities but also in running a network of Japanese agents in Malaya before the war.

Heenan was moved south under escort with the retreating British armies and taken to Singapore, where in January 1942 he was court-martialled for espionage, charged with having 'wilfully communicated information of value to an enemy while on active service in in Malaya in December 1941'. He was found guilty and sentenced to death.

Heenan was not alone in the intelligence he supplied. The British discovered to their horror after the war that the Japanese had seen all the most-secret traffic between Churchill and the War Cabinet in London and the Commander-in-Chief in Singapore in 1941.

To ensure that the most-secret and the highest-level documents of all were not hazarded or compromised by transmission or by aircraft overflights, in late September 1940 Whitehall despatched the direct correspondence to Singapore – which included a pessimistic 'eyes only' British chiefs of staff appreciation of Britain's real ability to defend Malaya – by a fast merchant ship, the 7,500 ton SS *Automedon*. (See page 147). The master, Captain McEwen, and the diplomatic courier,

Captain Evans, both had strict instructions to drop the weighted sack over the side if anything should go wrong.

It did. In November 1940 the *Automedon* was intercepted on the last leg of her journey off the Nicobar Islands in the Indian Ocean by the disguised German surface commerce raider, *Atlantis*, who had been reading British merchant codes.

The leader of the German boarding party, an English speaker called Mohr, could not believe his luck. The delighted Germans found that they were now in possession of a weighted official British diplomatic courier mailbag containing the top-secret personal correspondence and the intelligence crown jewels for the Far East, plus all the new British maritime code books, *and the British did not know*. The Admiralty assumed that *Automedon* had been torpedoed and sunk by a submarine as the victims of surface raider attacks usually were able to get off a signal; but not this time.

Naturally, the Germans were not much concerned with the details of British plans in the Far East at that time – although the new British Maritime (BAMS) codes were another matter – and so they passed all the relevant documents to their ally, Japan.

The British never knew that early in 1941 the Japanese had copies of all the high-level policy directions that passed between London and Singapore and in addition could read almost all the British secret maritime radio traffic.

As if superior Japanese military intelligence, bad security, under-estimation of the enemy and poor organisation was not enough, the British in Malaya were hampered in all their efforts by a self-inflicted wound: a divided and weak command. The final ingredient in the disaster of Malaya and Singapore appears to have been provided by the fragmentation of the colonial government itself. Just who really was running the Crown Colonies in Malaya as they prepared for war in 1941? It was most certainly not the armed services, neither before, nor, more seriously, after the Japanese invasion.

The real confusion lay firmly with the government itself. Under the leadership of Sir Shenton Thomas, Governor since 1934, the 'Straits Settlements' of Singapore and Malaya had stagnated into a kind of colonial torpor more concerned with the status quo and the social life of the colony than with harsh external realities. Described by a contemporary American observer as, 'a [pompous] slave to British civil service values . . . living in some kind of dream world where reality seldom enters and where the main effort is to restrict the entrance of anything disturbing . . .' Governor Thomas seems to embody the worst characteristics of early twentieth-century British values.

Much of the blame for the debacle in Malaya has been laid at his door, especially by the British armed forces. The Governor may however be at least partly a victim of poor leadership himself; Churchill's War Cabinet had given him strict instructions on Malaya's prime role in Britain's war with Germany – which was not to prepare for a war with Japan, but to make as much money as he could for the Empire by selling rubber to the Americans.

In this atmosphere the main priority was undoubtedly economic. It therefore followed that anything that impeded the production and sale of tin and rubber - such as calling up the local defence volunteers for guard duty or military training – was merely a costly distraction from Malaya's principal task.

The true reason perhaps for Malaya's problems, including its incompetent and desperately insecure intelligence organisation, can be found in this schizophrenic rule, where in the middle of a mortal threat to the colony the patterns of peacetime, social life and the civil service seem to have gone on unchanged. Imperturbability in the face of deadly danger is a quality much admired by the English: in Singapore in 1942 it found its limits.

Not all Britons were as complacent and confident as the Governor and his herbivorous civil service. At least one man, C. A. Vlieland, sounded a really accurate alarm before the war.

Unfortunately he was a civilian, and a member of Governor Thomas's staff. Vlieland, who was appointed Secretary for Defence for Malaya in 1938, was eventually to resign after some curious backstairs political intrigue in 1941 before war broke out. But by then Vlieland had predicted in great detail and with uncomfortable accuracy the probable route and outcome of any likely Japanese invasion from the north through Siam and Malaya. Equally accurately, he outlined the need for strong defences in the forests to the north of Singapore and virtually dismissed the notion of any assault from the sea. He even claimed that the 'Fortress of Singapore' was a complete white elephant and irrelevant to Malaya's real defence priorities, not a view likely to endear him to the mandarins of official British policy or the combined services.

Vlieland's real tragedy was to get caught up in the bureaucratic power play between the Governor, the British Army and RAF and the new Commander-in-Chief, General Bond, when he arrived in August 1939. Bond, a powerful and opinionated figure, promptly set about seizing back control of the defence strategy of his command from 'a bunch of damned civilians'. Bond's particular obsession was with Singapore, and he would have no truck with a mere colonial civil servant meddling in matters of defence policy, especially offering his own 'amateur' intelligence appreciations. The clash was inevitable, as was the outcome. An embittered Vlieland eventually resigned in early 1941.

Perhaps this clash between the military and the civil administration ensured the fall of Malaya more than any other single factor. The infighting and lack of a clear command structure meant that no organisation, be it intelligence operations or even civil defence, could survive the endless wrangles over who was really in charge and order forceful direct action. Even as the final convoys of reinforcements poured into the harbour in late January and early February 1942 it was already too late to save the campaign. To the Australian government's horror they found that their final reinforcements for the 8th Australian Division, disembarking in Singapore as late as 24 January 1942, were little more than more fuel for the fire. The battle for Malaya was already as good as lost.

The discovery that Churchill had been contemplating diverting the British 18th Division on the high seas and sending it to the Middle East instead of embattled Singapore turned out to be the last straw for John Curtin, the Australian Prime Minister, who had already seen Churchill sacrifice Australian troops twice in 1941, in Greece and Crete, and was alert to any backsliding or 'treachery' by the British. The word, incidentally, is his. In January 1942 he cabled Churchill, warning him that any attempt to divert the 18th Division from reinforcing the garrison in Singapore would be, in Australian eyes, an 'inexcusable betrayal'. Churchill backed down and sent the last drafts of the 9th,

11th and 18th Divisions virtually straight into captivity, to join their Australian comrades in the doomed 'impregnable fortress'. It was not Winston Churchill's finest hour.

Two stories sum up the atmosphere of those last days more than any other. As a tired British infantry battalion began to dig its fire trenches for the final defence of Singapore on a golf course, 'a colonial planter of the worst type' came up quivering with rage, demanding to know what was happening. On being told what was going on by the young officer in charge, he stormed off, 'apoplectic with rage, shouting that the Golf Club was private property and threatening to tell the Governor to get this nonsense stopped, and full compensation ...'

The second was the much mooted canard that it was really lack of water that finally convinced Lieutenant General Percival to capitulate. When the local civil works engineer said that 'nothing could be done' about the water supply, the Army's Commander Royal Engineers said that with a few lorries and a work party of a hundred men he could repair and maintain the reservoirs and pipelines, and guarantee water for as long as it was needed. He never got them: not from the hundreds of thousands of desperate civilians or from the thousands of drunken, defeated deserters roaming the streets amid the flames, chaos and *Götterdämmerung* of the doomed island of Singapore on that terrible Sunday in 1942.

Amid the chaos of the last days one grim final act was played out. British security in Malaya may have been bypassed and made a joke by the treacherous Captain Heenan, but British justice was inexorable and rough.

The day before Singapore fell, the convicted traitor, Captain Patrick Heenan of the 16th Punjab Regiment, was officially 'executed by firing squad'. Rumour has it that what *really* happened amid the smoke and chaos of the ruins of Singapore was that he was dragged onto the dockside between two military police sergeants during a Japanese air raid. An enraged Royal Military Police officer then blew Heenan's brains out with a revolver at point-blank range before kicking the body into the dock and melting back into the crowds of Australian deserters, drunks and terrified civilians trying to fight their way onto the last boats out of a doomed Singapore.

It took the victorious Japanese to eventually restore order and calm to the garrison of Singapore. They did so quickly and efficiently in their own brutal way, proving once again that it had been a very serious mistake to under-estimate the Japanese, even up to the very end.

Perhaps Churchill was wise after all not to have convened a parliamentary inquiry into the blunders and mismanagement that led up to the fall of Singapore. Some disasters are so shameful as to be best quietly ignored: but their lessons should not be forgotten. And British security in Malaya – or lack thereof from top to bottom – contributed massively to what Churchill rightly called, 'the greatest disaster ever to befall British arms'.

PART EIGHT

ON DECEPTION

CHAPTER 31

D-Day

Because every intelligence coup represents an intelligence disaster for the other side, let us now look at intelligence officers on both sides in the run-up to D Day in 1944. Some were working hard to fool their opponents by planting false intelligence. Their counterparts were totally deceived by the intelligence they had so conscientiously collected and collated. They not only misread it; they failed to interpret it correctly. These intelligence officers did their job: they just didn't do it very well.

And the reason was simple: a brilliant deception, planned and organised to the last detail. The Russians call it '*Maskirovka*', and woe betide the Russian or Israeli staff college student who fails to give full weight to 'deception' in his plan for battle.

If the D-Day landings had failed, then the rest of the twentieth century would have been very different. If there was one single event in the Second World War that could possibly have changed the course of history more than any other, an Allied repulse on the Normandy beaches would have had cataclysmic consequences. The German generals would have been unlikely to risk their bomb assassination plot against a victorious Adolf Hitler. Hitler could have redeployed east, bought time, new secret weapons would have been available and Stalin's Red Army would have faced the full might of a rearmed (German arms production peaked in September 1944) and victorious Wehrmacht.

Today we take it for granted that D-Day, 'Operation Overlord', was a success. But at the time there was a very real fear that the landings might fail and the Germans would be waiting to hurl the invaders back into the sea, as they had done at Dieppe in 1942. Churchill him-self feared another first day of the Somme, with its 60,000 casualties, telling his wife as they went to bed on 5 June 1944, 'By the time you wake up in the morning, 20,000 young men may have been killed.' We even know that on the morning of 6 June 1944, Eisenhower secretly began to draft a signal beginning, 'The landings in Normandy have failed . . .' just in case the invasion in the west was the disaster it could so easily have been. Neither pessimistic prognostication came true. The key to the success of D-Day was deception.

Military deception has two main goals: first, to lure or force the enemy into an action we can exploit; second, to provide the enemy with enough plausible misinformation to allow the attacker an entirely different and desirable course of action. D-Day's 'Bodyguard' deception plan was used to convince the Germans into looking in the wrong place, paving the way for the historic success of the actual invasion.

Sun Tzu got it right, observing that:

> All warfare is based on deception. Hence, when able to attack, we
> must seem unable; when using force, we must seem inactive; when
> we are near, we must make the adversary believe we are far away;
> when far away, we must make him believe we are near. Hold our
> baits to entice the adversary, feign disorder, and crush him.

The trick with deception operations is to use the enemy's own intelli-gence apparatus to fool him. If German intelligence had interpreted the evidence they had collected correctly, Eisenhower might indeed have gone down in history as a defeated and disgraced commander. However, blinded by the greatest deception operation in history, the German intelligence staff was confused, misled and tricked into mak-ing a calamitous misinterpretation of the Allies' intentions. To the key intelligence requirement questions of, 'Will the Allies invade? If so, when, where and in what strength?' the baffled German intelligence officers and their masters got all three answers wrong.

It was not as if the Germans did not realise the Allies were coming; on the contrary, they expected an invasion. Early in January 1944, the chief of *Fremde Heere West* (Foreign Armies West, or FHW) Oberkommando der Wehrmacht, (OKW) Colonel Baron Alexis von Roenne, received a crucial signal from one of the German military intelligence service's secret agents in England, telling him that General Eisenhower was expected back in Britain. After the catastrophic German defeat in North Africa in 1943, such an appointment could only signify one thing: 1944 was expected to be the year of the 'Second Front' and Ike was to command the invasion forces in the west.

The German Commander-in-Chief in the west, von Rundstedt, and his Atlantic wall deputy, Rommel, Commander of Army Group B, also understood the dangers of invasion only too well. But where would the Allies strike? If the Allies could not hide the fact that an invasion was imminent then they were determined to sow as much confusion in the German intelligence service as possible about the exact time and place. The organisation charged with this crucial task of deceiving the German High Command was a unique group, the 'Allied Deception Staff', better known by its cover name of the 'London Controlling Section' or LCS. The LCS's primary task was simple: to deceive and confuse the German High Command, and Hitler himself, as to the Allies intentions over the D-Day landings, Operation Overlord.

The LCS was a remarkable organisation. As befitted its extraordinary task – to 'puzzle and defeat' the German intelligence staff – it was staffed by some remarkable men. In Colonel John Bevan, its leader, supported by men like Dennis Wheatley, the novelist, Sir Reginald Hoare, the banker, and Bevan's brilliant multi-lingual deputy, Lieutenant Colonel Sir Ronald Wingate, the LCS boasted one of the most high-powered collections of talent and brains on any wartime staff.

More importantly, the LCS's members had an extraordinary network of personal contacts and links with nearly every centre of power and influence in the Allied camp. As a result, and perhaps most crucial of all, the LCS enjoyed the complete confidence of the Allied chiefs of staff, even Churchill and the War Cabinet. This trust was essential, because at times the LCS was effectively coordinating and directing the efforts of nearly all the argumentative and competing Allied intelligence and security agencies in their own personal attacks on the Germans' indicator and warning system.

Hitler himself, in March 1944, told his commanders in the west, 'Whatever concentrations of shipping exist, they cannot, and must not, be taken as evidence or any indication that the choice has fallen on any one sector of the "Long Western Front" from Norway to the Bay of Biscay . . .' Hitler and all his military experts were, however, convinced of one thing: in order for a successful invasion to work, the Allies would need to seize a port on landing. This preconception, based on sound German naval military advice, plus the experience of the Dieppe landing in 1942, was to seriously damage and skew any objective intelligence assessment. Across the other side of the Channel, an ingenious plan had been drawn up with the sole purpose of feeding these German preconceptions.

'Bodyguard' was the cover name for a comprehensive range of plans for strategic deception aimed at *using* the German intelligence system to pass false messages. It had two clear aims: firstly to disperse and weaken Hitler's forces by forcing him to spread out his key divisions and armies throughout Europe, from Norway to the Balkans; and secondly, to delay any German reaction to the invasion for as long as possible by keeping the German planners unsure whether the first landing was just a feint.

In order to do this, Bevan's LCS proposed an extraordinarily wide ranging series of deception operations designed to feed the German intelligence staff with exactly the information they were seeking. Moreover, by using real intelligence as far as possible, Bodyguard would even offer Oberst von Roenne a reasonably accurate picture of Allied troop strengths. The real subtleties lay in clever distortions designed to mislead and deceive the German staff about the exact time and place of the landings and the precise size and dispositions of the Allied units. These reports were embedded into the huge mass of conflicting intelligence reports that were to be pumped directly into the German intelligence system. Some of them, astonishingly, were true. The only problem for the German planners was, which ones? LCS's aim was, to use the modern language of intelligence, to overwhelm the German intelligence services with noise.

The sheer scope of the Bodyguard plan was vast, and in Anthony Cave Brown's words, 'resembled nothing less than a large-scale corporate fraud'. Bodyguard's plan split into sixteen main intelligence areas, each designed to feed the Germans' known collection plan, from HUMINT to electronic warfare, from bombing target analysis to French resistance activity. In this the British were helped immeasurably by Ultra, the highly secret code-breaking operation at Bletchley Park, that enabled the British to read Hitler's most secret Enigma-enciphered messages and instructions, sometimes even before the intended Nazi recipient had seen them. Using Ultra, the Allies were able to read precisely what information the Germans were looking for – and then, obligingly, to provide it for them; suitably doctored to mislead and misinform, of course. Armed with this invaluable tool, developed and refined to meet the changes that the war brought about, the British deception service could not only feed the Germans false information; their intelligence services could also monitor whether their enemy had taken the bait or not.

The LCS was also keenly aware of another vital fact: few intelligence organisations believe easily won information. Just as an art dealer will resolutely refuse to believe an expensively bought painting could possibly be a fake, so intelligence officers tend to believe that the harder it is to discover a secret, the more likely it is to be true. This is of course nonsense, but Bevan and his staff prepared a series of inspired leaks that would come to von Roenne and his staff only by the most round-about – and sometimes expensive – ways: through obscure agent-runners in Madrid, the Swedish stock exchange and hastily suppressed 'leaks' in the neutral press to name but three.

In all this, Bevan was aided by a remarkable HUMINT coup. Since 1940, the British Security Service, MI5, had effectively been running and controlling every known German agent in the UK. The Double Cross Committee, headed by Sir John Masterman could, through MI5's network of long established double agents, send the Germans whatever lies the Bodyguard plan required. Double agent Tate's message about Eisenhower's arrival in England was merely the first of an elaborately conceived series of complex lies that would continue until well after the D-Day landings themselves. At least six other trusted

Double Cross agents pumped messages direct to their Abwehr controllers in Hamburg or Madrid, giving such details as unit badges, tank and infantry landing-craft concentrations and sightings of troops.

In Operation 'Fortitude North', one of Bodyguard's major sub plans, a phantom 'British 4th Army' was reported around Edinburgh in Scotland, painstakingly recorded by two Abwehr Double Cross agents, 'Mutt' and 'Jeff'. From their mythical network of contacts and sub agents, the two Norwegians informed Hamburg about 4th Army's new 'commander', Lieutenant General Sir Andrew Thorne, (deliberately chosen because he was well known to Hitler personally as the British military attaché in Berlin before the war) and the local Scottish newspaper reports of civilian welcome committees and military traffic accidents. Meanwhile the Germans themselves could log its ceaseless administrative local radio chatter.

In fact the '4th Army' never amounted to more than about forty staff officers plus a few heavy-handed wireless operators diligently churning out a tightly controlled script. These wireless operators were the next stage in Bevan's complex deception. Knowing that the German staff would, like any professional intelligence operation, look for 'collateral' (reports from other sources, confirming the HUMINT agents' information) the ever helpful Bevan thoughtfully provided von Roenne and his people with just the material they were seeking. The fake '4th Army' headquarters and its busy sub units transmitted and received a stream of credible messages for the excellent Abwehr Signals Intelligence, or 'Y' Service, to intercept and plot. Here an officer – easily checked against the Army List – would be sent on compassionate leave; there an irate quartermaster would be indenting for quantities of missing ski equipment.

Whatever the variations, the messages, when carefully collated by the diligent Abwehr intelligence staff, all indicated that there was a major British army assembling in Scotland, preparing for a campaign in mountainous or Arctic terrain. Allied to the dangerous RAF photo-recce flights over the fjords and the increased Royal Navy destroyer activity off the Norwegian coast, it could only mean one thing. Hitler was eventually to tie down no fewer than twelve divisions in Norway against an invasion that never came, from an army that never existed.

These HUMINT and SIGINT reports had to be complemented by the other sources that the LCS knew that the Germans would use. While photographic reconnaissance was unlikely to be able to check the Fortitude North dispositions around Edinburgh – few German planes had the range, service ceiling or speed to survive after a long flight across the North Sea – in the south of England it was another matter. Specially equipped high-flying Luftwaffe photographic reconnaissance planes could easily overfly Kent. Bodyguard decided, as part of Operation Fortitude South, to offer them suitable 'targets' to feed into the Abwehr collection plan. Ever mindful of the German nervousness about an invasion across the short sea-crossing to the Pas de Calais, Bevan's team decided to strengthen the image of an army group massing in the south east. This would have the effect of diverting attention away from Normandy and reinforcing the Germans' anxieties about the Calais area.

A massive dummy oil depot was built on the coast near Dover, complete with pipes, valves, storage tanks and even well-publicised inspections by King George VI. From 34,000 feet the German aerial photographs would not reveal that what they were seeing was a wooden fake, whose building had been directed by the illusionist Jasper Maskelyne and Sir Basil Spence. The photographic interpreters could not spot that the hundreds of tanks parked in the Kentish orchards were really nothing more than inflatable rubber 'Shermans'. One farmer even saw his bull charge a 'tank' and watched in astonishment as the pierced dummy slowly deflated. And the lines of landing craft moored in the Medway, with their sailors' washing hanging on the lines looked real enough.

When the evidence of the aerial photography was added to the agent reports, the analysis of the signals traffic, (which showed that all over Kent, Essex and Sussex well known US Army radio operators were transmitting) plus the well-publicised presence of General George Patton in the area, it all indicated a clear message to the German intelligence analysts: Patton's 1st US Army Group (FUSAG) did exist, and it was poised in the south east of England just across from the Pas de Calais.

Masterman's double agents Brutus and Garbo enthusiastically reported every fictitious detail, while the ever loyal Tate faithfully confirmed their reports in his own radio messages from Wye in Kent; 'Something big is building in the Dover area . . .' It was; Bevan and his LCS were building an illusion that would pin down the bulk of German Panzer divisions in France to face an invasion that was happening 150 miles to the west.

By now the fastidious and aristocratic von Roenne had the key components of his collection plan collated: HUMINT, reporting a massive build-up; SIGINT, confirming new formations arriving in UK; and imagery intelligence, whose aerial photographs clearly indicated an enormous concentration of troops and materiel in the southeastern corner of England. All now depended on von Roenne and his experts' evaluation and interpretation of the mass of intelligence reports they were studying. Were they true? Who were they? What were the Allies doing? And what did it all mean?

Von Roenne's personal assessment was vital as he, unlike many of Hitler's inner circle of senior Army officers, was implicitly trusted by the Nazi dictator. But von Roenne was fighting two enemies as he sat in his Zossen office and tried to interpret the intelligence in front of him: the Allied deception staffs, clever, well-resourced and playing him like a fish on the hook, and amazingly, his own side – specifically the the Nazi Party's own security service, the Sicherheitsdienst (SD), who were now firmly in control of all Nazi Germany's intelligence services.

In early 1944, the head of the military intelligence service, the Abwehr, Admiral Canaris, had been quietly dismissed by Hitler and pensioned off.

Wilhelm Canaris was a complex character, and one of the real enigmas of the war. Sir Stuart Menzies, the head of the British secret service later described him as, 'a damned brave man and a true patriot . . .' an unusual accolade from an enemy. Was Canaris a leader of the anti-Nazi resistance and a British spy? It seems an astonishing question, and highly unlikely, and yet there is enough circumstantial evidence that he was in contact with Menzies to raise serious doubts about his role in the mysterious intelligence exchanges that seem to have taken place between the British and the 'non-Nazi' Germans. The role of these murky links between the Abwehr and the SIS may well have influenced the outcome of D-Day.

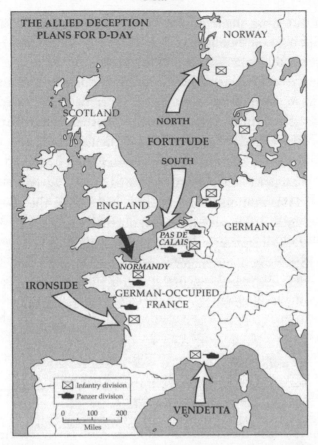

THE ALLIED DECEPTION
PLANS FOR D-DAY

After the Great War Canaris had dropped into the shadowy world
of the Reichswehr and its unofficial secret service. In 1934 Adolf Hitler
offered him the job of head of the Abwehr with the words, 'what I
want from you is an intelligence service like the British secret service'.
However, Canaris was no Nazi, and when war broke out, a series of
mysterious intelligence coups helped the British. For example, odd
packages of priceless technical information turned up anonymously
on the doorstep of the British Embassy in Oslo, among others.
(The information was so good that the British didn't believe it at first.)
As the war developed, the leaks and links between the Abwehr and its
supposed opposition became too obvious.

A suspicious Hitler finally gave Canaris's responsibility for intelligence to his arch-rival, and Nazi Party loyalist Walter Schellenberg,
the head of the SD. Canaris's discredited Abwehr were merged with

the SD to form a single unified Nazi intelligence organisation, The Reich Security and Intelligence Service, firmly under Party control.

However, the 'Amt Mil' or military section of the new service was still – just – under general staff control. Its British area intelligence officer was a cheerful extrovert called Oberstleutnant Roger Michel who, like all his brother officers, heartily detested his new Party bosses. Worse, Michel was labouring under a particular handicap – whenever he submitted an order of battle estimate to Führer headquarters, it was invariably sanitised and diluted by the SD party officials above him. They halved every estimate he made of Allied strength in Great Britain.

Oberst von Roenne had, however, devised a way for his frustrated subordinate to thwart their Nazi masters' tampering with, as they saw it, their perfectly good intelligence assessments. In the spring of 1944, von Roenne and Michel began to multiply their assessments of Allied strength by a factor of two, secure in the knowledge that the SD would then halve their report, thus ensuring that the report which went to Hitler's desk was an accurate reflection of the General Staff's original estimate. To add verisimilitude to this breathtaking scheme, the two plotters were only too grateful for the flood of fake Fortitude reports about 4th Army in Scotland, and Patton's mythical FUSAG and the build-up in the south east. Only the false Fortitude reports could be relied on to satisfy the Germans' desperate need for every scrap of collateral about troop dispositions in UK that they could get to support their inflated figures.

In May, von Roenne's crucial pre-invasion 'FHW Assessment of the Enemy's Order of Battle (ORBAT)' was published. To his horror, this time the SD did not halve his estimate of Allied strength. The reason was simple: the SD officer who had been cutting the Army's estimates had been posted. Von Roenne's assessment was sent out as the official top secret combined intelligence ORBAT to all Wehrmacht formations and headquarters in the west. Von Roenne dare not admit the deception – in the fevered atmosphere of suspicion and intrigue surrounding Hitler's court in the spring of 1944, to do so would be to invite summary Gestapo execution – and so he had to accept that the influential report issued under his name had effectively doubled the true known strength of the Allied forces from forty divisions to over eighty in the UK. It was a deception that would ultimately cost von Roenne his life.

But Bevan's ever resourceful intelligence hoaxers had one final trick up their sleeve. How much better, they reasoned, if a trusted *German* general could himself corroborate the mass of false intelligence reports they had fed into the German intelligence machine?

And, as chance would have it, the British just happened to have a spare German general.

General Hans Cramer had been captured in May 1943 as the Axis forces collapsed in Tunisia. As a prisoner of war in England his health had deteriorated, and in May 1944 the Red Cross arranged to repatriate him back to Germany in a neutral Swedish ship. Bevan's staff ensured that the general did not go empty handed. His drive to the docks took him through some of the heaviest troop concentrations in southern England, ending up at Patton's 'HQ' for his last night before embarkation. General Cramer hadn't the faintest idea where he had been, but was dined out, as a military courtesy to a sick man, by Patton himself. He also met some of Patton's 'divisional commanders' who were cool and correct to an enemy general officer, however ill, but gossipped away amongst themselves about 'Calais'.

The ruse worked. By 24 May, (only thirteen days before D-Day) Cramer was back in Berlin, faithfully reporting to General Zeitzler, Chief of Staff of the Wehrmacht, everything that he had seen and heard in England. Unsurprisingly, his information tallied with everything the Germans had collected and provided further collateral for von Roenne's intelligence estimate.

So, in the final days before the landings, the great LCS deception plan had, remarkably, become the basis for the German intelligence appreciation. Even Hitler himself, despite an almost feminine intuition that suddenly swung him towards Normandy at the last moment, forebore to change his dispositions. Of the German Army's 300 divisions, only sixty were active in France: less than 20 per cent. And of those, only eight divisions were in place to oppose the Allies directly as they came ashore. The remainder were spread between the Balkans, Italy, Russia, the south of France, Denmark, Holland, Norway and, most important of all, the Pas de Calais.

From their reading of the decrypted ULTRA intercepts on 1 and 2 June, Bevan's delighted staff could read that Baron Ōshima, (the Japanese envoy in Berlin) was reporting to Tokyo that no less a person than Adolf Hitler himself had assessed that the likely attack would fall in the Pas de Calais, with feints elsewhere.

For Bevan and his LCS, it had been an intelligence triumph. A small, highly talented and influential staff had successfully orchestrated the most complex deception in history against an alert and highly competent adversary. One slip, one mistake in the script, one piece of the story that did not quite fit, could have unravelled the whole fraudulent network that was Bodyguard, Fortitude and their interlocking layers of hoaxes. But, through a complete understanding of the German's professional intelligence methods, and aided by the ability to read the Enigma traffic, the LCS had effectively hijacked the German intelligence staff assessment for D-Day and forced von Roenne and the whole German intelligence machine to do precisely what the Allies wanted, by making a fatally wrong assessment at a critical moment.

The final German Intsums (intelligence summaries) for the end of May 1944 read like a catalogue of errors: the Germans were convinced that the Allies would attack in good weather, in the dark near a large port and at high tide. They also assessed that there would be *several* feint landings designed to draw German reserves away from the true landing – in the Pas de Calais.

The deception operations continued well after the Allied troops came ashore on D-Day. During 9 and 10 June, a fresh wave of resistance attacks, heavy air raids and an unheard of tempo of off-shore preparations hit the Calais area. Masterman's ever faithful Abwehr Double Cross agents sent extensive HUMINT 'collateral' explaining that the Normandy landings were merely a diversion, and the real blow – the landing of Patton's FUSAG – was just about to fall on the Pas de Calais.

To further compound this catalogue of errors, von Roenne personally contacted Hitler's intelligence liaison officer, Colonel Krummacher, and reinforced FHW's written intelligence estimate by insisting that any diversion of forces from the Pas de Calais to Normandy would be a mistake, as, 'von Roenne personally had definite intelligence that a new invasion was about to fall on the 15th Army sector, beginning with a wave of resistance attacks starting on the night 9/10 June'. Armed with this highly unusual special pleading from a senior staff intelligence officer, Krummacher agreed to represent FHW's view at Hitler's crucial midday situation and planning conference.

At that conference, Marshal Jodl reported FHW's assessment to Hitler and added to it the weight of General Kuhlenthal's (the Abwehr's senior agent controller in Portugal and Spain) latest secret radio message from his diligent agent Garbo, giving fresh collateral for an imminent attack on Calais by Patton's non-existent FUSAG.

Hitler took the bait. At the midnight staff conference on 9–10 June, he abruptly ordered a halt to any movement from the Pas de Calais to Normandy. Not only that, the Führer ordered extra divisions to the 15th Army Sector and not to the embattled Wehrmacht in Normandy.

Hitler might have been less happy with his decision and with the FHW/Kuhlenthal intelligence assessment if he had realised that Garbo's radio message had taken *two hours* to send. The critical question as to why the extremely efficient British 'Y' service had not been able to pinpoint a two-hour transmission and catch the illegal sender never seems to have occurred to the gullible Kuhlenthal and von Roenne.

Back in London, the delighted Bevan and his LCS saw the map lines heading towards Normandy suddenly stop, and over the following days coalesce into the Pas de Calais. Bodyguard and Fortitude had worked.

Even then, the great intelligence deception was not over, and continued well into July. As late as the last week in June there were more massive Allied spoof airborne and naval operations off Boulogne and Dieppe. These feints were successful enough for Hitler to personally authorise an order for all divisions still held back in the Pas de Calais a month after the D-Day landing to go onto full anti-invasion red alert for 8 July.

Was von Roenne an incompetent intelligence officer? Far from it. His track record before 1944 had been outstanding. His mistake was probably to allow his belief in his own system to overcome his doubts and to forget the need for critical analysis. The old intelligence assessment of source material – 'Is it true? Is it credible? Is it confirmed by other sources?' – seems to have either broken down, been ignored or just been saturated by an enemy intelligence deception operation that knew, thanks to Enigma, just how FHW's intelligence system worked and just how to fool it.

Faced by the key intelligence questions of 'Will the Allies invade? If so, when and where and in what strength?' the German intelligence staff got it completely wrong. It was a mistake that was to end in the ruins of Berlin and the collapse of Hitler's 'Thousand-year Reich'. Rarely can a bad intelligence estimate have had such serious consequences.

The great D-Day intelligence deception story has a postscript that elegantly sums up Bevan's cunning, Masterman's professionalism and the German tragedy. At 3 a.m. on the morning of D-Day, Masterman's trusted double agent, Garbo, frantically signalled his German controllers to inform them that one of his 'network of agents' had reported that the Allied troops had left camp, complete with sea-sickness bags. Only by dawn did the message get through to Berlin, by which time the Allies had begun to land, thus boosting Garbo's credibility as an agent without damaging the Allied operations. Bitterly, Garbo castigated his German controllers – 'I sent you this priceless information and it makes me seriously question your professionalism and responsibility.' Two months later, Garbo received a message awarding him the Iron Cross by Hitler's command.

Von Roenne was not so lucky. He was arrested in the aftermath of the 20 July Bomb Plot on Hitler. He was joined later by his old boss, Admiral Canaris, who may well have been a party to some of the deceptions, and who many post-war researchers suspect may have been in direct contact with Menzies.

Schellenberg knew that Canaris had been talking to a number of the generals who were later implicated in the 20 July bomb plot. Three days later Canaris was arrested by Schellenberg and his men. 'Hello' said the little admiral to his arresting officer; 'I've been expecting you . . .'

On 11 October 1944, Oberst Baron Alexis von Roenne was exe-cuted by the Nazi authorities for treason in the bomb plot's bloody aftermath. Rarely can an intelligence officer have paid such a high price for getting it so badly wrong. Canaris, whose role in the whole

D-Day deception has never been clear, was to follow. An SD search of the old Abwehr offices revealed records and diaries that showed the admiral and his staff to have been aware of many things they should have reported. The last head of the Abwehr was finally condemned for having been in contact with the enemy. In vain Canaris protested that that was the job of a secret intelligence service, and that he was a loyal German, no traitor to the Reich. It was to no avail; he was imprisoned and, as the Reich crashed around the deranged dictator, Hitler finally ordered him killed.

Canaris's end was not easy; after being beaten up by SD thugs, and with blood dripping from a smashed nose and jaw, he was slowly hanged from a meat hook on 9 April 1945, a lonely sacrifice to Nazi vengeance. In their own way, the two German intelligence officers, von Roenne and Canaris, were both among the final victims of the successful Allied deception to protect the secrets of D-Day.

PART NINE

ON TERROR

CHAPTER 32

On Terrorism

'Kill one – frighten ten thousand'.

Sun Tzu, and as brutally demonstrated by Lenin

As Westerners we are obsessed with battles. Napoleon and the Duke of Wellington have much to answer for. While the crushing defeat of the French Emperor at Waterloo was the final blow to the old European order, dear old von Clausewitz's writings also ushered in a very dangerous misunderstanding in Western minds: the myth of the 'great, decisive battle' that would end a war.

Others had different ideas, because the decisive head-to-head clash on the battlefield is by no means the only way for men to fight. Despite the risks, for the weak, the dispossessed and the just plain ruthless, sometimes the stiletto in the back can be just as efficient as the steamroller head-on – and has the great advantage of being easier to perform.

The truth is that terrorism has a long and bloody history and pinprick attacks on the rulers, the rich and the powerful are as old as humanity itself. The contemporary notion that terrorism is a new phenomenon is incorrect. As is the idea that terrorism is somehow not a 'legitimate' weapon for the 'continuation of politics by other means'.

It doesn't take any great capability or special weapons to be a successful terrorist. Terrorism is relatively easy provided the determination is there, although its consequences can be immense, as the 2015 Charlie Hebdo attacks in Paris showed.

A single knife or just one gun in the hands of a fanatic can change history. When Gavrilo Prinçip shot and killed Archduke Franz Ferdinand of Austria at Sarajevo in 1914, he lit a powder trail that led to the detonation and collapse of the whole European edifice. At the time his act was merely the latest in a long and depressing catalogue of atrocities.

There are two main elements to terrorism: 'terror tactics' and 'terrorism' itself. 'Terror tactics' are deliberately horrific acts of mass terror and have been used throughout recorded history to send a message to future foes: 'Don't resist too strongly, or this will happen to you.' Genghis Khan with his mounds of skulls stands as the arch practitioner of such a brutal method of waging war: but he was by no means the first national leader – nor the last – to indulge in such savage psychological operations.

Genghis Khan was not alone. Terror has always been the tool of tyranny. Mass terror has even been turned against a regime's own people. The French, the Russians, the Chinese and the Cambodian people have all been on the receiving end of a *domestic* terror meted out by their own government.

'Terrorism' however is something quite different. Terrorism nowadays means an act of specific act of violence to obtain political advantage. The phrase 'armed propaganda' is entirely accurate. Terror attacks are not intended to destroy an enemy's capacity to wage war: they are intended to communicate a clear threat, whether in pursuit of a grievance or to warn enemies off. The aim is always to frighten: but at the same time to send a message to three key constituencies: the enemy; the domestic population; and lastly, to overseas audiences.

Unlike normal warfare, the *message* is as important for modern terrorists as the actual violence itself. It is the oxygen of publicity that helped modern terrorism to become 'politics by other means'. Von Clausewitz would have approved of that. The truth is that, like it or not, terrorism is now recognised as just another part of mankind's brutal spectrum for resolving disputes – and a very cost-effective one for the determined terrorist.

'Terrorism' has been around in various forms for centuries. Jewish fanatics called '*sicarii*' plunged curved daggers into the backs of off-duty legionaries in the dark alleys of Jerusalem during the Roman occupation of first-century Palestine, and political murder has always been with us, as Guy Fawkes' 1605 Gunpowder Plot demonstrates.

Closer to our own time the *'Thuggees'* of India, with their murderous strangling attacks on travellers in the name of their bloodthirsty god, Kali, and the brutal way the Mafia traditionally held sway in Sicily are examples of historic terrorism in action, dominating whole populations by the use of fear as a weapon.

It was the industrial revolution of the nineteenth century that gave the terrorist three invaluable new tools: accurate, quick-loading fire-arms; reliable explosives; and a political theory.

This last, the 'political blueprint', really comes out of tsarist Russia. In the last half of the nineteenth century a number of revolutionary groups began to target politicians and officials in an attempt to bring down the tsarist state by a deliberate campaign to assassinate and terrorise its functionaries. And therein lies the true message of political terrorism – at heart it is an attack on the power of the state.

Terrorism nowadays owes its notoriety to the modern conjunction of an unholy Trinity.

> Political violence since the end of the Second World War has usually been successful.
>
> Modern media has helped to carry the terrorists' message more widely than they themselves could ever have hoped: in some cases the media have become virtually accomplices of their terrorist suppliers of 'big stories for the newsroom'.
>
> The technical potential of new weapons has offered the terrorist new and undreamed of ways to break things and hurt people. (For example, cell phones, computer triggering devices; and modern explosives.)

Terrorism is nothing more than the calculated use of violence to achieve a political goal by killing and maiming in order to terrify and intimidate as many people as possible. In this it is little different from war itself. The expert views of some practitioners of state terrorism are instructive: 'The death of one is a tragedy; a million a statistic.' said Stalin. And Lenin, who had clearly pondered at length on the subject of state terror, mused that 'the purpose of terror is, quite simply, to terrify'.

Most professional soldiers and policemen harbour a deep dislike of terrorism and its practitioners. They see all too clearly the clear distinction between the warrior and the murderer. Many normal people share this same feeling of unease and worry over the difference between killing in battle and murder. The difference is the grievance. Terrorists are invariably a minority of men – and women – with a deep and burning grievance.

What drives *most* terrorists is the 'cause', some deep grievance that can make reasonable human beings abandon their normal sense of values, transcends their natural human impulses and extinguishes all sense of proportion or mercy by imbuing the terrorist with a higher calling for their actions. The 'cause' can make men and women fanatics: and fanatics with a cause and a gun can be very dangerous indeed. For example, after one heated argument about tactics between the 'revolutionary' members of the Baader-Meinhof terrorist group in Germany in the early 1970s, their leader shouted, 'For God's sake stop arguing! Let's just go and kill a policeman . . .'

Their 'cause' absolves the terrorist from their actions, however dreadful. It can turn even nice old grandmothers into hate-filled fanatics with a suspended sense of Catholic values, as BBC reporter Fergal Keane realised, listening with growing unease to his Irish grandparents gleefully recounting their bloodthirsty tales of the IRA in the 1920s.

Terrorism is rarely a mass movement. The Provisional IRA and ETA, the Basque separatist movement in northern Spain, illustrate the point. In both cases no more than ten per cent of the population – if that? – was active in the terrorists' cause. Despite this, the terrorists ended up dictating the political agenda and swaying events, even though they were only a tiny minority. Terrorism has had an impact out of all proportion to the numbers involved.

Since 1945 the terrorists' belief in their cause, and their will to succeed, allied to the refusal of the state to use serious all-out armed force against them, has almost always ensured success for the determined terrorist.

Unlike the vengeful retribution of Nazi Germany, today's terrorist is usually operating in the belief that his enemy is unlikely to retaliate by taking the gloves off and unleashing the full force of the state against him. For example, there was very little terrorism in Stalin's USSR. The reason was simple: the totalitarian state would kill any dissidents they caught without a second thought and usually all their friends and family as well. The Provisional IRA would not have lasted three months in Pol Pot's Cambodia during the 'Year Zero'. Terrorists invariably are relying on government weakness, the media and political concessions to a much greater extent than they – or the general public – care to admit.

This exploitation of a reluctance by the authorities to come down hard and crush them is usually accompanied by a general sense that the terrorist's political grievances do actually contain a degree of truth. For example, Lenin and his fellow Bolsheviks' grievance against the authoritarian repression of tsarist Russia and their Marxist dream of a better Russia was shared by many. Lenin claimed to offer a better alternative – governed by Lenin and his chums, naturally. With other terrorists the alleged wrong that inspires and drives the 'cause' varies, but always there is the deep-seated political *grievance*, the sense of some burning injustice, which overrides morality and the laws of normal society.

For the Palestinians it is Israel; for the IRA it was the British in the Six Counties of Ulster; for the Pro-Lifers it is abortion clinics; for jihadis it is their perverted view of Islam. Carried to extremes, such logic can even encourage the militants of the Animal Liberation Front to believe that it is actually morally right to murder human beings in order to be kind to animals.

With logic like this to guide their actions it follows that terrorists are not like normal people. For whatever reason, their normal belief system has been distorted or bypassed. Normal people therefore have great difficulty understanding the terrorist mind.

Most grievances in most societies are resolved by a graduated range of responses and dialogue. For example, the local residents don't like the plans for a new wind farm being planned in the neighbourhood. 'Not in my backyard!' goes up the cry, and residents' associations are formed, public meetings are held, and soon appeals to government at both local and national level kick in. Protestors are organised by activists and leaders, frequently self-selecting from the most vociferous or just plain bloody-minded, with little better to do.

But these disaffected citizens have a just case: and *they are right*. The grievance is further mobilised by marches, banners, publicity on television, minor acts of damage or attacks on any policemen unlucky enough to get in the way. That is when the threshold of legality is effortlessly passed, once 'direct action' becomes part of the protest against the grievance.

Should the issue still not be resolved to the protestors' satisfaction (even when they are in a clear minority, as with the IRA or ETA) or should there be no mechanism for protest against perceived injustice – as in for example in the Israeli–Palestinian dispute – then the protestors with their grievance and their 'cause' face a hard choice.

Deeply alienated from society for whatever reason, they can either give up, or continue the fight by 'non-parliamentary means'. Historically the disaffected resort to terrorism when they believe all other avenues to have failed, or they see no other way forward. Direct action then swiftly becomes a targeted attack against an individual; if the grievance still festers, then a general attack on the 'enemy group' and its supporters is the obvious next step. The spectrum of disaffection and protest has now reached terrorism. Although every group is slightly different, the recipe always contains the same basic ingredients. There is a deeply held

THE LIMITS OF PROTEST:
A SPECTRUM OF DISAFFECTION

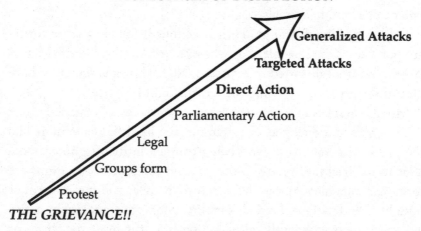

(For a good example, consider the Animal Liberation Front)

grievance; resentment at the inability to win their case by legal means or total alienation from a political system that offers no redress; and finally, a resort to very public violence to coerce the enemy to change its policy.

One major change over the past 150 years however has been the loss of restraint and the killing of the innocent. The attitude towards the terrorists' audience, the public, has hardened. For example, on several occasions in the nineteenth century the Russian radicals sometimes aborted assassination attacks on the tsar at the last moment out of concern for innocent bystanders. Nowadays their more ruthless successors deliberately target and kill innocent third parties in a conscious effort to get the attention of their real audience: not the public, but the government. The Omagh bombing in Northern Ireland in 1998 and the massacre of 132 innocent school children in Pakistan in 2014 stand as classic examples of targeting the innocent to garner publicity.

Worse still, the Islamic Fundamentalists of al Qaeda and its successor jihadis, such as ISIS and all the other Islamic terror groups, appear to have no intention of even attempting to try and modify their enemies' policy or to 'win their case'. For them the audience *is* the target and the almost nihilistic attack on the World Trade Center in 2001 and the Charlie Hebdo murders in Paris seem merely demonstrations of their hatred and contempt for the West, rather than any attempt to coerce governments into change. Much jihadi grievance admits of no redress and has uneasy parallels with some anarchist violence.

The heart of the problem revolves around this 'grievance' and what can actually spark it off. General Sir James Glover (who enjoyed considerable success commanding the British security forces against the Provisional IRA in the 1970s) had thought deeply about terrorism and the sources of disaffection. He believed potential grievances abounded at all times and in all societies, and felt that a skilful politician should be able to spot them early and defuse them before they became the triggers for social unrest and terrorism.

He called these triggers 'the catalysts for conflict'. These are, like terrorism, as old as mankind itself. Some classic examples of these grievances and catalysts for conflict are:

Survival – The Warsaw Ghetto

Food supplies – The depopulation war on Easter Island

Land – Western settlers and the Native Americans

Natural resources – Japan's invasion of Manchuria

Greed – The Conquistadors

Drugs – Colombia, Mexico and the cartels

Power – Hitler and Czechoslovakia

Self-determination – The American Civil War

Religion – The Crusades

Ideology – Pol Pot and Cambodia

Control – Kashmir

Revenge – Oklahoma City bombing

Autonomy – ETA and the Basques

Freedom – East Timor

Language – Walloon and Flemings, Belgium

Class – Lenin and the Kulaks

The list could be longer . . .

All these catalysts for conflict, if not addressed, can trigger some deep grievance and encourage wars or incite the terrorist to act.

With such a grievance and their 'righteous' cause, the profile of the average terrorist is surprisingly easy to discern. They believe in and have, a 'cause'. They are right and we are wrong. So they are, by definition, better people than the rest of us. Their cause and their 'struggle' legitimises their atrocities. Being members of a righteous cause, the 'struggle' against an unworthy enemy now defines their whole identity and existence and so the 'group' soon becomes their 'family'. Just like the Zionist terror groups of 1944–1948, the group exists for, and believes in, some hope-filled future, where victory for the cause is assured and always just around the corner.

For the committed terrorist, all it will take are a few more atrocities and a few more killings to bend the rest of humanity to see just why they should do what the terrorists want them to do. The mind of the committed terrorist is in fact clinically little different to that of a self-assured psychopath. Normal reality, let alone normal *morality*, is suspended.

Perhaps the most dangerous aspect of all is the terrorist's inability to turn back, to change his or her mind. Because the struggle is their very reason for living, the group and the cause gradually becomes everything to them. Sweet reason or other voices are excluded. Their whole life and being is now defined by the cause and by their guilty involvement in what is a criminal conspiracy.

With such a mindset, it soon follows therefore that anyone not with them, even moderates in their own camp, eventually become potential traitors and enemies. To those within the little bubble of criminal conspirators, eventually everyone *outside* their circle becomes a potential betrayer either of them or the cause. Paranoia and infighting follow murder and conspiracy as inevitably as night follows day. Terrorism, like revolution, tends to devour its children.

The success of terrorism as a weapon or tactic in the latter half of the twentieth century has changed the face of battle. The straws were in the wind immediately after the 1914–18 war, when the Irish Republican movement hounded the British out of Ireland by a deliberate campaign of murder and terror, with great brutality on both sides. By 1921, the British, sickened by the prospect of a bloody and open-ended campaign, and with war-weary voters at home, gave up the struggle with the Home Rulers and quit, leaving the Southern Irish to fight their own squalid little civil war and murder each other instead in their grab for political power. Terrorism by a minority of determined killers had worked.

In his memoirs, Field Marshal Montgomery saw very clearly the purpose and the inevitable logic of terrorism. Recalling his experiences of the Irish Republican Army's struggle to evict their English rulers in 1921, he wrote:

> In many ways this war [against Irish terrorists] was far worse than the Great War ... It developed into a murder campaign in which, in the end, the soldiers became very skilful and more than held their own ...

Two very clear indicators of the way in which terrorist wars would be fought in the future marked the IRA's early struggle. There was a deliberately targeted campaign of murders and atrocities against non-combatants on both sides; and it was that intelligence drove the war. For example, in 1919 in a series of spectacular coups the IRA murdered undercover British intelligence officers and Special Branch police officers as prime targets. From the very start the terrorists' war was an *intelligence* war. The IRA's leader Michael Collins planned and fought it as just that, before de Valera's own band of Irish terrorists eventually murdered him in his turn.

The achievements of the IRA's terrorist campaign that hounded the British out of Ireland in the 1920s, plus the successes of the irregular tactics of the Resistance movements and organisations like SOE during the Second World War, alerted new groups with a grievance after 1945 to the possibilities offered by guerrilla warfare and terror attacks.

In what is now Israel, two groups in particular, the Stern and Irgun gangs, prosecuted their terrorist operations with considerable ruthlessness to drive out the British, the Palestinians and even the UN itself. Jewish settlers who dared to disagree with the Zionist zealots became terrorist targets too.

It is one of the ironies of history that Israel's current government condemns Palestinian terrorists for using the very methods that the Israeli terror gangs used in 1945–48 to seize Palestine from the British and Arabs and consolidate their own Zionist rule.

By 1948 terrorism was everywhere, usually in the guise of an 'anti-colonialist struggle'. From Malaya to Vietnam, from EOKA murdering women and children in Cyprus to the Casbah in Algeria, guerrilla and terrorist wars marked the three decades after the Second World War. In virtually every case the European government backed down and compromised with the rebels. A combination of weakness, lack of determination, and domestic opposition at home forced them to give in.

The most successful campaign of all was the Viêt Công's bid to seize and take over South Vietnam. With a clear political aim, and veering between guerrilla and terrorist tactics and all-out war as the opportunity demanded, the North Vietnamese and their backers eventually wore down the resistance of American domestic opinion until even the global superpower finally quit the battlefield out of sheer weariness, leaving their South Vietnamese allies to their fate.

It was this 'war of the flea', not set-piece battles, which characterised warfare and conflict during the Cold War, as the long-running struggles in Northern Ireland, South America, the Basque country and the jihadi attacks in the Middle East clearly demonstrate. In Mao's words, the terrorists were able to 'swim in the sea' of a compliant or cowed population.

By the end of the twentieth century, terrorism as a phenomenon had become entrenched all round the world. The Tamil Tigers of Sri Lanka, the Hutus of Rwanda, the Colombian and Mexican drug cartels, and the Chechnyan rebels (who even took their fight up to the gates of the Kremlin) were all exploiting one of the oldest forms of warfare in their various attempts to intimidate the opposition. Terrorism had become a part of most people's lives.

By 1968, the majority of the Palestine people and their Arab friends realised that, after the Israel Defense Forces' victories in the 'Six Day War' of 1967, there was no real possibility of ejecting the Israelis from the land of Israel by force. Dispossessed, sullen, brooding in their filthy overcrowded camps in Gaza and the West Bank, by the mid 1960s the Palestinians looked for another way of bringing their cause to an uninterested world's attention. In a series of daring coups, televised live around the world, the militants of the Palestine Liberation Organisation (PLO) hijacked airliners and blew them up on prime time TV. An astonished world looked on amazed and insurance brokers wept into their champagne over lost profits.

In 1972, eleven Israeli athletes were kidnapped and gunned down at the Munich Olympic Games, along with five of their captors. This time the world recoiled in horror; but the 'armed propaganda' of the PLO was stunningly successful. Suddenly the world was very interested indeed in the Palestinians' problems.

Within two years of the Dawson's Field aircraft bombings, Yassar Arafat, the PLO's leader, was addressing the United Nations General Assembly in New York, pleading his cause. Clearly, terrorism worked.

In 1969 and 1970 the Provisional IRA's attempt to take over Northern Ireland, which started on the back of a civil rights movement in Ulster in 1968–69 was at first remarkably successful as a means of waging war. By the early 1970s, bombs exploded, policemen and soldiers were gunned down in cold blood and political violence and terrorism had become a way of life.

The first British reaction was appeasement. They tried to buy off the IRA by giving the terrorists what they wanted. The metropolitan *bien pensants* of London and Whitehall never really accepted that the raucous demagoguery of the Ulster Protestants was in fact the authentic voice of the democratic majority. At one stage in 1972 the British government was even considering re-drawing Ulster's border with the South in a desperate bid to rid itself of this combative minority of its citizens. Under the stern gaze of the Ulster Unionists they rejected this option, and were forced to fight on.

To defeat the terrorists, the British went underground. Led by men like General Sir Frank Kitson, who had learned his intelligence skills running counter gangs against the Mau Mau in Kenya in the 1950s, who recognised from the start that, like the original IRA campaign of the 1920s, the new campaign against the Provisional IRA was once again an intelligence war.

Undercover special intelligence operators took the Provisional IRA on in their own backyard, disrupting the terrorists by employing their own tactics against them. Terrorists were identified and followed by well-trained surveillance teams: terrorist arms caches were uncovered and booby trapped; and terrorists carrying out attacks were themselves ambushed and gunned down by undercover troops lying in wait. Above all, the IRA and their Unionist counterparts were penetrated from top to bottom by government spies and informers collecting intelligence on the terrorists.

Suddenly every IRA terrorist feared betrayal, the midnight raid or knock on the door just as much as their victims. Thanks to 'intelligence' the hunters became the hunted. The result of this long running undercover intelligence war was that terrorist leaders like Martin McGuinness and Gerry Adams realised that successive British governments really did have the stomach for a drawn-out and bloody campaign. Eventually, in a climate of political failure and mounting losses, the Provisional IRA's terrorist leaders were forced to seek new, more political, tactics to stay in the vanguard of their struggle. The price of terrorism in Northern Ireland was high, however. The Northern Irish terrorist campaign lasted over thirty years and claimed over three thousand lives.

From 1970 onwards, terrorism spread across the globe like a rash. From the Irish to the Basques, from the Baader-Meinhof gangs to the Red Brigades, 'terrorism' became the cutting-edge method of choice of groups with a grievance. Even criminal gangs and drug barons jumped onto the bandwagon. Technology, publicity, death and terror united when a tiny Japanese splinter group, the *Aum Shinrikyo* (effectively no more than a bunch of fanatical religious crackpots), released the nerve gas Sarin on the Tokyo subway in 1995 for no clear reason and succeeded in killing thirteen innocent people.

In this escalation of horrors one dispute remained as bedrock; the Arab–Israeli war, rumbling along at its various intensities. From a dispute over land in 1948, the Arab–Israeli war escalated into a full-blown clash of cultures, and by the end of the century had become an ideological crusade for Islam. By 1996 the PLO's war of terror against Israel had turned into something even more sinister: it had evolved into undeclared war against the United States of America, Israel's backer, by Islamic militants from all lands.

Islamic zealots seeking to strike at the West noted that they could exploit the vulnerabilities of Western liberal democracies. Open borders, relaxed and lengthy legal procedures, a culture of free speech, free association and free movement positively greased the slipway for terrorists to move and plan and work. Western states had for decades even turned a blind eye to terror. Pleas from Britain for American citizens to stop funding Irish terrorism fell on deaf ears. Basque separatists fled over the Pyrenees to sanctuary in France.

Even when governments struck back hard against killers and terrorists using undercover operators and good intelligence to target the terrorists in advance and stop them killing innocent bystanders, (as the British special forces did in Northern Ireland, London and Gibraltar) droves of well-paid lawyers and journalists strove to prove that their very own protector, the state, had in fact been acting outside the law. From such pusillanimous responses, Islamic terrorism took much comfort and planned accordingly.

Because Islam had a serious grievance against the West.

CHAPTER 33

Islam and the War on Terror

No greater dispute reared its head in the second half of the twentieth century than the Arab–Israeli conflict.

In the Middle East the bitter regional quarrels between Zionist colonial settlers and the dispossessed Palestinians mutated into a wider ideological crusade, this time of fanatical Islamic terrorists waging their own version of jihad against the global commercial and political influence of the West. The stage was set for catastrophe.

Islam has a long tradition of political violence and terrorism. Indeed, many Muslims genuinely believe that violence is somehow legitimate in defence of their faith because they belive that the Qur'an says they must wage jihad. The truth is that the real jihad of the Qur'an, as stated by the Prophet, is the individual's personal struggle to submit to the will of God. Ignorance, encouraged by the Western media, has instead blanketed all Islamic terrorism as 'jihad' and its fighters as 'jihadi'. It isn't and they aren't.

So now an explosive fourth factor had now been added to terrorism's unholy Trinity of success, the oxygen of publicity and efficient modern technology. From Algeria to Afghanistan, Islamic militants now had the supposed blessing of Holy Writ itself.

The fundamental roots of Islamic hostility to the West lie deep. A hundred years after the Prophet's death in 632 AD, his Muslim warriors had conquered most of the Middle East, Western Asia, the North African littoral and Spain. Over the next 500 years Islam

developed an advanced scientific and literary culture. Astronomy, bot-
any, geography mathematics, medicine, music, poetry and metallurgy
all flourished at a time when most Europeans lived in disease, despair
and darkness.

By 1095, Islam's dynamic cultural and military expansion towards
Constantinople and into Palestine triggered thousands of credulous
and ignorant Christians to set out on a long trek to evict the heathen
from the Holy Land. The First Crusade had begun.

The seven crusades that followed established a pattern of historic
enmity between Christian and Muslim. No sooner had the West
established its short-lived Crusader kingdoms in Palestine than the
Muslim leader Salah-ad-Din (Saladin), recaptured Jerusalem in 1187.
Over the next two centuries surviving crusaders came home to import
the wonders and learning of Islam into Western Europe.

The historic result was that although the Crusades may have been
militarily ineffective, their legacy was a dawning rebirth of knowledge
and enlightenment in the West. Europe prospered economically, politically and socially in the Enlightenment that followed the Renaissance.
By the beginning of the twentieth century, Western colonial expansion
had the crumbling Ottoman Empire and Islam in retreat on every
front; territorial, economic, cultural, scientific and, most dangerous of
all, religious.

Where force of arms had failed nine centuries before, Western commerce and colonialism now exploited and reigned triumphant over the
lands of Allah. For the true believer contemplating Islam's glorious
past, it was a deeply humiliating prospect.

The post-colonial leaders of the emerging Arab world now provided
another bone of contention for the faithful who had hoped that with
the end of colonialism true Islamic values would rule.

A tide of nationalism swept aside any ideas of a true Islamic state
as the new Arab leaders consolidated their hold: and they were as
authoritarian and corrupt as any of the pre-colonial regimes. The new
nationalist leaders' pleas for modernity and the London School of
Economics' enlightened belief in 'progress' meant nothing to the more
radical imams. For true believers, paradise was not some Western-
style secular state with the emancipation of women, well stocked

supermarkets and democracy. The true way was the Community of the Faithful, the *Umma*, based on an Islamic ideal and the revealed word of God. The ancient concept of a single 'Kingdom of God' (*Dar el Islam* – the land of Islam) had already been fragmented by the different nationalist priorities of states from Algeria to Pakistan. Now the Islamic world's new leaders were openly ignoring centuries of religious teaching and heritage.

Although they paid lip service to the mosque, the new Arab nationalist leaders were essentially secular. For men like Nasser of Egypt, Assad of Syria and the re-installed Shah in Iran, their radical Muslim clerics represented nothing but trouble. They resolved the clash between nationalism and 'Islamism' by ruthless repression. In Syria, outspoken Muslim opponents of the regime quietly disappeared into Damascus's version of the Lubyanka. In Egypt the Muslim Brotherhood was suppressed and in 1966 Sayyid Qutb, its great theoretical voice, hanged, and in Shi'ite Iran, opponents of the Shah's regime – who referred to the Shi'a imams contemptuously as 'his black crows' – fled to avoid prison. A clear fault line was emerging between the mosque and the state in the Islamic world.

To the burning grievance against the West for centuries of colonialism and humiliation was now added yet another cause for resentment: domestic oppression. From Algeria to Pakistan, Islam now trod carefully under the watchful eye of the state and its secret policemen and informers. The exploding populations of Algiers, Baghdad, Cairo, Damascus and Islamabad bred into a world of disease, poverty and powerlessness where dictators ruled. Inequalities were everywhere. For many of the young people there seemed no way out of the hopelessness of existence. But from the mosque came reassurance for the faithful: hope was at hand from Islam, and the establishment of God's kingdom on earth.

For the mosque had not been idle while it had appeared to be quiescent. The imams may have been forced to meekly bow their head to the state and the secular men of power, but they had preached sedition whenever they could. For, whatever their differences of class, nationalism, culture or language, every true believer across the Muslim world was now being told that there was one simple solution to all their problems of oppression and public corruption by their new rulers.

They only had to set up a single state with sharia law and the sacred texts of the Qur'an to bring about God's kingdom on earth, with freedom and justice for all. In simple, clear, modern language the radical Muslim clerics proclaimed a gospel of hope in the 1960s and 1970s and fired up a new generation of post-colonial Moslem youth imbued with a single burning slogan: 'The Qur'an is our constitution.' From an oppressed present the mosque brooded on its hopes for the future.

Events on the wider world stage eventually brought the extremists and fanatics the very opportunity for which they had been waiting and also the God-given enemy against which all Islam could unite – Israel. Ironically, it was the victory of the arch-enemy itself that indirectly triggered Islam's great rallying cry and call to arms.

The Yom Kippur War (see page 205) triggered a series of events that were to alter the balance of power in Islam's favour.

With the Suez Canal blocked economic chaos reigned. The price of oil suddenly rocketed from $12 a barrel in 1972, to $25 a barrel by December 1973. Sadat's Operation Badr had revealed a powerful new Arab weapon: oil. OPEC's restrictions on petroleum exports turned the screw still further. Money poured into the coffers of the oil states and the 1970s oil crisis brought Western economies to the brink of disaster. The Islamic world had rediscovered real global power – thanks to oil.

The result was that by the 1980s, Saudi Arabia became the epicentre of both OPEC and the Islamic world. With their newfound petro-dollar wealth, the Saudis and their rich Gulf state allies were able to fund a massive expansion of the faith, bankrolling thousands of mosques worldwide and making donations to Islamic charities through a network of Saudi controlled banks.

As well as money, the Saudis held another vital trump card in the Islamic world. They were also able to capitalise on their stewardship of the sacred places of Islam. The high-living but cautious Saudi rulers had always realised that their Wahhabite doctrine of asceticism and strict Islamic observance was essential for the guardians of Mecca. They had to be *seen* to behave as strict Muslims for the regime to survive. By 1986, when King Saud formally took the title of 'Custodian of the Holy Places' this combination of great wealth and public piety allowed the Saudis to become the focus of the hopes of the Islamic world.

But not all Muslims are Sunni. Shi'ite Iran was beginning to stir. Shi'ites, who make up about 15 per cent of the Islamic world, believe that the true path for Islam is the teachings of the Prophet's cousin and son-in-law Ali, murdered by Islamic rivals in the struggle for the succession and the soul of Islam. The imam traditionally exercises greater influence in Shi'a Islam, both over the faithful and, ideally, over society.

By the mid-1970s, despite the best efforts of his secret police, the Shah's regime in Iran was confronted by two major threats. The first was a group of young militant intellectuals heavily influenced by Marxist ideas and the other, revolutionary movements of the 1960s. Despairing of finding a democratic voice in the tightly controlled autocracy, the students plotted in their universities and colleges, hoping to mobilise the workers and peasants.

The second influence was an elderly cleric brooding in exile across the border in Iraq. His name was Ayatollah Khomenei. Khomenei's contribution to Islamic thought rests principally on his *Islamic Government under the Guidance of the Law*. While never a best seller in Western bookstores, Khomenei's collection of sermons advocated an Islamic revolution leading to the '*Dar el Islam*' ruled by godly men and following strict sharia law. Such a state would, of course, need to be guided by a wise supreme counsellor to whom all could turn for clarification over tricky points of the law and the real will of Allah. (Khomenei felt that this was a role to which he could perhaps make some modest contribution . . .) This combination of angry young middle-class students seeking to overthrow the Shah's regime and the revealed Shi'ite word of Allah proved an explosive mixture.

With falling oil revenues, unemployment, extra taxes and student unrest on the streets, by 1977 the Shah's regime was in serious trouble. As SAVAK, his secret police, cracked down, agitation increased. From abroad Khomenei stepped up his sermons, blasting bloodcurdling anathemas on the luckless Shah and appealing to the 'disinherited' of Iran to rise up against the godless dictator and his corrupt regime and seize power in the name of Allah the compassionate and the merciful.

The exiled Ayatollah became the symbol around which enemies of the Shah could rally. To cries of *'Allahu Akbar!'* the poor, the workers, the middle class, the students and finally the armed forces – even, astonishingly, Iranian Communists – united by despair at the Shah and hope for a better future, pledged allegiance to Allah and loyalty to Khomenei. In February 1979, the Shah abdicated and fled to Egypt to die in exile. Khomenei returned in triumph to adoring crowds in Teheran.

The brooding figure of a malevolent old ayatollah with dictatorial powers now ruled Iran and the Shi'a world. Khomenei's word was law.

With a ruthless single-mindedness at odds with his claims to otherworldly religious spirituality, Khomenei swiftly set about putting his own draconian version of the rule of Allah 'the compassionate and merciful' into action. The hangman and the firing squad found no shortage of work as a vengeful Khomenei took revenge on his opponents and let the mosque settle old scores under the pretext of cleaning out the stables. Political opponents and members of the old regime were butchered or fled at the same time as thieves lost their hands, homosexuals were executed and sophisticated Teheran women forced out of Yves Saint Laurent and Dior back into the chador and burka. Alcohol was poured into the drains and everywhere symbols of Western capitalism and decadence were torn down or defaced. Politics in Iran became synonymous with the mosque: and the mosque was synonymous with the Ayatollah's medieval view of God's kingdom on earth.

Within the year, Iran was officially declared an 'Islamic' republic with Khomenei as 'Supreme Guide of Allah'. All secular opposition had been crushed or sidelined. Even dissenting clerics were imprisoned, or worse. In a final explosive gesture of defiance and a demonstration of Khomenei's internal power, the American Embassy in Teheran was stormed and occupied in November 1979 by militant students of Khomenei's Party of the Iranian Revolution (PIR). The new Islamic regime sent shockwaves out both to the West and throughout the Muslim world.

Khomenei was stopped in his tracks by an unlikely adversary. Saddam Hussein ruled over a predominantly Shi'ite Iraq. Mindful of the adage that when your neighbour's house is on fire it is wise to take precautions, in 1980 he invaded Iran to seize the vital oil exporting installations in the Shatt al-Arab. Saddam may also have calculated that Khomenei's fanaticism needed to be stopped from sending too many revolutionary sparks onto Iraq's somewhat incendiary Shi'ite roof.

Faced with a mortal threat to his revolution, Khomenei once more turned to Iran's vast army of poor, young, working-class men and peasants. Like the alienated Iranian middle class they were now beginning to question the real benefits of Khomenei's emphasis on Islamist ideals at the expense of tangible prosperity and progress. Khomenei sent out a rallying call to divert them to their new holy task, invoking the Shi'ite concept of martyrdom in defence of the faith.

Hundreds of thousands of young Iranians volunteered to fight the Iraqis and, in a welter of bloodletting not seen since 1914–18 were hurled against the invader. The volunteers (*bassidjis*) died like flies in frontal attacks against the Iraqi army but stopped the advance. Khomenei trumpeted their sacrifice, claiming that they had been 'martyred for Allah' against the 'Godless Ba'athist of Baghdad'. Iranian blood, martyrdom and sacrifice again became the symbols of militant Islam.

The mantle of Islamic leadership now passed from the cautious but generous Saudis to the fiery and revolutionary Iranians. The new message to the faithful was clear: 'Rise up against your impious and corrupt leaders, take up arms against the foes of God, and jihad and martyrdom will win the day.' In images of blood and religious fervour Khomenei's Iran exported its revolution to the rest of the Islamic world.

Among the teeming millions of this Arab and Islamic world, where 50 per cent of the population is under thirty and dirt poor, the Iranian call to arms struck home. Nowhere did it have a greater impact than in Lebanon, Palestine, Gaza and the West Bank, where disaffected young Arabs, long without hope and searching for a means of hitting back at Israel, rallied to the fundamentalist cause. For the first time the 'call of Allah' became synonymous with opposition to Israel: with explosive consequences. Even the backers of Israel were now declared to be legitimate targets for the faithful.

Hezbollah, the popular movement backed by Iran, invoked the call of martyrdom and carried out a series of spectacular suicide bombings against Western targets. In one bombing in Beirut, 258 US Marines died and the Western powers rapidly withdrew from Lebanon leaving it to the locals to sort out their own arguments. The mullahs and imams proclaimed the victory: martyrdom and terror could even frighten off the mighty USA. Suddenly Khomenei's Islamic revolution was inspiring passions and uniting Arabs far beyond Persia's borders.

In the end, like many old men in a hurry, Khomenei overreached himself. He had long coveted the ownership and control of the Holy Places of Islam. After an abortive 'spontaneous uprising' at the 1987 Hajj in Mecca an appalled Muslim world surveyed the 400 dead pilgrims and unequivocally blamed the baleful old man of the Persian Mountains. Exhaustion on the battlefield and a renewed offensive in the long-running war with Iraq in 1988 finally forced Khomenei to 'drink the poisoned chalice' and sign a peace treaty with Saddam Hussein to ensure the survival of his regime. But his legacy of terror, martyrdom and jihad lived on.

The fanatics and the militants now looked for new causes. Afghanistan soon presented itself. In 1979 – the same year as Khomenei's revolution and the storming of the US Embassy in Teheran – the Soviet Union invaded the country of confused, backward and warring Islamic tribes that made up one of the world's most primitive states.

The invasion, on Boxing Day 1979, took NATO and the rest of the world completely by surprise. Astonished and worried intelligence officers were recalled from leave as planeload after planeload of Soviet special forces landed at Kabul to seize power. President Amin was murdered in his palace and a Soviet-style Communist regime seemed assured. But as the weeks progressed, a combination of Afghan nationalism and Islamic fervour united the mujahideen fighters from the tribes against the godless Marxists from the north. The Soviets found themselves embroiled in a war of national resistance against a determined and courageous enemy. Moreover, it was an increasingly well-armed enemy.

The mujahideen seemed to have endless supplies of good machine guns, good advisers and dangerously effective anti-helicopter missiles. Pakistan – backed by the CIA – was arming the Afghan resistance, in particular an Islamic group known as Hezbi Islami. America, 'the great Satan', was actually arming Islamic fundamentalists. One of America's clients was an obscure Saudi resistance organiser called Osama bin Laden.

Bin Laden was born in 1957, the son of a rich Yemeni contractor who had made a fortune from restoring Saudi Arabia's 'Holy Places'. Osama's mother had occupied a lowly place in his father's house, being referred to as the 'slave bride' by the senior wives, and the young boy, his mother's only child, had wandered the family mansion, alone and friendless. From such childish psychological scars, great consequences can follow.

Bin Laden's early career appears to have followed the standard pattern of rich young Saudis; university in Lebanon, wild drinking sprees with loose women and his friends, and cruising Jeddah in a canary-yellow Mercedes 450SL. The playboy's days of gladness ended abruptly in 1977 when made his Hajj to Mecca. Suddenly, Osama bin Laden became a born-again Muslim. Like many a fanatical convert before, his burning desire to atone for past misdeeds now went looking for some pious outlet to express his newfound zeal.

By the time of the Soviet invasion of Afghanistan, bin Laden was in his early twenties, devout, clever, ambitious and rich. He rapidly fell under the spell of a Palestinian, Abdullah Azzam. Azzam, as well as being a fiery preacher of Islam, was busy in the 1980s organising a supply of dedicated Muslim volunteers to fight in Afghanistan. Bin Laden now had his cause and his teacher. Osama learned his skills in Azzam's 'Office of Service', recruiting, training and moving the volunteers to a network of camps and bases in Pakistan and Afghanistan.

Bin Laden proved to be a good pupil and a skilful organiser, and the 'Office of Service' eventually pumped over 30,000 volunteer Islamic fighters from all over the world into Afghanistan, backed by a ready supply of Saudi Arabian government aid, Pakistani logistics, CIA intelligence and American Stinger missiles.

When the Soviets finally quit Afghanistan, in 1989, the battle-hardened veterans dispersed back to their home countries. These fighters took with them a radicalised, militarised view of Islam and a track record of victory fighting Islam's foes. From this network of veterans and Azzam's Office' sprang the idea of al Qaeda, 'the cell', a looser international grouping of like-minded Islamic warriors and men of action, all bound by their great calling and all determined to carry on their life's work, fighting in the name of Allah. As Azzam and Khomenei had made clear, jihad and martyrdom in Afghanistan were just the beginning of the fight to establish God's kingdom on earth.

Flushed with success, Bin Laden returned to his native Saudi Arabia and soon ran into trouble. By 1991, the desert kingdom was packed with foreign troops, mostly American, busy preparing for and then fighting the first Iraq war. To the devout bin Laden, raised in the Wahhabi tradition of strict puritanical observance of the Qur'an and the law, these impure foreigners so close to the Holy Places were a source of corruption and pollution in every way.

He said so openly, and offered his own wealth and organisation as a defensive bulwark to the House of Saud. Rejecting this poisoned cup, the Saudi regime found bin Laden and his followers too great a challenge and took steps to force him out. By 1991 a resentful Osama found himself exiled in the Sudan in a Khartoum office whose brass plate openly displayed the name of his business: 'al Qaeda'.

Al Qaeda's business remained what it had been when bin Laden worked for Azzam's 'office' in Afghanistan: raising funds, recruiting and training suitable volunteers, moving men and money round the world and creating an international organisation dedicated to fighting the foes of Islam. But by 1992, the year America invaded Somalia, the foes of Islam were no longer the godless Marxists of the Soviet Union. They had long gone. The new foe was the United States of America and the 'arch-oppressors' of the Palestinian people – the state of Israel.

Al Qaeda openly joined the warlords and clans fighting against American troops in Somalia and, by 1996, when bin Laden issued a fatwa against the US and was then forced to flee from East Africa to Afghanistan, the organisation had become a clearly identified terrorist threat. Afghanistan provided the perfect haven for bin Laden and his followers. The fanatical Taliban regime of young students, fired with missionary zeal in their madrasas, or religious schools, brought a brand of puritanical Islamic asceticism that echoed bin Laden's own Wahhabi views. Here in Afghanistan he could live a godly, quiet and sober life, plotting global murder and mayhem.

In 1998, the year al Qaeda began suicide bombings against American Embassies in Africa, he issued a rallying call to the faithful, proclaiming his 'World Islamic Front for Jihad against Jews and Crusaders' (WIFJ), an organisation whose title was also helpfully its mission statement. With al Qaeda and bin Laden at its heart, the WIFJ spelt out its aims: free the Holy Places of Arabia from foreign influence, drive the Jews out of Palestine and kill anyone who obstructs Allah's warriors or aids their enemies.

At a stroke, Israel, the USA, the West and any Muslim who disagreed with their view of the world became legitimate targets for al Qaeda. The battle lines for global terror and the horrors of 9/11 were now openly drawn up. On the one side stood the fanatical warriors of Allah, united by an historic grievance against the West, with access to millions of disaffected supporters, unlimited funds and a worldwide network of sympathetic organisations.

On the other stood the Great Satan and its allies, with its network of military bases, global capitalism and local collaborators, standing as an affront to Islam and its values while offering a feast of soft targets. Al Qaeda went looking for a target that would strike a deadly blow against America.

CHAPTER 34

The Greatest Atrocity – 9/11 and the Attack on the World Trade Center

The greatest single atrocity committed by Islamic terrorists was the attack on the World Trade Center in New York and the Pentagon on 11 September 2001 by hijacked airliners used as flying bombs. The terrorist attacks killed 2,996 in total, most of them innocent civilians, and caused more law enforcement deaths in the line of duty of than any other single incident in American history: 71 police officers, 343 firemen and paramedics died as the burning buildings collapsed on top of them.

The planning for the World Trade Center attack had started eight years earlier. On 26 February 1993, a half-ton truck bomb put together by an Arab called 'Youssef' detonated under the World Trade Center in New York, killing six and injuring over a thousand. Youssef fled. The bombing, timed to correspond with the anniversary of the ejection of Saddam Hussein's armies from Kuwait two years before, had all the hallmarks of a carefully planned terrorist attack and was almost certainly controlled by Iraqi agents based in the USA.

Youssef's massive bomb blasted down through six levels. The innovative architecture and the thousands of workers in the building survived the explosion. But the World Trade Center's vulnerabilities were openly exposed and explored in the extensive media coverage after the attack, especially its propensity to progressive collapse if hit higher up. The 1993 attack proved that the World Trade Center was a tempting target and, moreover, it also showed how the twin towers, symbol of America, Capitalism and the rule of the godless could be brought low.

The mysterious 'Youssef' had drawn up a blueprint for disaster.

By 2000 the CIA knew all about al Qaeda.

After the attack on the USS *Cole* off Yemen in June 2000, which killed seventeen American sailors, the world's intelligence agencies also knew that they were facing a well organised, clever and fanatical organisation that was prepared to deliver suicide bombs by unconventional means (the *Cole* had been blown open by a suicide boat coming alongside). They also had incontrovertible evidence that they were up against an enemy that was perfectly capable of planning and executing decisive attacks against well-defended Western targets.

The Qur'an strictly forbids suicide. *Intihar*, or killing oneself is specifically against the law. However, martyrdom, *shahid*, and acts of self-martyrdom – *istishhad* – for the cause of Allah are not only accepted but praiseworthy. Not every Muslim imam agrees; even Sheik Fadlallah of Hezbollah has condemned the practice of suicide bombings. However, bin Laden's mentor in Afghanistan, the Palestinian Abdullah Azzam, had laid great stress on the glories to be obtained by martyrdom, writing: 'Glory does not build its lofty edifice except with skulls,' and elsewhere, 'Those who think that they can change reality without blood sacrifice . . . do not understand our religion.' The concept of martyrdom is in fact deeply entrenched in Islamic tradition, especially the Shi'ite sect.

Hezbollah was the first modern Islamic group to use suicide bombers, or martyrs. Between 1982 and 1996 they waged a successful campaign against the Israelis, emulating the suicide bombers of the Tamil Tigers in Sri Lanka, who, in turn, modelled themselves on the Japanese Kamikaze pilots of 1945. Inside Palestine, suicide attacks are portrayed as heroic acts and families gain both honour and hard cash from their children's sacrifice. A poll in 2014 showed that 46 per cent of Palestinians supported suicide bombing as a tactic. It is regarded as both cost effective in terms of getting Israelis to pay attention (suicide bombers account for only 1 per cent of attacks on Israeli targets, but cause 44 per cent of Israeli casualties, according to Hamas) and also a good way of getting publicity for the Palestinian cause.

Fanatical young Muslims, many well educated and with at least 10 per cent young women in their ranks, volunteered to carry the fight to the Israeli camp. An instantaneous death, while smiting down the enemies of God, is believed by some Muslims to be a guaranteed passport to heaven. By their sacrificial act they also establish their true identity for all time: not as some worthless, half-educated unemployed youth, but as a religious warrior with a name that will live on forever. For impressionable young people imbued with, and schooled in, religious fanaticism since birth, this is an enticing prospect.

The martyr's last days are carefully controlled by the hard-eyed godfathers of terror to nurture and reinforce this idea. Like some human sacrifice of the Aztecs, the 'living martyr's' final glorious week is marked by feasting, one last – or even first – taste of earthly pleasures, adulation and admiration from all around and writing or videoing final emotional messages from the afterlife. Once trapped in this web of public commitment there is no going back for the suicide bomber.

Al Qaeda's suicide bombers followed a similar pattern to Hezbollah and Hamas, but with less frenzy and an altogether cooler determination to strike more significant targets than just small knots of hapless young IDF conscripts waiting at a bus stop. After the USS *Cole*, Osama bin Laden was after much bigger fish, a global audience and, thanks to 1993, he even knew the right target.

The World Trade Center beckoned.

In June 2002 members of the US Congress heard a detailed report on the most public, if not the worst (that doleful distinction falls to Pearl Harbor) intelligence blunder in American history.

In a closed-door top-secret session with the Directors of the NSA, CIA and FBI, both the Chairman and Deputy Chairman of the Senate Intelligence Committee heard an extraordinary tale of intelligence lapses and mistakes in the months before al Qaeda's attack on the twin towers. In their findings the inquiry concluded that there had been no single piece of evidence, no 'smoking gun' to indicate that al Qaeda was planning to use civil airliners as bombs and fly them into prestige US buildings on 11 September 2001. This chimed with the conventional wisdom that the terrorist kamikaze attacks on the World Trade Center and the Pentagon with airliners were so extraordinary that they just could not have been predicted.

Nothing could be further from the truth.

For, contrary to ideas that 'the attack could not have been foreseen', the Congressional report went on in the fine print to say that key intelligence which could have thwarted al Qaeda's plot had been only too available. Sadly it had been ignored, mishandled or just not distributed by the US intelligence agencies. The attack on the World Trade Center and the Pentagon was in fact a monumental intelligence blunder.

While it was true that there was no single piece of 100 per cent clear and accurate intelligence giving the exact date, time and location of the aircraft attacks, it is evident from the secret testimony at the Congressional inquiry that the old, familiar problems of the American intelligence agencies had reasserted themselves once again.

Astonished American intelligence committee members heard that there had in fact been an abundance of intelligence available to the US intelligence community before the atrocity. Literally dozens of clear indicators emerged of an impending al Qaeda terrorist attack by aircraft against prestige buildings inside continental USA.

The intelligence committee heard a litany as familiar as the story of Pearl Harbor.

Information that should have been communicated between intelligence and law enforcement agencies was not passed on; the significance of some intelligence reports was neither understood nor pursued; and key information that *had* been gathered was not even analysed or its significance assessed. From the post-attack analysis, the truth emerged of one of the greatest intelligence failures in American history. While the US – and other – intelligence organisations never identified the exact time and place of the impending World Trade Center attack in September 2001, the US Congressional inquiry revealed that their intelligence agencies had however amassed a very great deal of detail indeed about al Qaeda's capabilities and intentions well before the bombings. Somehow *collated* intelligence had not become *disseminated* intelligence.

Al Qaeda's plot went back a long way.

As early as December 1994 an Air France flight to Algiers was hijacked by Algerian terrorists who planned to crash the aircraft into the Eiffel Tower. French special forces took out the hijackers on the ground, but the warning both of terrorist capability and intention was there for all to see. In February 1995 the US Congress' Special Task Force on Terrorism and Unconventional Warfare actually published a warning that al Qaeda was planning a terrorist attack on lower Manhattan using hijacked civilian airliners as flying bombs. The US intelligence agencies all received copies of the report, which were duly filed away.

In January of 1995, as part of the precautionary security for Pope John Paul's visit, the Philippine police had burst into a Manila apartment shared by three known Islamic militants. Among the items they seized was a computer belonging to one Abdul Murad, a known terrorist suspect, containing specific details of an al Qaeda plan to hijack eleven airliners and either blow them up simultaneously or to fly them directly into prestige US buildings as suicide bombs. The plot was codenamed 'Bojinka', a Serbo-Croat term for a big bang.

This strange story was later confirmed in 1995 when Pakistan handed Murad over to the US as a wanted terrorist. Under questioning Murad turned out to the accomplice of 'Youssef', the mysterious 1993 World Trade Center bomber. Murad boasted openly to American federal agents about an al Qaeda plan to send airliners against US buildings. Rafael Garcia, the IT expert who had unbuttoned the captured computer for the Philippine National Bureau of Investigation later revealed that when he downloaded the target list the names of the White House, the Pentagon, CIA headquarters and the World Trade Center appeared. He passed the information to the FBI.

The FBI interrogated Murad and he confessed to being a trainee suicide pilot with orders to learn how to fly civilian airliners for attacks on US targets. Armed with the names of his accomplices the US authorities rapidly closed in on the 1993 World Trade Center bombers and yet again the Pakistani police were helpful: 'Youssef', al Qaeda's master bomber and their hero of the first World Trade Center bombing, was arrested while hiding in Islamabad and extradited to the USA.

In 1996 the Great Satan tried, convicted and sentenced him to a lifetime in an American prison.

The date of the first World Trade Center bomber's US conviction and sentence was 11 September.

With Youssef and Murad safely out of the way, Bojinka was filed away by the CIA, NSA and FBI. The FBI congratulated itself on yet another successful anti-terrorist conviction. There was no attempt by the Counterterrorism Center set up by the CIA in 1986 to issue new intelligence collection priorities. There is no record of any special watch being kept on young Muslims suddenly wanting to learn to fly civilian airliners. For the FBI, the case was closed.

The FBI did however take the threat seriously enough to issue special air-alert warnings during the 1996 Atlanta Olympic games. In particular they warned local law enforcement and security agencies to watch out for straying crop-dusting flights and demanded stronger than usual anti-hijack measures, 'to make sure that no-one hijacked a small aircraft and flew it into one of the [Olympic Games] venues'. This awareness of the changing threat is confirmed by the Federal Aviation Authority's (FAA) 1999 and 2000 annual reports, both of which specifically highlighted Bin Laden and al Qaeda as 'posing a specific threat to the security of US airliners'. The idea of an airborne attack was at least embedded somewhere in the collective US security consciousness.

Between June 1998 and September 2001 no fewer than seventeen separate reports linked bin Laden and al Qaeda with an attack on the USA, many indicating that an aircraft would be used. Reports were received from Israel, Pakistan, Germany the UK and Pakistan. This information failed to stimulate any reaction or a revised threat assessment, despite a secret briefing by the Director of the CIA, George Tenet, to his senior staff in the summer of 1998 at which he declared, apropos al Qaeda, 'we are now at war'. Unfortunately he doesn't appear to have lobbied to change the national intelligence collection priorities to reflect this historic judgement; nor did the head of the CIA allocate any extra resources to counter al Qaeda.

During the spring and summer of 2001 there was a 'significant increase' in reports of al Qaeda activity indicating a strike against the

US and possibly a prestige target within America itself. Even more damning evidence began to accumulate in both CIA and FBI files, reporting that the terrorists were still contemplating using airliners as flying bombs. The NSA had not been idle either. Their ECHELON intercept system, (which hoovers up all communications and then checks them against key words such as 'terrorism', 'bomb', 'targets', 'al Qaeda', 'spying', etc.) was clearly reading al Qaeda's communications.

Following the bombing of US embassies in Africa in 1996, al Qaeda had become a priority target and, after the events of 9/11, the NSA admitted that they had 'intercepted multiple phone conversations from al Qaeda operatives . . .' For example, early in 1999 NSA intercepted the name of one Nawaf al-Hazmi as a likely al Qaeda hijacker. The information was filed but apparently not passed on. More key telephone calls were intercepted, including calls from Abu Zubaida, al Qaeda's chief operational planner and even Osama bin Laden himself. During the course of the Congressional enquiry in 2002, an embarrassed director of the NSA, Michael Hayden, admitted that his agency had decoded thirty-three warnings of an al Qaeda attack between May and July 2001 – but had failed to pass them on for action.

In its turn, the CIA had little reason to crow at NSA's discomfiture. Although its Director, George Tenet, had been 'literally pounding on desks and warning of trouble' in the summer of 2001 and issuing apocalyptic warnings of war to his assistant directors, it transpired that he hadn't actually done much about his own warning.

A lack of suitable field officers meant that the CIA relied almost entirely on foreign agents and informers for its human intelligence on al Qaeda. There were few – if any – American spies working inside Islamic terror groups. In the words of one unnamed CIA source after 9/11, 'The agency no longer risked mainstream US field officers in what were known as "diarrhoea" postings.' As a result, a stream of uncoordinated reports in several languages, and of varying quality, poured into Langley, where understaffed and overworked analysts struggled to make sense of them. The truth was that there was a desperate shortage of Arabic-speaking analysts in the CIA's counterterrorist cell. Most of the existing manpower there was heavily tasked to the existing national intelligence priorities: the continuing operations against the 'no fly zone' in Saddam Hussein's Iraq, al Qaeda movements worldwide, WMD proliferation, Afghanistan, events in the Middle East and tracking the numerous militant Islamic groups popping up all over the world. To make matters worse, being a CIA analyst back in Langley was considered a low-status assignment compared with the prestige postings to 'Operations' and most officers posted there were moved on after only three years. The result was that, in the words of one critic:

> ... most [of the analysts] lacked any real ability ... to put the events they were seeing into any kind of true historical context ... It was all short-term tactical stuff ... to save lives ... It was a failure of comprehension as much as anything else ...

It transpired that, between 1994 and September 2001, the Counterterrorism Center (CTC) collated no fewer than twelve specific reports warning that terrorists were scheming to hijack an airliner and fly it into a prestige target. Several of the reports actually named bin Laden and al Qaeda. One of these reports came from a 'walk-in' to the FBI's New Jersey office, where a stunned FBI agent was told that al Qaeda were planning to hijack a plane and fly it into a building. Despite polygraph checks that proved the informant was telling the truth, nothing was done to alert other agencies. The idea was inconceivable; more like something out of a Tom Clancy novel than real life.

Despite all these clues as to al Qaeda's intentions, the intelligence analysts of CTC and the other agencies made no effort to update and amend their collection plan to include indicators that al Qaeda might be planning to use aeroplanes as bombs. No new CIR (critical intelligence requirements) were issued or called for. The US intelligence community remained fragmented and divided, complacently going about business as usual.

The truth is that the CTC was often not informed or involved in much of the intelligence reporting from the FBI or NSA, appearing to act merely as a Congressional figleaf to cover the lack of serious awareness of the threat. CTC attempts to task the National Reconnaissance satellites were sometimes overruled to keep them locked onto other, more important non-terrorist targets. Even attempts to track Osama bin Laden's funds and banking network were aborted for lack of manpower and financial expertise, despite the CIA's notoriously close links with Wall Street and 'big money'. This was later to prove a deadly weakness in the final days before the attack.

As 2001 wore on even more indicators of trouble loomed over the horizon. Even to the most overworked intelligence analysts, some were very clear indeed.

Early in 2001 the CIA's Malaysian station had detected two known senior al Qaeda terrorists, Khalid al Mihdhar and Nawaf al-Hazmi, meeting at an apartment in Malaysia and then travelling on to America. The importance of this meeting was not lost on the CIA as 'Khallad', the al Qaeda terrorist behind the bombing of the USS *Cole,* was present and in the chair. Al Hazmi was also well known to the NSA in Fort Meade, Maryland. Their signals intelligence operators had intercepted a message in 1999 proving that al Hazmi was an al Qaeda terrorist and that he was plotting to hijack American airliners. They had however, apparently not told the CIA or FBI.

In their turn, having watched this extraordinary gathering of terrorists at an al Qaeda planning meeting in Malaysia, the CIA now failed to notify the FBI to put the two terrorist suspects on the watch lists for entry into the US. The result was that the FBI and the US Immigration Service looked on with only routine curiosity as both these would-be hijackers and known al Qaeda terrorists flew openly into the USA.

They subsequently made close contacts with an identified al Qaeda paymaster, al-Bayoumi, in Los Angeles, and later with a third hijacker, Hani Hanjour. A complete terrorist support team swung into action under the FBI's very nose as two known Islamic terrorists were helpfully provided with an apartment, clothes, cars, driving licences and all the administrative paraphernalia needed to settle in a strange new country by a hitherto unidentified al Qaeda US logistics network. All those involved were careful to shave off their beards, 'go Western' and be seen drinking in clubs and bars. The FBI filed routine reports. After all, wasn't this the normal pattern for these 'Ay-rabs' loose in the fleshpots of the USA for the first time ... ?

Neither the CIA nor the FBI linked the significance of the group's activities in the West to al Qaeda's intentions. A frustrated FBI agent said later that if the CIA had ever told him that al Mihdhar and al Hazmi were known terrorist players and were travelling to California to meet other al Qaeda suspects, it would have made a 'huge difference'. (The FBI later admitted that fourteen known terrorist suspects had been identified making contact with the al Qaeda men roaming the West Coast, but that the reports 'had not been followed up'.) The Federal Aviation Authority later complained bitterly that if al Mihdhar and al Hazmi had been placed on the government's watch lists, then the two hijackers would never have been allowed to board Flight 77 on the morning of 11 September before it took off on its final flight.

To add insult to injury, it later turned out that the FBI could have found out a great deal more about al Qaeda's Western cell if they wanted to. For when all the pieces were later put together, it emerged that during this period both the al Qaeda terrorists had also met a key FBI undercover source in San Diego, California. The individual in question was an unnamed FBI Muslim informant whose primary mission was to report on Islamic terrorism in the US. This source was never tasked by the FBI to report on his new Islamic acquaintances, and so appears to have kept his distance and made no attempt to gain the two al Qaeda men's confidence. The result was that the FBI missed the chance to task a uniquely placed informant to collect intelligence on the al Qaeda hijackers' plans.

Other warnings crowded in during the summer of 2001.

In July 2001, the FBI field office in Phoenix, Arizona sent an urgent message to the counter-terrorist offices at FBI headquarters and the New York office, specifically alerting them that al Qaeda agents were now active in the US. It also warned that, according to the flight school owners, the two Arabs 'were showing an inordinate amount of interest in learning to fly' but 'weren't taking much interest in take-offs and landings'. The Phoenix FBI's e-mail, which later became famous at the Congressional inquiry as the 'electronic communication', then requested four specific actions:

> An immediate check on the background of all foreign students
> at flying schools in the US.

A check on the visas of foreign students learning to fly in the US.

The establishment of routine liaison reporting with all flying schools to keep watch and report on suspicious activity in future.

An urgent meeting with the CIA and other interested parties to discuss the significance of these intelligence reports.

The 'electronic communication' was sent to the FBI's RFU, (Radical Fundamentalist Unit) the NY field office (which had a lead responsibility on terrorism within the US), the FBI terrorist squad and the FBI's dedicated Osama bin Laden squad. No-one did anything. FBI ignored the intelligence and took no action. The agency was after all, as they tartly pointed out on several occasions, 'a law enforcement organisation, not an intelligence collection agency'.

Worse was to come. On 16 August 2001, the Minneapolis FBI was tipped off by a local flying school that a suspicious Arab had joined a flying training course in Minnesota and was 'interested in flying large commercial airliners'. Immediately suspecting preparations for a hijack, local FBI agents detained the Arab, Zacarias Moussaoui, who had entered the USA on 23 January 2001 on a ninety-day visa. That visa expired on 22 May, so when Moussaoui enrolled for a flying course on 11 August, he was quite clearly an illegal resident in the US.

The local FBI duly searched him and found that he had shin guards, padded gloves and a knife in his possession. When asked why he needed these, Moussaoui lamely said that he needed them 'for protection'. When asked 'what protection?' he had replied 'because a believer must be prepared to fight to defend the faith'. The Minneapolis FBI arrested him and carried out their standard checks. They discovered from his instructors and classmates that although Moussuoui had claimed he was of French origin he spoke no French. They also discovered that although he said he was going to be an airline pilot during the course, he also wasn't interested in take-offs or landings but only in flying the Boeing airliner simulator.

Suspecting that they had definitely bagged a would-be hijacker, the local FBI now alerted their headquarters and requested a court order to search Massaoui's rooms and place him under surveillance, using the Foreign Intelligence Surveillance Act (FISA). However, the FBI's Washington lawyers refused to apply for a court order against the suspect, citing legal technicalities with the FISA and again emphasising 'law enforcement, not intelligence' was the FBI's prime task.

Worse still, they totally ignored the intelligence value of the information. No attempt was made to collate or connect it with the activities of al Mihdhar or al Hazmi, despite a warning from the French authorities that Moussaoui was a well-known suspected terrorist and wanted by them. In vain the Minneapolis FBI office pleaded that Moussaoui had a suspicious collection of civil airliner operating manuals in his possession and a letter from one Yazid Sufaatt. Was there any trace on Yazid Sufaatt? The FBI in DC loftily ignored this fuss out in the boonies while their headquarters lawyers debated the legal niceties of the FISA.

The FBI might have reacted a lot more strongly if they had been realised that 'Yazid Suffatt' was in fact a well-known al Qaeda paymaster and the owner of the al Qaeda apartment in Malaysia. This was the apartment in which al Mihdhar, al Hazmi and 'Khaled' the *Cole* bomber had held their January 2001 meeting watched over by the CIA: but the CIA had never informed the FBI. In the world's only intelligence superpower, with the best computer links on the planet, no-one, not even the CIA's own analysts at their Counterterrorism Center, was bothering to collate the information and to make the intelligence connections, let alone warn their friends.

The CIA and FBI might as well have been operating in different countries.

As the summer of 2001 wore on, the CIA also gradually became aware of the importance of an al Qaeda cell based in Hamburg. The BfV, (German domestic security service, the Office for the Protection of the Constitution) informed the CIA that one of the Hamburg cell's members, a Mohamed Atta, had now moved to the USA. (Later, after the 9/11 attacks it emerged that at least three of the presumed hijacker pilots had lived together as part of the radical Islamic cell in Hamburg in the 1990s and had probably been recruited by al Qaeda while there. In all fairness this was hindsight. The CIA had not known this fact before 11 September.)

What the CIA *had* known however was that Mohamed Atta was a well-known al Qaeda terrorist suspect with a track record of smuggling explosives in Germany, and was wanted for a terrorist bombing in Israel. Yet, despite his blatant and known terrorist connections, Atta was allowed to enter and roam free in the US, even in violation of his expired entry visa, a fact which raises deep suspicions of incompetence at best, or something much more sinister at worst.

The puzzle as to what the CIA *really* did know about the al Qaeda plotters before the World Trade Center attack grows even more baffling when some of the other details are put under the microscope.

If their claims are to be believed, neither the CIA or the FBI were at any time aware that what was effectively a complete training programme for a cadre of would-be al Qaeda pilots was being held at Huffman Aviation's flying school in Venice, Florida. Quite how this managed to go unnoticed is a bit of a mystery, because at the time a CIA front company called Air Caribe was also operating out of the very same hangar at Venice airport as Huffman's flying school.

However, despite this, it appears that Mohamed Atta and his Arab friends' flying lessons somehow managed to go completely unreported by the Feds. This highly curious coincidence must inevitably raise some suspicions of just how much the CIA really did know before 9/11. Was the CIA hoping to infiltrate and 'double' the US-based al Qaeda cell, in the hope of using it against Osama bin Laden's organisation in the future?

The CIA was also very well aware that the real mastermind behind al Qaeda and Osama bin Laden was Khalid Sheikh Mohammed, whose nickname within al Qaeda was '*al Mukhtar*', 'the Brain' and he had a long record of terrorist involvement and planning with Osama bin Laden. He was well known to the CIA as the mastermind behind the Philippines Bojinka plot of 1995 and had even been indicted by the US authorities in 1996. 'KSM' was one of the most wanted terrorists in the world.

In spring 2001 several foreign intelligence services warned the US that Khalid Sheikh Mohammed was not only positively identified as the key planner for al Qaeda but that he was also actively organising a major strike against a prestige US target. Instead of issuing revised warnings to the FBI and NSA and drawing up a new collection plan to meet this emerging threat, the CIA analysts and the CTC continued doggedly on through the summer, even failing to appreciate the significance of Khalid Sheikh Mohammed ordering extra al Qaeda terrorists into the US during June 2001.

From late July onwards, the indicators of an impending terrorist attack against the US began to flow thick and fast.

These intelligence indicators were quite clear at the time – not just with the benefit of the 'retroscope' of hindsight either:

1. The White House National Coordinator for Counterterrorism Richard Clark had issued a warning of impending attack to all agencies.

2. The NSA had collected clear intelligence from ECHELON that the White House, Pentagon and World Trade Center were being targeted by al Qaeda.

3. The FBI knew that al Qaeda terrorists were at large and active in the US.

4. The CIA was well aware that high-level dedicated Islamic terrorists were planning another atrocity and had moved to the USA.

5. The FBI and the CIA knew that suspected terrorists were learning to fly in the US and were interested in flying airliners.

6. There was a plentiful intelligence that al Qaeda had been planning for years to attack US targets using civilian airliners as flying bombs.

7. The Israeli intelligence liaison in Washington warned the US of 'imminent attacks against highly visible US targets'.

8. The Russian government had warned the US 'in the strongest possible terms' that the USA was 'at imminent risk from an Islamic strike by terrorist aeroplanes against civilian

buildings ...' and that 'twenty-five suicide pilots have been trained for this task ...'

9. The French Secret Service (DST) warned that 'very specific information indicates an imminent terrorist strike against the USA with the order coming from within Afghanistan'.

10. Egyptian President Mubarak formally warned the White House at the end of August that his intelligence services were expecting an attack on America 'in the near future'.

11. Al Qaeda's internal traffic was warning of 'impending Hiroshima against the great Satan of America'.

12. The Philippine government had warned CIA liaison that 11 September was a likely anniversary for some kind of retaliation for the imprisonment of 'Youssef'.

13. To add insult to injury, in late June 2001 Osma bin Laden had, in the Arab press, openly boasted that, 'within the next two months, an attack against the great Satan that will shake the world.' (Even allowing for Arab rhetoric, this must be considered to be a bit of a clue as to terrorist intentions.)

All these intelligence indicators that al Qaeda's long-cherished Bojinka plan was now up and running were in the hands of US intelligence officers by 7 September 2001. This was the day when the US issued a general alert that; 'American citizens may be a target of a terrorist threat from extreme groups with links to Osama bin Laden's al Qaeda organisation ...' There was no mention of any specific areas at risk, there was no mention of the well-advertised threat to Lower Manhattan, and the FAA were not briefed on the real threat from kamikaze hijacked airliners.

Two final clues that something really big was cooking came in the week before 11 September. The NSA allegedly picked up a telephone conversation between bin Laden and his mother on 8 or 9 September, in which the Saudi terrorist leader said: 'In two days you are going to hear big, big news and then you're not going to hear from me for a while ...' This piece of SIGINT from within one of the most secretive organisations in the US government cannot be corroborated; but if true, this was a crucial piece of evidence that something big really was going down from al Qaeda, particularly when combined with all the other pieces of intelligence.

The second clue that really was an indicator that something was afoot came from that well-known source of good intelligence, the New York Stock exchange.

Every experienced intelligence officer knows that the real weakness of 'OPSEC', operational security, always lies in the administration. For example, the maps that are issued before an attack are a complete give-away as to where you are going to attack. Even money can betray operations.

Thus in Northern Ireland, the IRA soon learned to look out for the 'extra duty claims' from British intelligence operators working under-cover. Even for the most dangerous clandestine work, MoD civil servants in Northern Ireland insisted on detailed 'claims' and pored suspiciously over government forms for money spent. Their jobs were to make sure that an Intelligence Corps corporal working at great risk under cover on the local economy was not defrauding the taxpayer of the price of a pint of beer, let alone the cost of a civilian hire car. Every penny spent needed the appropriate MoD 'claims form' with the oper-ator's date, place and time. IRA spies in the Vehicle Registration Department and the Northern Ireland Claims Office rapidly discov-ered this Achille's heel of Whitehall finance, and used it to find out about the Army's secret operations and try to murder the undercover soldiers.

Operation Bojinka was no exception to this golden rule: follow the money. In the last week before the attack some very odd financial transactions swept the US stock markets. If anything gave away that something was imminent, the flurry of last-minute share dealing by those in the know pointed to some imminent major event that would shake the financial markets to their core.

A 'put option' is a contract giving the owner the right, *but not the obligation*, to sell a specified amount of an underlying security at a specified price within a specified time. Because the investor has agreed a guaranteed selling price in advance, he makes his margin from the

difference between this price and the actual value of the shares on day
of sale. Essentially, the investor is gambling that the share price in the
future will go down. Options, for those without strong nerves or a
crystal ball, are little more than bets on the future.

In the days just before the World Trade Center attack something
remarkable took place. In Chicago, on 10 September, over four and a
half thousand United Airlines 'put options' were signed off. Normally
there would only be a few dozen. In New York there was a positive run
against the share price of United Airlines and American Airlines – the
companies whose planes were used to attack the Twin Towers – in the
three days before 11 September. Someone was staking a lot of money
on the chance that the share price of the big US airlines would plunge.

Morgan Stanley – who sadly traded from the World Trade Center
building itself – reported 'put options' suddenly leaping from twen-
ty-seven contracts per day on 5 September to over two thousand one
hundred in the last three days before the attack on the World Trade
Center. Whoever made just these trading deals alone was guaranteed
to make well over a million dollars when they closed their option.
Merrill Lynch reported a 1,200 per cent jump in 'put options' on
American and United Airlines. It appears that al Qaeda was actually
planning to 'make a killing' in more ways than one. In Europe alarmed
investors like the French insurance giant AXA blew the whistle for the
regulatory authorities to step in and investigate what was going on.

It was too late.

The seismic shock waves of the attack when it came are too well
known to need detailed re-examination. In a series of devastating
attacks watched live on television by a stunned and shocked world, on
11 September 2001 al Qaeda's operation swung into action. In a carefully planned and executed operation, four heavily-laden US airliners
with passengers and crew on board, were hijacked simultaneously on
the US eastern seaboard. Two airliners plunged into the twin towers of
the World Trade Center in Manhattan bringing them crashing to the
ground. One plunged into the Pentagon in Washington DC and one
crashed upside down in a field in Pennsylvania following a struggle
between brave passengers and their hijackers. All 246 on board the
four hijacked planes, including the nineteen hijackers, were killed.

One hundred and twenty-five died in the Pentagon and 2,606 workers and 373 foreign nationals from sixty-two countries died at the World Trade Center. Total casualties were 2,977 fatalities. It was terrorism's most spectacular and grievous blow against the West.

There is some evidence that the apocalyptic images of 11 September shocked even bin Laden and his followers. When the Taliban were later ejected from Jalalabad as part of the US's carefully measured retaliation, an al.Qaeda videotape was discovered, on which bin Laden admits that even he had been surprised at the effectiveness of the attack.

As the recriminations flew thick and fast after the attack there was little doubt that the attacks had been a monumental intelligence blunder. For a variety of reasons, the US intelligence community, despite the establishment of a dedicated counter-terrorist centre in 1986, specifically intended to monitor this sort of activity, completely failed to piece together the jigsaw so painstakingly collected by its three key national intelligence agencies. The NSA heard what the terrorists were up to; the CIA learned what the terrorists were up to, and the FBI saw the terrorists training and meeting in the US. No-one bothered to connect the three.

No single US agency was maintaining an indicator and warning board for the emerging terrorist threat, let alone coordinating the US national effort against terrorism. By the first week of September 2001 the US intelligence agencies had failed to appreciate the intelligence reports that they had in their hands, indicating that some kind of major terrorist aircraft-borne attack against a prestige target in the US was being contemplated, even if they didn't know all the details. Yet again, no-one was putting the jigsaw together.

The truth was that the US intelligence ccommunity was neither organised nor equipped to meet a terrorist attack on the US before September 2001. Worse still, lack of communication, insularity and competition between the competing agencies, plus an inability to be flexible and adapt to new threats, meant that US intelligence, despite all the money lavished upon it, was unable to carry out one of its prime functions: warn the president and the people of threats to the nation.

There was no counter-terrorist plan, no counter-terrorist strategy, no counter-terrorist warning system. In the command bunker at Cheyenne Mountain the USAF's impressive automated indicator and warning radar warning display could track space junk over the pole, let alone incoming nuclear missiles. But, inside the USA, determined killers were running around planning an equally deadly strike and there was no comparable system of early warning.

Even the extra funding voted by Congress to beef up the US's counter-terrorism efforts during the late 1990s had been misapplied or wasted. Although the counter-terrorism budget had leapt from $5 billion in 1996 to nearly $11 billion in 2000 there was still no national database, the agencies' computers were not compatible and there was a grievous lack of analysts and therefore *analysis* of the threat. In particular, the level of Arabic speakers was lamentable; only 30 per cent of some key Arabic and Pashto speaking posts were actually manned. When pilloried later at the Congressional inquiry, the CTC's Director angrily flung the criticisms back in his accusers' faces, agreeing that he could have indeed have done something if he had only had three things right before 9/11: 'the right people, the right budget and the right operational support with political approval . . .' The committee wisely backed off.

It was not just resources. The American effort was also hampered by legal considerations. While NSA could intercept al Qaeda transmissions from Kabul and Quetta, it was theoretically prevented by law from monitoring transmissions inside the USA without specific legal authority. The CIA didn't talk to the FBI, the FBI were prohibited by law from collecting intelligence on American citizens, no matter how dangerous, and the whole counter-terrorist system was completely fragmented. The US didn't even have a national focus to which everyone had to report, let alone a national counter-terrorist strategy. In such circumstances it comes as no surprise that the President was never even offered a national intelligence estimate (NIE) spelling out the terrorist threat. After all the money, all the lessons of the past and all the work of dedicated men and women American intelligence was still, sixty years after Pearl Harbor, in an uncoordinated mess.

In the welter of recriminations, claim and counter-claim in the days immediately after the bombing, it was clear that al Qaeda was the only suspect. America's response to the outrage surprised no-one except those who had anticipated a blind knee-jerk spasm of rage. President George W. Bush declared open war on global terrorism. In a series of carefully calculated measures, the US then moved later in 2001 against al Qaeda and its sanctuary base among the Taliban regime in Afghanistan. The American president followed this with a ringing denunciation of an 'axis of evil' naming North Korea, Iraq, al Qaeda and Iran. This last was a dangerous choice, as yet again it alienated Iran's Shi'ite leadership and moderates. After Iran's discreet help in ousting the Taliban from Afghanistan, this was not only ungenerous but unwise.

American policy was not to be swayed from its tough new policies, however. In the spring of 2003 the United States and its closest allies moved decisively into the Middle East, invading Iraq, ousting its dictator Saddam Hussein and, coincidentally, providing al Qaeda and its Islamic fanatics with a 'target enriched environment'. US policy had come full circle, confronting the Islamic world and the Middle East head on and providing al Qaeda with US soldiers and plump western civilian aid organisations as fresh targets for terrorism on their doorstep.

The US was now involved in a new world war. From bombs in Bali to Baghdad, from French tankers off Yemen and attacks on Christians at worship in Pakistan; from explosive shoes in airliners over the Atlantic to stabbing police officers in leafy British suburbs, the sons of Allah locked themselves into a titanic worldwide struggle with the Western forces of law and order. In its blind hatred of the US, Israel and all it stands for, al Qaeda and ISIS have transformed themselves into a global movement of autonomous local fanatics. Just as the World Trade Organisation has transformed global Capitalism, so then has Osama bin Laden and his Islamic fundamental followers globalised terrorism.

In thirty years terrorism has evolved from cowardly Irish gunmen, sneaking up to shoot unsuspecting policemen in the back amid the dreary spires of Omagh and Armagh, into worldwide groups of suicidal religious fanatics armed with endless supplies of money, guns, mobile phones, the Internet and a burning grievance. The organisation

can call on a seemingly limitless worldwide pool of supporters prepared to give their lives for the 'cause' and access to weapons that have
hitherto been the monopoly of nation states.

The global Islamic insurgency rumbles on, fuelled by the inter-
Islamic war between Shia and Sunni in what used to be Iraq and Syria,
and a determination by the jihadi to take their religious war to the
West. And the jihadi have struck some telling blows. In 2015 Islamic
fanatics murdered seventeen people in Paris because a satirical magazine had dared to publish a cartoon of the Prophet Mohammed. The
country mourned, and global leaders joined an estimated 3.7 million
people on its streets to march in a show of unity.

Meanwhile, a world away in Nigeria, after an attack by another
Jihadi group calling itself 'Boko Haram', (literally, 'Books are Banned')
Islamist militants slaughtered an estimated 2,000 people around the
remote town of Baga. Amnesty International described it as the terror
group's 'deadliest massacre' to date, and local defence groups said they
had given up counting the bodies left lying on the streets. The clash of
cultures shows little sign of receding.

By 2015 Europol, the EU's crime agency, had collected the names of
2,500 suspected extremists from Europe. They warned the potential
terrorists are mainly young men who went overseas and could return
home to carry out attacks similar to those seen in Paris. Europol director Rob Wainwright said: 'We're talking about 3,000–5,000 EU
nationals. Clearly, we're dealing with a large body of mainly young
men who have the potential to come back and have the potential or the
intent and capability to carry out attacks we have seen in Paris.'

Jürgen Todenhöfer, the first Western journalist in the world to be
allowed extensive access to ISIS territories in Syria and Iraq agreed.
He warned that ISIS is 'much stronger and much more dangerous'
than anyone in the West appreciated, and added that 'Each day, hundreds of willing fighters arrive from all over the world.'

He added that ISIS's open ambition was to 'conquer the world' and
all who did not believe in the group's interpretation of the Qur'an
would be killed. 'To listen to ISIS, they are the largest religious cleans-
ing strategy that has ever been planned in human history.'

Radical Islam's terrorist war with the West goes on. By 2015 Western intelligence agencies had identified an army of up to 200,000 ISIS fighters and sympathisers worldwide – and growing. Should there be any doubt as to the Islamist warriors' future plans, the chilling words of Hussein Massaur, one of the early leaders of Hezbollah, spell out the intentions of Islamic terrorists clearly enough: 'We are not fighting to wring some concession from our enemy: we are fighting to wipe out our enemy . . .'

PART TEN

ON INTELLIGENCE FIASCOS

CHAPTER 35

The Sơn Tây raid

On 21 November 1970, at the height of the Vietnam War a small elite force of helicopter-borne American special forces crash-landed inside the walls of Sơn Tây, a North Vietnamese prisoner of war camp only twenty-three miles from Hanoi, in the middle of an area swarming with North Vietnamese troops; over twelve thousand were stationed within five miles.

Operation Polar Circle's mission was to rescue the sixty-one American POWs being held in brutal conditions in the Sơn Tây compound. It was the first joint military operation in United States history ever to be conducted under the direct control of the Chairman of the Joint Chiefs of Staff. Planning had been thorough; security was tight.

The assault force had been training for weeks. The fifty-six heavily armed special forces troopers selected to conduct the raid were organised into three groups: a fourteen-man assault group, which would crash-land within the prison compound; a twenty-two-man support group, which would provide immediate support for the assault team, and a twenty-man security group, to protect the prison area from NVA reaction forces and provide support if needed for either of the other two groups.

The raid took the North Vietnamese completely by surprise. The assault team crash-landed their helicopter directly into the courtyard of Sơn Tây prison just after 0200 hours with, literally, all guns blazing. The only casualty was the helicopter's flight engineer; a loose fire extinguisher broke his ankle. An officer used a bullhorn to tell the POWs to lie down on the floor and the well-rehearsed attackers stormed the prison compound, killing the guards and searching the prisoners' blocks cell by cell. Unfortunately, they were all empty.

Nearby the second assault force was having problems of its own. The helicopter 'Apple-1' landed by mistake in the dark about 450 metres south of the prison, near what intelligence briefings had identified as a 'secondary school.' But to everyone's surprise it was no 'secondary school' – it was a barracks; and moreover, one swarming with well-armed enemy soldiers. A savage fire-fight erupted and over a hundred of the occupants were killed in five minutes.

While this was going on the main assault force re-boarded their helicopters and flew off – empty-handed. The intelligence was wrong. There were no American prisoners; they had all been moved weeks before.

Although the mission was rightly deemed a 'tactical success' because of its execution, it was equally clearly an 'intelligence failure'. The sixty-five prisoners at Sơn Tây had been moved on 14 July to a camp fifteen miles closer to Hanoi because its wells had been contaminated by flooding.

Even then the failure of intelligence to spot the move of the POWs should not obscure the rest of the extraordinarily good intelligence on which the raid was based. The gathering of accurate intelligence for the operation, in both quality and quantity, had been remarkably successful. The intelligence failure lay in over 'compartmentalisation' of the information. The rescue planning staff had been deliberately isolated and closely monitored to prevent accidental leaks that might harm security. They had even been removed from the normal flow of intelligence to concentrate on their task in hand. As one planner later said: 'The raid was allowed to take place because those who had the correct intelligence information were not aware that someone else was contemplating a POW rescue.'

Sơn Tây stands as a classic example of a successful, text-book military operation; but one that failed in its primary mission because of faulty intelligence. But even then the raid had an unexpected bonus. Although no POWs were rescued, the raid sent a clear message to

North Vietnam that Americans would go to any lengths to bring their men home.

The North Vietnamese got the message.

The Sơn Tây raid triggered important changes in their treatment of American POWs. Within days, all of the POWs in the outlying camps had been moved to Hanoi. Men who had spent years in a cell on their own found themselves sharing a cell with dozens of others. From the prisoners' point of view the raid was the best thing that could have happened to them, short of their freedom.

In the final assessment, the Sơn Tây raid may not have been such a failure after all.

CHAPTER 36

Operation Eagle Claw

Operation Eagle Claw in April 1980 was an extraordinarily ambitious and complex plan by the US to rescue the Americans held hostage in Teheran by the Ayatollah Khomeini following the Iranian Islamic revolution of 1979. In the last days of the Carter presidency there was enormous political pressure to rescue the captives and teach Khomeini a sharp lesson. The operation depended on good intelligence throughout.

Eagle Claw turned out to be a humiliating failure. The secret rescue attempt had to be aborted in the Iranian desert, with mechanical failures and eight American servicemen dead in an aircraft collision on the ground. Official White House and Department of Defense statements claimed that the mission was cancelled because of a series of unfortunate events beyond human control.

However, the reality was that the plan was far too complex and came unravelled from the start through lack of intelligence, mechanical breakdowns, accidents and above all, a lack of unity of command. The idea was that American agents would infiltrate Teheran before the operation to support the main force when it arrived. The actual rescue mission was the responsibility of a new Department of Defense multi-service anti-terrorist force called Delta Force. The plan was for USAF C-130 Hercules transport aircraft to fly from Egyptian airfields to an abandoned airstrip in the Iranian desert called Desert One. Along with the Delta Force troopers the planes would bring additional aviation fuel and refuelling gear, and electronic equipment to jam Iranian radar and radio communications.

At the desert strip they were to meet up with eight US Marine and Navy RH-53 helicopters from the carrier *Nimitz*. The helicopters would remain at Desert One all day Thursday, resting the men and refuelling the helicopters.

Next day Delta Force would board the helicopters and fly to a second landing zone about fifty miles northeast of Teheran. There they would meet some of the Green Beret infiltrators, who would have acquired trucks from friendly Iranian sources in order to take Delta Force to a warehouse on the outskirts of Teheran.

There the assault teams would go in: one to the Foreign Ministry building, where three senior American diplomats were being held; the second to the American Embassy compound, where they would storm the Embassy and free the captives.

The attackers would then be lifted out by helicopters and fly to a third landing zone near Teheran, where they would rendezvous with the C-130s from Desert One, destroy the helicopters, and leave Iran.

Throughout the raid, an E-3 AWACS aircraft would maintain command and control, monitoring Iranian airspace and maintaining direct communications between the carrier task force, the White House, and the mission commander on the ground.

It didn't work out that way.

On the way to Desert One, one of the helicopters ran into a dust storm, suffered a rotor failure and was forced to land and had to be abandoned in the desert. Another helicopter had an electrical failure which disabled its gyrocompass and navigation equipment and was forced to return to the *Nimitz*. The remaining six helicopters and six C-130s arrived at Desert One.

The next day a busload of Iranian civilians drove down a road that ran straight through Desert One. Intelligence had reported that the road was unused. They were wrong. American guards stopped the bus and detained its bemused passengers. That evening it was discovered that one of the remaining helicopters was unserviceable due to a hydraulic system failure. At this point a smugglers' tanker truck towing a jeep blundered down the supposedly unused road into the middle of

Desert One. US soldiers stopped it at a roadblock, but the smugglers took off across country in the jeep.

Realising that security was now hopelessly compromised and knowing that a minimum of six RH-53s were needed to ensure the mission's success, the mission commander, Colonel Charles Beckwith, and the White House and Pentagon between them agreed to abort the mission.

Suddenly everyone was in a rush in the dark to get the hell out. The helicopters were to have been topped-up and flown out of Iran; but while taxiing to refuel, an RH-53 struck a stationary Hercules. It was carrying fuel and detonated in a fireball, killing eight men and seriously wounding five. Beckwith now dropped everything, got his men on the remaining C-130s, and took off, leaving behind the bodies of eight American servicemen, a cache of secret documents, five intact helicopters, and America's military reputation.

Both the Carter administration and the Pentagon tried to excuse the fiasco by referring its failures to 'equipment failure', and unforeseen events. The truth is that the conception and execution of the mission broke one of the cardinal rules of war: KISS – keep it simple, stupid! The complicated operation had been doomed from the start by a lack of accurate and up-to-date intelligence, and further hampered by the wrong equipment and a complex chain of command involving all four US services as well as the CIA, NSA and Washington itself.

Eagle Claw stands as a text-book example of how not to manage a complicated military operation.

points because the Judge Lord Hutton claimed that they were outside his narrow remit. Since the inquiry exonerated Blair and forced the BBC Chairman to resign in 2004, serious accusations of the misuse of intelligence by the Blair government have intensified. The result is that the whole question of intelligence's objectivity, truthfulness and trust-worthiness was exposed to the harsh illumination of public and media scrutiny. For the traditionally secretive intelligence community and for the British public, the whole affair came as a startling experience.

The first issue, of Saddam Hussein's possession of nuclear, biological or chemical weapons, was almost certainly an intelligence blunder by the various intelligence staffs all round the world, not just in the UK. That Saddam possessed chemical weapons (CW) was never in ques-tion: his use of CW in the Iran–Iraq war and his gassing of the hapless Kurds in 1988 was a potent reminder of Iraq's capability to deploy lethal CW agents and his intention to use them. The international intelligence community was merely being prudent in assuming that Saddam still retained that deadly and demonstrated capability. That Iraq had been experimenting with Biological Weapons (BW) was never in any doubt either: there was ample evidence that Saddam's scientists were developing and storing Anthrax and probably other dangerous bio-agents as well in Iraq's government laboratories.

Finally, the idea of an Iraqi nuclear bomb was no great mystery: that Saddam had the clear intention to develop nuclear weapons was a mat-ter of record. The Israelis did not go to the trouble of bombing the Osirak nuclear plant in 1981 because they were concerned about enhanced sup-plies of nuclear energy to the Iraqi national electricity grid. The existence of, or the intention to develop, these weapons of mass destruction were either clear capabilities or on the Iraqi dictator's wish list.

So where were they? The answer is, no-one knows. Saddam's WMDs, the very casus belli of Britain's surprise attack on a sovereign nation in the Middle East, had become invisible.

There were two possible explanations: either Saddam got rid of them long before the war, (as the UNSCOM inspectors and the Iraq Survey Group maintained) or he had hidden them. There was however a possible third explanation: Iraq's *Raïs* may no longer have had WMD but was playing a fatal game of bluff to pretend that that he was more

CHAPTER 37

Blair's Dodgy Dossier, Iraq 2003

Sometimes intelligence fiascos serve a purpose by reminding us what intelligence is not.

It is certainly not the popular cinematic image of James Bond. That is fantasy HUMINT. Neither is it occasional intuitive leaps of genius by eccentric scientists in mysterious secret chambers. That is brilliant analysis. It is certainly not spun public relations to promote government policy. That is called propaganda. But, above all, it is not selective; intelligence is merely impartial facts and objective assessments. If there are really any 'buzzwords' about intelligence apart from 'accuracy' and 'timeliness', then they are objectivity, trust and truth.

The invasion of Iraq in the spring of 2003 was, certainly for the United Kingdom, the first time that a war had been instigated by an elected government solely on the basis of an intelligence assessment. Prime Minister Blair swayed a dubious electorate and a sceptical Parliament on the need for war by referring to a 'direct threat to British interests' from Saddam Hussein's possession of, and intention to employ, Weapons of Mass Destruction. (WMD). Parliament, and the British people, believed him – at the time.

In 2003, a BBC report alleging that the Government had 'sexed up' an intelligence dossier to justify war, sparked a chain of events that ended with the tragic death of Dr David Kelly. The subsequent Hutton Inquiry threw this debate into sharp focus in the UK for several reasons. First, the Hutton Inquiry failed to address a number of key intelligence powerful than he really was. It would not be the first time that a bull frog from the Iraqi marshes had over-inflated himself to frighten and impress his Arab and Persian neighbours.

The point is that the intelligence communities of France, Germany, the UK and USA all assessed that Saddam still had WMDs – and they were all wrong.

The analysts may have, not unreasonably, inferred that what Saddam had once possessed he still had. Iraq's leader was always an unlikely candidate for beating his swords into ploughshares. But intelligence should have found out the truth. Whether it was because the West relied too much on technical intelligence and not enough on human intelligence is merely a point for investigation. The fact is that there appear to have been no WMDs.

The result is that Britain went to war on a false prospectus because, unlike the USA, Great Britain launched her unprecedented pre-emptive attack, not to remove Saddam Hussein, but specifically to prevent the Iraqi leader from striking at British interests with WMDs. The Prime Minister had said so to Parliament. Even though many were surprised by Blair's claims, even experienced intelligence analysts tended to believe the Prime Minister on the grounds that he must have seen highly-classified intelligence which they had not.

There was clearly a serious failure of intelligence and British soldiers died as a result. The intelligence process appears to have made a false assessment of the threat. It is certainly not why the taxpayers of the UK invest over ten billion pounds a year in their intelligence bureaucracy.

The second area that still needs to be clarified are those intelligence issues which Lord Hutton did not address at the time. The most contentious question is whether any changes were made to the JIC's assessment of the threat. This was helped by the comprehensive documentary coverage of the whole affair, which Lord Hutton obligingly placed in the public domain. As a result the public could make their own judgements by reading most of the evidence themselves. That readership constituted one vast jury.

Public opinion polls made it clear that the majority of this national jury still remains unconvinced that the Blair government was justified in going to war without the express justification of the UN.

Why, for example, did the Prime Minister's staff amend an intelligence assessment by the senior 'Court of Intelligence' in the land, the Joint Intelligence Committee (JIC)? On whose instructions? And on what grounds? The documentary trail is plain to read. An unelected Party official in the Prime Minister's office encouraged the Chairman of the JIC to change the wording of its national intelligence assessment: an unheard of interference.

Worse still, the government's (and Party political) Director of Communications chaired what was effectively a sub-committee or working group of the JIC to amend the wording of a professional intelligence staff's assessment of the threat and how it 'should be presented'. Again this was unprecedented. Changing an objective intelligence assessment for party policy reasons is the start of a very slippery slope indeed. Intelligence is not propaganda, however much politicians would wish it to be so. Intelligence assessments exist to tell the policy makers the truth and nothing but the truth, not what the government would like it to say.

That is the very reason why intelligence assessments are worded so very carefully. To the constant frustration of many of their readers in both Whitehall and Washington, JIC assessments are models of carefully weighed language. Americans frequently criticise the JIC as an example of 'intelligence by committee' and the lowest common denominator. American intelligence follows a more robust model. For those within the Beltway an 'intelligence market' reigns, with the various agencies fighting for the president's attention like so many medieval barons squabbling at the court of a powerful ruler.

The JIC is essentially a careful group of career civil servants and its tone and advice usually reflect this, as any reader of their highly classified products will know. Not for nothing did one of Blair's cabinet ministers denounce the JIC's reports as 'boring'.

To tamper with the wording of such a JIC assessment is therefore to alter its meaning. Changing the words changes the national assessment. That such changes were made to the September 2002 national assessment disseminated by the JIC to strengthen the document at the insistence of the Prime Minister's Office is beyond question. Lord Hutton may have not considered it his task to examine these changes, or chose to announce that they fell outside his remit. But for the pro-fessional intelligence community and the nation at large, such decisions are both profound and potentially very dangerous. They crossed a Rubicon of immense political significance. Under Blair and his propa-ganda chief Campbell, 'intelligence' had suddenly become a tool of governmental policy. Intelligence had effectively become a branch of government public relations, albeit dressed up as 'presentational aspects'. The Hutton report, despite what many commentators then and now consider to be its obvious attempt to whitewash the government's case, confirmed that, uniquely, the JIC's report on Saddam Hussein's WMDs was used to 'present the case for war' to the British people.

Intelligence has often been twisted for policy reasons before, usually with disastrous results. During the Nazi era Dr Goebbels ensured that all information, true or false, that went before the German people was carefully controlled to influence and mould public opinion by his Ministry of Information. It was called 'propaganda'.

Intelligence exists only to inform decision makers: not to publicise their policies. This brings us to the third charge against 'intelligence' under JIC Chairman Scarlett – that it allowed itself to be misused by the government of the day to bolster an administration's policy agenda. This is probably the most serious charge of all and one that carries the greatest responsibility. Any intelligence assessment can be wrong: they frequently are. Intelligence can be misused by governments: they are the paying customer, after all.

But what is unacceptable is that the national intelligence organisa-tion should allow itself to be seduced into cooperating in the executive's news management and propaganda process to become political cheer-leaders for the government. That is not what intelligence is for.

Sadly, even on the whitewashed facts presented by the Hutton Inquiry, this charge stands. The weight of evidence is overwhelming. The ambitious MI6 officer John Scarlett, Chairman of the JIC, appears to have allowed himself to be manipulated by a man he himself described as his mate to change his JIC assessment. Shortly afterwards Scarlett was promoted by a grateful Blair to become head of SIS and knighted for his pains on behalf of a highly manipulative government. A government that openly boasted that, during its time in office, it had

gone to hitherto unheard of lengths to get its own message across –
whatever the cost.

The facts of Alastair Campbell's attempted efforts to amend the JIC
report on behalf of Blair are a matter of public record. This was an
administration that was obsessed by 'spin', misrepresentation and presentation. It was a government that even issued a second hilarious
'Dodgy Dossier', a cobbled together farrago of carefully chosen half-
truths and selected readings from *Jane's Defence Review*, centred round
a twelve-year-old academic PhD thesis, all claiming to be 'an intelligence assessment about Iraq'. This blatant piece of false propaganda by
Number 10's Director of Communications soon became a laughing
stock and was ignominiously withdrawn.

In the circumstances, 'intelligence' should not have touched any of
Downing Street's 'presentational' nonsense with a barge pole. When
you sup with the devil, use a long spoon. Unfortunately, Britain's JIC
under the leadership of John Scarlett did not. Misgivings from
within the intelligence community that the Iraq WMD Assessment
was being distorted for political purposes, and did not reflect the
view of the experts, were suppressed. At one point officials from one
single intelligence agency – Scarlett's MI6, naturally – were even
marched into Downing Street to solemnly assure Tony Blair that
there was 'no dissent from within the intelligence community at
large'. Coming from the SIS, Britain's human intelligence agency,
which had cheerfully propagated crude and obvious forgeries about
uranium ore from Niger as 'proof' of Saddam's nuclear programme,
this was rich.

Even more bizarre was the attempt by the Chairman of the JIC to
pretend that such an assurance actually did faithfully reflect the views
of GCHQ, the Joint Air Reconnaissance Centre, the FCO, and the
Scientific and Technical Intelligence Staff of the MoD. It did not.
There were grave doubts in Whitehall. The very serious concerns of
senior scientists such as Dr Kelly on the Defence Intelligence Staff,
Britain's only all-source assessment agency outside the Cabinet Office,
were brushed aside and ignored. Downing Street was allowed to dictate
changes to a national intelligence assessment to suit its own purposes.
Crucially, the JIC connived in all these political meddlings.

We will never know if this was because John Scarlett at the JIC was trying to curry favour with his political masters in the hope of preferment, or because he simply lacked the moral courage to stand up to an assertive Number 10 bully. The fact is that, collectively, the JIC allowed themselves to be sucked into the political process, for whatever motive. That is unacceptable. That is the hinge point where intelligence was deliberately 'laundered' to become government propaganda. That is the point at which the JIC, and the intelligence community it represents, failed the taxpayers who pay for it and who placed implicit trust in its objectivity to defend the realm.

Since that date 179 British soldiers died in the war in Iraq and over 2,100 were wounded. In the follow-on war in Afghanistan, 453 were killed and thousands maimed. All these tragedies are indirectly linked with the false intelligence starting with Blair's changed dossier. Saddam's removal, although greatly to be celebrated, was not why Britain went to war and invaded Iraq. The Prime Minister said so. Britain went to war on a specific intelligence assessment that said that the country was at risk from Saddam Hussein's weapons of mass destruction. The Prime Minister said so. Many both in the country at large and within the informed intelligence community came to believe that such claims were grotesquely inflated for political reasons. The truth is that intelligence on Iraq was laundered and twisted to suit the propaganda agenda of the government of the day.

There was nothing 'subconscious' about it, as Judge Hutton bizarrely claimed. It was deliberate and blatant 'spinning' of intelligence to support government policy and no amount of weasel words can alter that fact. That is not what the JIC is for and it represents a serious perversion and betrayal of both the British intelligence community and the taxpayers. If a foreign secret service had suborned John Scarlett to lie and act as an agent for their country he would have been, rightly, guilty of treason. If the Chairman of the JIC distorted a national intelligence assessment in the hope of getting promotion, that is just as serious a betrayal of his trust.

The job of the JIC is to go to Downing Street, thrust an impartial, objective assessment through its iron gates, and walk briskly away to let the elected policy makers do with it as they will. It is not for members of the JIC to be invited by their 'mates' to participate in the machinations of government. It is not for the JIC to be invited into the golden circle of policy making and power in Number 10, to be flattered or bullied into changing its mind or its intelligence assessment to please the prime minister of the day. Easy to say: hard for ambitious men to do, especially with an administration addicted to the presentation of its message above all else, with a defence lawyer's flexible view of the truth and with the juicy plums of preferment and promotion to offer weak and ambitious men.

But the indictment stands. For whatever reason, the JIC crossed the line from assessment staff to political puppet. At least in the United States the Bush administration was forced to set up its own 'alternative' intelligence assessment group – the Office of Special Projects, (OSP) based in the Pentagon – to tell President Bush what they wanted to hear, because the US intelligence community was robust enough to tell politicians the truth as they saw it, however unpalatable.

The indictment therefore follows logically and forensically from Judge Hutton's much-derided inquiry: the intelligence on which the UK went to war was both wrong, and was manipulated for political purposes by the civil servant John Scarlett at the behest of Prime Minister Blair and his rottweiler press adviser, Alastair Campbell. Truth, objectivity, and trust in Whitehall's intelligence process were all compromised as a result. This poses critical implications for the future. In the twenty-first century, Western societies are unlikely to be threatened by all-out blitzkrieg. The real risk is more likely to come from regimes and terrorist movements capable of inflicting great harm without overtly breaching national frontiers.

This places an unprecedented responsibility on our intelligence services to be honest. The governments of the US and Britain will be chiefly dependent on the CIA and SIS for information about what our enemies are doing. The threat will always be visible. Its gravity will have to be judged in cold blood by national leaders, advised by intelligence and defence chiefs and without political distortion to suit tomorrow's headlines.

'Intelligence laundering' is a charge that ex-prime minister Blair and the once proud JIC will have to answer one day, because distorting intelligence no matter for what purpose, is tantamount to treason. Britain went to war, launching thousands of British soldiers into Iraq, on a pretext now conclusively exposed as false.

British – and other – lives were put at risk as a result of the JIC and the government presenting a false case for war, based on inaccurate intelligence manipulated by men who should have known better.

It remains a serious charge.

PART ELEVEN

NEW HORIZONS — NEW HORRORS?

CHAPTER 38

On Cyberwar:
When is a War Not a War?

Intelligence is no more immune to technical progress than any other field of human endeavour. The third industrial revolution, which began with the invention of the transistor in 1947, opened the door to a flood of technological change that has revolutionised the economies and the societies of the developed world. By the 1950s and 1960s many governments, the military, and numerous other civilian organisations had invested heavily to make computer systems an essential component of their normal operations.

By the 1980s, digital technology proliferated and, as the switch from analog to digital record keeping and operating became the new standard, computers invaded all aspects of life in the West. From automated teller cash machines in banks, through traffic and electricity grid control, industrial robots, down to video games and computer-generated graphics for entertainment, computers took over every aspect of our lives. By 1995 the new world wide web was becoming widely available. The Internet grew to become ubiquitous and necessary in every office and many homes, and expanded across the globe as people made it their favoured means of communication.

This technological revolution accelerated in the early years of the twenty-first century as mobile smartphones became commonplace and text messaging became part of modern life. By 2012 experts calculated that there were over five billion cell phones in use, and the Internet was regularly accessed by more than two billion users. The world was interconnected as never before with a widespread reliance on mobile networked devices such as tablets, smartphones and many other advanced computer-based devices to share information on an unprecedented scale. Social networking on individual smartphones became the norm for many. By 2015, tablet computers and smartphones exceeded personal computers for Internet access. All this was supported by new advanced systems based on cloud computing, which brings together groups of remote servers and software networks to enable different data sources to be uploaded in real time, crucially without the need to store processed data on individual computers.

The implications of modern advanced societies' growing reliance on this expanding high-tech infrastructure has not been ignored by the hard-nosed. Once again, the money men and the armourers moved in and thrived. From the start, defence manufacturers and governments realised the potential of the so-called 'smart weapons' and a new generation of missiles and technological military systems, from radar to global navigation systems, exploited the potential of the new digital devices.

Inevitably, intelligence got in on the act from the start. As early as 1946, the United States Army Ordnance Corps financed and developed the world's first true reprogrammable computer, the Electronic Numerical Integrator and Computer, or ENIAC. Once the NSA was formally established by President Truman in 1952, the new Signals Intelligence Agency became a major customer and investor in primitive computers, and by 1985 had merged with the National Computer Security Center (NCSC) (responsible for computer security for the US government) to become what the *Baltimore Sun* described in 1995 as 'the owner of the single largest group of supercomputers in the world.'

Supercomputers were first introduced in the 1960s by the Cray Data Corporation, specifically to serve intelligence. They are, without exaggeration, fantastically fast – and fantastically expensive. For example, today's massive Cray computers and their Chinese imitators have the ability to process an unimaginable 33 quadrillion floating point operations *per second:* and a state of the art 'entry level' Cray will cost you a trifling $500,000 a piece. At half a billion dollars a throw, that puts the Cray in the hands of well-funded governments and a handful of the biggest banks and corporations in the world.

NSA's reliance on digital technology expanded rapidly over the years to keep pace with these advances in digital technology. The Agency's latest facility is a dedicated High Performance Computing Center at Fort Meade, costing $3.2 billion. This new NSA computing centre has its own dedicated 150 megawatt power substation to provide 60 megawatts of electricity – just to work the NSA's massive and power-hungry computers. And it is just the first of three similar centres. Where America leads, others follow. In Britain GCHQ has expanded in step with the digital revolution, as have the associated signals intelligence agencies of all members of the UN Security Council. The Chinese in particular seem to have placed digital intelligence, in all its forms, very high on their list of national priorities.

The US intelligence community understands very well that real time digital intelligence is here to stay and will revolutionise the way 'intelligence' does business in future. It has already begun to implement the necessary structural changes and is even now discussing abandoning the traditional Int Cycle approach as too slow. David Cacner, deputy director, US National System for the Geospatial-Intelligence Program Management Office, and director of NSG Expeditionary Activities at the National Geospatial-Intelligence Agency pointed out the impending revolution in intelligence in 2015:

> The traditional Intelligence Cycle of TPED [Tasking, Processing, Evaluation, Dissemination] is dead . . . What's dead about it is 'let's wait to collect and process and send it to my buffer and then exploit it.' But no longer are we limited to a couple of forms and sources; we've got multiple sources and we can't afford to wait. We need applications and algorithms to work on data, provide recommendations to us and then act on it, dig into it deeper.

For the military intelligence officer, this means that the world of intelligence is changing rapidly. Action Information, Targeting and

Intelligence are rapidly fusing into one big digital communications and intelligence system before our eyes; certainly on the battlefield. In 2015 US Defense Secretary Ash Carter suggested that a new 'cyber corps' may ultimately become its own service branch:

> There may come a time when that makes sense . . . And I think you have to look at this as the first step in a journey that may, over time, lead to the decision to break out cyber the way that you saw the Army Air Corps became the US Air Force, the way Special Operations Command was created . . . with a somewhat separate thing, although that still has service parts to it.

Founded in 2009, US Cyber Command reflects the growing need for specialists who can operate in the digital battlespace. Carter went on to suggest that major reform of the military personnel system will be necessary to recruit and retain the new and technically qualified cyber force, such as allowing some highly skilled recruits to enter service at higher ranks or changing some recruiting standards such as screening out young people with high-tech skills. Any future successful defence effort will need geeks and nerds as never before. The idea of creating a new separate cyber corps risks an epic struggle among military bureaucracies worldwide. Any new service branch would mean reassessing annual budgets and reassigning thousands of jobs, with the inevitable wails of departmental misery and turf wars.

The key question for tomorrow's intelligence officers is how defence ministries and intelligence agencies will react to the necessary organisational changes confronting governments and their armed services. It is rapidly becoming clear that all traditional intelligence methods need to be re-examined to determine whether they are still relevant as the delicate relationship between the intelligencers and the communicators is brought into focus and intelligence bureaucrats battle for budgets. The pressure is not just on collectors of intelligence and the old-fashioned intelligence agencies to adapt to the digital age. The digital revolution has exposed a whole new raft of vulnerabilities for governments, indeed for whole societies: vulnerabilities that are inherently digital and therefore will have to be addressed, certainly in the first instance, by digital means.

Or, as it is now known, cyberwar.

In 2013 Thomas Rid, a highly respected academic theorist of King's College, London, specialising in strategy and technical innovation, published a book whose unfortunate title, *Cyber War Will Not Take Place* was to prove him spectacularly wrong.

For years, military experts have been warning us that our ideas about expectations of warfare are dangerously out of date. War is no longer something that happens on a foreign battlefield, fought out between massed armies with tanks, aeroplanes and guns.

For more than a century, the front line has been moving closer and closer to the ordinary Western household. From the German shelling of Hartlepool in 1914 through the horrors of the Blitz and the pub bombings of the IRA, down to the bombing of the World Trade Center in 2001, Western illusions of living in a safe civilian fortress have been slowly blown away.

Cyber war is merely the latest frightening development in the history of human conflict — a threat to society everywhere, but one that could have potentially devastating consequences for millions of families far from any war zone. We cannot pretend that we have not been warned. As early as 1979, the first aggressive hacker group emerged, using a crude electronic messaging forum. In 1988 Robert Morris (who said he was only trying to work out how big the Internet was becoming) became the first person to be convicted under the US's computer fraud and abuse act. The 'Morris Worm' – one of the first recognised computer worms to affect the world's primitive cyber infrastructure – spread around a number of American computers. The worm used weaknesses in the UNIX system 'Noun 1' to replicate itself. It slowed down computers to the point of being unusable. Morris was last heard of working as a professor at MIT. Hacking into computers was here to stay, feeding off the world's hunger for the Internet and the world wide web.

Inevitably, by 1994 the criminal fraternity had spotted their opportunity, too. A Russian called Vladimir Levin, working as a computer programmer for a St Petersburg-based computer company, used a laptop computer in London to access the Citibank network. He obtained a list of customer codes and passwords and passed them to his friends.

He then logged on and used wire transfers to steal at least $3.7 million from Citibank though its dial-up wire transfer service. The money was sent to accounts set up by accomplices in Finland, the United States, the Netherlands, Germany and Israel. Three of his accomplices were later arrested attempting to withdraw funds in Tel Aviv, Rotterdam and San Francisco. They implicated Levin.

In March 1995 Levin was detained by British police at London's Stansted Airport en route from Moscow. He was extradited to the US, and tried in New York on a single count of conspiracy to defraud and steal $3.7 million. In February 1998 he was convicted and sentenced to three years in jail; Citibank claimed that all but $400,000 of the stolen $10.7 million that had disappeared had been recovered.

Since those early days computer hacking has grown to become something much more widespread and dangerous than just stealing money. It has now developed into a genuine international threat to security with the potential to attack the classic security targets of espionage, sabotage and, to a lesser extent, subversion. Perhaps more dangerously for the intelligence officers of every country, cyber attacks are hard to blame on any adversary. For this very modern way of warfare it is only too easy to hide behind a different adversary or concoct a false flag attack. 'Who exactly is wrecking our computer infrastructure, Minister? It's hard to tell . . .'

By far the most damaging cyber attack is sabotage, using what is called a denial-of-service attack (DoS attack) to make a machine or network unavailable to its intended users. DoS attacks typically target sites or services hosted on high-profile web servers such as banks, credit card payment gateways and financial transactions. DoS attacks may not be limited to attacking financial targets, as strategic physical attacks against infrastructure can be just as devastating. For example, power, water, fuel, communications, and transportation infrastructure are all intensely vulnerable to disruption. To take just one example, modern railway systems rely totally on computer programs to manage their signals to trains. Interfere with the signals and points and chaos and carnage will follow. Computers and satellites that coordinate other communication activities are particularly vulnerable, and attacks to compromise military systems, such as command and control systems that are responsible for orders and communications, are prime targets. Even nuclear release codes could be at risk.

Away from the military, civilian services taken for granted are also at risk; computer security breaches have now gone way beyond stolen credit card numbers, and potential targets can also include the electric power grid, water treatment plants, as well as the banks and stock markets. In 2009, reports surfaced that China and Russia had allegedly infiltrated the US electrical grid and left behind software programs that could be used to disrupt the system. China denied intruding into the US electrical grid; but then, any prudent attacker would deny responsibility. It is the intelligence officer's worst nightmare and the most basic question of all: who is the enemy?

As well as these attacks to disable national systems, the danger of espionage to obtain secret information for military, political, or economic advantage using illegal exploitation methods on the Internet, other networks, software or computers remains high. There is a particular danger here, as classified information that is not handled securely can be intercepted and even modified, making espionage possible from the other side of the world and without knowing who is really responsible – or whether the information is genuine or not.

The first inkling of the real dangers posed by Cyberwar surfaced as early as 1999 when US officials accidentally discovered someone trying to access their computer systems at the Pentagon, NASA, the US Department of Energy, private universities, and research labs. The attacks had been first reported in 1998. The US called the attacks 'Moonlight Maze' and reported that the invaders were systematically marauding through tens of thousands of files – including maps of military installations, troop configurations and military hardware designs. The United States Department of Defense traced the trail back to a mainframe computer in the former Soviet Union, but the sponsor of the attacks is unknown and Russia hotly denied any involvement. Moonlight Maze was still being actively investigated by US intelligence in 2003. Shortly afterwards *Newsweek* magazine printed a story on Moonlight Maze that was entitled, 'We're in the middle of a Cyberwar.'

In that same year, a series of coordinated attacks on American computer systems gained access to many United States defence contractor computer networks who were targeted for their sensitive information, including those at Lockheed Martin, Sandia National Laboratories, Redstone Arsenal, and NASA. The attacks were labelled 'Titan Rain'. In 2005 the director of the SANS Institute, a US security institute, said that the attacks were 'most likely the result of Chinese military hackers attempting to gather information on U.S. systems', although their precise nature, e.g. state-sponsored espionage, corporate espionage, or random hacker attacks, and their real identities – which were masked by masked by proxy sites, 'zombie computers', and infected spyware/viruses – still remain officially unknown.

The realities of Cyber war were brought home in 2007 when a well-coordinated series of cyber attacks suddenly swamped a wide selection of Estonian websites. The little Baltic state was in dispute with the Russian Federation at the time about Russian war graves and monuments left after the Great Patriotic War.

The cyber attack blanked out the Estonian parliament, banks, ministries, newspapers and broadcasters' computer networks. Most of the attacks were denial of service type attacks ranging from single individuals to spamming of news organisations' commentaries and defacements of political parties' websites. Thousands of computers from all over the world were used in the cyber assault. The attack was comprehensive and lasted for several weeks.

Russia called accusations of its involvement 'unfounded', and neither NATO nor European Commission experts were able to find any proof of official Russian government participation. Estonia's defence minister admitted that he had no evidence that the cyber attacks were carried out by official Russian government agencies. However, the head of the Russian military forecasting centre later confirmed Russia's ability to conduct such an attack when he stated: 'These attacks have been quite successful, and today the alliance had nothing to oppose Russia's virtual attacks.'

Colonel Anatoly Tsyganok added, perfectly correctly, that the attacks did not violate any international agreement. A startled world took note and NATO set up a new multinational cyber defence group – based in Estonia.

The challenge to the intelligence community was obvious: who really was the perpetrator of the cyber attacks? The question came to the fore in 2010 when an unprecedented attack was launched against Iran's army of centrifuges, busy spinning to refine weapons-grade uranium. A malicious computer worm called Stuxnet was identified as the culprit, programmed to disrupt the automated industrial programmable logic controllers (PLCs) used to control the hi-tech machinery. The attack caused 25 per cent of Iran's fast-spinning centrifuges to tear themselves apart. The *New York Times* described it as 'the first attack on critical industrial infrastructure that sits at the foundation of modern economies'.

The Stuxnet attack was a serious and disturbing development on at least three levels; first, no-one knew where it had come from originally (although most people had a good idea – Israel). Second, it was a very sophisticated program. IT targeted machines by using the widely distributed Microsoft Windows operating system and networks to get in, and then sought out the Siemens Step7 software that controlled the centrifuges and told them to accelerate. Last, but not least, who were the victims? Siemens correctly claimed industrial sabotage against their business; and Iran claimed, equally correctly, that their nuclear programme had been sabotaged.

Perhaps most worrying of all was the simplicity of its initiation. Experts later discovered that it had been introduced by a single memory-stick flash-drive. Once in, Stuxnet propagated itself automatically. The truth emerged slowly. In May 2011 Gary Samore, the White House Coordinator for Arms Control and Weapons of Mass Destruction, admitted, 'we're glad they [the Iranians] are having trouble with their centrifuge machine and that we – the US and its allies – are doing everything we can to make sure that we complicate matters for them,' thereby acknowledging some US involvement. And at the 2011 retirement party for General Gabi Ashkenazi, the outgoing head of the IDF, a video was shown that included references to Stuxnet as one of his operational successes.

By 2011 the threats and dangers from cyber war were being openly debated. Richard Clarke, a former White House counter-terrorism chief who worked for the Reagan, Clinton and Bush administrations, published *Cyber War*, a book warning that the West might have lost the new cyber war before it had even officially started. Clarke pointed out that the Russians, the Chinese and the North Koreans had already recruited legions of hackers, while Iran even boasts of having the world's largest cyber army.

Clarke identified a worst-case scenario where the Russians or North Koreans launch an all-out cyber attack. That could effectively bring Western society to its knees within just fifteen minutes, according to Clarke, because we are so utterly dependent on electronics, which run everything from nuclear power stations to our bedside alarm clocks. He painted an apocalyptic picture where bugs and viruses disrupt major computer systems, leaving the military and the police paralysed as trains crash, pipelines explode, the financial markets go into meltdown, the National Grid might crash, hospitals could fall dark, cash dispensers might go dead and ordinary life would come to a grinding halt.

He had a point; not long after the book came out the People's Liberation Army's Shanghai-based cyber unit was caught hacking into major American corporations such as the nuclear power company Westinghouse Electric and the United States Steel Corporation.

Since then cyber attacks have become regular features of an undeclared war. In 2011 the Canadian government reported a major cyber attack against its agencies, including Defence Research and Development Canada, a research agency for Canada's Department of National Defence. The attack forced the Finance Department and Treasury Board, Canada's main economic agencies, to disconnect from the Internet for a time.

In 2012 Kaspersky, a major Russian IT security company, identified a worldwide cyber attack dubbed 'Red October', which had been operating since at least 2007. It used Microsoft's Word and Excel programs to gather information from government embassies, research firms, military installations, energy providers, nuclear and other critical infrastructures.

Awareness of the threat has grown. In Britain, the head of MI5 and the Director-General of GCHQ sent a letter to the bosses of all the FTSE 350 companies stating that cyber attacks against UK companies are causing significant damage to their reputations and revenues. And in America the head of the US DoD's new Cyber Command noted that his big problem was trying to determine who exactly was trying to attack the US and whether things like commercial espionage or theft of intellectual property are criminal activities or genuine 'breaches of national security'.

Matters came to a head at the end of 2014 when the giant Sony corporation was hacked and disrupted by a well-organised and orchestrated cyber attack. Sony had been about to release a low-budget B movie poking fun at Kim Jong-Un, the dictator of North Korea. The unstable Kim flew into a rage and unleashed his cyber army of 6,000 hackers against Sony. The most serious cyber attack up to that time, the Sony incident cost the company an estimated $100 million. The affair swiftly escalated. The FBI announced that they had discovered conclusive evidence proving the North Korean government was behind the Sony hacking; US President Obama then openly blamed North Korea and informed them that the United States would retaliate, which America did with a controlled cyber strike at North Vietnam's weak Internet. Almost immediately the North Korean leader issued a statement denying involvement and demanding an apology from the United States for their 'evil doings'.

Not everyone agreed with the FBI that North Korea was responsible. Kurt Stammberger of cyber-security firm Norse claimed that, given the severity of the hack, it had to have been an inside job, adding, 'We are very confident that this was not an attack master-minded by North Korea and that insiders were key to the implementation of one of the most devastating attacks in history,' once again underlining the difficulty of identifying the real cyber aggressor.

The success of the Sony cyber attack, the massive media attention the attack received, and a relatively weak retaliation by the US risked emboldening others to launch similar attacks. There is little doubt that the Sony case represented a threshold-level event and has changed the landscape of cyber conflict. Certainly things could never be the same after Sony's experience.

Those who worked in cyber security pointed out that they had been warning of an attack like this for years. One individual, working at the highest levels of national cyber security, when asked to rate the threat of cyber war on a scale of one to ten replied dryly, 'About twelve!'

One of the problems is characterising the Sony attack. Was it an act of cyber war, cyber terrorism, or a cyber *crime*? The FBI's turgid definition of cyber-terrorism is both all-embracing and clear:

> A criminal act perpetrated by the use of computers and telecommunications capabilities, resulting in violence, destruction and/or disruption of services to create fear by causing confusion and uncertainty within a given population, with the goal of influencing a government or population to conform to a particular political, social, or ideological agenda.

What is inevitable is that lawmakers will have to pass legislation enabling cyber-threat intelligence-sharing between the intelligence community and the private sector: the very thing that Edward Snowden had been warning about. From his Moscow eyrie the whistleblower/traitor Snowden pointed out the problem:

> It is important to highlight that we [the US] really started this trend in many ways when we launched the Stuxnet campaign against the Iranian nuclear program. It actually kicked off a response, sort of retaliatory action from Iran, where they realized they had been caught unprepared. They were far behind the technological curve as compared to the United States and most other countries. And this is happening across the world nowadays, where they realize that they're caught out. They're vulnerable. They have no capacity to retaliate to any sort of cyber campaign brought against them.
>
> We spend much more on research and development, compared to the rest of the world. So when it comes to our cyber security . . . We have more to lose than any other nation on Earth.

Snowden was right. Hacking was not just a defence problem for the US. For Americans it went to the heart of their national economy too. In 2014 hacking went viral. Big US retailers like Neiman Marcus Inc., Michaels, Home Depot Inc., and eBay Inc. announced major breaches of computer security and millions of customers were helpless to stop the flow of credit card information and personal data to cyber attackers. And it wasn't just retail giants: health care, finance, utilities, they all joined Sony as major victims of cyber attack and cyber crime.

However the very intensity of the attacks spawned an upsurge in computer security and counter-measures alongside moves designed to disrupt attackers. For example, in the US Operation Onymous resulted in several arrests and disruption of dozens of black market sites, including the latest resurrection of Silk Road, an anonymous marketplace known for its illegal drug trade.

Cyber security became a new priority, not just for intelligence and security officers working on national defence, but for commercial organisations too. Persistent, unanswered questions made it hard for companies as well as nations to make the right decisions: How much security is enough? How much should be spent? Should security be run internally or outsourced? What tools and people are most effective?

The problem is that Cyber war is no longer a matter just for national intelligence. Cyber attacks now threaten corporate and national economic success as well. The majority (60 per cent) of known attacks are aimed at commercial targets. According to US security company CISCO, cyber criminals are increasingly looking for intellectual property that they can either sell on the black market or use to inform decisions about competing products or plans. The uncomfortable truth is that these attacks could be by 'criminals' or 'nation states' reacting to events. It's very hard to tell. As researcher Levi Gundert pointed out, 'Nowadays you almost need to have *The Economist* or the *FT* in hand while looking at some of these [cyber attacks] – they correspond to geo-political events.'

Cyber attacks have now become the twenty-first century's preferred form of international trade theft. Hackers can easily target any intellectual property from which they can benefit. IT, electronics, software, defence, and aerospace secrets are only the most obvious targets; nowadays biomedical and pharmaceutical breakthroughs, energy, finance, banks and even agriculture offer new economic gain and state-related advantage. And the threat is growing exponentially: by 2015 the increase in the malware targeted at these sectors was more than 600 per cent over a three-year period, while attempts to breach security in the energy, oil and gas industries rose by more than 400 per cent. The onslaught is massive – and growing. The threat to national, not just commercial, security is obvious.

SECURITY CHALLENGES AND THREATS

In places like China, the state and economy are so intertwined that illicit intelligence-gathering invariably doubles as national security. For Russia, the pressure of Western economic sanctions in response to its military actions in Ukraine have encouraged a ruthless and determined cyber onslaught against targets of opportunity in the West.

The problem is that it is very difficult to pin down the culprits. The digital world is too interconnected. Theft and sabotage in the digital world leave no DNA sample or fingerprints to identify the perpetrator. But the results can be economically disastrous. One American bio-medical company took five years to bring a new series of revolutionary replacement heart valves to market. By the time the product could be manufactured and sold to hospitals it had been through the extensive – and very expensive – processes of research and development, testing to ensure it was safe, and then the long-winded bureaucratic hurdles of US regulatory scrutiny and accreditation.

To the company's horror, within eighteen months a Chinese competitor was marketing an identical product at half the cost. Heart valves and prosthetics take less time to produce when you can steal the idea and the technology. As one industry insider put it, 'A team of digital cat burglars can sneak into the American company's mainframe and pop out with schematics for a fully tested product, beating the original innovators to market.' Shawn Henry, President of Services and Chief Security Officer of CrowdStrike, a cyber security firm explained 'It happens with every industry. Cyber theft is a lot like bank robbing . . . We see foreign hackers worm their way into their mainframes and facilities on a regular basis.'

Cyber theft can be grouped into three categories: independent hackers, hackers financially backed by states, and purely state-employed hackers. Each prefers to operate in a different corner of the international market. For example, independent hackers usually often break into consumer-based industries for financial gain. The theft of data from JPMorgan Chase and the theft of 1.2 billion digital financial credentials by a Russian crime ring in 2015 is another expensive financial example of electronic theft.

However, contract-based and state-backed hackers tend to be targeted at information with national strategic value. Examples have been attempts to acquire oil-drilling maps, software source codes, or military technology for the next generation of fighter jets. (This last has plagued US aircraft development since the start of the twenty-first century.) Other cyber attackers are suspected of sabotaging the mergers and acquisitions of US companies with their Russian or Chinese counterparts at the behest of their government.

These cyber attacks have become more frequent and widespread.

In 2013 and 2014, a series of well-planned 'Dragonfly' attacks once again targeted energy companies in the US (as well as Spain, France, Italy, Germany, Turkey, and Poland) in an attempt to gain access to the power grid and related infrastructure. This followed a similar series of cyber attacks believed to emanate from Russia during 2013 against US energy companies. These economic infrastructure onslaughts were

CYBER ATTACKS – GROWTH
MAJOR REPORTED ATTACKS 2009–2014

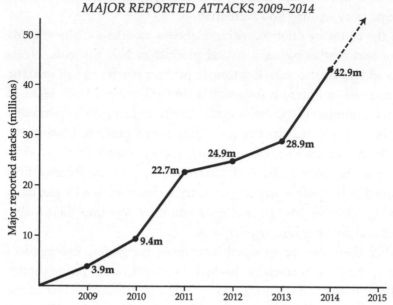

paralled by a series of simultaneous attacks on the foreign embassies of former Eastern Bloc nations. Diplomats and foreign agents were spied on for at least four years. As there was no economic motive for such activity it has unsurprisingly been attributed to government-controlled operations.

International agreements to limit such behaviour are widely held to be ineffective. Russia and China stoutly deny accusations of theft or cyber espionage and, in the wake of disclosures about the activities of the National Security Agency by the former contractor Edward Snowden, have even accused the US of blatant hypocrisy.

David Gorodyansky, chief executive of the privacy software developer AnchorFree, agreed, lamenting what he saw as America's dangerously disingenuous foreign cyber policy. 'The [NSA spying scandal] kind of prompted Russia and China to do the same thing,' he said. 'We spied on Germany and Brazil and all these other places, so they have no reason not to do the same thing. We need to take the high ground and say, "Look, we're not going to play this game."'

The problem for Cyber theft, as for Cyber war, is that it is easy to do, deniable and risk free. The benefits of easy pickings are just too tempting. Nations that can steal intellectual property are merely plucking low-hanging commercial fruit under a cloak of invisibilty and gaining considerable economic advantage for themselves in the process.

That the United States, Russia, China, Israel and North Korea have all been engaged in a secret, ruthless and potentially dangerous struggle since the late 1990s is no longer any secret. In response to this new strategic threat, the US Military's Strategic Command commissioned the creation of a new and well funded US Cyber Command in 2009, with one of its stated objectives being the 'defense of specified Department of Defense information networks'.

Within a very short time these new digital warriors discovered that the most important task once a cyber attack was identified was an *intelligence* problem, and a new one in warfare at that: who precisely was the aggressor? If you don't know who the enemy is, than it is hard – if not impossible – to retaliate.

Governments around the world took note. The reality and threat of cyber war took concrete form in terms of hard cash. The US Defense Department's backing for IT services got a boost in President Barack Obama's 2016 defense budget, with the Pentagon's IT and cyber programmes receiving more than a sixfold increase in spending.

Funding for the Joint Information Enterprise under the US Defense Information Systems Agency's budget exploded sevenfold from $13.3 million in 2015 to $84 million in 2016, and other IT spending plans quadrupled to nearly $1 billion. Even Britain's MoD's cash-strapped budget was upped to £1.1 billion in 2015 on Prime Minister Cameron's direct orders as the scale of the Cyber war threat sank in.

All this money reflects a growing recognition of a growing threat. However, like all new challenges to national security, it tends to pander to nervous politicians' perception of public insecurities. Although no-one knows exactly what the real threat is, the temptation to hurl taxpayers' money at some ill-defined enemy is strong. It is a brave politician who rejects the securocrats' demand for more money to counter terrorism or the cyber threat, to hear their reluctant reply, 'Well, it's your responsibility, Minister.' The unspoken threat hangs in the air. And, regrettably, as with terrorism, it is all too easy to spook ministers and hype up the threat to the public. Unscrupulous defence contractors are only too willing to exaggerate and sell their products in order to suck money from the public teat. The result is that, too often, IT procurement focuses on getting any product into service to prove that those in charge are doing something, rather than obtaining what is really needed. Nowhere is this more true than in the high-tech digital world of computer geekdom, where very often even product managers don't understand what their whizzkid operators are up to. What the managers do understand however, is the need to make a profit.

MOTIVATIONS BEHIND ATTACKS
January 2015

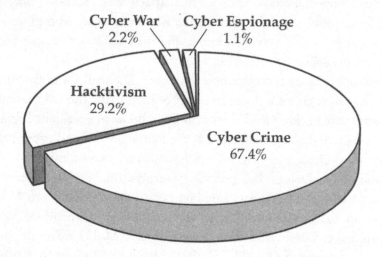

But the growing cyber threat demands something more than government money. Cyber war in its myriad forms represents nothing less than a new and ill-defined form of warfare with intelligence at its cutting edge.

This was recognised in 2015 by the establishment in the US of a 'federal intelligence integration center' in an effort to identify and combat cyber attacks. The new Cyber Threat Intelligence Integration Center (CTIIC), controlled by the Office of the Director of National Intelligence, works much like the National Counterterrorism Center, collating threat information into a single agency and then disseminating it as needed. The new centre is not an intelligence collecting agency. Instead, the CTIIC 'will analyze and integrate intelligence already collected . . . That will enable the existing cyber centers to be more effective.'

This addition to the intelligence battle is concrete recognition that cyber warfare in its many forms increasingly represents an alternative to conventional warfare as we have understood it. There is no longer any need for blitzkrieg, tanks and aeroplanes in the limited warfare of the future. Now it is all too easy to launch a cyber attack to complement a call for help from some allegedly oppressed minority with deniable masked 'volunteers' coming to their aid. For low-level conflict, 'hybrid' warfare looks to be soon replacing conventional warfare as the aggression of choice, with the cyber attack as its principal disabling weapon.

The threat is very real and growing. US President Barack Obama clearly defined the threat that cyber attacks pose to the economy and the state, in both the private and public sectors, when he said that the 'cyber threat is one of the most serious economic and national security challenges we face as a nation'.

To complicate matters still further, cyberwar can be an asymmetric conflict. For China and other autocratic governments, the priority is to control citizens' access to information; whereas for the more liberal west, the key concern is the struggle to protect intellectual property rights and technological supremacy.

Digital warfare – commercial, economic and strategic – is now developing so fast that it is hard for lumbering government bureaucracies to reorganise in order to meet technological advances. In late 2015 the CIA announced its first new Directorate in more than 50 years, the Directorate for Digital Innovation. And although in 2009 the US fielded a new joint-service cyber command, by 2016 a completely new US cyber service looks almost inevitable. Everyone is desperately seeking new answers to the exploding threat of cyber war.

But we can be sure of one thing in the cyber war being waged all around us – if decisions are put off until the threat is real and until we have 100 per cent correct answers – it will be too late.

PART TWELVE

A DANGEROUS TRADE

CHAPTER 39

The Secret War for ELINT

Intelligence collection has always had its hazardous side. From the secret agents of the Special Operations Executive pursuing their dangerous trade under the very noses of the Gestapo in occupied Europe to the undercover agents infiltrating the Provisional IRA in Northern Ireland, detection and capture has always meant one thing: death. But the dangers are not just confined to the brave individual agent. Since the Second World War the technical collectors have frequently risked their lives, too.

Between 1950 and 1970 there were a score of US military aircraft shot down by the military of the Soviet Union in an undeclared war.

On 8 April 1950 a pair of Soviet Lavochkin La-11 fighters homed in on a US Navy PB4Y-2 Privateer over the Baltic Sea off Latvia and blasted it out of the sky. The ten-man crew was presumed dead until information obtained from German, Austrian, and Japanese POWs repatriated from the Soviet Union in 1953 reported that at least one member of this aircraft's crew had been sighted in Soviet 'Camp #20' near Taishet, USSR, and 'Collective Farm #25', fifty-four kilometres from Taishet, 'said to be under sentence for alleged espionage. This American national was described as having suffered burns on the face and legs in the crash of his aircraft and using crutches or a cane.'

One of these Americans stated that he was serving a twenty-five-year sentence for espionage and had been a crewmember of a downed US aircraft. The US protested but in 1956 the Soviet government, stated that an 'exhaustive enquiry' into the charges of the US note had been carried out and that no such American military personnel were being held on Soviet territory.

After that the gloves were off. By 1972 nineteen US planes, mainly reconnaissance aircraft, had been destroyed in one-sided clashes with Russian fighters. These hazardous incursions were repeated over the Far East. In December 1950 a USAF RB-45C Tornado was shot down by Soviet MiG-15s over China near the North Korean border. A year later the Soviets shot down a US Navy P2V-3 Neptune near Vladivostok by Soviet fighters. The crew disappeared.

More seriously, in October 1952 a USAF RB-29 Superfortress was shot down by Soviet fighters over the Kurile Islands. Although the eight-man crew was presumed dead, in 1994 the remains of Captain John R. Dunham were returned to the US after former Soviet documents revealed that a dead crewman had been found and buried on Yuri Island. Former Soviet KGB Maritime Border Guards sailor Vasili Saiko came forward in 1993 and produced a ring that he took from Captain Dunham's body in 1952 to be passed onto Captain Dunham's widow.

Over 250 ELINT aircrew gave their lives during the Cold War from several nations. The missions they flew and lives they lost were shrouded in secrecy for decades. Now, their story of dedication and sacrifice can be told, and commemorated.

ELINT was a very dangerous trade during the Cold War.

CHAPTER 40

USS *Pueblo*

On 11 January 1968, the tiny (895 tons fully laden) SIGINT collector USS *Pueblo* left her base at Sasebo in Japan and headed north with orders to intercept and conduct surveillance of Soviet Union naval activity and to gather signal and electronic intelligence from North Korea.

On board the *Pueblo* were several top-secret US KW-7 encryption machines. However, without the daily one-time key settings the machines were just big teleprinters. The real secrets were the Americans' key settings. As long as the daily top-secret one-time cipher keylists used to 'set' the KW-7 machines were kept safe, the communications traffic would still be still secure. But as a technical source, the tiny, unprotected top-secret spyship was stuffed full of highly classified radio recording equipment and documents.

On 23 January, off the coast of Wonsan, *Pueblo* was approached by a North Korean sub chaser and ordered to heave-to. *Pueblo* raised the US flag and began to manoeuvre for open waters at her top speed of only 12 knots. The sub chaser fired several warning shots as she was joined by three more fast patrol boats and a pair of MiG 21 fighters.

After about two hours of attempting to escape, the North Koreans lost patience and opened fire, killing a crewman. Trapped and hopelessly outgunned, the tiny and vulnerable *Pueblo* surrendered. Something like panic then ensued as the small crew tried to destroy the huge quantity of top-secret communications equipment, signals, manuals and other sensitive material on board. It was a hopeless task.

In the end only a tiny percentage of the classified material onboard was destroyed as the *Pueblo* with her captured crew was escorted to Wonsan. The SIGINT material was flown straight to Moscow. As the CIA history notes, within a month of John Walker volunteering his services (see page 74), the Soviets had managed to hijack a United States Navy SIGINT ship along with its priceless cipher machines and ensure that they could read every US Navy classified signal.

Eventually in 1968 and following an apology, a written admission by the US that *Pueblo* had been spying, and an assurance that the US would not spy in the future, the North Korean government decided to release the eighty-two remaining crew members.

The US promptly retracted the ransom admission and the North Koreans blanked out the paragraph above the signature which read: 'and this hereby receipts for eighty-two crewmen and one dead body'.

Bucher and his crew subsequently appeared before a Navy Court of Inquiry. The Secretary of the Navy decided that the Navy and NSA men had suffered enough. Commander Bucher continued his Navy career until retirement.

The *Pueblo* is now a tourist attraction in North Korea.

CHAPTER 41

The Attack on the USS *Liberty*: With Friends Like This, Who Needs Enemies?

The *Pueblo* was just one of the SIGINT ships that the NSA and US Navy used. Both the US and the USSR used spy ships to intercept and collect electronic transmissions during the Cold War. There were numerous incidents at sea between submarines as well as the occasional near miss as warships manoeuvred at high speed. However, the worst incident was against a US SIGINT collection ship during the 1967 Arab–Israeli War.

On 8 June 1967 at the height of the Six-Day War between Israel and the United Arab Republic the USS *Liberty* Signal Intelligence collection ship ATGR 5 was attacked by Israeli aircraft and torpedo boats while in international waters off the coast of El Arish, south of Gaza.

The attack caused 70 per cent casualties on board – the biggest US Navy peacetime loss of life, with thirty-four crewmembers dead (officers, seamen, two Marines, and one civilian), 171 crewmembers wounded – and severely damaged the ship.

Israel eventually apologised for the attack, claiming that the USS *Liberty* had been attacked in error after being mistaken for an Egyptian ship.

Both the official US and Israeli government inquiries claimed that it was an 'unfortunate accident' caused by Israeli confusion about the ship's identity. This version is now widely discredited, as evidence has since emerged that the Israeli attack was in fact premeditated and deliberate, for reasons that still remain unclear.

We have a number of first-hand sources for the attack, discounting the mendacious official Israeli version: the testimony of the *Liberty*'s crew; the accounts of some of the IDF pilots who eventually came forward with the truth; the signals intelligence collected by an American EC-121 spy plane that monitored the incident from above; and reports from an American submarine that was secretly shadowing the *Liberty*.

The drama started at about 0930 on 8 June 1967. *Liberty*, a 7,700 ton Victory class freighter converted as an US Navy-NSA SIGINT collector, was sailing in international waters about thirteen miles off shore, in the curve of land between Egypt and Gaza. The minaret at El Arish could be seen with the naked eye, like a solitary mast in a sea of sand. Visibility in the crystal clear air was twenty-five miles or better. Through a pair of binoculars, individual buildings were clearly visible. *Liberty*'s captain, Commander McGonagle, used the 'quite conspicuous' tower as a navigational aid to determine the ship's position throughout the morning and afternoon.

What no-one realised at the time was that *Liberty* was almost a ringside spectator to a major Israeli war crime. At that very moment, near the minaret at El Arish, Israeli forces were engaged in a massacre of prisoners. As the *Liberty* sat within sight of El Arish, eavesdropping on surrounding communications, Israeli soldiers turned the town into a slaughterhouse, systematically butchering their prisoners. An eyewitness recounted how in the shadow of the El Arish mosque, they lined up about sixty unarmed Egyptian prisoners, hands tied behind their backs, and then opened fire with machine guns. Accounts differ, but the various reports plus the subsequent discovery of mass graves indicate that the IDF killed at least a thousand captured Egyptian prisoners of war out of hand; a major war crime.

Then they forced other prisoners to bury the victims in mass graves. 'I saw a line of prisoners, civilians and military,' said Abdelsalam Moussa, one of those who dug the graves, 'and they opened fire at them all at once. When they were dead, they told us to bury them.'

Nearby, another group of Israelis gunned down thirty more prisoners and then ordered some Bedouins to cover them with sand.

The Israeli journalist Gabi Bron saw about 150 Egyptian POWs sitting on the ground, crowded together with their hands held at the backs of their necks. 'The Egyptian prisoners of war were ordered to dig pits and then army police shot them to death,' Bron said. 'I witnessed the executions with my own eyes on the morning of June eighth, in the airport area of El Arish.'

The Israeli military historian Aryeh Yitzhaki, who worked in the IDF's history department after the war, said he and other officers collected testimony from dozens of soldiers who admitted killing POWs. According to Yitzhaki, Israeli troops killed, in cold blood, as many as 1,000 Egyptian prisoners in the Sinai, including some 400 in the sand dunes of El Arish.

On board the *Liberty*, just after sun-up, Duty Officer John Scott noticed an Israeli Noratlas 'Flying Boxcar' making several circles near the ship and then heading off northeast. Down in the secret NSA spaces, Chief Melvin Smith apparently also picked up radio signals from the plane, later identified as Israeli. Shortly after the plane departed, he called up Scott and asked if he had seen a close air-contact recently. Scott told him he had, and checked the wind direction by watching the American flag ruffling in a twelve-knot breeze.

On board, the forenoon continued quiet. At about 1000 hours the officer of the watch recorded two unmarked, rocket-armed, delta-winged jets circle *Liberty* three times. *Liberty* officers counted the rockets and could see the pilots, but see no identifying marks on the planes. The jets radioed IDF headquarters and confirmed that the ship was flying an American flag and with hull markings reading 'GTR-5'.

At about 1030 the Israeli marked 'Flying Boxcar' came back and circled the *Liberty* at about 200 feet. Crewmember Larry Weaver recorded that 'I was actually able to wave to the co-pilot, a fellow on the right-hand side of the plane. He waved back, and actually smiled at me.' Half an hour later Pinchas Pinchasy, the naval liaison officer at Israeli Air Force headquarters, confirmed to naval headquarters that the ship cruising slowly off El Arish is 'an electromagnetic audio-surveillance ship of the US Navy, named *Liberty*, whose marking was GTR-5'.

About noon, as the *Liberty* was again in sight of El Arish, the Israeli Navy and Air Force had conducted more than six hours of close surveillance of the *Liberty* off the Sinai and must have positively identified it as an American electronic spy ship.

At 1400 three unmarked Dassault Mystère IIIC jets attacked with napalm and rockets. The attack lasted approximately twenty-two minutes, involving thirty to thirty-five sorties, killing nine men and wounding around sixty. One Israeli pilot reported to base: 'Great, wonderful, she's burning, she's burning.'

As the jets struck the *Liberty*, a Lieutenant Painter attempted to reach the men manning the gun mounts, but it was too late. 'I was trying to contact these two kids,' he recalled, 'and I saw them both; well, I didn't exactly see them as such. They were blown apart, but I saw the whole area go up in smoke and scattered metal.' The Mirages raked the ship from bow to stern. A bomb exploded near the whaleboat aft of the bridge, and those in the pilothouse and the bridge were thrown from their feet. Commander William L. McGonagle rang up for all-ahead flank speed and ordered a distress call: 'Under attack by unidentified jet aircraft, require immediate assistance.'

In the communications spaces, *Liberty's* Chief Radioman, Wayne Smith and his team were desperately trying to patch together the broken antennae to get a distress call off to the Sixth Fleet. To their horror they discovered that someone was using powerful jammers to block *Liberty's* signals. Five of the ship's six shore circuits were very quickly jammed and then whoever was doing it 'went searching' for the last circuit. It was only at 1410 hours, five minutes after the attack started, that *Liberty* succeeded in transmitting an open-channel 'Mayday' distress call for assistance, despite intense jamming by the Israelis. 'Any station, this is Rockstar,' Halman shouted, using the *Liberty's* voice call sign. 'We are under attack by unidentified jet aircraft and require immediate assistance.'

At 1409 hours, the aircraft carrier USS *Saratoga*, operating near Crete, acknowledged *Liberty's* cry for help. 'I am standing by for further traffic,' it signalled.

After taking out the gun mounts, the Israeli fighter pilots turned their attention to the antennae so the ship could not call for help or pick up any more revealing interceptions. Then the planes attacked the bridge, killing the ship's executive officer. With the *Liberty* now deaf, blind, and silenced, unable to call for help or move, the Israeli pilots proceeded to close in for the kill. Designed to punch holes in the toughest tanks, the aircrafts' shells tore through the *Liberty*'s steel plating like hot nails through butter, exploding into jagged bits of shrapnel and butchering men deep in their living quarters.

As the slaughter continued, neither the Israelis nor the *Liberty* crew had any idea that witnesses were present high above. For nearly thirty-five years the NSA hid the fact that one of its spy planes – a Navy EC-121 ferret – was overhead at the time of the incident, eavesdropping on what was going on below. The interceptions from that plane, which answer some of the key questions about the attack, are among the NSA's deepest secrets.

Navy Chief Petty Officer Marvin Nowicki heard one of the other Hebrew linguists on the plane excitedly trying to get his attention on the secure intercom. 'Hey, chief,' he shouted, 'I've got really odd activity on UHF. They mentioned an American flag. I don't know what's going on.' Nowicki asked the linguist for the frequency and 'rolled up to it'. 'Sure as the devil,' said Nowicki, 'Israeli aircraft were completing an attack on some object.'

Deep down in *Liberty*, Terry McFarland, head encased in earphones, was vaguely aware of flickers of light coming through the bulkhead above him. He had no idea that they were armour-piercing tracer bullets slicing through the ship's skin. Larry Weaver had run to his general quarters station but it was located on an old helicopter pad that left him exposed and vulnerable. He grabbed a dazed shipmate and pushed him into a safe corner. 'I said, "Fred, stay here, you've just got to because he's coming up the centre,"' Weaver recalled. 'I got in the foetal position,' he said, 'and before I closed my eyes I looked up and I saw the American flag and that was the last thing I saw before I was hit.'

As soon as the Mirages pulled away, they were replaced by Super Mystère fighters, which raked the ship with rocket, cannon, and machine-gun fire, 1,000-pound bombs and napalm. Commander McGonagle was hit in the right thigh and arm by shrapnel, his blood draining into his shoe. A later analysis would show 821 separate hits on the hull and superstructure.

There was then a lull as the aircraft disappeared. During the interval, crewmen aboard the *Liberty* hoisted a large American flag (a thirteen foot 'holiday' ensign) to clearly identify and *Liberty* managed to get off another distress message that was received by the Sixth Fleet aircraft carrier USS *Saratoga*.

Captain McGonagle later explained 'three high speed boats were approaching the ship from the north east at about 14:20' and that it 'appeared that they were approaching the ship in a torpedo launch attitude.' He turned the ship hard to manoeuvre, but at 1435 *Liberty* was hit by a torpedo launched from one of the torpedo boats. It struck the starboard side forward, blowing a hole in the ship's classified research spaces and killing twenty-five servicemen, almost all of them from the intelligence section, and wounding dozens more.

The Israeli torpedo boats then closed in to close range and strafed the ship's hull with their cannons and machine guns, even deliberately firing on sailors preparing life rafts for launch and damage control parties. Petty Officer Charles Rowley recorded the concentration of machine-gun fire on the lifeboats still stored on deck. The order 'Prepare to abandon ship!' was followed, naturally, by the lowering of the first lifeboats. As they touched the water the Israeli MTBs moved closer and shot them to pieces. One of the attackers even swooped in and recovered a shot-up rescue dinghy, clearly marked with US Navy markings. After the attack Rowley carefully photographed the shredded boats, thinking that one day his pictures would help to tell a story.

The *Liberty* now had no engines, no rudder, no power and was taking in water. Nine of its officers and crew were known dead; another twenty-five were missing and correctly presumed to be dead (in the communications room that had taken the torpedo); and 171 were wounded. Those who were wounded but not incapacitated joined with the other ninety who had survived unscathed and set about collecting bodies, dressing wounds, fighting fires, stringing lights and hand-operated phone sets, repairing the engines and, above all, trying to keep the *Liberty* afloat.

While they worked on those tasks, two large Israeli SA-321 Super Frelon helicopters put in an appearance and slowly circled the stricken ship. Both were clearly marked with a large Star of David. The cargo bay doors were open and *Liberty* crewmen could see that both helicopters were crammed with armed troops (Israeli special forces) and a machine gun was trained on the ship. On the *Liberty* Captain McGonagle gave the order 'Standby to repel borders!' The helicopters circled the *Liberty* and then flew off north.

On board the *Liberty* at 1600 the crew was still screaming for help. 'Flash, flash, flash,' Radioman Joe Ward shouted into his microphone. 'I pass in the blind. [That is, he didn't know who was picking up the transmission.] We are under attack by aircraft and high-speed surface craft. I say again, flash, flash, flash.' By then, unencrypted voice messages had been filling the open airwaves for two hours. Attempts by Sixth Fleet to launch aircraft to assist *Liberty* were inexplicably recalled by presidential order.

There was another unknown witness to the whole affair. Several *Liberty* crewmembers testified that they had briefly seen a periscope during the attack. In February 1997, a senior member of the crew of the submarine USS *Amberjack* told James Ennes that he had watched the attack through the periscope and took pictures. According to the official ship's history from the Department of Defense, *Amberjack*'s mission between 23 April and 24 July was reconnaissance in the Mediterranean off the coast of the UAR.

When contacted, four crewmen stated that they were so close to USS *Liberty* when it came under attack that some of the crew believed *Amberjack* itself was under depth charge assault. However, August Hubal, Captain of the *Amberjack*, insisted that the vessel was 160 kilometres from the *Liberty* and when told the crew believed they were closer replied: 'They must be mistaken.'

In 2003, as a result of a Freedom of Information Act request by the Israel News Agency demanding any evidence that the US submarine *Amberjack* had gathered by means of its periscope, the National Security Agency stated that 'no radio intercepts were made by the US submarine *Amberjack*'. But that carefully begged the question of what they had *seen* ...

Eventually at about 1600, two hours after the attack began, Israel informed the US embassy in Tel Aviv that its military forces had mistakenly attacked a US Navy ship. When the ship was 'confirmed to be

American' the torpedo boats returned at about 1640 to offer help. It was refused by the *Liberty*.

At about 1730 an angry Rear Admiral Lawrence Geis, commander of the Sixth Fleet in the Mediterranean, personally protested to Secretary of Defense McNamara about the decision to recall the US Navy rescue planes. At that point President Johnson came on the radio-ophone and to Geis's astonishment says 'he doesn't care if the ship is sunk, he would not embarrass his allies'. A stunned Admiral Geis told Lieutenant Commander David Lewis, head of the *Liberty*'s NSA group, of the remark, but asked him not to repeat it.

Back in Washington a bizarre scene was played out. According to Deputy Director Louis Tordella of the NSA 'One of my immediate concerns, considering the depth of the water and the distance of the ship off shore, had to do with the classified materials which she had on board.' Tordella got on the phone to the Joint Reconnaissance Center and spoke to the deputy director, a Navy captain named Vineyard about the NSA's major fear: 'I expressed my concern that the written material be burned if at all possible and that the electronic equipment be salvaged if that were possible.'

But Tordella was not prepared for what he heard. According to NSA documents classified top-secret/Umbra, Tordella was told that 'some senior officials in Washington wanted above all to protect Israel from embarrassment; Captain Vineyard had mentioned during this conversation,' wrote Tordella, 'that consideration was then being given by some unnamed Washington authorities to sink[ing] the *Liberty* in order that newspaper men would be unable to photograph her and thus inflame public opinion against the Israelis. I made an impolite comment about the idea.' Almost immediately Tordella wrote a memorandum for the record, describing the conversation, and then locked it away.

Later, Israel provided a helicopter to fly US naval attaché Commander Castle to the ship. He found a scene of carnage. A wounded and exhausted Captain McGonagle, managed to dictate his first report on estimated casualties: ten dead; fifteen severely wounded; seventy-five total wounded; undetermined missing. His estimate would prove low. Only then did he leave the wreck of his bridge and seek treatment.

Lieutenant Ennes took over and conned the stricken vessel north and west heading for the open sea. For one day and night when the ship was slowly moving northward, no other ships or planes could be seen. At midnight, the *Liberty* came across the Soviet missile destroyer 626/4, which signalled a flashing-light message in English: 'Do you need help?' *Liberty* responded: 'No, thank you.' The Soviets answered: 'I will stand by on the horizon and be ready to help in case you need me.'

The Soviet ship followed a parallel course for the next six hours acting as guard ship. At dawn, the *Liberty* radar detected the American destroyers *Massey* and *Davis* and the cruiser USS *Little Rock*. Medical personnel were transferred to the *Liberty* and wounded sailors from the *Liberty* were delivered by helicopters to the fleet aircraft carriers. The *Liberty* was escorted westwards and limped back to Malta for temporary repairs where the crew was told, 'the assault would be investigated by a Navy court'.

However, once the *Liberty* docked at Malta on 14 June, the effort to bury the incident went to full-speed ahead. A total news blackout was imposed. Crewmembers were threatened with courts-martial and jail time if they ever breathed a word of the episode to anyone – including family members and even fellow crewmembers. 'If you ever repeat this to anyone else ever again you will be put in prison and forgotten about,' Larry Weaver said he was warned.

Rear Admiral Isaac Kidd was assigned the task of presiding over the Naval Board of Inquiry and promptly swore the crew to secrecy. Confirming a gagging order issued by Defense Secretary McNamara about not speaking to the media, Kidd ordered *Liberty* survivors who were to give evidence to refer all questions to the commanding officer or executive officer or to himself. He added: 'Answer no questions. If you are backed into a corner, then you may say that it was an accident and that Israel has apologised. You may say nothing else.' Marked 'Top Secret', the Naval Board's report was completed on 18 June 1967. It has not been fully declassified to this day.

That the attack was deliberate is no longer in doubt, despite the determined efforts of America's pro-Israeli apologists to hide the truth. Fifteen years after the attack, a retired Israeli pilot approached *Liberty* survivors and then held extensive interviews with former Congressman

Paul N. (Pete) McCloskey about his role in the attack. According to the senior Israeli lead pilot, he recognized the *Liberty* as American immediately, so informed his headquarters, and was told to ignore the American flag and continue his attack. He refused to do so and returned to base, where he was arrested. Later, a dual-citizen Israeli major told survivors that he was in an Israeli war room where he heard that pilot's radio report. 'The attacking pilots and everyone in the Israeli war room knew that they were attacking an American ship,' the major said. He recanted the statement only after he received threatening phone calls from Israel.

Why did the Israelis do it? There is evidence, circumstantial but clear, of a relationship between the attack on the *Liberty* and a postponement of a planned Israeli offensive to capture the Syrian-held Golan Heights. The timing of the Israeli assault on the Golan was intended to seize this key Israeli objective before any UN ceasefire came into effect. The United Nations had scheduled a ceasefire for 9 June. On his own admission, Moshe Dayan and the IDF leadership feared the *Liberty* might intercept some of the many signals then filling the air that would expose Israel's secret preparations for the invasion of Syria. Israel might then be forced into a ceasefire before they conquered the coveted territory on the Golan. So they determined to silence the US spy ship.

The various inquiries support this view. In 2002, Captain Ward Boston, JAGC, US Navy, Senior Counsel for the Court of Inquiry, said that the Court of Inquiry's findings were intended to cover up what was a deliberate attack by Israel on a ship that the Israelis knew to be American. In 2004, Boston signed an affidavit in which he said that Admiral Kidd had told him that the government ordered Kidd to falsely report that the attack was a mistake, and that Boston and Kidd both believed the attack was deliberate. Boston wrote:

Both Admiral Kidd and I believed with certainty that this attack, which killed 34 American sailors and injured 172 others, was a deliberate effort to sink an American ship and murder its entire crew. Each evening, after hearing testimony all day, we often spoke our private thoughts concerning what we had seen and heard. I recall Admiral Kidd repeatedly referring to the Israeli forces responsible for the attack as 'murderous bastards.' It was our shared belief, based on the documentary evidence and testimony we received first hand, that the Israeli attack was planned and deliberate, and could not possibly have been an accident.

They were not alone. The testimony of the following senior US officials make the truth more clear than anything else.

Lieutenant General Marshall S. Carter, Director of the National Security Agency at the time: 'There was no other answer than it was deliberate.'

Dr Louis Tordella, the Deputy Director of NSA at the time: 'I believed the attack might have been ordered by some senior commander on the Sinai Peninsula [where the massacres were taking place] who wrongly suspected that the *Liberty* was monitoring his activities.' Tordella also scrawled across the top page of the formal Israeli 'mistake' report, 'A nice whitewash.'

Major General John Morrison, NSA Deputy Director of Operations at the time: 'Nobody believes that explanation. The only conjecture that we ever made that made any near sense is that the Israelis did not want us to intercept their communications at that time.'

Walter Deeley, the senior NSA official who conducted an internal NSA investigation of the incident: 'There is no way that they didn't know that the *Liberty* was American.'

Admiral Thomas H. Moorer, former Chairman of the Joint Chiefs of Staff: 'I have to conclude that it was Israel's intent to sink the *Liberty* and leave as few survivors as possible. Israel knew perfectly well that the ship was American.'

Captain William L. McGonagle, the *Liberty*'s commander: 'After many years I finally believe that the attack was deliberate.'

Phillip F. Tourney, President of the USS *Liberty* Veterans

Association and a survivor of the attack: 'The Israelis got by with cold-blooded, premeditated murder of Americans.'

George Christian, press secretary to President Johnson at the time: 'I became convinced that an accident of this magnitude was too much to swallow.'

Paul C. Warnke, Under Secretary of the Navy at the time: 'I found it hard to believe that it was, in fact, an honest mistake on the part of the Israeli air force units ... I suspect that in the heat of battle they figured that the presence of this American ship was inimical to their interests.'

Dean Rusk, Secretary of State at the time: 'The *Liberty* was flying an American flag. It was not all that difficult to identify, and my judgment was that somewhere along the line some fairly senior Israeli official gave the go-ahead for these attacks.'

David G. Nes, the deputy head of the American mission in Cairo at the time: 'I don't think that there's any doubt that it was deliberate ... [It is] one of the great cover-ups of our military history.'

George Ball, Under Secretary of State at the time: 'American leaders did not have the courage to punish Israel for the blatant murder of its citizens.'

Although Captain McGonagle was awarded the Congressional Medal of Honor for his heroism in saving the ship and bringing it back to safety, senior White House officials decided to keep the occasion as quiet as possible.

Because the medal, the nation's highest honour, is only rarely awarded, it is almost always presented by the president in a high-profile White House ceremony. But McGonagle's award was given by the secretary of the Navy in a low-profile, hastily arranged gathering at the Washington Navy Yard, a scrappy base on the banks of the smelly Anacostia River.

I must have gone to the White House fifteen times or more to watch the president personally award the Congressional Medal of Honor to Americans of special valor [said Admiral Thomas H. Moorer, who became Chief of Naval Operations within weeks of the attack]. So it irked the hell out of me when McGonagle's ceremony was relegated to the obscurity of the Washington Navy Yard and the medal was presented by the Secretary of the Navy. This was a back-handed slap. Everyone else received their medal at the White House. President Johnson must have been concerned about the reaction of the Israeli lobby.

Later, a naval officer connected with the awards told Jim Ennes, a lieutenant on the ship, the reason. 'The government is pretty jumpy about Israel,' he said. 'The State Department even asked the Israeli ambassador if his government had any objections to McGonagle getting the medal. "Certainly not!" Israel said. But to avoid any possible offense. McGonagle's citation does not mention Israel at all, and the award ceremony kept the lowest possible profile.' LBJ was so determined not to offend Israel that the crewmembers' graves are inscribed, 'died in the Eastern Mediterranean', as if they had been killed by disease, rather than an unprovoked Israeli attack on an innocent Allied ship on the high seas.

Israel has never wavered on one critical point: that no-one ever saw a flag flying from the *Liberty* during either the air or sea attack, despite the virtually unanimous agreement among survivors that flags were flying during both periods. 'Throughout the contact,' said the 'mistake' report, 'no Israeli plane or torpedo boat saw an American or any other flag on the ship.'

But Marvin Nowicki, the senior Hebrew linguist on the EC-121 flying above the scene, knows what he heard and the NSA tapes prove it. 'As I recall, we recorded most, if not all, of the attack,' he said. 'I heard a couple of references to the flag during an apparent attack.'

Given his knowledge of Israel's intelligence capabilities NSA Director Carter's view stands as the ultimate indictment 'There is no way that the Israelis didn't know that the *Liberty* was American,' he told James Bamford, author of *Body of Secrets*, in a 1980 interview. Let Ward Boston, the Navy Investigating Judge Advocate General have the last word.

In 2012 he swore an affidavit:

I have examined the released version of the transcript and I did not see any pages that bore my hand corrections and initials. Also the original did not have any deliberately blank pages as the released version does. Finally the testimony of Lt Painter concerning the deliberate machine gunning of the life rafts by the Israeli torpedo boats, which I distinctly recall being given at the Court of Enquiry and included in the original transcript is now missing and has been excised.

In May 1968, the Israeli government finally paid US$ 3,323,500 (US$ 22.5 million 2015) in compensation to the families of the 34 men killed in the attack. In March 1969, Israel paid a further $3,566,457 to the men who had been wounded. On 18 December 1980, it agreed to pay $6 million as settlement for the final U.S. bill of $17,132,709 for material damage to the *Liberty* herself plus thirteen years' interest.

CHAPTER 42

Disaster at Forward Operating Base Chapman

In one key area of intelligence – HUMINT – things have changed surprisingly little. Modern technology, and technical gizmos aimed at making the laborious tradecraft of the secret agent easier are no substitute for the trusted undercover agent in place with access in the enemy's camp.

Sometimes in HUMINT things go badly wrong. In January 2010 Jordanian Dr Humam al-Belawi, blew himself up at the CIA's Forward Operating Base Chapman on the Afgahnistan-Pakistan border. FOB Chapman was located about ten miles northwest of the Pakistani border. One of the main tasks of the CIA personnel stationed at the base was to provide intelligence supporting drone attacks against Taliban targets in Pakistan. The suicide bomber took with him three security contractors, four CIA officers, included the CIA's chief of the base at Khost, and an analyst from headquarters who reportedly was the agency's foremost expert on al Qaeda, as well as the Jordanian General Intelligence Department (GID) officer who was al-Balawi's handler.

Humam Khalil Abu-Malal al-Balawi was a Jordanian doctor from Zarqa. Jordanian officers from the General Intelligence Directorate (GID) had arrested him in 2007 because of his close involvement with radical jihadi online forums, which is illegal in Jordan. The GID subsequently approached al-Balawi while he was in a Jordanian prison and recruited him to work as an undercover intelligence agent. The Jordanians ran him: the CIA bankrolled the operation. The GID had what appeared to be a real gem of a source on their hands: a turned jihadi agent who could lead them into the heart of al Qaeda's ruling hierarchy. For the CIA and their political masters demanding answers it must have seemed like manna from heaven, and almost too good to be true. It was.

Al Belawi was regarded by the CIA as a real catch, and a gold mine on Islamic terrorism. He was the first agency mole ever to infiltrate al Qaeda at a high level. The truth, as ever, was more complex. From his Jordanian prison al-Balawi was sent under control to Pakistan. He established himself in Pakistan as a medical student to receive advanced medical training. Under his pseudonym of 'al-Khurasani,' al-Balawi began to make contact with jihadists and in September 2009, in an interview on a jihadist Internet forum, declared that he had officially joined the Afghan Taliban.

The Jordanians and the CIA were delighted with their success. They should have been more cautious, because al-Balawi had secretly approached the Tehrik-i-Taliban Pakistan (TTP), the main Pakistani Taliban group, confessing all, and warned them that he was being run by the CIA and GID. The Taliban decided to play him back against the CIA.

Al-Balawi played his part. From Pakistan, Al-Belawi called his handler claiming that he had urgent information and needed to brief the top CIA team. He told his Jordanian handler that he had good intelligence on the location of Ayman al-Zawahiri, the al Qaeda second-in-command, as well as detailed battle damage assessments of the US drone strikes in Pakistan. He also claimed to have access to high-level jihadi sources. The prospect of finally receiving such crucial and long-sought information explains the urgency and eagerness of the CIA at FOB Chapman to meet their wonderful new source. They called him to a secret meeting to brief their top people.

And the CIA was genuinely eager to meet him. As he arrived on the afternoon of 30 December 2009, fourteen people in all gathered outside, in front of a makeshift interrogation centre. The mole was due any minute. The point of the welcoming committee was apparently to show respect for their top agent and to make him understand how important he was to the CIA's war on Osama bin Laden. The result was an extraordinary failure to follow routine security procedures.

Normally, an outer ring of Afghan military security was the first line of defence around the base, charged with searching anybody who wanted to enter FOB Chapman. The US military then searched again at the outer perimeter of the US portion of the base. Al-Balawi, a high-value CIA asset, was allowed to skip these external layers of security to avoid exposing his identity to Afghan troops and US military personnel. Instead, the team of civilian security contractors from Blackwater were to search al-Balawi only as he arrived at the CIA's facility. Nearly every security rule in the book when operating in Bandit Country was broken in the agency's thirst for high-level information, and al Qaeda took full advantage of their opponents' deadly weakness. Once surrounded by his enemies, Al-Belawi blew himself up.

The subsequent investigation revealed that Al-Belawi was an al Qaeda double agent all along. The media reaction was instant and critical: 'Another intelligence blunder!' But the story was not as simple as the media made out. With this in mind it is easy to see how the CIA was fooled by Dr Belawi and al Qaeda.

The isolated CIA station was run by a desk officer, Jennifer Lynne Matthews. She was forty-five years old and a divorced mother of three. She'd spent the vast majority of her career driving a desk in Langley, where she became a national expert on al Qaeda. Michael Scheuer, her boss in the CIA unit that tracked bin Laden, said that despite her training at the Farm, she was always slotted to be a reports officer, someone who edits reports coming in from the field. She was never intended to meet and debrief informants.

Matthews was an acknowledged al Qaeda expert. But Khost was her first field command, her first real chance to run informants. She lived in a trailer, ate in a common mess, experienced the isolation of life behind blast walls and razor wire, surrounded by the dreary countryside of eastern Afghanistan. The chance of a one-to-one with the CIA's top agent inside the Taliban was just too good to miss.

On coming back from his 'dangerous mission' the double agent was not searched, not checked and then allowed to brief a meeting of fourteen CIA operatives within a secure CIA Base, including experts who had been flown in especially from Kabul. He knew that high-value targets would be present because he had set the stage for the meeting by dangling vital information before the agency. He went to the meeting to carry out his true mission, which was to deliver a blow against the CIA. He succeeded. Surrounded by the CIA's best under-cover agent handlers in the region, he achieved lethal results.

However, this CIA intelligence blunder is really no better and no worse than the British Double Cross programme, which played dou-bled German agents back to the Abwehr in the 1940s. What we can observe are the very human reasons why agencies are duped. These remain constants: first, a desperate desire to believe in the agents, despite warnings and misgivings; second, an urgency to gain valuable information; and lastly, a gullibility that over-rides the essential scep-ticism and inherent mistrust that should be the guiding principle behind any double-agent operation. The agency wants to believe the information so mouth-wateringly on offer. Therefore it does. It lowers its guard and is fooled.

Therein lies the enemy's opportunity, as al Qaeda had proved once again. Following the 30 December 2009 attack at FOB Chapman, the CIA conducted an extensive investigation into its procedures and tra-decraft leading up to the calamity. That investigation found that many normal operating procedures had been ignored in anticipation of what was seen as the most promising lead against al Qaeda in years.

HUMINT is always going to be messy, dangerous and full of ambi-guities. Relying as it does on people, not machines, HUMINT will always be to intelligence what 'fuzzy logic' is to mathematics: the domain of uncertainty, imponderables and risk.

It is also the realm of betrayal.

WILL IT EVER GET ANY BETTER?

When the Cold War fizzled out in the early 1990s, the question of what to do with all the various intelligence agencies arose – in every nation. The politicians were keen to save money, the 'securocrats' to save their jobs.

However, it soon became clear that the new political landscape had not diminished the quest for intelligence. If anything it had widened and diversified it to encompass new targets, such as national economic rivalries. America's NSA suddenly found itself collecting SIGINT on AirBus's commercial plans in order to help Boeing sell more planes. The number of intelligence targets now takes in WMD proliferation, terrorism, rogue states, criminal arms trafficking and drug dealing, as well as new threats like cyber war and the seemingly endless threat of Islamic jihad.

Intelligence is back in business, monitoring the 'bewildering variety of poisonous snakes' that have replaced 'the dead dragon'. Old-style intelligence has never gone away. Nowhere was this better demonstrated than when, in 2015, the Arabic news station Al Jazeera released what it called 'the spy cables', offering a remarkable – and embarrassing – glimpse into the modern world of intelligence and espionage.

Al Jazeera claimed that came into the possession of leaks of 'hundreds of secret intelligence documents from the world's spy agencies'.

It reported that, 'unlike the Edward Snowden documents that focus on electronic signals intelligence, commonly referred to in intelligence circles as "SIGINT", the spy cables deal with human intelligence, or "HUMINT".'

'Rather than chronicling spy-movie style tales of ruthless efficiency of intelligence agencies,' Al Jazeera reported, the files 'offer an unprecedented glimpse into the daily working lives of people whose jobs are kept secret from the public.'

Al Jazeera claimed that the leaked files come from intelligence agencies around the world, including: Israel's Mossad, Britain's MI6, Russia's FSB, Australia's ASIO and South Africa's SSA.

Israels's *Haaretz* newspaper reported that one of the revelations contained within the documents was Mossad's 'true assessment' of Iran's nuclear programme – an explosive piece of information because it showed how, behind the scenes, Mossad's actual intelligence assessment of the threat from Iran differed widely from alarmist public statements by Israel's political leaders.

Although not on the same scale as the earlier leaks exposed by the former CIA employee Edward Snowden, the leaks offered a tantalising glimpse into the shadowy world of espionage, focusing on human intelligence rather than digital intelligence.

The revelations covered from 2006 until December 2014, and included detailed briefings and internal analyses written by South Africa's state security agency. They also revealed South Africa's secret correspondence with the CIA, MI6, Mossad, FSB and Iran.

Other revelations included how Britain worked closely with South Africa to recruit a North Korean spy, how South Korean intelligence targeted the leader of Greenpeace, how South African agents spied on Russia over a £65 million joint satellite deal, and why President Obama openly threatened the Palestinian leader Mahmoud Abbas over the Palestinian bid to win formal recognition and statehood for Palestine.

The source of the leaks would appear to have been South African, because they exposed several embarrassing incidents from that country, prompting the comment from South Africa's Shadow Defence Minister, 'The state security agency has now become a state within a state beyond effective scrutiny and oversight of parliament.' In this the Al Jazeera leaks were merely reinforcing an oft-forgotten fact: national intelligence agencies all too often tend to take on a life of their own, immune to taxpayers and governments alike. But as intelligence is the servant of government and not the other way around, the leaks once again emphasise the need for oversight and control of intelligence and security agencies. The changing sources of intelligence reinforce the need to police this rapidly changing landscape.

One of the problems for 'intelligence' in the future will be this changing array of potential threats and problems. The pace of scientific and technological change is accelerating as we head into our new century and the digital revolution is but one example of how rapidly our world and society is evolving. Who would have guessed, even twenty years ago, that it would be possible to read every citizen's private mail and snoop on their personal habits by the mass monitoring of emails, the Internet and social media? No longer do we need a legal warrant to steam open and read other people's post, when a technician with a computer and some slick software can now do it at the press of a keyboard. Or do we? The digital age has opened up new visions of society beyond the comprehension of many existing laws. New legislation will be needed, and new debates will have to decide what are the legal limits of state intrusion into our everyday lives in this brave new world. What are the acceptable limits of government snooping in a supposedly free, democratic society? What controls do we need on our intelligence and security services? Perhaps more importantly, what do we want to permit them to do on our behalf? Because, in the final analysis, intelligence and security services exist for the sole purpose of protecting the citizen and the taxpayer: the prime purpose of government.

Different countries have reacted differently to their changed needs. For most developed countries, technical intelligence and open-source information now provide the bulk of intelligence being processed, where once diplomacy and HUMINT reigned supreme. But the problem remains: in order to target clandestine information, you have to know what you don't know. And therein lies the problem for policy makers and intelligence officers alike. Government ministers don't like 'black swan' moments. We all like to know what we don't know and politicians more than most, detest and fear sudden nasty surprises. But that is precisely what 'intelligence' and its many agencies exist for.

If the definition of responsible intelligence is 'to speak truth unto power' then it looks as if intelligence in the future will face the very same problems that intelligence has faced in the past. Walsingham, Richelieu, Washington, Stieber, Dzerzhinsky and Markus Wolf all faced the same challenges that will confront tomorrow's intelligence officers: how to collect, collate, interpret and disseminate timely, accurate intelligence to convince policy makers and decision makers to do their job in a dangerous, fast-changing world.

The internal problems of intelligence will not change, either. The perennial conflicts over inter-agency feuding, competition for budgets, disagreements over priorities, hubris, human frailty and vanity, bureaucratic inefficiency, poor security and under-estimation of potential enemies will always remain, in their various forms. Human nature will not change, any more than the relationship between bureaucrats and their political masters.

The truth is that the intelligence problem will get worse, not better. Intelligence blunders in the twenty-first century will be very expensive and potentially very dangerous. We need to keep a very close eye on just who has usable nuclear weapons and how they intend to use them. The greatest threat of all has always been 'the fanatic armed with power', whether a lone killer with a grievance, a terrorist group, or a nation's leader bent on war. Because today's technology knows no boundaries, today's sophisticated technical toys put deadly new capabilities into uncertain, uncontrolled hands.

For good or ill, intelligence will remain at the heart of the world's affairs.

Select Bibliography

This book was written primarily for the interested general reader and not as an academic textbook.

On a subject as vast as intelligence it is only too easy to drown in the flood of authoritative – and some not so authoritative – sources and references from every quarter. However, if more detail or further reading is required, then I have found the following books and other references to be especially useful or interesting.

Many of these sources of information can be found nowadays on the Internet. Although I have not listed every site's complete URL in mind-numbing detail, for the dedicated researcher a trawl through any good Internet search engine using key words will reveal many of the references below, plus many, many more.

The Internet archive now includes so many primary source documents that it stands as an important research tool. For example, to read in the original *exactly* what the Soviet Ambassador said at the height of the Cuban Missile crisis in his top-secret telegram to the Kremlin is of huge significance when trying to cut through the fog of what *really* went on, whether the telegram in question happens to be online or in some dusty archive.

I have also included some seminal television productions as primary references. While some in the academic community deride modern media (and particularly television) as 'not a real source', it seems perfectly reasonable to me to accept the on-camera testimony of someone who is recording his or her memories of events as a primary source. Of course, old soldiers do sometimes forget or embellish their stories. It is not unknown either for politicians to polish their recollections of events in order to show themselves in the best light.

To maintain however that somehow such recordings are inferior to the written word strikes me as a conceit, and a misguided one at that. It implies that written documents are the 'only true record', as if written records of meetings, telegrams, policy documents and position papers are somehow never 'polished' by their authors, corrupted, or are guilty of omissions or embellishments. Anyone who has ever worked in a bureaucracy, military or civilian, will know immediately how unlikely that is. I have myself been guilty of writing up the minutes of the odd senior policy meeting to reflect what the participants *wished* that they had said, rather than reflecting exactly what they did say . . .

Finally, I agree with my colleague Max Hastings that lengthy bibliographies are sometimes more evidence of some kind of academic 'virility parade' than any real help to those looking for sensible guidance for further reading. For this reason I have confined myself only to those books and sources that I felt had most to offer, rather than every single possible reference. Life, and the reader's attention span (let alone the reader's budget) is just too short . . .

On Intelligence

Chandler, David. *The Campaigns of Napoleon*, Weidenfeld & Nicolson, 1967.

Herman, Michael. *Intelligence Power in Peace and War*, Frank Cass, 2001.

JIS (NE), Intelligence briefs (various), 1974–1975.

Marshall-Cornwall, General Sir James, personal interview with the author, Ashford, 1976.

Polmar and Allen. *The Spy Book*, Greenhill, 1997.

SACEUR's Briefing, Exercise WINTEX, NATO, 1979. School of Service Intelligence, Intelligence Training (Restricted), Ashford, Kent,1974 et seq.

Shulsky, Abram. *Silent Warfare*, Brassey's, USA, 1991.

Urquhart, Brian, personal interview with the author, UNFICYP, Cyprus, 1975.

On HUMINT and Spies

Andrew, Christopher *Defence of the Realm: The Authorized History of MI5*, Penguin, 2010.

Bearden, Milton. *The Main Enemy*, Presidio Press; Reprint edition, 2004.

Crumpton, Henry. *The Art of Intelligence: Lessons from a Life in the CIA's Clandestine Service*, Penguin, 2013.

Hughes-Wilson, John. *The Puppet Masters: the Secret History of Intelligence*, Weidenfeld and Nicolson, 2004.

Hennessey, Thomas. S*pooks: the Unofficial History of MI5*, Amberley Publishing, 2011.

Money: The Walker Family's Unusual Business

Blum, Howard. *I Pledge Allegiance: The True Story of the Walkers: an American Spy Family*, Simon & Schuster Books, 1987.

Earley, Peter. *Family of Spies: Inside the John Walker Spy Ring*, Bantam, 1988.

Kneece, Jack; *Family Treason: The Walker Spy Case.* Paperjacks, 1988.

O'Connor, John J. TV View; American spies in pursuit of the American dream, 4 February 1990.

Where Ideology and Ego Mix: Ana Montes

Carmichael, Scott. *True Believer: Inside the Investigation and Capture of Ana Montes, Cuba's Master Spy*, US Naval Institute Press, 2009.

Gertz, Bill. 'DIA Official Warns About Cuban Spies' *Washington Times*, 15 March 2007.

Popkin, Jim. 'Ana Montes did much harm spying for Cuba. Chances are, you haven't heard of her,' *Washington Post*, 18 April 2013.

The Centre for Counterintelligence and Security Studies. 'An Unrepentant Montes Sentenced to 25 Years', October 2002.

The One Who Got Away: Melita Norwood

The Mitrokhin Inquiry Report, UK Intelligence and Security Committee. 27 April 2008.

Burke, David. *The spy who came in from the Co-op: Melita Norwood and the ending of Cold War espionage* Boydell Press, 2013.

Clinton and Pollard

'The Jonathan Pollard Case' http://www.crimelibrary.com/terrorists_spies/spies/pollard/11.html

Hersh, Seymour. 'Annals of Espionage: The Traitor. The case against Jonathan Pollard', The New Yorker, 18 January 1999.

Olive, Ronald. *Capturing Jonathan Pollard: How One of the Most Notorious Spies in American History Was Brought to Justice*, Naval Institute Press, 2009.

US archives.gov. 1987 (Heavily redacted)

'The Jonathan Jay Pollard Espionage Case: A Damage Assessment', (CIA).

Ego: Hanssen

Vise, David A. (2001), *The Bureau and the Mole: The Unmasking of Robert Philip Hanssen, the Most Dangerous Double Agent in FBI History*, Grove Publishers, 2001 and 2003.

Wise, David. *Spy: The Inside Story of How the FBI's Robert Hanssen Betrayed America*, Random House, 2003.

U.S. Department of Justice 'A Review of the FBI's Performance in Deterring, Detecting, and Investigating the Espionage Activities of Robert Philip Hanssen', 14 August 2003.

The Grievance: Penkovsky

Oleg Penkovsky, Oral History of Joseph J. Bulik, Penkovsky's CIA case officer.

Penkovsky, Oleg. *The Penkovsky Papers: The Russian Who Spied for the West*, Doubleday, (NY) 1966.

Wynne, Greville. The Man from Moscow, Hutchinson & Co, 1967.

Espionage and the Cold War: Oleg Penkovsky and the Cuban missile crisis. Intelligence and National Security, (Taylor and Francis) 1999, Vol. 14, Issue 3.

On SIGINT

Aldrich, Richard. *GCHQ*, Harper Press, 2011.

Parshal, Jon. *Shattered Sword: The Untold Story of the Battle of Midway*, Potomac Books Inc; Reprint edition, 2008.

Prange, Gordon. 'Miracle at Midway,' Penguin, 1983.

Symonds, Craig. *The Battle of Midway*, OUP, 2011.

On Technical Intelligence

Chester, Richard. A History of the HEXAGON Program, National Reconnaissance Office, 1985.

Chiriba, Abel. *Military Satellites: Issues, Goals and Challenges (Defense, Security and Strategy Series)*, Nova Science Pub Inc., 2009.

Doyle, John M. 'Big Bird, Uncaged' Air and Space, December 2011/ January 2012.

Drew, Christopher and Sontag, Sherry. Blind Man's Bluff: The Untold Story of American Submarine Espionage, William Morrow, 2000.

Graham, Richard. *SR-71 Revealed: The Inside Story*, Zenith Press; 1996.

Maini, Varsha Agrawal. *Satellite Technology: Principles and Applications*, Wiley and Sons, 2011.

Rich, Ben. *Skunk Works: A Personal Memoir of My Years at Lockheed*, Back Bay Books, 1996.

Welti, Robert. *Satellite Basics For Everyone: An Illustrated Guide to Satellites for Non-Technical and Technical People*, iUniverse, 2012

'Military Satellite Systems: A History.' *MilSat* Magazine, May 2008.

'Why Military Satellites Matter', *National Defense Magazine*, March 2014.

On Collation: Vietnam and Tet Offensive

Bonds, Ray. *The Vietnam War*, London, Salamander Books, 1979.

Braestrup, Peter. *Vietnam as History*, Washington DC, University Press of America, 1984.

Colby, William. *Lost Victory*, Chicago, IL, Contemporary Books, 1990.

Fall, Bernard. *A Street Without Joy*, London, Greenhill Books, 1994.

Gilbert, Marc Jason and Head, William (eds). *The Tet Offensive*, Westport, CN, Praeger/Greenwood, 1996.

Gittinger, E. (ed.). *The Johnson Years: a Vietnam Roundtable*, Austin, TX, LBJ Library, 1993.

Historical Division of the Joint Secretariat. The Joint Chiefs of Staff and the War in Vietnam, Washington DC, 1970.

MACV (J2): Command briefing, 8 May 1972.

MACV (J2): Command Intelligence Centre Study, Viet Cong Infrastructure, 1 April 1967.

McMaster, H.R. *Dereliction of Duty: Lyndon Johnson, Robert McNamara, the Joint Chiefs of Staff, and the lies that led to Vietnam*, New York, HarperCollins, 1997.

McNamara, Robert. *In Retrospect: The Tragedy of Vietnam*, New York, Times Books, 1995.

Miller, Nathan. *Spying for America: The Hidden History of US Intelligence*, New York, Dell Books, 1989.

Oberdorfer, Don. *Tet! The Turning Point in the Vietnam War*, New York, Da Capo Press, 1995.

The Recollections of Colonel J.K. Moon, US Intelligence Corps, personal correspondence with the author.

The Recollections of Colonel John Robbins, US Artillery, personal correspondence with the author.

US Department of State. Foreign Relations of the United States, US Government Printing Office, 1994.

Westmoreland, William. *A Soldier Reports*, New York, Dell, 1976.

Wirtz, Colonel James. *The Tet Offensive: Intelligence Failure in War*, Ithaca, NY, Cornell University Press, 1991.

On Interpretation: Yom Kippur

Badri, Magdoub and Zohdy. *The Ramadan War 1973*, Dupuy Assoc., VA, 1974.

Barnett, Corelli. *The Desert Generals*, London, William Kimber, 1960, and Bloomington, Indiana University Press, 1982.

Bickerton and Pearson. *The Arab-Israeli Conflict*, London, 1993.

Dupuy, Colonel Trevor. *Elusive Victory*, London, 1978.

Fraser, T.G. *The Arab-Israeli Conflict*, London, 1995.

Handel, Michael I. *Perception, Deception and Surprise; The Case of Yom Kippur*, Jerusalem, Leonard Daw Institute, 1976.

Herzog, Chaim. *The War of Atonement: The Inside Story of the Yom Kippur War*, 1973, Mechanicsburg, PA, Stackpole Books, 1998.

Perlmutter, Amos. *Politics and the Military in Israel 1967–1977*, Portland, OR, ISBS, 1978.

Recollections of an Israeli Intelligence Officer (name withheld).

Private correspondence with the author, 2001.

The Agranat Commission. *A Report into the Failures Before and During the 1973 October War*, Government Printing Office, Tel Aviv, 1975.

Telling the User: Barbarossa and Stalin

Andrew and Gordievsky. *KGB: The Inside Story*, Hodder & Stoughton, 1990.

Bialer, Seweryn. *Stalin and his Generals*, Boulder, Colorado, USA, 1994.

Bullock, Alan. *Hitler and Stalin*, London, 1991.

Carrell, Paul. *Der RusslandKrieg*, Ullstein Verlag Frankfurt, 1964.

Deacon, Richard. *A History of the Russian Secret Service*, Grafton, 1987.

Erickson, John. *The Road to Stalingrad: Stalin's War with Germany*, London, Weidenfeld & Nicolson, 1993.

Erickson and Dilks (eds). *Barbarossa, the Axis and the Allies*, Edinburgh, 1994.

Finkel, G. 'Red Moles', (unpublished MS), personal correspondence, Calgary.

Halder, Franz. *Hitler as Warlord*, New York, Putnam, 1950.

Harrison, Mark. *Soviet Planning in War and Peace*, Cambridge University Press, 1985.

Hinsley, Sir Harry. *British Intelligence in the Second World War*, abridged edition, London, HMSO, 1993. The official history, originally published in five volumes. (various authors)

Irving, David. *Churchill's War*, New York, Avon Books, 1987.

Kahn, David. *Hitler's Spies: German Military Intelligence in WW2*, Macmillan, 1978.

Philippi and Heim. *Der Feldzug Gegen SowjetRussland*, Stuttgart, 1962.

Polmar and Allen. *The Spy Book*, Greenhill, 1997.

Seaton, Albert and Barker, Arthur. *The Russo-Japanese War 1941–45*, London, Arthur Barker, 1971.

Uberberschar and Wette (eds). *Unternehmen Barbarossa*, Frankfurt, 1993.

West, Nigel. *Unreliable Witness*, London, Weidenfeld & Nicolson, 1984.

Whaley, Barton. Codeword Barbarossa, Cambridge, MA, MIT Press, 1973.

On Dissemination: Pearl Harbor

Beach, Ed L. *Scapegoats: A Defence of Kimmel and Short at Pearl Harbor*, USNI Press, 2000.

Betts, Richard. *Surprise Attack: Lessons for Defense Planning*, Washington DC, Brookings Institute, 1982.

Burtness and Ober. *The Puzzle of Pearl Harbor*, Peterson, 1962.

Clausen, Henry. *Pearl Harbor: Final Judgement*, New York, Crown, 1992.

Elphick, Peter. *Far Eastern File*, Hodder & Stoughton, 1997.

Kahn, David. *The Intelligence Failure at Pearl Harbor*, Foreign Affairs, Vol. 70, #5, 1991.

Knorr, *Klaus and Morgan*, Patrick (eds). *Strategic Military Surprise*, New Brunswick, Transaction, 1984.

Prange, Gordon. *At Dawn We Slept*, McGraw Hill, 1981, and Viking, 1991.

Rusbridger, James and Nave, Eric. *Betrayal at Pearl Harbor: How Churchill Lured Roosevelt into WWII*, New York, Summit Books, 1991.

Stafford, David. *Churchill and Secret Service*, John Murray, 1997.

Stinnet, Robert. *Day of Deceit*, London, Constable & Robinson, 2000.

Toland, John. *Infamy*, London, Methuen, 1982.

On Security

Dhillon, G., *Principles of Information Systems Security: Text and Cases*, John Wiley & Sons, 2007.

Imbus, Michael T. 'Identifying Threats: Improving Intelligence and Counterintelligence Support to Force Protection' (PDF), USAFCSC-Imbus- April 2002.

van Ginkel, Bibi. 'Towards the intelligent use of intelligence: Quis Custodiet ipsos Custodes?' International Centre for Counter-Terrorism – The Hague, 2014.

'Operations Security' (JP 3-13.3) U.S. DoD Operations Security Doctrine.

Joint Chiefs of Staff 'Joint Publication 2-0: Intelligence' (PDF), US JP 2-0. 2007.

'Physical Security Challenges. (Field Manual 3-19.30: Physical Security) Headquarters, United States Department of Army, 2001.

'Purple Dragon: The Origin & Development of the United States OPSEC Program', NSA, 1993.

One Who Slipped Through The Net: Aldrich Hazen Ames

Barron, John. *Confessions of a Spy*. Houghton Mifflin, 1987.

Grimes, Sandra. *Circle of Treason: A CIA Account of Traitor Aldrich Ames and the Men He Betrayed*, Naval Institute Press, 2013.

Weiner, Tim. *Betrayal: The Story of Aldrich Ames, an American Spy*, Random House, 2014.

WikiLeaks and the Appalling Assange

Assange, Julian. *Julian Assange: The Unauthorised Autobiography*, Canongate Books, 2011.

Gavett, Gretchen. 'New Evidence of Assange–Manning Link', PBS, 19 December 2011

Nakashima, Ellen, 'Bradley Manning case: Investigators show evidence of WikiLeaks link, Assange . . .', *Washington Post*, 20 December 2011.

'Kissinger Cables: Wikileaks publishes 1.7m US diplomatic documents from 1970s', Daily Telegraph, 8 April 2013.

Snowden and the Surveillance State

Bigo and Delmas-Marty. 'The State and Surveillance: Fear and Control', *La Clé des Langues*, 23 September 2011.

Electronic Frontier Foundation. 'Mass Surveillance Technologies'. 15 September 2013.

Greenwald, Glenn. *No Place to Hide: Edward Snowden, the NSA and the Surveillance State*, Hamish Hamilton 2014.

'UK–US surveillance regime was unlawful "for seven years",' *Guardian*, 6 February 2015.

Harding, Luke. *The Snowden Files: The Inside Story of the World's Most Wanted Man*, Guardian, Faber, 2014.

Strategic Security: Insecure From Top to Bottom – Singapore, 1941–2

Allen, Louis. *Singapore*, London, Frank Cass, 1997.

Bauer and Barnett. *History of WW2*, Monaco, Polus, 1966, and Galley Press, 1984.

Crawford, Edward. The Malayan recollections of the late Brigadier V.R.W. Crawford MC. Private correspondence to the author, November 1999.

David, Saul. *Military Blunders*, London, Robinson Publishing, 1997.

Elphick, Peter. *Singapore: The Pregnable Fortress*, London, Sceptre, 1995.

Gilchrist, Sir Andrew. *Malaya 1941*, London, Hale, 1992.

Kirby, *Official History of the War against Japan*, Vol 1, HMSO, 1957.

Lewin, R. *The Other Ultra*, Hutchinson, 1982.

UK-NA (PRO): CRMC 34300 (G), 19 July 1938 (GOC Malaya, WO 106/2440). UK-NA (PRO): Defence of Malaya and Johore (GOC Malaya, WO 106/2440). UK-NA (PRO): 106/2432, 4/38.

Owen, Frank. *The Fall of Singapore*, London, Michael Joseph, 1960.

Shepherd, Peter J. *Three Days to Pearl*, Annapolis, US Naval Institute Press, 2000. Smith, Michael. *Odd Man Out; The Story of the Singapore Traitor*, London, Coronet, 1994.

Stafford, David. *Churchill and Secret Service*, John Murray, 1997.

Tsuji, Colonel Masanobu. *Japan's Greatest Victory, Britain's Worst Defeat*, Staplehurst, Spellmount Publishers, 1995.

Young, Peter. *World War 1939–45*, London, Barker, 1966.

D-Day

Brown, Anthony Cave. *Bodyguard of Lies*, New York, Harper & Row, 1975.

Bennett, Ralph. *Ultra in the West*, London, Hutchinson, 1979.

Bennett, Ralph. *Behind the Battle*, Pimlico, 1999.

Cruickshank, Charles. *Deception in WW2*, London, 1979.

Harwell, Jack. *The Intelligence & Deception of the D-Day Landings*, Batsford, 1979.

Haswell, Jock. *British Military Intelligence*, Weidenfeld & Nicolson, 1973.

Hastings, Max. *Overlord*, London, Pan Books, 1985.

Hinsley (ed.). *British Intelligence in the Second World War*, 6 vols, HMSO, 1990.

Howard, Sir Michael. *Strategic Deception in the Second World War*, London HMSO, 1990 and Pimlico, 1992.

Kahn, David. *The Codebreakers*, Weidenfeld & Nicolson, 1968.

Masterman, Sir John. *The Double Cross System*, Yale University Press, 1972.

National Archive (NA) (formerly PRO) CAB 80/63, CofS (42) 180(0), 21 June1942. UK-NA: (PRO) JIC (43) 385(0), 25 September 1943. UK-NA: CAB 80/77, CofS (43) 779(0) Final, 23 January 1944.

Perrault, Gilles. *The Secrets of D-Day*, English edition, Arthur Barker, 1965.

Skillen, Hugh. *Enigma and its Achilles Heel*, c/o The Intelligence Corps Museum, Chicksands (by application only).

Tute, Warren, et al. *D-Day*, London, Sidgwick & Jackson, 1974.

Winterbotham, F.W. *The Ultra Secret*, London, 1974.

On Terror

Griffin, David Ray. *The Mysterious Collapse of World Trade Center 7: Why the Final Official Report About 9/11 Is Unscientific and False*, Olive Branch Press, 2009.

Hoffman, Bruce. *Inside Terrorism*, Columbia University Press, 1998.

Nunberg, Geoffrey 'Head Games / It All Started with Robespierre. "Terrorism": The history of a very frightening word', *San Francisco Chronicle*, 28 October 2001.

Risen, James. *Pay Any Price: Greed, Power, and Endless War*, Houghton Mifflin Harcourt, 2014

Weiss and Hassan. *ISIS; Inside the Empire of Terror*, Regan Arts, 2015.

Wright, Lawrence. *The Looming Tower: Al-Qaeda and the Road to 9/11*, Vintage 2007.

The Greatest Atrocity – 9/11 and the Attack on the World Trade Center

Given the global impact, there are inevitably more books and website articles on the events surrounding '9/11' than most people can cope with. These are the best that I have found and used for this book.

Baxter and Downing. *The Day that Shook the World*, London, BBC, 2001.

Bergen, Peter. *Holy War: Inside the Secret World of Osama bin Laden*, London, 2001.

Bodansky, Josef, et al. *Bin Laden, the Man Who Declared War on America*, 2003. Channel 4. *Why the Twin Towers Collapsed*, UK TV Documentary, November 2001.

Cooley, John K. *Unholy Wars: Afghanistan, America and International Terrorism*, London and Virginia, 2000.

Hoffman, B. *The Modern Terrorist Mind*, Centre for the Study of Terrorism, St Andrew's University, 1997.

Ibrahim, Sa'd al-din. *The New Arab Order: Oil and Wealth*, Boulder, CO, 1982. Jurgensmeyer. *Jihad! Terror in the Mind of God*, Berkeley, CA, 2000.

Metzer, Milton. *The Day the Sky Fell: A History of Terrorism*, Landmark Books, 2002.

Petesr, Rudolph. *Islam and Colonialism, Den Haag and New York*, 1979.

Reeve, Simon. *The New Jackals: bin Laden and the Future of Terrorism*, London, 1999.

Roy, Oliver. *The Failure of Political Islam, London*, 1994.

RUSI. 'Weapons of Catastrophic Effect', Whitehall seminar, 2003.

RUSI. 'Homeland Security and Terrorism', Whitehall seminar, 2003.

Sinclair, Andrew. *An Anatomy of Terror*, Macmillan, 2003.

Stern, Jessica. 'Terror's Future', Foreign Affairs, July 2003.

The Encyclopedia of World Terrorism, New York, Armonk Publications, 1997.

US Department of State. *Patterns of Global Terrorism*, Langley, 2001 and 2002.

US Government Printing Office website. 'Congressional Report into the Events of "9/11"', 2002.

Wilkinson, Paul. *Political Terrorism*, London, 1974.

The Sơn Tây raid

Amidon, Mark. 'Groupthink, Politics, and the Decision to Attempt the Son Tay Rescue', *Parameters, Journal of the US Army War College*, 2005.

Gargus, John. *The Son Tay Raid: American POWs in Vietnam Were Not Forgotten*, Williams-Ford Texas A&M University Military History Series, 2007.

Schemmer, Benjamin. *The Raid: The Son Tay Prison Rescue Mission*. Ballantine, 2002.

Operation Eagle Claw

Lenahan, Rod. *Crippled Eagle: A Historical Perspective Of U.S. Special Operations 1976–1996*, Narwhal Press, 1998.

Kamps, Charles Tustin. 'Operation Eagle Claw: The Iran Hostage Rescue Mission', *Air & Space Power Journal*, 2006.

Radvanyi, Richard, A. Maj. Operation Eagle Claw: Lessons Learned. USMC Command and Staff College, 2002.

Ryan, Paul B. *The Iranian Rescue Mission: Why it Failed*, Annapolis: Naval Institute Press, 1985

'The Desert One Debacle.' *The Atlantic Magazine*, May, 2006.

On Cyberwar: When is a War Not a War?

Clarke, Richard. *Cyber War: The Next Threat to National Security and What to Do About It*, HarperCollins, 2010.

Harris, Shane. *@War: The Rise of the Military-Internet Complex*, Houghton Mifflin Harcourt, 2014.

Rid, Thomas. *Cyber War Will Not Take Place*, OUP, 2013.

Singer, P. W. *Cybersecurity and Cyberwar: What Everyone Needs to Know*, OUP, 2014

Zetter, Kim. *Countdown to Zero Day: Stuxnet and the Launch of the World's First Digital Weapon*, Crown Books, 2014.

Disaster at Forward Operating Base Chapman

Dilanian, Ken. 'CIA inquiry cites failures in Afghan bombing that killed agents', *Los Angeles Times,* 19 October 2010.

Gorman, Siobhan. 'Suicide Bombing in Afghanistan Devastates Critical Hub for CIA Activities', *Wall Street Journal,* 1 January 2010.

Mazzetti, Mark and Stolberg, Sheryl Gay. 'Suicide Bombing Puts a Rare Face on C.I.A.'s Work', *New York Times,* 7 January 2010.

Panetta, Leo. 'Statement on CIA Casualties in Afghanistan', Central Intelligence Agency, 31 December 2009.

Stein, Jeff. 'The Mole's Manual', *New York Times* (International) 5 July 1994.

'Intelligence Fiasco in Afghanistan', *Financial Times,* 11 January 2010.

Will It Ever Get Any Better?

Herman, Michael. *Intelligence Services in the Information Age,* Frank Cass, 2001. Shukman, Harold (ed.). *Agents for Change: Intelligence Services* in the 21st Century, St Ermin's Press, 2000.

Glossary

Russian Secret Police and Intelligence Service Titles
The name of what is effectively the same organisation changes (confusingly) over the period:

OCHRANA	Czarist secret police	pre-1917
CHEKA	Soviet secret service	1917–22
OGPU	Soviet secret service	1923–34
NKGB	Soviet secret service	1934–41
NKVD	Soviet secret service	1941–6
MGB	Soviet secret service	1946–54
KGB	Soviet secret service	1954–91
GRU	Russian/Soviet military intelligence and security staff	
FSB	Russian federal counter-intelligence service	1991–
SVR	Foreign intelligence service of the Russian Federation	1991–

Glossary, General

AGER	US Navy auxiliary intelligence gathering ship
AQ	al Qaeda (transliteration)
ASIO	Australian security and intelligence organisation
BfV	modern German domestic security service (*Bundesamt für Verfassungschutze*)
black programme	unadmitted, 'off the books' intelligence operation
Bletchley Park	location of UK SIGINT service (WWII)

BND	German foreign intelligence service (*Bundesnachrichtendienst*)
C-130	Hercules four-engined transport plane
Cheka	Soviet secret service 1917–22
C4ISTAR	Command, Control, Communications, Computers, Surveillance, Target Acquisition & Reconnaissance
CIA	Central Intelligence Agency – US foreign intelligence service
CIR	critical intelligence requirements
COMINT	communications intelligence
CPGB	Communist Party of Great Britain
CPO	chief petty officer
CPSU	Communist Party of the Soviet Union
CTIIC	Cyber Threat Intelligence Integration Center
DIA	US Defence Intelligence Agency
DNI	Director of National Intelligence (US)
DoD	Department of Defense (US)
DoS attack	denial-of-service cyber attack
Dragonfly	state sponsored espionage and sabotage cyber attack
EC-121	US ELINT plane (based on Lockheed Constellation)
ECHELON	secret SIGINT collection and monitoring system
ECHR	European Court of Human Rights
EEIs	essential elements of information
ENIGMA	German encoding machine (WWII)
FAA	Federal Aviation Authority
FBI	US Federal Bureau of Investigation – US domestic security service
FCO	Foreign and Commonwealth Office (UK)
FOB	forward operating base
GRU	Russian/Soviet military intelligence and security staff
Hanoi	capital, North Vietnam
HUMINT	human intelligence – agents, debriefings, POW interrogation

ICBM	inter-continental ballistic missile
INO	Soviet Foreign Ministry intelligence department
ISIS/IS	Islamic State of Iraq and Syria
I & W	indicators and warnings
J2	joint military staff intelligence and security branch
Keylist	top-secret cypher and code machine settings
KW-7	US top-secret coding machine
KW Series	US top-secret cipher machines
JFK	John Fitzgerald Kennedy
JIC	Joint Intelligence Committee (UK)
KSM	Khalid Sheikh Mohammed (terrorist)
Langley	CIA headquarters, near Washington, DC
LBJ	Lyndon Baines Johnson
MFS	Ministry of State Security (East German – See also *Stasi*)
MGB	Soviet secret service 1946
MI	military intelligence
MI 5	UK domestic security service
MI 6	UK foreign intelligence service (see also, 'SIS')
MoD	Ministry of Defence (UK)
MVD	Soviet secret service (1953)
NATO	North Atlantic Treaty Organisation
NGO	non-governmental organisation
NIE	national intelligence estimate
NIS	US Navy's investigation service (now NCIS)
NKGB	Soviet secret service (1943)
NKVD	Soviet secret service (1934)
NRO	National Reconnaissance Office (satellites) (US)
NSA	National Security Agency; US SIGINT service
NVA	North Vietnamese Liberation Army
OCHRANA	Czarist secret service
OGPU	Soviet secret service (1923–34)
OKW	*Ober Kommand Wehrmacht* (German WWII)
OSA	Official Secrets Act

OSS	Office of Special Services (US, WWII)
PB4Y-2 Privateer	US ELINT collection plane
PI	photographic interpretation
PIRA	Provisional IRA
PLA	Peoples' Liberation Army (Chinese)
PLO	Palestine Liberation Organisation
POW	prisoner of war
PRC	Peoples' Republic of China
PSYOPS	psychological operations
P2V-3 NEPTUNE	US ELINT collection plane
RAF	Royal Air Force *or* Red Army Faction (German terrorists)
RB-45C Tornado	US ELINT collection plane
RB-47	USAF reconnaissance jet, 1949–1960
RCMP	Royal Canadian Mounted Police
RFU	Radical Fundamentalist Unit (FBI)
Saigon	capital, South Vietnam, pre-1975
SAM	surface to air missile
SAS	British Army Special Air Service
Savak	Shah of Iran's secret police
SCI	Special Compartmented Intelligence (US)
SHAPE	Supreme Headquarters Allied Powers Europe
SIGINT	signals intelligence – intercept, analysis, code breaking
SIS	UK Secret Intelligence Service (See also 'MI 6')
SNIE	special national intelligence estimate (US)
SOE	Special Operations Executive (UK WWII)
Sputnik	popular name for first orbiting satellite (Soviet)
SS	*Schutzstaffel* – Himmler's Nazi Party army
SSA	State Security Agency (South Africa)
Stasi	East German (DDR) state intelligence and security service
Stinger	US hand-held anti-aircraft missile

TECHINT	technical intelligence – equipment, electronics, weapons
top-secret Umbra	code-word protected information
TTP	Tehrik-i-Taliban; principal Pakistani Taliban
U2	Lockheed very high-altitude reconnaissance plane
UKAEA	UK atomic energy authority
UNDP	United Nations Development Programme
UNHCR	UN High Commission for Refugees
USAF	United States Air Force
USSR	Union Of Soviet Socialist Republics
VC	Viêt Công
Venona	code name for intercepted Soviet espionage traffic (WWII)
WMD	weapons of mass destruction

INDEX